Reader in Marxist Philosophy

Reader in Marxist Philosophy

From the Writings of Marx, Engels, and Lenin

Selected and Edited with Introductions and Notes by

Howard Selsam

Harry Martel

AAKAR

Reader in Marxist Philosophy
Howard Selsam and Harry Martel

First Published in India 2018
Reprinted 2020
Reprinted 2025

ISBN 978-93-5002-571-0

Published with the permission from International Publishers, New York for publication and sale only in South Asia.

Published by
AAKAR BOOKS
28 E Pocket IV, Mayur Vihar Phase I
Delhi 110 091, India
www.aakarbooks.com

Printed at
D.K. Fine Art Press, Delhi

Prefatory Note

The materials from Marx, Engels, and Lenin presented in this volume are divided into seven parts, plus two lengthy Appendices. The reason for the latter is explained in the General Introduction. The editors have also supplied a separate introduction for each part and for each of the two Appendices.

In the main body of the work, the editors have frequently departed from a chronological presentation in the interests of the logical development of Marxist philosophy. Since, however, the chronology is often significant, the year in which the work was completed—though not necessarily published—is given after each entry.

The Contents gives the source of all entries, which is repeated, for the convenience of the reader, at the end of each selection in the text, together with page references. Inasmuch as many of these works have appeared in numerous editions, the list of Sources at the end identifies the editions used. Throughout, the editors have sought to use those most readily available in the United States today. In most cases these are also the best and most authentic translations.

All cuts within a given selection are marked with three dots. All footnotes not marked "—*Ed.*" are from the original texts. Inserts within square brackets [ ] in the text are by the editors.

A biographical index identifies persons referred to. The major concepts are, for the most part, contained in the detailed table of contents.

THE EDITORS

Contents

PART THREE

DIALECTICS AND THE DIALECTICAL METHOD

PART FIVE

THE MATERIALIST INTERPRETATION OF HISTORY

PART SIX

RELIGION

PART SEVEN

ETHICS

APPENDIX I

THE FORMATIVE PERIOD

APPENDIX II
LENIN'S PHILOSOPHICAL NOTEBOOKS

GENERAL INTRODUCTION

This volume is a systematic presentation of the principal philosophical statements of Marx, Engels, and Lenin. The materials were selected to give the student and the general reader a clear understanding of the Marxist world-outlook as a whole, and at the same time the Marxist approach to such special branches of philosophy as logic, theory of knowledge, theory of history, and ethics. Most of the selections, we believe, are relatively self-explanatory, but the reader must remember that, as in all scientific and philosophical innovations, there is a distinctive terminology which must be understood. Such terms as "materialism," "idealism," "ideology," "metaphysics," "alienation," or even "philosophy" itself, are used differently in Marxist thought than they are conventionally.

The problem of selection was difficult, for the writings of Marx, Engels, and Lenin at times deal simultaneously with the most immediate tactical and political considerations, and with the broadest historical and philosophical generalizations. Some of Marxism's most basic concepts were formulated in the course of discussions on monopolies, the labor theory of value, trade unions, the organization of political parties, and a host of other practical problems. Thus it was necessary to examine virtually all of the writings of Marx, Engels, and Lenin, and not rely exclusively on those relatively few works wherein they deal explicitly with philosophy.

Some scholars, guided by their professional interests, have not sufficiently understood this interrelation of the theoretical and practical in Marxism. This accounts for the frequent complaint that Marx, Engels, and Lenin failed to deal with this or that philosophical question in a systematic way. The complaint would have a certain justification if we were examining the work of professional philosophers, of men whose main concern was philosophy as a specialized discipline. But the classic Marxists were not philosophers of that kind. On the contrary, although they knew philosophy well (Marx, it should be remembered, had a Doctorate in philosophy) and always gave due recognition to the thinkers who had preceded them, from Aristotle to Hegel, they insisted that a radically different way of dealing with philosophical questions was imperative. They came to believe that philosophy, in the old sense of the term, had come to an end, and that the solutions offered by conventional philosophy, brilliant as many of them were, were nevertheless infected with an alienation from reality. The time had come, they maintained, for the emergence of a new type of philosopher, one whose feet were on the ground, and who regarded the social practice of mankind as both the source of philosophical concepts and the criterion of their truth. Because Marx, Engels, and Lenin rejected the traditional modes of philosophical thinking, the editors had to employ non-traditional procedures in order to present a more or less systematic grasp of Marxist philosophy.

In limiting the selections to Marx, Engels, and Lenin, there is no implication that many others did not contribute to the expansion and development of this philosophy. No one can deny that Joseph Dietzgen, Paul Lafargue, George Plekhanov, and in more recent times Antonio Gramsci, enriched Marxism with specialized contributions. Nor that Joseph Stalin, especially in his *Dialectical and Historical Materialism* and his *Marxism and Linguistics* made contributions of considerable pedagogical significance. One must also mention Mao Tse-tung's penetrating studies of knowledge theory and of dialectical contradiction.

The classic formulations of Marxist philosophy included here are today, even more than in the past, the basis for a tremendous amount of philosophical work, both in the socialist countries and in the capitalist world. More and more this work is covering the whole gamut of philosophical questions, from re-interpretations of the history of philosophy and major thinkers to problems of the relation of formal logic to dialectics, from the basis of moral judgments to cybernetics. Unfortunately, most of this work is unknown in our country. The increasing number of books and periodical literature reveals a new flourishing of Marxist philosophy accompanied by a decided attack on those who in the past tended to make a new form of scholasticism out of Marxism.

There were many problems in the organization of these selections. The same passage sometimes could be placed in different parts of the work. In a few instances the editors found it desirable to break up a passage, using different portions of the same statement under different headings. These problems were accentuated by the fact that many statements of philosophical import appear in a discussion of contemporary problems, as already indicated. Such philosophical reflections, however, when linked to broader and more generalized statements reveal the breadth and scope of Marxist philosophical thought.

Originally, the editors planned to open the volume with such materials as now appear in *Appendix I* under the title "The Formative Period." But further consideration forced a change of mind. Even though this section comes first chronologically, the editors feared that the reader would find it too formidable an obstacle, not only because of its content, but even more because of its language. This material, dating from 1844 to 1845, was written in the Hegelian German of that period. *The Economic and Philosophic Manuscripts of 1844,* written by Marx when he was barely 26, is exciting as one of the first presentations of some of his major philosophical, sociological, and economic concepts. These can best be understood in the light of Marx's mature thinking, and not the other way around, as some maintain. The most varied conclusions have been drawn from the *Manuscripts,* based fundamentally on a complete separation of the young Marx from the later Marx. Once this separation is achieved—always at the expense of the mature Marx—it is then possible to re-make the young Marx into an existentialist, a pragmatist, a Freudian, or even a believer in religion. One can indeed find many isolated statements to support the pet notions of some of these commentators. But the editors believe that careful study will confirm the conclusion that the *Economic and Philosophic Manuscripts* reveal Marx approaching his final separation from all traces of the *speculative* philosophizing of Hegel and the Young Hegelians. He, together with Engels, reached this goal in *The German Ideology,* as Marx himself stated. The materials of this Appendix do add a new dimension to the later thought of Marx and Engels, namely a passionate humanism that they do not explicitly discuss later—in the interest of an objective, scientific approach to their problems—but which nevertheless underlies and pervades all their subsequent thought.

Then there was the problem of Lenin's *Philosophical Notebooks,* which first appeared in English in 1961. They consist of scattered, often cryptic notes in connection with passages Lenin copied from Hegel's *Logic,* Aristotle's *Metaphysics,* and other philosophical works. The entries are almost always too short to be incorporated into other sections of the book. Yet their importance for the understanding of dialectical materialism cannot be overestimated. For not only do they illuminate certain problems, resolved and unresolved, in that philosophy; they at times present new problems and new insights for its further development. We have placed virtually all excerpts from the *Notebooks* that can stand alone in a separate section, *Appendix II,* for the benefit of the more advanced student. Notes in the body of the work refer to Lenin's passages wherever relevant.

One cannot know the world we live in today without knowing Marxist philosophy. The editors have sought to provide the essential materials for such knowledge in the most cogent passages they could find in the writings of Marx, Engels, and Lenin. Only through first-hand acquaintance can one understand why this particular philosophy has become a world phenomenon that is shaping the destinies of a third of mankind and influences both intellectuals and unlettered people everywhere. It safely can be said that no other philosophy has ever been studied so assiduously by so many people under such different circumstances. It is studied in universities, in rice fields, in factory schools, and on sugar plantations. In one land it is an authoritative creed; in another it is anathematized and persecuted. It arouses passionate loyalty or heated condemnation, but it is recognized, even by opponents, to be one of the most significant developments in modern thought.

January, 1963 —THE EDITORS

PART ONE

WHAT MARXISM IS

The philosophers have only interpreted *the world differently, the point is to* change *it.*

—MARX, *Theses on Feuerbach, XI* (1845).

Introduction

THE FIRST question that must be asked of any philosophy is: What does it conceive itself to be doing? Is it what it professes to be? Does it succeed in accomplishing its stated aims? These questions can be answered only in the light of a philosophy's basic conception of itself. Marxism began with a clear idea of what it aimed to be and do. Earlier even than the opening selection from *The Poverty of Philosophy,* written in the winter of 1846–47, in answer to Proudhon's *Philosophy of Poverty,* Marx and Engels regarded themselves as the theoreticians or philosophers of a new kind of socialism. This was to be scientific rather than based on blueprints of the future society or any expression of utopianism. In their minds, as we see two years later in the *Communist Manifesto,* they were neither inventing nor discovering anything, but only giving expression to the actual realities of the world as it then existed. They believed that for this they needed a definite, clear-cut world-outlook and methodology.

The main principles of this philosophy were not formulated until later, but its outlines were already clear. The essential fact for the reader to bear in mind is that the "new materialism" was intended by Marx and Engels from the beginning to be objectively and scientifically true and, at the same time, thoroughly revolutionary. For them it would be revolutionary because it was true, and true because it was revolutionary.

The socialist movement became scientific, Engels explained many years later in *Anti-Dühring,* by embracing the best philosophical achievements to date—notably materialism as developed by the eighteenth century French philosophers and the dialectics of the German philosopher Hegel. Philosophy, in turn, fulfilled itself and began to move towards its "withering away" by identifying itself with the cause of the proletariat, the class that was destined to do away with classes.

Marxist philosophy thus appears in these opening selections as a world-view and a scientific method, as the product of past history and as predicting and creating future history, as both objective truth and a fighting partisan in the working class and socialist struggles. One danger facing any theory that claims so much is its hardening into dogma. This problem is discussed in the last entry in this section from post-revolutionary Russia where Lenin warns the youth against any temptation to believe that Marxism is something that can be learned by rote.

[1]

MARXISM: THE THEORY OF THE PROLETARIAT

A. Science Becomes Revolutionary

Just as the *economists* are the scientific representatives of the bourgeois class, so the *Socialists* and the *Communists* are the theoreticians of the proletarian class. So long as the proletariat is not yet sufficiently developed to constitute itself as a class, and consequently so long as the struggle itself of the proletariat with the bourgeoisie has not yet assumed a political character, and the productive forces are not yet sufficiently developed in the bosom of the bourgeoisie itself as to enable us to catch a glimpse of the material conditions necessary for the emancipation of the proletariat and for the formation of a new society, these theoreticians are merely utopians who, to meet the wants of the oppressed classes, improvise systems and go in search of a regenerating science. But in the measure that history moves forward, and with it the struggle of the proletariat assumes clearer outlines, they no longer need to seek science in their minds; they have only to take note of what is happening before their eyes and to become the mouthpiece of this. So long as they look for science and merely make systems, so long as they are at the beginning of the struggle, they see in poverty nothing but poverty, without seeing in it the revolutionary, subversive side, which will overthrow the old society. From this moment, science, produced by the historical movement and associating itself with it in full recognition of its cause, has ceased to be doctrinaire and has become revolutionary.

—MARX, *The Poverty of Philosophy* (1847), pp. 140*f*.

B. MODERN SOCIALISM REFLECTS AN ACTUAL CONFLICT

The new forces of production have already outgrown the bourgeois form of using them; and this conflict between productive forces and mode of production is not a conflict which has risen in men's heads, as for example the conflict between original sin and divine justice; but it exists in the facts, objectively, outside of us, independently of the will or purpose even of the men who brought it about. Modern socialism is nothing but the reflex in thought of this actual conflict, its ideal reflection in the minds first of the class which is directly suffering under it—the working class.

—ENGELS, *Anti-Dühring* (1878), p. 293.

[2]

"THE MOST RADICAL RUPTURE WITH TRADITIONAL IDEAS"

The theoretical conclusions of the Communists are in no way based on ideas or principles that have been invented, or discovered, by this or that would-be universal reformer.

They merely express, in general terms, actual relations springing from an existing class struggle, from a historical movement going on under our very eyes. The abolition of existing property relations is not at all a distinctive feature of communism.

All property relations in the past have continually been subject to historical change consequent upon the change in historical conditions.

The French Revolution, for example, abolished feudal property in favor of bourgeois property.

The distinguishing feature of communism is not the abolition of property generally, but the abolition of bourgeois property. But modern bourgeois private property is the final and most complete expression of the system of producing and appropriating products that is based on class antagonisms, on the exploitation of the many by the few.

In this sense, the theory of the Communists may be summed up in the single sentence: Abolition of private property.

We Communists have been reproached with the desire of abolishing the right of personally acquiring property as the fruit of a man's own labor, which property is alleged to be the groundwork of all personal freedom, activity, and independence.

Hard-won, self-acquired, self-earned property! Do you mean the property of the petty artisan and the small peasant, a form of property that preceded the bourgeois form? There is no need to abolish that; the development of industry has to a great extent already destroyed it, and is still destroying it daily.

Or do you mean modern bourgeois private property?

But does wage labor create any property for the laborer? Not a bit. It creates capital, i.e., that kind of property which exploits wage labor, and which cannot increase except upon condition of begetting a new supply of wage labor for fresh exploitation. Property, in its present form, is based on the antagonism of capital and wage labor. Let us examine both sides of this antagonism.

To be a capitalist, is to have not only a purely personal, but a social *status* in production. Capital is a collective product, and only by the united action of many members, nay, in the last resort, only by the united action of all members of society, can it be set in motion.

Capital is therefore not a personal, it is a social, power.

When, therefore, capital is converted into common property, into the property of all members of society, personal property is not thereby transformed into social property. It is only the social character of the property that is changed. It loses its class character. . . .

All objections urged against the communist mode of producing and appropriating material products, have, in the same way, been urged against the communist modes of producing and appropriating intellectual products. Just as, to the bourgeois, the disappearance of class property is the disappearance of production itself, so the disappearance of class culture is to him identical with the disappearance of all culture.

That culture, the loss of which he laments, is, for the enormous majority, a mere training to act as a machine.

But don't wrangle with us so long as you apply, to our intended abolition of bourgeois property, the standard of your bourgeois notions of freedom, culture, law, etc. Your very ideas are but the outgrowth of the conditions of your bourgeois production and bourgeois property, just as your jurisprudence is but the will of your class made into a law for all, a will whose essential character and direction are determined by the economic conditions of existence of your class.

The selfish misconception that induces you to transform into eternal laws of nature and of reason, the social forms springing from your present mode of production and form of property—historical relations that rise and disappear in the progress of production—this misconception you share with every ruling class that has preceded you. What you see clearly in the case of ancient property, what you admit in the case of feudal property, you are of course forbidden to admit in the case of your own bourgeois form of property. . . .

The charges against communism made from a religious, a philosophical, and, generally, from an ideological standpoint, are not deserving of serious examination.

Does it require deep intuition to comprehend that man's ideas, views, and conceptions, in one word, man's consciousness, changes with every change in the conditions of his material existence, in his social relations and in his social life?

What else does the history of ideas prove, than that intellectual production changes its character in proportion as material production is changed? The ruling ideas of each age have ever been the ideas of its ruling class.

When people speak of ideas that revolutionize society, they do but express the fact that within the old society the elements of a new one have been created, and that the dissolution of the old ideas keeps even pace with the dissolution of the old conditions of existence.

When the ancient world was in its last throes, the ancient

religions were overcome by Christianity. When Christian ideas succumbed in the 18th century to rationalist ideas, feudal society fought its death-battle with the then revolutionary bourgeoisie. The ideas of religious liberty and freedom of conscience, merely gave expression to the sway of free competition within the domain of knowledge.

"Undoubtedly," it will be said, "religion, moral, philosophical and juridical ideas have been modified in the course of historical development. But religion, morality, philosophy, political science, and law, constantly survived this change."

"There are, besides, eternal truths, such as Freedom, Justice, etc., that are common to all states of society. But communism abolishes eternal truths, it abolishes all religion, and all morality, instead of constituting them on a new basis; it therefore acts in contradiction to all past historical experience."

What does this accusation reduce itself to? The history of all past society has consisted in the development of class antagonisms, antagonisms that assumed different forms at different epochs.

But whatever form they may have taken, one fact is common to all past ages, *viz.*, the exploitation of one part of society by the other. No wonder, then, that the social consciousness of past ages, despite all the multiplicity and variety it displays, moves within certain common forms, or general ideas, which cannot completely vanish except with the total disappearance of class antagonisms.

The communist revolution is the most radical rupture with traditional property relations; no wonder that its development involves the most radical rupture with traditional ideas.

—MARX and ENGELS, *Communist Manifesto* (1848), pp. 23*f*, 26, 28*f*.

[3]

THE GENESIS OF MARXISM: HOW SOCIALISM BECAME A SCIENCE

Modern socialism is, in its content, primarily the product of the perception on the one hand of the class antagonisms existing in modern society, between possessors and non-possessors, wage workers and bourgeois; and on the other hand, of the anarchy ruling in production. In its theoretical form, however, it originally appears as a further and ostensibly more consistent extension of the principles established by the great French philosophers of the eighteenth century. Like every new theory, it had at first to link itself on to the intellectual material which lay ready to its hand, however deep its roots lay in economic facts.

The great men who in France were clearing the minds of men for the coming revolution themselves acted in an extremely revolutionary fashion. They recognized no external authority of any kind. Religion, conceptions of nature, society, political systems, everything was subjected to the most merciless criticism; everything had to justify its existence at the bar of reason or renounce all claim to existence. The reasoning intellect was applied to everything as the sole measure. It was the time when, as Hegel says, the world was stood upon its head; first, in the sense that the human head and the principles arrived at by its thought claimed to be the basis of all human action and association; and then later on also in the wider sense, that the reality which was in contradiction with these principles was in fact turned upside down from top to bottom. All previous forms of society and government, all the old ideas handed down by tradition, were flung into the lumber room as irrational; the world had hitherto allowed itself to be guided solely by prejudices; everything in the past deserved only pity and contempt. Now for the first time appeared the light of day; henceforth, superstition, injustice, privilege, and oppression were to be superseded by eternal truth, eternal justice, equality grounded in Nature, and the inalienable rights of man.

We know today that this kingdom of reason was nothing more than the idealized kingdom of the bourgeoisie; that eternal justice found its realization in bourgeois justice; that equality reduced itself to bourgeois equality before the law; that bourgeois property was proclaimed as one of the essential rights of man; and that the government of reason, the Social Contract of Rousseau, came into existence and could only come into existence as a bourgeois democratic republic. No more than their predecessors could the great thinkers of the 18th century pass beyond the limits imposed on them by their own epoch.

But side by side with the antagonism between the feudal nobility and the bourgeoisie was the general antagonism between the exploiters and the exploited, the rich idlers and the toiling poor.

And it was precisely this circumstance that enabled the representatives of the bourgeoisie to put themselves forward as the representatives not of a special class but of the whole of suffering humanity. Still more; from its origin the bourgeoisie had been saddled with its antithesis: that capitalists cannot exist without wage workers, and in the same degree as the medieval burgher of the guild developed into the modern bourgeois, so the guild journeyman and the day laborer outside the guilds developed into the proletarian. And although, on the whole, the bourgeoisie in their struggle with the nobility could claim to represent at the same time the interests of the different sections of workers of that period, yet in every great bourgeois movement there were independent outbursts of that class which was the more or less developed forerunner of the modern proletariat. For example, the Thomas Münzer tendency in the period of the reformation and peasant war in Germany; the Levellers in the great English revolution; in the great French revolution, Babeuf. Alongside of these revolutionary armed uprisings of a class which was as yet undeveloped, the corresponding theoretical manifestations made their appearance; in the 16th and 17th centuries, utopian portrayals of ideal social conditions; in the 18th century, actual communistic theories (Morelly and Mably). The demand for equality was no longer limited to political rights, but was extended also to the social conditions of individuals; it was not merely class privileges that were to be abolished, but class distinctions themselves. An ascetic communism, linked to Spartan conceptions, was the first form in which the new doctrine made its appearance. Then came the three great utopians: Saint-Simon, with whom bourgeois tendencies still had a certain influence, side by side with proletarian; Fourier, and Owen, who, in the country where capitalist production was most developed, and under the influence of the antagonisms begotten of this, worked out his schemes for the removal of class distinctions systematically and in direct relation to French materialism.

It is common to all three of these that they do not come forward as representatives of the interests of the proletariat which in the meantime history has brought into being. Like the philosophers of the Enlightenment they aim at the emancipation not of a definite class but of all humanity. Like them, they wish to establish the kingdom of reason and eternal justice; but their kingdom is spheres apart from that of the French philosophers. To them the bourgeois world based on the principles of these philosophers is also irrational and unjust, and therefore finds its way to the rubbish bin just as readily as feudalism and all earlier forms of society. If pure reason and justice have not hitherto ruled the world, this has been due only to the fact that until now men have not rightly understood them. What was lacking was just the individual man of genius, who has now arisen and has recognized the truth; the fact that he has now arisen, that the truth has been recognized precisely at this moment, is not an inevitable event, following of necessity in the chain of historical development, but a mere happy accident. He might just as well have been born 500 years earlier, and would then have saved humanity 500 years of errors, strife and suffering.

This mode of outlook is essentially that of all English and French and of the first German Socialists, including Weitling. To all these socialism is the expression of absolute truth, reason, and justice, and needs only to be discovered to conquer the world by virtue of its own power; as absolute truth is independent of time and space and of the historical development of man, it is a mere accident when and where it is discovered. At the same time, absolute truth, reason, and justice are different for the founder of each different school; and as each one's special kind of absolute truth, reason and justice is in turn conditioned by his subjective understanding, his conditions of existence, the measure of his knowledge and intellectual training, so the only solution possible in this conflict of absolute truths is that they should grind each other down. And from this nothing could emerge but a kind of eclectic average socialism, such as in fact dominated the minds of most socialist workers in France and England up to the present time; a mixture, admitting of the most manifold shades, of such of the critical observations, economic doctrines and delineations of future society made by the various founders of sects as excite the least opposition; a mixture which is the more easily produced the more its individual constituents have the sharp edges of precision rubbed off in the stream of debate, as pebbles are rounded in a brook. In order to make socialism into a science it had first to be placed upon a real basis.

Meanwhile, along with and after the French philosophy of the 18th century, the newer German philosophy had arisen, culminating in Hegel. Its greatest merit was the re-adoption of dialectics as the highest form of thinking. The old Greek philosophers were all natural born dialecticians, and Aristotle, the most encyclopedic intellect of them, had even already analyzed the most essential forms of dialectic thought. The newer philosophy, on the other hand, although it too included brilliant exponents of dialectics (*e.g.*, Descartes and Spinoza), had become especially under English influence, more and more rigidly fixed in the so-called metaphysical mode of reasoning, by which also the French of the 18th century, at all events in their special philosophical works, were almost exclusively dominated. But outside philosophy in the restricted sense, the French were nevertheless able to produce masterpieces of dialectic; we need only recall Diderot's *Le Neveu de Rameau* [*Rameau's Nephew*] and Rousseau's *Discourse on the Origin of Inequality among Men*. We give here, in brief, the essential character of these two modes of thought; we shall have to return to them later in greater detail.

When we reflect on nature, or the history of mankind, or our own intellectual activity, the first picture presented to us is of an endless maze of relations and interactions, in which nothing remains what, where and as it was, but everything moves, changes, comes into being, and passes out of existence. This primitive, naive, yet intrinsically correct conception of the world was that of ancient Greek philosophy, and was first clearly formulated by Heraclitus: everything is and also is not, for everything is in *flux*, is constantly changing, constantly coming into being and passing away. But this conception, correctly as it covers the general character of the picture of phenomena as a whole, is yet inadequate to explain the details of which this total picture is composed; and so long as we do not understand these, we also have no clear idea of the picture as a whole. In order to understand these details, we must detach them from their natural or historical connections, and examine each one separately, as to its nature, its special causes and effects, etc. This is primarily the task of natural science and historical research; branches of science which the Greeks of the classical period, on very good grounds, relegated to a merely subordinate position, because they had first of all to collect materials for these sciences to work upon. The beginnings of the exact investigation of nature were first developed by the Greeks of the Alexandrian period, and later on, in the Middle Ages, were further developed by the Arabs. Real natural science, however, dates only from the second half of the 15th century, and from then on it has advanced with constantly increasing rapidity.

The analysis of nature into its individual parts, the grouping of the different natural processes and natural objects in definite classes, the study of the internal anatomy of organic bodies in their manifold forms—these were the fundamental conditions of the gigantic strides in our knowledge of nature which have been made during the last 400 years. But this method of investigation has also left us as a legacy the habit of observing natural objects and natural processes in their isolation, detached from the whole vast interconnection of things; and therefore not in their motion, but in their repose; not as essentially changing, but as fixed constants; not in their life, but in their death. And when, as was the case with Bacon and Locke, this way of looking at things was transferred from natural science to philosophy, it produced the specific narrow-mindedness of the last centuries, the metaphysical mode of thought.

To the metaphysician, things and their mental images, ideas, are isolated, to be considered one after the other apart from each other, rigid, fixed objects of investigation given once for all. He thinks in absolutely discontinuous antitheses. His communication is: "Yea, yea, Nay, nay, for whatsoever is more than these cometh of evil." For him a thing either exists, or it does not exist; it is equally impossible for a thing to be itself and at the same time something else. Positive and negative absolutely exclude one another; cause and effect stand in an equally rigid antithesis one to the other.

At first sight this mode of thought seems to us extremely plausible, because it is the mode of thought of so-called sound common sense. But sound common sense, respectable fellow as he is within the homely precincts of his own four walls, has most wonderful adventures as soon as he ventures out into the wide world of scientific research. Here the metaphysical mode of outlook, justifiable and even necessary as it is in domains whose extent varies according to the nature of the object under investigation, nevertheless sooner or later always reaches a limit beyond which it becomes one-sided, limited, abstract, and loses its way in insoluble contradictions. And this is so because in considering individual things it loses sight of their connections; in contemplating their existence it forgets their coming into being and passing away; in looking at them at rest it leaves their motion out of account; because it cannot see the wood for the trees. For everyday purposes we know, for example, and can say with certainty whether an animal is alive or not; but when we look more closely we find that this is often an extremely complex question, as jurists know very well. They have cudgelled their brains in vain to discover some rational limit beyond which the killing of a child in its mother's womb is murder; and it is equally impossible to determine the moment of death, as physiology has established that death is not a sudden, instantaneous event, but a very protracted process. In the same way every organic being is at each moment the same and not the same; at each moment it is assimilating matter drawn from without, and excreting other matter; at each moment the cells of its body are dying and new ones are being formed; in fact, within a longer or shorter period the matter of its body is completely renewed and is replaced by other atoms of matter, so that every organic being is at all times itself and yet something other than itself. Closer investigation also shows us that the two poles of an antithesis, like positive and negative, are just as inseparable from each other as they are opposed, and that despite all their opposition they mutually penetrate each other. It is just the same with cause and effect; these are conceptions which only have validity in their application to a particular case as such, but when we consider the particular case in its general connection with the world as a whole they merge and dissolve in the conception of universal action and interaction, in which causes and effects are constantly changing places, and what is now or here an effect becomes there or then a cause, and *vice versa*.

None of these processes and methods of thought fit into the frame of metaphysical thinking. But for dialectics, which grasps things and their images, ideas, essentially in their interconnection, in their sequence, their movement, their birth and death, such processes as those mentioned above are so many corroborations of its own method of treatment. Nature is the test of dialectics, and it must be said for modern natural science that it has furnished extremely rich and daily increasing materials for this test, and has thus proved that in the last analysis nature's process is dialectical and not metaphysical. But the scientists who have learnt to think dialectically are still few and far between, and hence the conflict between the discoveries made and the old traditional mode of thought is the explanation of the boundless confusion which now reigns in theoretical natural science and reduces both teachers and students, writers and readers to despair.

An exact representation of the universe, of its evolution and that of mankind, as well as of the reflection of this evolution in the human mind, can therefore only be built up in a dialectical way, taking constantly into account the general actions and reactions of becoming and ceasing to be, of progressive or retrogressive changes. And the more recent German philosophy worked with this standpoint from the first. Kant began his career by resolving the stable solar system of Newton and its eternal permanence—after the famous initial impulse had once been given—into a historical process: the formation of the sun and of all the planets out of a rotating nebulous mass.* Together with this he already drew the conclusion that given this origin of the solar system, its ultimate dissolution was also inevitable. Half a century later his views were given a mathematical basis by Laplace, and another 50 years later the spectroscope proved the existence in space of such incandescent masses of gas in various stages of condensation.

This newer German philosophy culminated in the Hegelian system, in which for the first time—and this is its great merit—the whole natural, historical, and spiritual world was presented as a process, that is, as in constant motion, change, transformation, and development; and the attempt was made to show the internal interconnections in this motion and development. From this standpoint the history of mankind no longer appeared as a confused whirl of senseless deeds of violence, all equally condemnable before the judgment seat of the now matured philosophic reason, and best forgotten as quickly as possible, but as the process of development of humanity itself. It now became the task of thought to follow the gradual stages of this process through all its devious ways, and to trace out the inner regularities running through all its apparently fortuitous phenomena.

That Hegel did not succeed in this task is here immaterial. His epoch-making service was that he propounded it. It is indeed a task which no individual will ever be able to solve. Although Hegel—with Saint-Simon—was the most encyclopedic mind of his age, yet he was limited, in the first place, by the necessarily restricted compass of his own knowledge, and, secondly, by the

* *General Natural History and Theory of the Heavens* (1755). See below, pp. 164*f*.—*Ed.*

similarly restricted scope and depth of the knowledge and ideas of his age. But there was also a third factor. Hegel was an idealist, that is to say, the thoughts within his mind were to him not the more or less abstract images of real things and processes, but, on the contrary, things and their development were to him only the images made real of the "Idea" existing somewhere or other already before the world existed. This mode of thought placed everything on its head, and completely reversed the real connections of things in the world. And although Hegel grasped correctly and with insight many individual interconnections, yet, for the reasons just given, there is also much that in point of detail also is botched, artificial, labored, in a word, wrong. The Hegelian system as such was a colossal miscarriage—but it was also the last of its kind. It suffered, in fact, from an internal and insoluble contradiction. On the one hand, its basic assumption was the historical outlook, that human history is a process of evolution, which by its very nature cannot find intellectual finality in the discovery of any so-called absolute truth; but on the other hand, it laid claim to being the very sum-total of precisely this absolute truth. A system of natural and historical knowledge which is all-embracing and final for all time is in contradiction to the fundamental laws of dialectical thinking; which, however, far from excluding, on the contrary includes, the idea that the systematic knowledge of the external universe can make giant strides from generation to generation.

The realization of the entire incorrectness of previous German idealism led necessarily to materialism, but, it must be noted, not to the simple metaphysical and exclusively mechanical materialism of the 18th century. Instead of the simple and naively revolutionary rejection of all previous history, modern materialism sees history as the process of the evolution of humanity, and its own problem as the discovery of laws of motion of this process. The conception was prevalent among the French of the 18th century, as well as with Hegel, of nature as a whole, moving in narrow circles and remaining immutable, with its eternal celestial bodies, as Newton taught, and unalterable species of organic beings, as Linnaeus taught. In opposition to this conception, modern materialism embraces the more recent advances of natural science, according to which nature also has its history in time, the celestial bodies, like the organic species which under favorable circumstances people them, coming into being and passing away, and the recurrent circles, in so far as they are in any way admissible, assuming infinitely vaster dimensions. In both cases modern materialism is essentially dialectical, and no longer needs any philosophy standing above the other sciences. As soon as each separate science is required to get clarity as to its position in the great totality of things and of our knowledge of things, a special science dealing with this totality is superfluous. What still independently survives of all former philosophy is the science of thought and its laws—formal logic and dialectics. Everything else is merged in the positive science of nature and history.

While, however, the revolution in the conception of nature could only be carried through to the extent that research furnished the corresponding positive materials of knowledge, already much earlier certain historical facts had occurred which led to a decisive change in the conception of history. In 1831, the first working class rising had taken place in Lyons; between 1838 and 1842 the first national workers' movement, that of the English Chartists, reached its height. The class struggle between proletariat and bourgeoisie came to the front in the history of the most advanced European countries, in proportion to the development there, on the one hand, of large-scale industry, and on the other, of the newly-won political domination of the bourgeoisie. Facts more and more forcibly stamped as lies the teachings of bourgeois economics as to the identity of the interests of capital and labor, as to the universal harmony and universal prosperity that free competition brings. All these things could no longer be ignored, any more than the French and English socialism which was their theoretical, even though extremely imperfect, expression. But the old idealist conception of history, which was not yet displaced, knew nothing of class struggles based on material interests, in fact knew nothing at all of material interests; production and all economic relations appeared in it only incidentally, as subordinate elements in the "history of civilization." The new facts made imperative a new examination of all past history, and then it was seen that *all* past history was the history of class struggles, that these warring classes of society are always the product of the conditions of production and exchange, in a word, of the *economic* conditions of their time; that therefore the economic structure of society always forms the real basis from which, in the last analysis, is to be explained the whole superstructure of legal and political institutions, as well as of the religious, philosophical, and other conceptions of each historical period. Now idealism was driven from its last refuge, the philosophy of history; now a materialist conception of history was propounded, and the way found to explain man's consciousness by his being, instead of, as heretofore, his being by his consciousness.

But the socialism of earlier days was just as incompatible with this materialist conception of history as the French materialist conception of nature was with dialectics and modern natural science. It is true that the earlier socialism criticized the existing capitalist mode of production and its consequences, but it could not explain them, and so also could not get the mastery over them; it could only simply reject them as evil. But what had to be done was to show this capitalist mode of production on the one hand in its historical sequence and in its inevitability for a definite historical period, and therefore also the inevitability of its downfall, and on the other hand also to lay bare its essential character, which was still hidden, as its critics had hitherto attacked its evil consequences rather than the process of the thing itself. This was done by the discovery of *surplus value*. It was shown that the appropriation of unpaid labor is the basic form of the capitalist mode of production and of the exploitation of the worker effected through it; that even if the capitalist buys the labor power of his laborer at its full value as a commodity on the market, he yet extracts more value from it than he paid for; and that in the ultimate analysis this surplus value forms those sums of value from which are heaped up the constantly increasing masses of capital in the hands of the possessing classes. The process both of capitalist production and of the production of capital was explained.

These two great discoveries, the materialist conception of history and the revelation of the secret of capitalist production by means of surplus value, we owe to *Marx*. With these discoveries socialism became a science, which had in the first place to be developed in all its details and relations.

—ENGELS, *Anti-Dühring* (1878), pp. 23–33.

[4]

THE THREE COMPONENT PARTS OF MARXISM

Throughout the civilized world the teachings of Marx evoke the utmost hostility and hatred of all bourgeois science (both official and liberal), which regards Marxism as a kind of "pernicious sect." And no other attitude is to be expected, for there can be no "impartial" social science in a society based on class struggle. In one way or another, *all* official and liberal science *defends* wage slavery, whereas Marxism has declared relentless war on wage slavery. To expect science to be impartial in a wage-slave society is as silly and naive as to expect impartiality from manufacturers on the question whether workers' wages should be increased by decreasing the profits of capital.

But this is not all. The history of philosophy and the history of social science show with perfect clarity that there is nothing resembling "sectarianism" in Marxism, in the sense of its being a hidebound, petrified doctrine, a doctrine which arose *away from* the highroad of development of world civilization. On the contrary, the genius of Marx consists precisely in the fact that he furnished answers to questions which had already engrossed the foremost minds of humanity. His teachings arose as a direct and immediate *continuation* of the teachings of the greatest representatives of philosophy, political economy and socialism.

The Marxist doctrine is omnipotent because it is true. It is complete and harmonious, and provides men with an integral world conception which is irreconcilable with any form of superstition, reaction, or defense of bourgeois oppression. It is the legitimate successor of the best that was created by humanity in the 19th century in the shape of German philosophy, English political economy, and French socialism.

On these three sources of Marxism, which are at the same time its component parts, we shall briefly dwell.

I

The philosophy of Marxism is *materialism*. Throughout the modern history of Europe, and especially at the end of the 18th century in France, which was the scene of a decisive battle against every kind of medieval rubbish, against feudalism in institutions and ideas, materialism has proved to be the only philosophy that is consistent, true to all the teachings of natural science and hostile to superstition, cant and so forth. The enemies of democracy therefore tried in every way to "refute," undermine, and defame materialism, and advocated various forms of philosophical idealism, which always, in one way or another, amounts to an advocacy or support of religion.

Marx and Engels always defended philosophical materialism in the most determined manner and repeatedly explained the profound erroneousness of every deviation from this basis. Their views are most clearly and fully expounded in the works of Engels, *Ludwig Feuerbach* and *Anti-Dühring*, which, like the *Communist Manifesto*, are handbooks for every class-conscious worker.

But Marx did not stop at the materialism of the 18th century; he advanced philosophy. He enriched it with the acquisitions of German classical philosophy, especially of the Hegelian system, which in its turn led to the materialism of Feuerbach. The chief of these acquisitions is *dialectics, i.e.*, the doctrine of development in its fullest and deepest form, free of one-sidedness—the doctrine of the relativity of human knowledge, which provides us with a reflection of eternally developing matter. The latest discoveries of natural science—radium, electrons, the transmutation of elements—have remarkably confirmed Marx's dialectical materialism, despite the teachings of the bourgeois philosophers with their "new" reversions to old and rotten idealism.

Deepening and developing philosophical materialism, Marx completed it, extended its knowledge of nature to the knowledge of *human society*. Marx's *historical materialism* was one of the greatest achievements of scientific thought. The chaos and arbitrariness that had previously reigned in the views on history and politics gave way to a strikingly integral and harmonious scientific theory, which shows how, in consequence of the growth of productive forces, out of one system of social life another and higher system develops—how capitalism, for instance, grows out of feudalism.

Just as man's knowledge reflects nature (i.e., developing matter), which exists independently of him, so man's *social knowledge* (i.e., the various views and doctrines—philosophical, religious, political, and so forth) reflects the *economic system* of society. Political institutions are a superstructure on the economic foundation. We see, for example, that the various political forms of the modern European states serve to fortify the rule of the bourgeoisie over the proletariat.

Marx's philosophy is finished philosophical materialism, which has provided humanity, and especially the working class, with powerful instruments of knowledge.

II

Having recognized that the economic system is the foundation on which the political superstructure is erected, Marx devoted most attention to the study of this economic system. Marx's principal work, *Capital,* is devoted to a study of the economic system of modern, i.e., capitalist, society.

Classical political economy, before Marx, evolved in England, the most developed of the capitalist countries. Adam Smith and David Ricardo, by their investigations of the economic system, laid the foundations of the *labor theory of value*. Marx continued their work. He rigidly proved and consistently developed this theory. He showed that the value of every commodity is determined by the quantity of socially necessary labor time spent on its production.

Where the bourgeois economists saw a relation of things (the exchange of one commodity for another), Marx revealed a *relation of men*. The exchange of commodities expresses the tie by which individual producers are bound through the market. *Money* signifies that this tie is becoming closer and closer, inseparably binding the entire economic life of the individual producers into one whole. *Capital* signifies a further development of this tie: man's labor power becomes a commodity. The wage worker sells his labor power to the owner of the land, factories and instruments of labor. The worker uses one part of the labor day to cover the expenses of maintaining himself and his family (wages), while the other part of the day the worker toils without remuneration, creating *surplus value* for the capitalist, the source of profit, the source of the wealth of the capitalist class.

The doctrine of surplus value is the cornerstone of Marx's economic theory.

Capital, created by the labor of the worker, presses on the worker by ruining the small masters and creating an army of unemployed. In industry, the victory of large-scale production is at once apparent, but we observe the same phenomenon in agriculture as well: the superiority of large-scale capitalist agriculture increases, the application of machinery grows, peasant economy falls into the noose of money capital, it declines and sinks into ruin, burdened by its backward technique. In agriculture, the decline of small-scale production assumes different forms, but the decline itself is an indisputable fact.

By destroying small-scale production, capital leads to an increase in productivity of labor and to the creation of a monopoly position for the associations of big capitalists. Production itself becomes more and more social—hundreds of thousands and millions of workers become bound together in a systematic economic organism—but the product of the collective labor is appropriated by a handful of capitalists. The anarchy of production grows, as do crises, the furious chase after markets, and the insecurity of existence of the mass of the population.

While increasing the dependence of the workers on capital, the capitalist system creates the great power of united labor.

Marx traced the development of capitalism from the first germs of commodity economy, from simple exchange, to its highest forms, to large-scale production.

And the experience of all capitalist countries, old and new, is clearly demonstrating the truth of this Marxist doctrine to increasing numbers of workers every year.

Capitalism has triumphed all over the world, but this triumph is only the prelude to the triumph of labor over capital.

III

When feudalism was overthrown, and "*free*" capitalist society appeared on God's earth, it at once became apparent that this freedom meant a new system of oppression and exploitation of the toilers. Various socialist doctrines immediately began to arise as a reflection of and protest against this oppression. But early socialism was *utopian* socialism. It criticized capitalist society, it condemned and damned it, it dreamed of its destruction, it indulged in fancies of a better order and endeavored to convince the rich of the immorality of exploitation.

But utopian socialism could not point the real way out. It could not explain the essence of wage slavery under capitalism, nor discover the laws of its development, nor point to the *social force* which is capable of becoming the creator of a new society.

Meanwhile, the stormy revolutions which everywhere in Europe, and especially in France, accompanied the fall of feudalism, of serfdom, more and more clearly revealed the *struggle of classes* as the basis and the motive force of the whole development.

Not a single victory of political freedom over the feudal class was won except against desperate resistance. Not a single capitalist country evolved on a more or less free and democratic basis except by a life and death struggle between the various classes of capitalist society.

The genius of Marx consists in the fact that he was able before anybody else to draw from this and consistently apply the deduction that world history teaches. This deduction is the doctrine of the *class struggle*.

People always were and always will be the stupid victims of deceit and self-deceit in politics until they learn to discover the *interests* of some class behind all moral, religious, political, and social phrases, declarations, and promises. The supporters of reforms and improvements will always be fooled by the defenders of the old order until they realize that every old institution, however barbarous and rotten it may appear to be, is maintained by the forces of some ruling classes. And there is *only one* way of smashing the resistance of these classes, and that is to find, in the very society which surrounds us, and to enlighten and organize for the struggle, the forces which can—and, owing to their social position, *must*—constitute a power capable of sweeping away the old and creating the new.

Marx's philosophical materialism has alone shown the proletariat the way out of the spiritual slavery in which all oppressed classes have hitherto languished. Marx's economic theory has alone explained the true position of the proletariat in the general system of capitalism.

Independent organizations of the proletariat are multiplying all over the world, from America to Japan and from Sweden to South Africa. The proletariat is becoming enlightened and educated by waging its class struggle; it is ridding itself of the prejudices of bourgeois society; it is rallying its ranks ever more closely and is learning to gauge the measure of its successes; it is steeling its forces and is growing irresistibly.

—Lenin, "The Three Sources and Three Component Parts of Marxism" (1913), *Selected Works,* vol. xi, pp. 3–8.

[5]

COMMUNISM CANNOT BE LEARNED BY ROTE

What do we need in order to learn communism? What must be singled out from the sum total of general knowledge to acquire a knowledge of communism? Here a number of dangers threaten us, which invariably crop up whenever the task of learning communism is presented incorrectly, or when it is interpreted *too one-sidedly*.

Naturally, the first thought that enters one's mind is that learning communism means imbibing the sum total of knowledge that is contained in communist textbooks, pamphlets, and books. But such a definition of the study of communism would be too crude and inadequate.

If the study of communism solely consisted in imbibing what is contained in communist books and pamphlets, we might all too easily obtain communist text-jugglers or braggarts, and this would very often cause us harm and damage, because such people, having learned by rote what is contained in communist books and pamphlets would be incapable of combining this knowledge, and would be unable to act in the way communism really demands.

One of the greatest evils and misfortunes bequeathed to us by the old capitalist society is the complete divorcement of books from practical life; for we have had books in which everything was described in the best possible manner, yet these books in the majority of cases were most disgusting and hypocritical lies that described communist society falsely. That is why the mere routine absorption of what is written in books about communism would be utterly wrong. In our speeches and articles we do not now merely repeat what was formerly said about communism, because our speeches and articles are connected with daily, all-around work. Without work, without struggle, a routine knowledge of communism obtained from communist pamphlets and books would be worthless, for it would continue the old divorcement of theory from practice, that old separation which constituted the most disgusting feature of the old bourgeois society. . . .

The old school was a school of cramming; it compelled pupils to imbibe a mass of useless, superfluous, barren knowledge, which clogged the brain and transformed the younger generation into officials turned out to pattern. But you would be committing a great mistake if you attempted to draw the conclusion that one can become a Communist without acquiring what human knowledge has accumulated. It would be a mistake to think that it is enough to imbibe communist slogans, the conclusions of communist science, without acquiring the sum total of knowledge of which communism itself is a consequence.

Marxism is an example of how communism arose out of the sum total of human knowledge.

You have read and heard that communist theory, the science of communism, mainly created by Marx, that this doctrine of Marxism has ceased to be the product of a single Socialist of the 19th century, even though he was a genius, and that it has become the doctrine of millions and tens of millions of proletarians all over the world, who are applying this doctrine in their struggle against capitalism.

And if you were to ask why the Marxist doctrine was able to capture the hearts of millions and tens of millions of the most revolutionary class, you would receive only one answer: It was because Marx took his stand on the firm foundation of the human knowledge acquired under capitalism. Having studied the laws of development of human society, Marx realized that the development of capitalism was inevitably leading to communism. And the principal thing is that he proved this only on the basis of the most exact, most detailed and most profound study of this capitalist society; and this he was able to do because he had fully assimilated all that earlier science had taught.

We studied critically everything that had been created by human society, not ignoring a single item. We studied everything that had been created by human thought, criticized it, put it to the test of the working class movement, and drew conclusions which people hemmed in by bourgeois limitations or bound by bourgeois prejudices could not draw. . . .

We must not take from the old school the system of loading young people's minds with an immense amount of knowledge, nine-tenths of which was useless and one-tenth distorted. But this does not mean that we can confine ourselves to communist conclusions and imbibe only communist slogans. You will not create communism that way. You can become a Communist only by enriching your mind with the knowledge of all the treasures created by mankind.

We do not need cramming; but we do need to develop and perfect the mind of every student by a knowledge of the principal facts. For communism would become a void, a mere signboard, and a Communist would become a mere braggart, if all the knowledge he had obtained were not digested in his mind. You must not only assimilate this knowledge, you must assimilate it critically, so as not to cram your mind with useless lumber, but enrich it with all those facts that are indispensable to the modern man of education.

If a Communist took it into his head to boast about his communism because of the ready-made conclusions he had absorbed, without putting in a great deal of serious and hard work, without understanding the facts which he must examine critically, he would be a very sorry Communist. Such superficiality would be decidedly fatal. If I know that I know little, I shall strive to learn more; but if a man says that he is a Communist and that he need know nothing thoroughly, he will never be anything like a Communist.

—LENIN, "Address at Congress of Russian Young Communist League" (1920), *The Young Generation,* pp. 28–32.

PART TWO

MATERIALISM *VERSUS* IDEALISM

> *The materialistic outlook on nature means no more than simply conceiving nature just as it exists without any foreign admixture.*
>
> —ENGELS, *Ludwig Feuerbach* (1888), p. 68.

Introduction

THE BASIC principles of Marxist materialism are easy to understand. Like all previous materialism, it holds that the world exists independent of our knowing it, and that it is material—not mental or spiritual—in origin and nature. Marxism differs from previous materialism in three major respects.

First, it has no commitments as to what matter is. *Matter* is simply the name for what exists objectively, with the one proviso that mind, thought, consciousness are its products. All further questions as to the nature of matter, its structure or composition, the relation of mass, energy, space, time, etc., are not primarily philosophical, but are to be resolved by the natural sciences themselves.

Secondly, unlike virtually all previous materialism, it is not reductive. It does not deny qualities. Neither does it seek to reduce higher levels of organization, or "integration" as they are now called, to lower ones. In conceiving nature "as it is, without reservations," to use Engels' expression, Marxist or dialectical materialism accepts the myriad qualities we find in our world as having an objective basis that the sciences can ascertain. In short, we have here a materialism which loses nothing of the qualitative richness of our experience.

Finally, in addition to a world of infinite qualitative variety, we have in this materialism a world of infinitely complex interaction. Unlike most previous materialism, thanks to its dialectical method, Marxist materialism holds to no "billiard-ball" universe, in which A strikes B, B strikes C, and so on in an endless succession of mechanical causes. Things interact in such ways that an organism which is a product of its environment may also react upon and change its environment, and man can be a product of history and in turn make history and change himself in the process.

Thus its founders called it a "new" materialism, and later "dialectical" materialism, to distinguish it from traditional materialism which in their eyes was bogged down in a "mechanical" or "metaphysical" approach. It could have been designated by many other names, such as evolutionary naturalism, scientific materialism, or naturalistic humanism. These and other possible appellations correctly designate aspects and leading features of this philosophy, but Engels at least would have found them insufficiently precise and insufficiently inclusive, even though he once referred to it simply as "modern materialism." Marx and Engels had the highest respect and admiration for Democritus, Epicurus, and Lucretius, the great materialists of the ancient world. But, they believed, there had to be added to the permanent foundations of materialism these men had laid "the whole thought content of two thousand years of development of philosophy and natural science" and of history too. (Engels, *Anti-Dühring*, p. 152.)

This was not a mere "addition," however, but a radical transformation. This new or modern materialism would have been all but unrecognizable by its ancient forebears. It was no longer a whole system of the world, with atoms in infinite motion in an infinite void, and the attempt to explain all things, including human thought, by their motions. This new materialism "is in fact," wrote Engels, "no longer a philosophy, but a simple world outlook which has to establish its validity and be applied not in a science of sciences [*i.e.*, a philosophical system] standing apart, but within the positive sciences." (*idem.*)

One feature of most of the materials in this section that strikes the unprepared reader with special force is their intense partisanship. Two considerations concerning this must be borne in mind. The first is that from the very beginning of philosophy, at least in the West, philosophers have taken their positions with great earnestness, passionately contending for one kind of outlook on the world against another. In the second place, it must be remembered that Marx, Engels, and Lenin were not academic philosophers but fighters in what they regarded as the greatest revolutionary struggle of all history. For them the philosophical issues of materialism and idealism were deeply intertwined with the class struggle. The philosophical agnostics who avoid a commitment to either materialism or idealism seemed to them to be nothing but fence-sitters in the class struggle. Engels calls them "shamefaced materialists." In a different period, Lenin regards them as helpers of "reactionary idealism" and clericalism. This latter view appears here in the selections from Lenin's *Materialism and Empirio-Criticism,* in which work, early in this century, he defended Marxist materialism against prevailing forms of positivism and empiricism.

[1]

MATERIALISM AND IDEALISM: THE TWO BASIC SCHOOLS OF PHILOSOPHY

The great basic question of all philosophy, especially of modern philosophy, is that concerning the relation of thinking and being. From the very early times when men, still completely ignorant of the structure of their own bodies, under the stimulus of dream apparitions, came to believe that their thinking and sensation were not activities of their bodies, but of a distinct soul which inhabits the body and leaves it at death—from this time, men have been driven to reflect about the relation between this soul and the outside world. . . .

This question could for the first time be put forward in its whole acuteness, could achieve its full significance, only after European society had awakened from the long hibernation of the Christian Middle Ages. The question of the position of thinking in relation to being, a question which, by the way, had played a great part also in the scholasticism of the Middle Ages, the question, which is primary, spirit or nature—that question, in relation to the Church, was sharpened into this: "Did God create the world or has the world been in existence eternally?"

The answers which the philosophers gave to this question split them into two great camps. Those who asserted the primacy of spirit to nature and, therefore, in the last instance, assumed world creation in some form or other—(and among the philosophers, Hegel, for example, this creation often becomes still more intricate and impossible than in Christianity)—comprised the camp of idealism. The others, who regarded nature as primary, belong to the various schools of materialism.

These two expressions, idealism and materialism, primarily signify nothing more than this; and here also they are not used in any other sense. What confusion arises when some other meaning is put into them will be seen below.

But the question of the relation of thinking and being has yet another side: In what relation do our thoughts about the world surrounding us stand to this world itself? Is our thinking capable of the cognition of the real world? Are we able in our ideas and notions of the real world to produce a correct reflection of reality? In philosophical language this question is called the question of the "identity of thinking and being," and the overwhelming majority of philosophers give an affirmative answer to this question. With Hegel, for example, its affirmation is self-evident; for what we perceive in the real world is precisely its thought-content—that which makes the world a gradual realization of the absolute idea which absolute idea has existed somewhere from eternity, independent of the world and before the world. But it is manifest without more ado that thought can know a content which is from the outset a thought-content. It is equally manifest that what is here to be proved is already tacitly contained in the presupposition. But that in no way prevents Hegel from drawing the further conclusion from his proof of the identity of thinking and being that his philosophy, because it is correct for his own thinking, is therefore the only correct one, and that the identity of thinking and being must prove its validity by mankind immediately translating his philosophy from theory into practice and transforming the whole world according to Hegelian principles. This is an illusion which he shares with well-nigh all philosophers.

In addition there is yet another set of different philosophers—

those who question the possibility of any cognition (or at least of an exhaustive cognition) of the world. To them, among the moderns, belong Hume and Kant, and they have played a very important role in philosophical development. What is decisive in the refutation of this view has already been said by Hegel—in so far as this was possible from an idealist standpoint. The materialistic additions made by Feuerbach are more ingenious than profound. The most telling refutation of this as of all other philosophical fancies is practice, *viz.*, experiment and industry. If we are able to prove the correctness of our conception of a natural process by making it ourselves, bringing it into being out of its conditions and using it for our own purposes into the bargain, then there is an end of the Kantian incomprehensible "thing-in-itself." The chemical substances produced in the bodies of plants and animals remained just such "things-in-themselves" until organic chemistry began to produce them one after another, whereupon the "thing-in-itself" became a thing for us, as, for instance, alizarin, the coloring matter of the madder, which we no longer trouble to grow in the madder roots in the field, but produce much more cheaply and simply from coal tar. . . . If, nevertheless, the Neo-Kantians are attempting to resurrect the Kantian conception in Germany and the agnostics that of Hume in England (where in fact it had never ceased to survive), this is—in view of their theoretical and practical refutation accomplished long ago—scientifically a regression and practically merely a shamefaced way of surreptitiously accepting materialism, while denying it before the world.

But during this long period from Descartes to Hegel and from Hobbes to Feuerbach, the philosophers were by no means impelled, as they thought they were, solely by the force of pure reason. On the contrary. What really pushed them forward was the powerful and ever more rapidly onrushing progress of natural science and industry. Among the materialists this was plain on the surface, but the idealist systems also filled themselves more and more with a materialist content and attempted pantheistically to reconcile the antithesis between mind and matter. Thus, ultimately, the Hegelian system represents merely a materialism idealistically turned upside down in method and content. . . .

The course of evolution of Feuerbach is that of a Hegelian—a never quite orthodox Hegelian, it is true—into a materialist; an evolution which at a definite stage necessitates a complete rupture with the idealist system of his predecessor. With irresistible force Feuerbach is finally forced to the realization that the Hegelian pre-mundane existence of the "absolute idea," the "pre-existence of the logical categories"* before the world existed, is nothing more than the fantastic survival of the belief in the existence of an extra-mundane creator; that the material, sensuously perceptible world to which we ourselves belong is the only reality; and that our consciousness and thinking, however supra-sensuous they may seem, are the product of a material, bodily organ, the brain. Matter is not a product of mind, but mind itself is merely the highest product of matter. This is, of course, pure materialism. But, having got so far, Feuerbach stops short. He cannot overcome the customary philosophical prejudice, prejudice not against the thing but against the name materialism. He says: "To me materialism is the foundation of the edifice of human essence and knowledge, but to me it is not what it is to the physiologist, to the natural scientist in the narrower sense, for example, Moleschott, and necessarily so indeed from their standpoint and profession, the building itself. Backwards I fully agree with the materialists; but not forwards."

Here Feuerbach lumps together the materialism that is a general world outlook resting upon a definite conception of the relation between matter and mind, and the special form in which this world outlook was expressed at a definite stage of historical development, *viz.*, in the eighteenth century. More than that, he confuses it with the shallow and vulgarized form in which the materialism of the 18th century continues to exist today in the minds of naturalists and physicians, the form which was preached on their tours in the 'fifties by Büchner, Vogt and Moleschott. But just as idealism underwent a series of stages of development, so also did materialism. With each epoch-making discovery even in the sphere of natural science it has to change its form; and after history also was subjected to materialistic treatment, here also a new avenue of development has opened.

The materialism of the last century was predominantly mechanical, because at that time, of all natural sciences, mechanics and indeed only the mechanics of solid bodies—celestial and

* For Hegel the categories of logical thought were conceived as the driving force and inner substance of the world of nature, society, and mind, whereas for Marxian materialism they are nothing else than the abstract reflection in the human mind of the material world.—*Ed.*

terrestrial—in short, the mechanics of gravity, had come to any definite close. Chemistry at that time existed only in its infantile, phlogistic form. Biology still lay in swaddling clothes; vegetable and animal organisms had been only roughly examined and were explained as the result of purely mechanical causes. As the animal was to Descartes, so was man a machine to the materialists of the 18th century.* This exclusive application of the standards of mechanics to processes of a chemical and organic nature—in which processes, it is true, the laws of mechanics are also valid, but are pushed into the background by other and higher laws—constitutes a specific but at that time inevitable limitation of classical French materialism.

The second specific limitation of this materialism lay in its inability to comprehend the universe as a process—as matter developing in an historical process. This was in accordance with the level of the natural science of that time, and with the metaphysical, i.e., anti-dialectical manner of philosophizing connected with it. Nature, it was known, was in constant motion. But according to the ideas of that time, this motion turned eternally in a circle and therefore never moved from the spot; it produced the same results over and over again. This conception was at that time inevitable. The Kantian theory of the origin of the solar system † had been put forward but recently and was regarded merely as a curiosity. The history of the development of the earth, geology, was still totally unknown, and the conception that the animate natural beings of today are the result of a long sequence of development from the simple to the complex could not at that time scientifically be put forward at all. The unhistorical view of nature was therefore inevitable. We have the less reason to reproach the philosophers of the 18th century on this account, since the same thing is found in Hegel. According to him, nature, as a mere "alienation" of the idea, is incapable of development in time—capable only of extending its manifoldness in space, so that it displays simultaneously and alongside of one another all the stages of development comprised in it, and is condemned to an eternal repetition of the same process. This absurdity of a development in space, but outside of time—the fundamental condition of all development—Hegel imposes upon na-

* For example, Lamettrie's *Man a Machine* (1748).—*Ed.*

† The nebular hypothesis of the origin of the solar system.—*Ed.*

ture just at the very time when geology, embryology, the physiology of plants and animals, and organic chemistry were being built up, and when everywhere on the basis of these new sciences brilliant foreshadowings of the later theory of evolution were appearing (*e.g.*, Goethe and Lamarck). But the system demanded it; hence the method, for the sake of the system, had to become untrue to itself.

This same unhistorical conception prevailed also in the domain of history. Here the struggle against the remnants of the Middle Ages blurred the view. The Middle Ages were regarded as a mere interruption of history by a thousand years of universal barbarism. The great progress made in the Middle Ages—the extension of the area of European culture, the bringing into existence there of great nations, capable of survival, and finally the enormous technical progress of the 14th and 15th centuries—all this was not seen. Consequently a rational insight into the great historical inter-connections was made impossible, and history served at best as a collection of examples and illustrations for the use of philosophers.

The vulgarizing pedlars who in Germany in the 'fifties busied themselves with materialism by no means overcame the limitations of their teachers. All the advances of natural science which had been made in the meantime served them only as new proofs against the existence of a creator of the world; and, in truth, it was quite outside their scope to develop the theory any further. Though idealism was at the end of its tether and was dealt a death blow by the Revolution of 1848, it had the satisfaction of seeing that materialism had for the moment fallen lower still. Feuerbach was unquestionably right when he refused to take responsibility for this materialism; only he should not have confounded the doctrines of these hedge-preachers with materialism in general. . . .

Here, however, two things must be pointed out.

First, during Feuerbach's lifetime, natural science was still involved in a process of violent fermentation—which only during the last 15 years has reached a relatively clear conclusion. New scientific data were acquired to a hitherto unheard-of extent, but the establishing of inter-relations, and thereby the bringing of order into this chaos of discoveries following closely upon each other's heels has only quite recently become possible for the first time. It is true that Feuerbach had lived to see all three of the decisive discoveries—that of the cell, the transformation of energy, and the theory of evolution named after Darwin. But how could the lonely philosopher, living in rural solitude, be able sufficiently to follow scientific developments in order to appreciate at their full value discoveries which scientists themselves at that time either contested or did not adequately know how to make use of? The blame for this falls solely upon the wretched conditions in Germany, in consequence of which cobweb-spinning eclectic flea-crackers had taken possession of the chairs of philosophy, while Feuerbach, who towered above them all, had to rusticate and grow sour in a little village. It is therefore not Feuerbach's fault that the historical conception of nature, which had now become possible and which removed all the one-sidedness of French materialism, remained inaccessible to him.

Secondly, Feuerbach is quite correct in asserting that the exclusively natural-scientific materialism was indeed "the foundation of the edifice of human . . . knowledge, but . . . not . . . the building itself." For we live not only in nature but also in human society, and this also no less than nature has its history of development and its science. It was therefore a question of bringing the science of society (i.e., the sum total of the so-called historical and philosophical sciences) into harmony with the materialist foundation, and of reconstructing it thereupon. But it did not fall to Feuerbach's lot to do this. In spite of the "foundation," he remained here bound by the traditional idealist fetters, a fact which he recognizes in these words: "Backwards I . . . agree with the materialists; but not forwards!"

—ENGELS, *Ludwig Feuerbach* (1888), pp. 20–29.

[2]

THE DEVELOPMENT OF MODERN MATERIALISM IN FRANCE AND ENGLAND

The French Enlightenment of the 18th century, in particular French materialism, was not only a struggle against the existing political institutions and the existing religion and theology; it was just as much an open struggle against metaphysics of the 17th century, and against all metaphysics, in particular that of Descartes, Malebranche, Spinoza and Leibniz. Philosophy was opposed to metaphysics as Feuerbach, in his first decisive attack on Hegel opposed sober philosophy to drunken speculation. Seventeenth century metaphysics, beaten off the field by the French Enlightenment, to be precise, by French materialism of the 18th century, was given a victorious and solid restoration in German philosophy, particularly in speculative German philosophy of the 19th century. After Hegel linked it in so masterly a fashion with all subsequent metaphysics and with German idealism and founded a metaphysical universal kingdom, the attack on speculative metaphysics and metaphysics in general again corresponded, as in the 18th century, to the attack on theology. It will be defeated forever by materialism which has now been perfected by the work of speculation itself and coincides with humanism. As Feuerbach represented materialism in the theoretical domain, French and English socialism and communism in the practical field represent materialism which now coincides with humanism.

There are two trends in French materialism; one traces its origin to Descartes, the other to Locke. The latter is mainly a French development and leads direct to socialism. The former, mechanical materialism, merges with what is properly French natural science. The two trends cross in the course of development. We have no need here to go deep into French materialism, which comes direct from Descartes, any more than into the French Newton school or the development of French natural science in general.

We shall therefore just note the following:

Descartes in his physics endowed matter with self-creative power and conceived mechanical motion as the act of its life. He completely separated his physics from his metaphysics. Within his physics matter is the only substance, the only basis of being and of knowledge.

Mechanical French materialism followed Descartes' physics in opposition to his metaphysics. His followers were by profession anti-metaphysicists, i.e., physicists.

The school begins with the physician Leroy, reaches its zenith with the physician Cabanis, and the physician Lamettrie is its center. Descartes was still living when Leroy, like Lamettrie in the 18th century, transposed the Cartesian structure of animals to the human soul and affirmed that the soul is a modus of the body and ideas are mechanical motions. Leroy even thought Descartes had kept his real opinion secret. Descartes protested. At the end of the 18th century Cabanis perfected Cartesian materialism in his treatise: *Les Rapports du Physique et du Moral de l'homme* [Relationships of the Physical and Moral in Man].

Cartesian materialism still exists today in France. It had great success in mechanical natural science which will be least of all reproached with romanticism.

Metaphysics of the 17th century, represented in France by Descartes, had materialism as its antagonist from its very birth. It personally opposed Descartes in Gassendi, the restorer of Epicurean materialism. French and English materialism was always closely related to Democritus and Epicurus. Cartesian metaphysics had another opponent in the English materialist Hobbes. Gassendi and Hobbes were victorious over their opponent long after their death when metaphysics was already officially dominant in all French schools.

Voltaire observed that the indifference of Frenchmen to the disputes between Jesuits and Jansenists in the 18th century was due less to philosophy than to Law's financial speculation. And, in fact, the downfall of 17th century metaphysics can be explained by the materialistic theory of the 18th century only as far as that theoretical movement itself is explained by the practical nature of French life at the time. That life was turned to the immediate present, worldly enjoyment and worldly interests, the earthly world. Its anti-theological, anti-metaphysical, and materialistic practice demanded corresponding anti-theological, anti-metaphysical and materialistic theories. Metaphysics had in practice lost all credit. Here we have only to indicate briefly the theoretical process.

In the 17th century metaphysics (*cf.* Descartes, Leibniz, and others) still had an element of positive, profane content. It made discoveries in mathematics, physics, and other exact sciences which seemed to come within its pale. This appearance was done away with as early as the beginning of the 18th century. The positive sciences broke off from it and determined their own separate fields. The whole wealth of metaphysics was reduced to beings of thought and heavenly things, although this was the very time when real beings and earthly things began to be the center of all interest. Metaphysics had gone stale. In the very year in which Malebranche and Arnauld, the last great French metaphysicians of the 17th century, died, Helvetius and Condillac were born.

The man who deprived 17th century metaphysics of all credit in the domain of theory was Pierre Bayle. His weapon was skepticism which he forged out of metaphysics' own magic formulae. He at first proceeded from Cartesian metaphysics. As Feuerbach was driven by the fight against speculative theology to the fight against speculative philosophy precisely because he recognized in speculation the last prop of theology, because he had to force theology to turn back from pretended science to coarse, repulsive faith, so Bayle too was driven by religious doubt to doubt about metaphysics which was the support of that faith. He therefore critically investigated metaphysics from its very origin. He became its historian in order to write the history of its death. He mainly refuted Spinoza and Leibniz.

Pierre Bayle did not only prepare the reception of materialism and the philosophy of common sense in France by shattering metaphysics with his skepticism. He heralded atheistic society, which was soon to come to existence, by proving that a society consisting only of atheists is possible, that an atheist can be a respectable man and that it is not by atheism but by superstition and idolatry that man debases himself.

To quote the expression of a French writer, Pierre Bayle was "the last metaphysician in the 17th century sense of the word and the first philosopher in the sense of the 18th century."

Besides the negative refutation of 17th century theology and metaphysics, a positive, anti-metaphysical system was required. A book was needed which would systematize and theoretically justify the practice of life of the time. Locke's treatise on the origin of human reason came from across the Channel as if in answer to a call. It was welcomed enthusiastically like a long-awaited guest.

To the question: Was Locke perchance a follower of Spinoza? "profane" history may answer:

Materialism is the son of Great Britain by birth. Even Britain's scholastic Duns Scotus wondered: "Can matter think?"

In order to bring about that miracle he had recourse to God's omnipotence, i.e., he forced theology itself to preach materialism. In addition he was a nominalist. Nominalism is a main component of English materialism and is in general the first expression of materialism.

The real founder of English materialism and all modern experimental science was Bacon. For him natural science was true science and physics based on perception was the most excellent part of natural science. Anaxagoras with his homoeomeria * and Democritus with his atoms are often the authorities he refers to. According to his teaching the senses are infallible and are the source of all knowledge. Science is experimental and consists in applying a rational method to the data provided by the senses. Induction, analysis, comparison, observation, and experiment are the principal requisites of rational method. The first and most important of the inherent qualities of matter is motion, not only mechanical and mathematical movement, but still more impulse, vital life-spirit, tension, or, to use Jacob Boehme's expression, the throes (Qual) of matter. The primary forms of matter are the living, individualizing forces of being inherent in it and producing the distinctions between the species.

In Bacon, its first creator, materialism contained latent and still in a naive way the germs of all-round development. Matter smiled at man with poetic sensuous brightness. The aphoristic doctrine itself, on the other hand, was full of the inconsistencies of theology.

In its further development materialism became one-sided. Hobbes was the one who systematized Bacon's materialism. Sensuousness lost its bloom and became the abstract sensuousness of the geometrician. Physical motion was sacrificed to the mechanical or mathematical, geometry was proclaimed the principal science. Materialism became hostile to humanity. In order to overcome the anti-human incorporeal spirit in its own field, materialism itself was obliged to mortify its flesh and become an ascetic. It appeared as a being of reason, but it also developed the implacable logic of reason.

If man's senses are the source of all his knowledge, Hobbes argues, proceeding from Bacon, then conception, thought, imagination, etc., are nothing but phantoms of the material world more or less divested of its sensuous form. Science can only give a name to these phantoms. One name can be applied to several phantoms. There can even be names of names. But it would be a contradic-

* A term used by Aristotle to describe the particles or "seeds" which Anaxagoras held made up all things.—*Ed.*

tion to say, on the one hand, that all ideas have their origin in the world of the senses, and to maintain, on the other hand, that a word is more than a word, that besides the beings represented, which are always individual, there exist also general beings. An incorporeal substance is just as much a nonsense as an incorporeal body. Body, being, substance, are one and the same real idea. One cannot separate the thought from matter which thinks. Matter is the subject of all changes. The word infinite is meaningless unless it means the capacity of our mind to go on adding without end. Since only what is material is perceptible, knowable, nothing is known of the existence of God. I am sure only of my own existence. Every human passion is a mechanical motion ending or beginning. The objects of impulses are what is called good. Man is subject to the same laws as nature; might and freedom are identical.

Hobbes systematized Bacon, but did not give a more precise proof of his basic principle that our knowledge and our ideas have their source in the world of the senses.

Locke proved the principle of Bacon and Hobbes in his essay on the origin of human reason.

Just as Hobbes did away with the theistic prejudices in Bacon's materialism, so Collins, Dodwell, Coward, Hartley, Priestley, and others broke down the last bounds of Locke's sensualism. For materialists, at least, deism is no more than a convenient and easy way of getting rid of religion.

We have already mentioned how opportune Locke's work was for the French. Locke founded the philosophy of *bon sens,* of common sense; i.e., he said indirectly that no philosopher can be at variance with the healthy human senses and reason based on them.

Locke's immediate follower, Condillac, who also translated him into French, at once opposed Locke's sensualism to 17th century metaphysics. He proved that the French had quite rightly rejected metaphysics as the mere bungling of fancy and theological prejudice. He published a refutation of the systems of Descartes, Spinoza, Leibniz, and Malebranche.

In his *Essai sur l'origine des connaissances humaines* he expounded Locke's ideas and proved that not only the soul, but the senses too, not only the art of creating ideas, but also the art of sensuous perception are matters of experience and habit. The whole development of man therefore depends on education and environment. It was only by eclectic philosophy that Condillac was ousted from the French schools.

The difference between French and English materialism follows from the difference between the two nations. The French imparted to English materialism wit, flesh and blood, and eloquence. They gave it the temperament and grace that it lacked. They civilized it.

In Helvetius, who also based himself on Locke, materialism became really French. Helvetius conceived it immediately in its application to social life (Helvetius, *De l'homme, de ses facultés intellectuelles et de son éducation*). Sensuous qualities and self-love, enjoyment and correctly understood personal interests are the bases of morality. The natural equality of human intelligence, the unity of progress of reason and progress of industry, the natural goodness of man and the omnipotence of education are the main points of his system.

In Lamettrie's work we find a combination of Descartes' system and English materialism. He makes use of Descartes' physics in detail. His *Man Machine* is a treatise after the model of Descartes' beast-machine. The physical part of Holbach's *Système de la Nature* is also a result of the combination of French and English materialism, while the moral part is based substantially on the ethics of Helvetius. Robinet (*De la Nature*), the French materialist who had the most connection with metaphysics and was therefore praised by Hegel, refers explicitly to Leibniz.

We need not dwell on Volney, Dupuis, Diderot and others any more than on the physiocrats, having already proved the dual origin of French materialism from Descartes' physics and English materialism, and the opposition of French materialism to 17th century metaphysics and to the metaphysics of Descartes, Spinoza, Malebranche, and Leibniz. The Germans could not see this opposition before they came into the same opposition with speculative metaphysics.

As Cartesian materialism merges into natural science proper, the other branch of French materialism leads direct to socialism and communism.

There is no need of any great penetration to see from the teaching of materialism on the original goodness and equal intellectual endowment of man, the omnipotence of experience, habit, and education, and the influence of environment on man, the great significance of industry, the justification of enjoyment, etc., how necessarily materialism is connected with communism and socialism.* If man draws all his knowledge, sensation, etc., from the world of the senses and the experience gained in it, the empirical world must be arranged so that in it man experiences and gets used to what is really human and that he becomes aware of himself as man. If correctly understood interest is the principle of all morality, man's private interest must be made to coincide with the interest of humanity. If man is unfree in the materialist sense, i.e., is free not through the negative power to avoid this or that, but through the positive power to assert his true individuality, crime must not be punished in the individual, but the anti-social source of crime must be destroyed, and each man must be given social scope for the vital manifestation of his being. If man is shaped by his surroundings, his surroundings must be made human. If man is social by nature, he will develop his true nature only in society, and the power of his nature must be measured not by the power of separate individuals but by the power of society.

This and similar propositions are to be found almost literally even in the oldest French materialists. This is not the place to assess them. *Fable of the Bees* or *Private Vices Made Public Benefits* by Mandeville, one of the early English followers of Locke, is typical of the social tendencies of materialism. He proves that in modern society vice is indispensable and useful. This was by no means an apology for modern society.

Fourier proceeds immediately from the teaching of the French materialists. The Babouvists were coarse, uncivilized materialists, but mature communism too comes directly from French materialism. The latter returned to its mother country, England, in the form Helvetius gave it. Bentham based his system of correctly understood interest on Helvetius's ethics, and Owen proceeded from Bentham's system to found English communism. Exiled to England, the Frenchman Cabet came under the influence of communist ideas there and on his return to France became the most popular, although the most superficial, representative of communism. Like Owen, the more scientific French communists, Dezamy, Gay and others, developed the teaching of materialism as the teaching of real humanism and the logical basis of communism.

—MARX and ENGELS, *The Holy Family* (1845), pp. 168–77.

* Marx and Engels refer here, of course, to pre-Marxian socialism and communism. The reader will recall that this was written in 1844—*Ed.*

[3]

THE RELATION OF AGNOSTICISM, MATERIALISM, AND RELIGION TO MODERN CLASS STRUGGLES

I am perfectly aware that the contents of this work will meet with objection from a considerable portion of the British public. But if we Continentals had taken the slightest notice of the prejudices of British "respectability," we should be even worse off than we are. This book defends what we call "historical materialism," and the word materialism grates upon the ears of the immense majority of British readers. "Agnosticism" might be tolerated, but materialism is utterly inadmissible.

And yet the original home of all modern materialism, from the 17th century onwards, is England.

"Materialism is the natural-born son of Great Britain. . . ." *

Thus Karl Marx wrote about the British origin of modern materialism. If Englishmen nowadays do not exactly relish the compliment he paid their ancestors, more's the pity. It is none the less undeniable that Bacon, Hobbes, and Locke are the fathers of that brilliant school of French materialists which made the 18th century, in spite of all battles on land and sea won over Frenchmen by Germans and Englishmen, a preeminently French century, even before that crowning French Revolution, the results of which we outsiders, in England as well as in Germany, are still trying to acclimatize.

There is no denying it. About the middle of this century, what struck every cultivated foreigner who set up his residence in England was what he was then bound to consider the religious bigotry and stupidity of the English respectable middle class. We, at that time, were all materialists, or, at least, very advanced freethinkers, and to us it appeared inconceivable that almost all educated people in England should believe in all sorts of impossible miracles and that even geologists like Buckland and Mantell should contort the facts of their science so as not to clash too much with the myths of the book of Genesis; while,

* See pp. 56–60 for remainder of quotation, omitted here, from *The Holy Family*.—*Ed.*

in order to find people who dared to use their own intellectual faculties with regard to religious matters, you had to go amongst the uneducated, the "great unwashed," as they were then called, the working people, especially the Owenite socialists.

But England has been "civilized" since then. The exhibition of 1851 sounded the knell of English insular exclusiveness. England became gradually internationalized, in diet, in manners, in ideas; so much so that I begin to wish that some English manners and customs had made as much headway on the Continent as other Continental habits have made here. Anyhow, the introduction and spread of salad oil (before 1851 known only to the aristocracy) has been accompanied by a fatal spread of continental skepticism in matters religious, and it has come to this, that agnosticism, though not yet considered "the thing" quite as much as the Church of England, is yet very nearly on a par, as far as respectability goes, with Baptism, and decidedly ranks above the Salvation Army. And I cannot help believing that under these circumstances it will be consoling to many who sincerely regret and condemn this progress of infidelity, to learn that these "new-fangled notions" are not of foreign origin, are not "made in Germany," like so many other articles of daily use, but are undoubtedly Old English, and that their British originators 200 years ago went a good deal further than their descendants now dare to venture.

What, indeed, is agnosticism, but, to use an expressive Lancashire term, "shamefaced" materialism? The agnostic's conception of nature is materialistic throughout. The entire natural world is governed by law, and absolutely excludes the intervention of action from without. But, he adds, we have no means either of ascertaining or of disproving the existence of some supreme being beyond the known universe. Now, this might hold good at the time when Laplace, to Napoleon's question, why in the great astronomer's *Mécanique céleste* the Creator was not even mentioned, proudly replied: "*Je n'avais pas besoin de cette hypothèse.*" [I had no need for that hypothesis.] But nowadays, in our evolutionary conception of the universe, there is absolutely no room for either a creator or a ruler; and to talk of a supreme being shut out from the whole existing world implies a contradiction in terms, and as it seems to me, a gratuitous insult to the feelings of religious people. . . .

As soon, however, as our agnostic has made these formal mental reservations, he talks and acts as the rank materialist he at bottom is. He may say that, as far as *we* know, matter and motion, or as it is now called, energy, can neither be created nor destroyed, but that we have no proof of their not having been created at some time or other. But if you try to use this admission against him in any particular case, he will quickly put you out of court. If he admits the possibility of spiritualism *in abstracto,* he will have none of it *in concreto.* As far as we know and can know, he will tell you there is no Creator and no Ruler of the universe; as far as we are concerned, matter and energy can neither be created nor annihilated; for us, mind is a mode of energy, a function of the brain; all we know is that the material world is governed by immutable laws, and so forth. Thus, as far as he is a scientific man, as far as he *knows* anything, he is a materialist; outside his science, in spheres about which he knows nothing, he translates his ignorance into Greek and calls it agnosticism.

At all events, one thing seems clear: even if I were an agnostic, it is evident that I could not describe the conception of history sketched out in this little book, as "historical agnosticism." Religious people would laugh at me, agnostics would indignantly ask, was I going to make fun of them? And thus I hope even British respectability will not be overshocked if I use, in English, as well as in so many other languages the term "historical materialism," to designate that view of the course of history, which seeks the ultimate cause and the great moving power of all important historic events in the economic development of society, in the changes in the modes of production and exchange, in the consequent division of society into distinct classes, and in the struggles of these classes against one another.

—ENGELS, *Socialism, Utopian and Scientific,* Intro. to 1st Eng. ed. (1892), pp. 10–13, 15*f.*

[4]

LENIN DEFENDS MARXIST MATERIALISM AGAINST REVISIONISTS

A number of writers, would-be Marxists, have this year undertaken a veritable campaign against the philosophy of Marxism. In the course of less than half a year four books devoted mainly and almost exclusively to attacks on dialectical materialism have made their appearance. These include first and foremost *Studies in* (?—it would have been more proper to say "against") *the Philosophy of Marxism* (St. Petersburg, 1908), a symposium by Bazarov, Bogdanov, Lunacharsky, Berman, Helfond, Yushkevich and Suvorov; Yushkevich's *Materialism and Critical Realism;* Berman's *Dialectics in the Light of the Modern Theory of Knowledge* and Valentinov's *The Philosophical Constructions of Marxism.*

All these people could not have been ignorant of the fact that Marx and Engels scores of times termed their philosophical views dialectical materialism. Yet all these people, who, despite the sharp divergence of their political views, are united in their hostility toward dialectical materialism, at the same time claim that in philosophy they are Marxists! Engels' dialectics is "mysticism," says Berman. Engels' views have become "antiquated," remarks Bazarov casually, as though it were a self-evident fact. Materialism thus appears to be refuted by our bold warriors, who proudly allude to the "modern theory of knowledge," "recent philosophy" (or "recent positivism"), the "philosophy of modern natural science," or even the "philosophy of natural science of the twentieth century." Supported by all these supposedly recent doctrines, our destroyers of dialectical materialism proceed fearlessly to downright fideism* (in the case of Lunacharsky it is most evident, but by no means in his case alone!). Yet when it comes to an explicit definition of their attitude towards Marx and Engels, all their courage and all their respect for their own convictions at once disappear. In deed—a complete renunciation of dialectical materialism, i.e., of Marxism; in word—endless subterfuges, attempts to evade the essence of the question, to cover their retreat, to put some materialist or other in place of materialism in general, and a determined refusal to make a direct analysis of the innumerable materialist declarations of Marx and Engels. This is truly "mutiny on one's knees," as it was justly characterized by one Marxist. This is typical philosophical revisionism, for it was only the revisionists who gained a sad notoriety for themselves by their departure from the fundamental views of Marxism and by their fear, or inability, to "settle accounts" openly, explicitly, resolutely, and clearly with the views they had abandoned. When

* The reliance on faith rather than reason in questions of philosophy and religion.—*Ed.*

orthodox Marxists had occasion to pronounce against some antiquated views of Marx (for instance, Mehring when he opposed certain historical propositions), it was always done with such precision and thoroughness that no one has ever found anything ambiguous in such literary utterances.

For the rest, there is in the *Studies "in" the Philosophy of Marxism* one phrase which resembles the truth. This is Lunacharsky's phrase: "Perhaps we [i.e., all the collaborators of the *Studies* evidently] have gone astray, but we are seeking" (p. 161). That the first half of this phrase contains an absolute and the second a relative truth, I shall endeavor to demonstrate circumstantially in the present book. At the moment I would only remark that if our philosophers had spoken not in the name of Marxism but in the name of a few "seeking" Marxists, they would have shown more respect for themselves and for Marxism.

As for myself, I too am a "seeker" in philosophy. Namely, the task I have set myself in these comments is to seek for the stumbling block to people who under the guise of Marxism are offering something incredibly muddled, confused, and reactionary.

—LENIN, *Materialism and Empirio-Criticism* (1908), pp. 9*f*.

[5]

"REFUTATION OF MATERIALISM" FROM BERKELEY TO THE MACHIANS

Anyone in the least acquainted with philosophical literature must know that scarcely a single contemporary professor of philosophy (or of theology) can be found who is not directly or indirectly engaged in refuting materialism. They have declared materialism refuted a thousand times, yet are continuing to refute it for the thousand and first time. All our revisionists are engaged in refuting materialism, pretending, however, that actually they are only refuting the materialist Plekhanov, and not the materialist Engels, nor the materialist Feuerbach, nor the materialist views of Dietzgen—and, moreover, that they are refuting materialism from the standpoint of "recent" and "modern" positivism, natural science, and so forth. . . .

The materialists, we are told, recognize something unthinkable and unknowable—"things-in-themselves"—matter "outside of experience" and outside of our knowledge. They lapse into genuine mysticism by admitting the existence of something beyond, something transcending the bounds of "experience" and knowledge. When they say that matter, by acting upon our sense-organs, produces sensations, the materialists take as their basis the "unknown," nothingness; for do they not themselves declare our sensations to be the only source of knowledge? The materialists lapse into "Kantianism" (Plekhanov, by recognizing the existence of "things-in-themselves," i.e., things outside of our consciousness); they "duplicate" the world and preach "dualism," for the materialists hold that beyond the appearance there is the thing-in-itself; beyond the immediate sense data there is something else, some fetish, an "idol," an absolute, a source of "metaphysics," a double of religion ("holy matter," as Bazarov says).

Such are the arguments levelled by the Machians against materialism, as repeated and retold in varying keys by the aforementioned writers.

In order to test whether these arguments are new, and whether they are really directed against only one Russian materialist who "lapsed into Kantianism," we shall give some detailed quotations from the works of an old idealist, George Berkeley. This historical inquiry is all the more necessary in the introduction to our comments since we shall have frequent occasion to refer to Berkeley and his trend in philosophy, for the Machians misrepresent both the relation of Mach to Berkeley and the essence of Berkeley's philosophical line.

The work of Bishop George Berkeley, published in 1710 under the title *Treatise Concerning the Principles of Human Knowledge,** begins with the following argument:

"It is evident to anyone who takes a survey of the *objects* of human knowledge, that they are either ideas actually imprinted on the senses; or else such as are perceived by attending to the passions and operations of the mind; or lastly, ideas formed by help of memory and imagination. . . . By sight I have the ideas of light and colours, with their several degrees and variations. By touch I perceive hard and soft, heat and cold, motion and resistance. . . . Smelling furnishes me with odours; the palate with tastes; and hearing conveys sounds. . . .

"And as several of these are observed to accompany each other, they

* *Works of George Berkeley,* edited by A. C. Fraser, Oxford, 1871, Vol. I, p. 155.

come to be marked by one name, and so to be reputed as one thing. Thus, for example, a certain colour, taste, smell, figure and consistence having been observed to go together, are accounted one distinct thing, signified by the name *apple;* other collections of ideas constitute a stone, a tree, a book, and the like sensible things. . ." (§ 1).

Such is the content of the first section of Berkeley's work.

We must remember that Berkeley takes as the basis of his philosophy hard, soft, heat, cold, colors, tastes, odors, etc. For Berkeley, things are "collections of ideas," this expression designating the aforesaid, let us say, qualities or sensations, and not abstract thoughts.

Berkeley goes on to say that besides these "ideas or objects of knowledge" there exists something that perceives them—"mind, spirit, soul or myself" (§ 2). It is self-evident, the philosopher concludes, that "ideas" cannot exist outside of the mind that perceives them. In order to convince ourselves of this it is enough to consider the meaning of the word "exist."

"The table I write on I say exists, that is, I see and feel it; and if I were out of my study I should say it existed; meaning thereby that if I was in my study I might perceive it." That is what Berkeley says in § 3 of his work; and thereupon he begins a polemic against the people whom he calls materialists (§§ 18, 19, etc.).

"I cannot conceive," he says, "how it is possible to speak of the absolute existence of things without their relation to the fact that somebody perceives them. To exist means to be perceived" (their *esse* is *percipi,* § 3—a dictum of Berkeley's frequently quoted in textbooks on the history of philosophy).

"It is indeed an opinion strangely prevailing amongst men, that houses, mountains, rivers, and in a word all sensible objects have an existence, natural or real, distinct from their being perceived by the understanding" (§ 4).

This opinion is a "manifest contradiction," says Berkeley. "For, what are the aforementioned objects but the things we perceive by sense? and what do we perceive besides our own ideas or sensations? and is it not plainly repugnant that any one of these, or any combination of them, should exist unperceived?" (§ 4).

The expression "collection of ideas" Berkeley now replaces by what to him is an equivalent expression, *combination of sensations,* and accuses the materialists of an "absurd" tendency to go still further, of seeking some source of this complex—that is, of this combination of sensations. In § 5 the materialists are accused of trifling with an abstraction, for to divorce the sensation from the object, according to Berkeley, is an empty abstraction. "In truth," he says at the end of § 5, omitted in the second edition, "the object and the sensation are the same thing, and cannot therefore be abstracted from each other." Berkeley goes on:

"But, say you, though the ideas themselves do not exist without the mind, yet there may be things like them, whereof they are copies or resemblances, which things exist without the mind, in an unthinking substance. I answer, an idea can be like nothing but an idea; a colour or figure can be like nothing but another colour or figure. . . . I ask whether those supposed originals, or external things, of which our ideas are the pictures or representations, be themselves perceivable or no? If they are, then they are ideas and we have gained our point; but if you say they are not, I appeal to anyone whether it be sense to assert a colour is like something which is invisible; hard or soft, like something which is intangible; and so of the rest" (§ 8).

As the reader sees, Bazarov's "arguments" against Plekhanov concerning the problem of whether things can exist apart from their action on us do not differ in the least from Berkeley's arguments against the materialists whom he does not mention by name. Berkeley considers the notion of the existence of "matter or corporeal substance" (§ 9) such a "contradiction," such an "absurdity," that it is really not worth wasting time exposing it. He says:

"But because the tenet of the existence of Matter seems to have taken so deep a root in the minds of philosophers, and draws after it so many ill consequences, I choose rather to be thought prolix and tedious than omit anything that might conduce to the full discovery and extirpation of that prejudice" (§ 9).

We shall presently see to what "ill consequences" Berkeley is referring. Let us first finish with his theoretical arguments against the materialists. Denying the "absolute" existence of objects, that is, the existence of things outside human knowledge, Berkeley deliberately represents the views of his opponents as though they recognized the "thing-in-itself." In § 24 Berkeley writes in italics that the opinion which he is refuting recognizes *"the absolute existence of sensible objects in themselves, or without the mind"* (pp. 167–68, *op. cit.*). The two fundamental lines of philosophical outlook are here depicted with the straightforwardness, clarity and precision that distinguish the classical philosophers from the inventors of "new" systems in our day. Materialism is the recognition of "objects in themselves," or outside the mind; ideas and sensations are copies or images of these objects. The opposite doctrine (idealism) claims that objects do not exist "without the mind"; objects are "combinations of sensations."

This was written in 1710, fourteen years before the birth of Immanuel Kant, yet our Machians, supposedly on the basis of "recent" philosophy, made the discovery that the recognition of "objects in themselves" is a result of the infection or distortion of materialism by Kantianism! The "new" discoveries of the Machians are the product of an astounding ignorance of the history of the basic philosophical trends.

Their next "new" thought consists in this: that the concepts "matter" or "substance" are remnants of old uncritical views. Mach and Avenarius, you see, advanced philosophical thought, deepened analysis and eliminated these "absolutes," "unchangeable entities," etc. If you wish to check such assertions with the original sources, go to Berkeley and you will see that they are pretentious fictions. Berkeley says quite definitely that matter is "nonentity" (§ 68), that matter is *nothing* (§ 80). "You may," thus Berkeley ridicules the materialists, "if so it shall seem good, use the word *matter* in the same sense as other men use *nothing*" (pp. 196–97). At the beginning, says Berkeley, it was believed that colors, odors, etc., "really exist," but subsequently such views were renounced, and it was seen that they only exist in dependence on our sensations. But this elimination of old erroneous concepts was not completed; a remnant is the concept "substance" (§ 73), which is also a "prejudice" (p. 195), and which was finally exposed by Bishop Berkeley in 1710! In 1908 there are still wags who seriously believe Avenarius, Petzoldt, Mach and the rest, when they maintain that it was only "recent positivism" and "recent natural science" which at last succeeded in eliminating these "metaphysical" conceptions.

These same wags (among them Bogdanov) assure their readers that it was the new philosophy that corrected the error of the "duplication of the world" in the doctrine of the eternally refuted materialists, who speak of some sort of a "reflection" by the human consciousness of things existing outside the consciousness. A mass of sentimental verbiage has been written by the above-named authors about this "duplication." Owing to forgetfulness or ignorance, they failed to add that these new discoveries had already been discovered in 1710. Berkeley says:

"Our knowledge of these [*i.e.*, ideas or things] has been very much obscured and confounded, and we have been led into very dangerous errors by supposing a two-fold existence of the objects of sense—the one *intelligible* or in the mind, the other *real* and without the mind" (*i.e.*, outside consciousness) (§ 86).

And Berkeley ridicules this "absurd" notion, which admits the possibility of thinking the unthinkable! The source of the "absurdity," of course, "follows from our supposing a difference between *things* and *ideas* . . . the supposition of external objects" (§ 87). This same source—as discovered by Berkeley in 1710 and rediscovered by Bogdanov in 1908—engenders a faith in fetishes and idols.

"The existence of Matter," says Berkeley, "or bodies unperceived, has not only been the main support of Atheists and Fatalists, but on the same principle doth Idolatry likewise in all its various forms depend" (§ 94). Here we arrive at those "ill consequences" derived from the "absurd" doctrine of the existence of an external world which compelled Bishop Berkeley not only to refute this doctrine theoretically, but passionately to persecute its adherents as enemies.

"For as we have shewn the doctrine of Matter or corporeal Substance to have been the main pillar and support of Scepticism, so likewise upon the same foundation have been raised all the impious schemes of Atheism and Irreligion. . . . How great a friend *material substance* has been to Atheists in all ages were needless to relate. All their monstrous systems have so visible and necessary a dependence on it, that when this cornerstone is once removed, the whole fabric cannot choose but fall to the ground, insomuch that it is no longer worth while to bestow a particular consideration on the absurdities of every wretched sect of Atheists (§ 92, p. 203).

"Matter being once expelled out of nature drags with it so many sceptical and impious notions, such an incredible number of disputes and puzzling questions ["the principle of economy of thought," discovered by Mach in the 'seventies, "philosophy as a conception of the world according to the principle of minimum expenditure of effort"—Avenarius in 1876!] which have been thorns in the sides of divines as well as philosophers, and made so much fruitless work for mankind, that if the arguments we have produced against it are not found equal to demonstration (as to me they evidently seem), yet I am sure all friends to knowledge, peace, and religion have reason to wish they were" (§ 96).

Frankly and bluntly did Bishop Berkeley argue! In our time these very same thoughts on the "economical" elimination of "matter" from philosophy are enveloped in a much more artful form, and confused by the use of a "new" terminology, so that these thoughts may be taken by naive people for "recent" philosophy!

But Berkeley was not only candid as to the tendencies of his philosophy, he also endeavored to cover its idealistic nakedness, to represent it as being free from absurdities and acceptable to "common sense." Instinctively defending himself against the accusation of what would nowadays be called subjective idealism and solipsism, he says that by our philosophy "we are not deprived of any one thing in nature" (§ 34). Nature remains, and the distinction between realities and chimeras remains, only "they both equally exist in the mind" (§ 34).

"I do not argue against the existence of any one thing that we can apprehend either by sense or reflection. That the things I see with my eyes and touch with my hands do exist, really exist, I make not the least question. The only thing whose existence we deny is that which *philosophers* [Berkeley's italics] call Matter or corporeal substance. And in doing this there is no damage done to the rest of mankind, who, I dare say, will never miss it. The Atheist indeed will want the colour of an empty name to support his impiety" (§ 35).

This thought is made still clearer in § 37, where Berkeley replies to the charge that his philosophy destroys corporeal substance:

". . . if the word *substance* be taken in the vulgar sense, for a *combination* of sensible qualities, such as extension, solidity, weight, and the like—this we cannot be accused of taking away; but if it be taken in a philosophic sense, for the support of accidents or qualities without the mind—then indeed I acknowledge that we take it away, if one may be said to take away that which never had any existence, not even in the imagination."

Not without good cause did the English philosopher Fraser, an idealist and adherent of Berkeleianism, who edited Berkeley's works and supplied them with his own annotations, designate Berkeley's doctrine by the term "natural realism" (*op. cit.*, p. x).

This amusing terminology must by all means be noted, for it in fact expresses Berkeley's intention to counterfeit realism. In our further exposition we shall frequently find the "recent positivists" repeating the same stratagem or counterfeit in a different form and in a different verbal wrapping. Berkeley does not deny the existence of real things! Berkeley does not go counter to the opinion of all humanity! Berkeley denies "only" the teaching of the philosophers, *viz.*, the theory of knowledge, which seriously and resolutely takes as the foundation of all its reasoning the recognition of the external world and the reflection thereof in the minds of men. Berkeley does not deny natural science, which has always adhered (mostly unconsciously) to this, i.e., the materialist, theory of knowledge. We read in § 59:

> "We may, from the experience* [Berkeley—a philosophy of "pure experience"] we have had of the train and succession of ideas in our minds . . . make . . . well-grounded predictions concerning the ideas we shall be affected with pursuant to a great train of actions, and be enabled to pass a right judgment of what would have appeared to us, in case we were placed in circumstances very different from those we are in at present. Herein consists the knowledge of nature, which [listen to this!] may preserve its use and certainty very consistently with what hath been said."

Let us regard the external world, nature, as "a combination of sensations" evoked in our mind by a deity. Acknowledge this and give up searching for the "ground" of these sensations outside the mind, outside men, and I will acknowledge within the framework of my idealist theory of knowledge *all* natural science and all the importance and authenticity of its deductions. It is precisely this framework, and only this framework, that I need for my deductions in favor of "peace and religion." Such is Berkeley's train of thought. It correctly expresses the essence of idealist philosophy and its social significance, and we shall encounter it later when we come to speak of the relation of Machism to natural science.

Let us now consider another recent discovery that was borrowed from Bishop Berkeley in the 20th century by the recent positivist and critical realist, P. Yushkevich. This discovery is "empiriosymbolism." "Berkeley," says Fraser, "thus reverts to his favourite theory of a Universal Natural Symbolism" (*op. cit.*, p. 190). Did

* In his preface Fraser insists that both Berkeley and Locke "appeal exclusively to experience" (p. 117).

these words not occur in an edition of 1871, one might have suspected the English fideist philosopher Fraser of plagiarism from both the modern mathematician and physicist Poincaré and the Russian "Marxist" Yushkevich!

This theory of Berkeley's, which threw Fraser into raptures, is set forth by the Bishop as follows:

"The connexion of ideas [do not forget that for Berkeley ideas and things are identical] does not imply the relation of *cause* and *effect,* but only of a mark or *sign* with the thing *signified"* (§ 65).

"Hence, it is evident that those things, which under the notion of a cause co-operating or concurring to the production of effects, are altogether inexplicable, and run us into great absurdities, may be very naturally explained . . . when they are considered only as marks or signs for our information" (§ 66).

Of course, in the opinion of Berkeley and Fraser, it is no other than the deity who informs us by means of these "empirio-symbols." The epistemological significance of *symbolism* in Berkeley's theory, however, consists in this, that it is to replace "the doctrine" which "pretends to explain things by corporeal causes" (§ 66).

We have before us two philosophical trends in the question of causality. One "pretends to explain things by corporeal causes." It is clear that it is connected with the "absurd doctrine of matter" refuted by Bishop Berkeley. The other reduces the "notion of causality" to the notion of a "mark or sign" which serves for "our information" (supplied by God). We shall meet these two trends in a 20th century garb when we analyze the attitude of Machism and dialectical materialism to this question.

Further, as regards the question of reality, it ought also to be remarked that Berkeley, refusing as he does to recognize the existence of things outside the mind, tries to find a criterion for distinguishing between the real and the fictitious. In § 36 he says that those "ideas" which the human mind evokes at pleasure

"are faint, weak, and unsteady in respect to others they perceive by sense: which, being impressed upon them according to certain rules or laws of nature, speak themselves about the effects of a Mind more powerful and wise than human spirits. These latter are said to have *more reality* in them than the former; by which is meant that they are more affecting, orderly and distinct, and that they are not fictions of the mind perceiving them. . . ."

Elsewhere (§ 84) Berkeley tries to connect the notion of reality with the simultaneous perception of the same sensations by many people. For instance, how shall we resolve the question as to whether the transformation of water into wine, of which we are being told, is real? "If at the table all who were present should see, and smell, and taste, and drink wine, and find the effects of it, with me there could be no doubt of its reality." And Fraser explains: "The simultaneous consciousness of . . . the 'same' *sense*-ideas by *different persons*, as distinguished from the purely individual or personal consciousness of *imaginary* objects and emotions, is here referred to as a test of the *reality* of the former."

From this it is evident that Berkeley's subjective idealism is not to be interpreted as though it ignored the distinction between individual and collective perception. On the contrary, he attempts on the basis of this distinction to construct a criterion of reality. Deriving "ideas" from the action of the deity upon the human mind, Berkeley thus approaches objective idealism: The world proves to be not my idea but the product of a single supreme spiritual cause that creates both the "laws of nature" and the laws distinguishing "more real" ideas from those less real, and so forth.

In another work, *The Three Dialogues Between Hylas and Philonous* (1713), where he endeavors to present his views in an especially popular form, Berkeley sets forth the opposition between his doctrine and the materialist doctrine in the following way:

> "I assert as well as you [materialists] that, since we are affected from without, we must allow Powers to be without, in a Being distinct from ourselves. . . . But then we differ as to the kind of this powerful being. I will have it to be Spirit, you Matter, or I know not what (I may add too, you know not what) third nature. . ." (p. 335).

Fraser comments:

> "This is the gist of the whole question. According to the Materialists, sensible phenomena are due to *material substance,* or to some unknown 'third nature'; according to Berkeley, to Rational Will; according to Hume and the Positivists, their origin is absolutely unknown, and we can only generalise them inductively, through custom, as facts."

Here the English Berkeleian, Fraser, approaches from his consistent idealist standpoint the same fundamental "lines" in philosophy which were so clearly characterized by the materialist Engels. In his work *Ludwig Feuerbach* Engels divides philosophers into "two great camps"—materialists and idealists. Engels—dealing with theories of the two trends much more developed, varied and rich in content than Fraser dealt with—sees the fundamental distinction between them in the fact that while for the materialists nature is primary and spirit secondary, for the idealists the reverse is the case. In between these two camps Engels places the adherents of Hume and Kant, who deny the possibility of knowing the world, or at least of knowing it fully, and calls them *agnostics*. In his *Ludwig Feuerbach* Engels applies this term only to the adherents of Hume (those people whom Fraser calls, and who like to call themselves, "positivists"). But in his article "On Historical Materialism," * Engels explicitly speaks of the standpoint of "*the Neo-Kantian agnostic,*" regarding Neo-Kantianism as a variety of agnosticism.

We cannot dwell here on this remarkably correct and profound judgment of Engels' (a judgment which is shamelessly ignored by the Machians). We shall discuss it in detail later on. For the present we shall confine ourselves to pointing to this Marxian terminology and to this meeting of extremes: The views of a consistent materialist and of a consistent idealist on the fundamental philosophical trends. In order to illustrate these trends (with which we shall constantly have to deal in our further exposition) let us briefly note the views of outstanding philosophers of the 18th century who pursued a different path from Berkeley.

Here are Hume's arguments. In his *An Enquiry Concerning Human Understanding,* in the chapter (XII) on skeptical philosophy, he says:

"It seems evident, that men are carried, by a natural instinct or prepossession, to repose faith in their senses; and that, without any reasoning, or even almost before the use of reason, we always suppose an external universe, which depends not on our perception, but would exist though we and every sensible creature were absent or annihilated. Even the animal creations are governed by a like opinion, and preserve this belief of external objects, in all their thoughts, designs, and actions. . . .

"But this universal and primary opinion of all men is soon destroyed by the slightest philosophy, which teaches us, that nothing can ever be present to the mind but an image or perception, and that the senses are only the inlets, through which these images are conveyed, without being able to produce any immediate intercourse between the mind and the

* See pp. 142*f*.—*Ed.*

object. The table, which we see, seems to diminish, as we remove farther from it: But the real table, which exists independent of us, suffers no alteration: It was, therefore, nothing but its image, which was present to the mind. These are the obvious dictates of reason; and no man, who reflects, ever doubted, that the existences, which we consider, when we say, 'this house,' and 'that tree,' are nothing but perceptions in the mind. . . .

"By what argument can it be proved, that the perceptions of the mind must be caused by external objects, entirely different from them, though resembling them (if that be possible), and could not arise either from the energy of the mind itself, or from the suggestion of some invisible and unknown spirit, or from some other cause still more unknown to us? . . .

"How shall the question be determined? By experience surely; as all other questions of a like nature. But here experience is, and must be entirely silent. The mind has never anything present to it but the perceptions, and cannot possibly reach any experience of their connection with objects. This supposition of such a connection is, therefore, without any foundation in reasoning.

"To have recourse to the veracity of the Supreme Being, in order to prove the veracity of our senses, is surely making a very unexpected circuit . . . if the external world be once called in question, we shall be at a loss to find arguments, by which we may prove the existence of that Being, or any of his attributes." *

He says the same thing in his *Treatise of Human Nature* (Part IV, Sec. II, "On Scepticism Towards Sensations"): "There is only a single existence, which I shall call indifferently *objects or perceptions*." By skepticism Hume means the refusal to explain sensations as the effects of objects, spirit, etc., a refusal to reduce perceptions to the external world, on the one hand, and to a deity or to an unknown spirit, on the other. And the author of the introduction to the French translation of Hume, F. Pillon—a philosopher of a trend akin to Mach (as we shall see below)—justly remarks that for Hume the subject and the object are reduced to "groups of various perceptions," to "elements of consciousness, to impressions, ideas, etc."; that the only concern should be with the "groupings and combinations of these elements." † The English Humean, Huxley, who coined the apt

* David Hume, *An Enquiry Concerning Human Understanding. Essays and Treatises,* London, 1882, Vol. II, pp. 151–53.

† *Psychologie de Hume. Traité de la nature humaine, etc.* Trad. par Ch. Renouvier et F. Pillon, Paris 1878. Introduction, p. x.

and correct term "agnosticism," in his *Hume* also emphasizes the fact that Hume, regarding "sensations" as the "primary and irreducible states of consciousness," is not entirely consistent on the question how the origin of sensations is to be explained, whether by the effect of objects on man or by the creative power of the mind. "Realism and idealism are equally probable hypotheses" (i.e., for Hume).* Hume does not go beyond sensations. "Thus the colors red and blue, and the odor of a rose, are simple impressions. . . . A red rose gives us a complex impression, capable of resolution into the simple impressions of red color, rose-scent, and numerous others" (pp. 64–65, *op. cit.*). Hume admits both the "materialist position" and the "idealist position" (p. 82); the "collection of perceptions" may be generated by the Fichtean "ego" or may be a "signification and even a symbol" of "something real." This is how Huxley interprets Hume.

As for the materialists, here is an opinion of Berkeley given by Diderot, the leader of the Encyclopedists:

> "Those philosophers are called *idealists* who, being conscious only of their existence and of the sensations which succeed each other within themselves, do not admit anything else. An extravagant system which, to my thinking, only the blind could have originated; a system which, to the shame of human intelligence and philosophy, is the most difficult to combat, although the most absurd of all."†

And Diderot, who came very close to the standpoint of contemporary materialism that arguments and syllogisms alone do not suffice to refute idealism, and that here it is not a question for theoretical argument), notes the similarity of the premises both of the idealist Berkeley and the sensationalist Condillac. In his opinion, Condillac should have undertaken a refutation of Berkeley in order to avoid such absurd conclusions being drawn from the treatment of sensations as the only source of our knowledge. . . .

For the present we shall confine ourselves to one conclusion: The "recent" Machians have not adduced a single argument against the materialists that had not been adduced by Bishop Berkeley.

—LENIN, *Materialism and Empirio-Criticism* (1908), pp. 13–30.

* Thomas Huxley, *Hume*, London, 1879, p. 74.

† *Œuvres complètes de Diderot*, ed. par J. Assézat. Paris, 1875, Vol. I, p. 304.

[6]

MATERIALISM VERSUS IDEALISM: NON-PARTISANSHIP AND RECONCILIATION IMPOSSIBLE

Throughout the preceding exposition,* in connection with every problem of epistemology touched upon and in connection with every philosophical question raised by the new physics, we traced the struggle between *materialism* and *idealism*. Behind the mass of new terminological devices, behind the litter of erudite scholasticism, we invariably discerned *two* principal alignments, two fundamental trends in the solution of philosophical problems. Whether nature, matter, the physical, the external world be taken as primary, and mind, spirit, sensation (experience—as the widespread terminology of our time has it), the psychical, etc., be regarded as secondary—that is the root question which *in fact* continues to divide the philosophers into *two great camps*. The source of thousands upon thousands of mistakes and of the confusion reigning in this sphere is the fact that beneath the envelope of terms, definitions, scholastic devices and verbal artifices, these two fundamental trends are *overlooked*. (Bogdanov, for instance, refuses to acknowledge his idealism, because, you see, instead of the "metaphysical" concepts "nature" and "mind," he has taken the "experiential" physical and psychical. A word has been changed!)

The genius of Marx and Engels consisted in the very fact that in the course of a long period, *nearly half a century*, they developed materialism, that they further advanced one fundamental trend in philosophy, that they did not confine themselves to reiterating epistemological problems that had already been solved, but consistently applied—and showed *how* to apply—*this same* materialism in the sphere of the social sciences, mercilessly brushing aside as litter and rubbish the pretentious rigmarole, the innumerable attempts to "discover" a "new" line in philosophy, to invent a "new" trend and so forth. The verbal nature of such

* This section, which appears near the end of *Materialism and Empirio-Criticism*, summarizes Lenin's view of the social significance of what he regards as the two main camps in philosophy.—*Ed.*

attempts, the scholastic play with new philosophical "isms," the clogging of the issue by pretentious devices, the inability to comprehend and clearly present the struggle between the two fundamental epistemological trends—this is what Marx and Engels persistently pursued and combated throughout their entire activity.

We said, "nearly half a century." And, indeed, as far back as 1843, when Marx had only just become Marx, i.e., the founder of scientific Socialism, the founder of *modern materialism,* which is immeasurably richer in content and incomparably more consistent than all preceding forms of materialism, even at that time Marx pointed out with amazing clarity the basic trends in philosophy. Karl Grün quotes a letter from Marx to Feuerbach dated October 30, 1843, in which Marx invites Feuerbach to write an article for the *Deutsch-Französische Jahrbücher* against Schelling. This Schelling, writes Marx, is a shallow braggart with his claims to having embraced and transcended all previous philosophical trends. "To the French romanticists and mystics he [Schelling] says: I am the union of philosophy and theology; to the French materialists: I am the union of the flesh and the idea; to the French skeptics: I am the destroyer of dogmatism." *

That the "skeptics," be they called Humeans or Kantians (or, in the 20th century, Machians), cry out against the "dogmatism" of both materialism and idealism, Marx at that time already realized; and, without letting himself be diverted by any one of a thousand wretched little philosophical systems, he was able with the help of Feuerbach to take the direct materialist road against idealism. Thirty years later, in the afterword to the second edition of the first volume of *Capital,* Marx just as clearly and definitely contrasted *his materialism* to *Hegel's idealism,* the most consistent and developed idealism of all; he contemptuously brushed Comtian "positivism" aside and dubbed as wretched epigoni the modern philosophers who imagine that they have destroyed Hegel when in reality they have reverted to a repetition of the pre-Hegelian errors of Kant and Hume. In the letter to Kugelmann of June 27, 1870, Marx refers contemptuously to Büchner, Lange, Dühring, Fechner, etc., because they understood nothing of Hegel's dialectics and treated him with scorn. And finally, take the various philosophical utterances by Marx in *Capital* and other

* Karl Grün, *Ludwig Feuerbach in seinem Briefwechsel und Nachlass, sowie in seiner philosophischen Charakterentwicklung,* Vol. I, Leipzig 1874, p. 361.

works, and you will find an *invariable* basic motif, *viz.,* insistence upon *materialism* and contemptuous derision of all obscurantism, of all confusion and all deviations towards *idealism*. All Marx's philosophical utterances revolve within these fundamental opposites, and, in the eyes of professorial philosophy, their defect lies in this "narrowness" and "one-sidedness." As a matter of fact, this refusal to recognize the hybrid projects for reconciling materialism and idealism constitutes the great merit of Marx, who moved *forward* along a sharply-defined philosophical road.

Entirely in the spirit of Marx, and in close collaboration with him, Engels in all his philosophical works briefly and clearly contrasts the materialist and idealist lines in regard to *all* questions, without, in 1878, 1888, or 1892,* taking seriously the endless attempts to "transcend" the "one-sidedness" of materialism and idealism, to proclaim a *new* trend—"positivism," "realism," or some other professorial charlatanism. Engels based his *whole* fight against Dühring on the demand for consistent adherence to materialism, accusing the materialist Dühring of verbally confusing the issue, of phrasemongering, of methods of reasoning which involved a compromise with idealism and adoption of the position of idealism. Either materialism consistent to the end, or the falsehood and confusion of philosophical idealism—such is the formulation of the question given in *every paragraph* of *Anti-Dühring*; and only people whose minds had already been corrupted by reactionary professorial philosophy could fail to notice it. And right down to 1894, when the last preface was written to *Anti-Dühring,* revised and enlarged by the author for the last time, Engels continued to follow the latest developments both in philosophy and science, and continued with all his former resoluteness to hold to his lucid and firm position, brushing away the litter of new systems, big and little.

That Engels followed the new developments in philosophy is evident from *Ludwig Feuerbach*. In the 1888 preface, mention is even made of such a phenomenon as the rebirth of classical German philosophy in England and Scandinavia, whereas Engels (both in the preface and in the text of the book) has nothing but contempt for the prevailing Neo-Kantianism and Humism. It is quite obvious that Engels, observing the repetition by *fashion-*

* These dates refer to the publication of *Anti-Dühring, Ludwig Feuerbach,* and the introduction to the English edition of *Socialism, Utopian and Scientific,* respectively.—*Ed.*

able German and English philosophy of the old pre-Hegelian errors of Kantianism and Humism, was prepared to expect some good even *from the turn to Hegel* (in England and Scandinavia), hoping that the great idealist and dialectician would help to disclose petty idealist and metaphysical errors.

Without undertaking an examination of the vast number of shades of Neo-Kantianism in Germany and of Humism in England, Engels *from the very outset* refutes their fundamental deviation from materialism. Engels declares that the *entire tendency* of these two schools is "scientifically a step backward." And what is his opinion of the undoubtedly "positivist," according to the current terminology, the undoubtedly "realist" tendencies of these Neo-Kantians and Humeans, among whose number, for instance, he could not help knowing Huxley? That "positivism" and that "realism" which attracted, and which continue to attract, an infinite number of muddleheads, Engels declared to be *at best a philistine method of smuggling in materialism* while criticising and abjuring it publicly! One has to reflect only very little on *such* an appraisal of Thomas Huxley—a very great scientist and an incomparably more realistic realist and positive positivist than Mach, Avenarius and Co.—in order to understand how contemptuously Engels would have greeted the present infatuation of a group of Marxists with "recent positivism," the "latest realism," etc.

Marx and Engels were partisans in philosophy from start to finish; they were able to detect the deviations from materialism and concessions to idealism and fideism in each and every "new" tendency. They therefore appraised Huxley *exclusively* from the standpoint of his materialist consistency. They therefore rebuked Feuerbach for not pursuing materialism to the end, for renouncing materialism because of the errors of individual materialists, for combating religion in order to renovate it or invent a new religion, for being unable, in sociology, to rid himself of idealist phraseology and become a materialist. . . .

Let us now examine Mach, Avenarius, and their school from the standpoint of parties in philosophy. Oh, these gentlemen boast of their non-partisanship, and if they have an antipodes, it is the *materialist* . . . and *only* the materialist. A red thread that runs through *all* the writings of *all* the Machians is the stupid claim to have "risen above" materialism and idealism, to have transcended this "obsolete" antithesis; but *in fact* the whole fraternity are *continually* sliding into idealism and are conducting a steady and incessant struggle against materialism. The subtle epistemological crochets of a man like Avenarius are but professorial inventions, an attempt to form a small philosophical sect "of his own"; but, *as a matter of fact,* in the general circumstances of the struggle of ideas and trends in modern society, the *objective* part played by these epistemological artifices is in every case the same, namely, to clear the way for idealism and fideism, and to serve them faithfully. In fact, it cannot be an accident that the small school of empirio-criticists is acclaimed by the English spiritualists, like Ward, by the French neo-criticists, who praise Mach for his attack on materialism, and by the German immanentists! Dietzgen's expression, "graduated flunkeys of fideism," hits the nail on the head in the case of Mach, Avenarius and their whole school.*

It is the misfortune of the Russian Machians, who undertook to "reconcile" Machism and Marxism, that they trusted the reactionary professors of philosophy and as a result slipped down an inclined plane. The methods of operation employed in the various attempts to develop and supplement Marx were not very ingenious. They read Ostwald, believe Ostwald, paraphrase Ostwald and call it Marxism. They read Mach, believe Mach, paraphrase Mach and call it Marxism. They read Poincaré, believe Poincaré, paraphrase Poincaré and call it Marxism! *Not a single one* of these professors, who are capable of making very

* Here is another example of how the widespread currents of reactionary bourgeois philosophy make use of Machism in practice. Perhaps the "latest fashion" in the latest American philosophy is "pragmatism" (from the Greek word "pragma"—action; that is, a philosophy of action). The philosophical journals perhaps speak more of pragmatism than of anything else. Pragmatism ridicules the metaphysics both of idealism and materialism, acclaims experience and only experience, recognizes practice as the only criterion, refers to the positivist movement in general, *especially turns for support to Ostwald, Mach, Pearson, Poincaré* and *Duhem* for the belief that science is not an "absolute copy of reality" and . . . successfully deduces from all this a God for practical purposes, and only for practical purposes, without any metaphysics, and without transcending the bounds of experience (*cf.* William James, *Pragmatism, A New Name for Some Old Ways of Thinking,* New York, 1907, pp. 57 and 106 especially). From the standpoint of materialism the difference between Machism and pragmatism is as insignificant and unimportant as the difference between empirio-criticism and empirio-monism. Compare, for example, Bogdanov's definition of truth with the pragmatist definition of truth, which is: "Truth for a pragmatist becomes a class-name for all sorts of definite working values in experience" (*ibid.,* p. 68).

valuable contributions in the special fields of chemistry, history, or physics, *can be trusted one iota* when it comes to philosophy. Why? For the same reason that *not a single* professor of political economy, who may be capable of very valuable contributions in the field of factual and specialized investigations, *can be trusted one iota* when it comes to the general theory of political economy. For in modern society the latter is as much a *partisan* science as is epistemology. Taken as a whole, the professors of economics are nothing but scientific salesmen of the capitalist class, while the professors of philosophy are scientific salesmen of the theologians.

The task of Marxists in both cases is to be able to master and adapt the achievements of these "salesmen" (for instance, you will not make the slightest progress in the investigation of new economic phenomena unless you have recourse to the works of these salesmen) and to be able to lop off their reactionary tendency, to pursue one's own line and to combat the *whole alignment* of forces and classes hostile to us. And this is just what our Machians were unable to do; they *slavishly* followed the lead of the reactionary professorial *philosophy*. "Perhaps we have gone astray, but we are seeking," wrote Lunacharsky in the name of the authors of the *Studies*. The trouble is that it is not *you* who are *seeking*, but you who are *being sought*! You do not go with your, i.e., Marxist (for you want to be Marxists), standpoint to every change in the bourgeois philosophical fashion; the fashion comes to you, foists upon you its new surrogates got up in the idealist taste, one day à la Ostwald, the next day à la Mach, and the day after à la Poincaré. These silly "theoretical" devices ("energetics," "elements," "introjections," etc.) in which you so naively believe are confined to a narrow and tiny school, while the ideological and *social tendency* of these devices is immediately spotted by the Wards, the neo-criticists, the immanentists, the Lopatins and the pragmatists, and *serves their purposes*. The infatuation for empirio-criticism and "physical" idealism passes as rapidly as the infatuation for Neo-Kantianism and "physiological" idealism; but fideism takes its toll from every such infatuation and modifies its devices in a thousand ways for the benefit of philosophical idealism.

The attitude towards religion and the attitude towards natural science excellently illustrate the *actual* class use made of empirio-criticism by bourgeois reactionaries.

Take the first question. Do you think it is an accident that in a collective work directed *against* the philosophy of Marxism Lunacharsky went so far as to speak of the "apotheosis of the higher human potentialities," of "religious atheism," etc.? If you do, it is only because the Russian Machians have not informed the public correctly regarding the *whole* Machian current in Europe and the attitude of this current to religion. Not only is this attitude in no way similar to the attitude of Marx, Engels, J. Dietzgen and even Feuerbach, but it is its *very opposite,* beginning with Petzoldt's statement to the effect that empirio-criticism "contradicts neither theism nor atheism" (*Einführung in die Philosophie der reinen Erfahrung,* v. I, p. 351), or Mach's declaration that "religious opinion is a private affair," and ending with the explicit fideism, the explicitly *arch-reactionary* views of Cornelius, who praises Mach and whom Mach praises, of Carus and of all the immanentists. The neutrality of a *philosopher* in this question *is in itself* servility to fideism, and Mach and Avenarius, because of the very premises of their epistemology, do not and cannot rise above neutrality.

Once you deny objective reality, given us in sensation, you have already lost every one of your weapons against fideism, for you have slipped into agnosticism or subjectivism—and that is all fideism wants. If the perceptual world is objective reality, then the door is closed to every other "reality" or quasi-reality (remember that Bazarov believed the "realism" of the immanentists, who declare God to be a "real concept"). If the world is matter in motion, matter can and must be infinitely studied in the infinitely complex and detailed manifestations and ramifications of *this* motion, the motion of *this* matter; but beyond it, beyond the "physical," external world, with which everyone is familiar, there can be nothing. And the hostility to materialism and the showers of abuse heaped on the materialists are all in the order of things in civilized and democratic Europe. All this is going on to this day. All this is being *concealed* from the public by the Russian Machians, who have *not once* attempted even simply to compare the attacks made on materialism by Mach, Avenarius, Petzoldt and Co. with the statements made *in favor of* materialism by Feuerbach, Marx, Engels and J. Dietzgen. . . .

One must be blind not to see the ideological affinity between Lunacharsky's "apotheosis of the higher human potentialities" and Bogdanov's "general substitution" of the psychical for physical nature. This is one and the same thought; in the one case it is expressed from the esthetic standpoint, and in the other from the epistemological standpoint. "Substitution," approaching the subject *tacitly* and from a different angle, *already deifies* the "higher human potentialities," by divorcing the "psychical" from man and by substituting an immensely extended, abstract, divinely lifeless "psychical in general" *for all physical nature.* And what of Yushkevich's "Logos" introduced into the "irrational stream of experience"?

A single claw ensnared, and the bird is lost. And our Machians have all become ensnared in idealism, that is, in a diluted and subtle fideism; they became ensnared from the moment they took "sensation" not as the image of the external world but as a special "element." It is nobody's sensation, nobody's mind, nobody's spirit, nobody's will—this is what one inevitably comes to if one does not recognize the materialist theory that the human mind *reflects* an objectively real external world.

—LENIN, *Materialism and Empirio-Criticism* (1908), pp. 348–59.

[7]

DOES THE NEW PHYSICS REFUTE MATERIALISM?

You cannot take up any of the writings of the Machians or about Machism without encountering pretentious references to the new physics, which is said to have refuted materialism, and so on and so forth. Whether these assertions are well-founded is another question, but the connection between the new physics, or rather a definite school of the new physics, and Machism and other varieties of modern idealist philosophy is beyond doubt. To analyze Machism and at the same time to ignore this connection—as Plekhanov does—is to scoff at the spirit of dialectical materialism, i.e., to sacrifice the method of Engels to the letter of Engels. Engels says explicitly that "with each epoch-making discovery even in the sphere of natural science ["not to speak of the history of mankind"], it [materialism] has to change its form" (*Ludwig Feuerbach,* p. 26). Hence, a revision of the "form" of

Engels' materialism, a revision of his natural-philosophical propositions is not only not "revisionism," in the accepted meaning of the term, but, on the contrary, is demanded by Marxism. We criticize the Machians not for making such a revision, but for their *purely revisionist method* of changing the *essence* of materialism under the guise of criticizing its *form* and of adopting the fundamental precepts of reactionary bourgeois philosophy without making the slightest attempt to deal directly, frankly and definitely with assertions of Engels' which are unquestionably extremely important to the given question, as, for example, his assertion that ". . . motion without matter is unthinkable" (*Anti-Dühring*, p. 71).

It goes without saying that in examining the connection between one of the schools of modern physics and the rebirth of philosophical idealism it is far from being our intention to deal with special physical theories. What interests us exclusively is the epistemological conclusions that follow from certain definite propositions and generally known discoveries. These epistemological conclusions are of themselves so insistent that many physicists are already reaching for them. What is more, there are already various trends among the physicists, and definite schools are beginning to be formed on this basis. Our object, therefore, will be confined to explaining clearly the essence of the difference between these various trends and the relation in which they stand to the fundamental lines of philosophy.

1. The Crisis in Modern Physics

In his book *La valeur de la science,* the famous French physicist Henri Poincaré says that there are "symptoms of a serious crisis" in physics, and he devotes a special chapter to this crisis (Chap. VIII, *cf.* also p. 171). This crisis is not confined to the fact that "radium, the great revolutionary," is undermining the principle of the conservation of energy. "All the other principles are equally endangered" (p. 180). For instance, Lavoisier's principle, or the principle of the conservation of mass, has been undermined by the electron theory of matter. According to this theory atoms are composed of very minute particles called electrons, which are charged with positive or negative electricity and "are immersed in a medium which we call the ether." The experiments of physicists provide data for calculating the velocity of the electrons and their mass (or the relation of their mass to their electrical charge). The velocity proves to be comparable with the velocity of light (186,000 miles per second), attaining, for instance, one-third of the latter. Under such circumstances the twofold mass of the electron has to be taken into account, corresponding to the necessity of overcoming the inertia, firstly, of the electron itself and, secondly, of the ether. The former mass will be the real or mechanical mass of the electron, the latter the "electrodynamic mass which represents the inertia of the ether." And it turns out that the former mass is equal to zero. The entire mass of the electrons, or, at least, of the negative electrons, proves to be totally and exclusively electrodynamic in its origin. Mass disappears. The foundations of mechanics are undermined. Newton's principle, the equality of action and reaction, is undermined, and so on.

We are faced, says Poincaré, with the "ruins" of the old principles of physics, "a debacle of principles." It is true, he remarks, that all the mentioned departures from principles refer to infinitesimal magnitudes; it is possible that we are still ignorant of other infinitesimals counteracting the undermining of the old principles. Moreover, radium is very rare. But at any rate we have reached a "*period of doubt.*" We have already seen what epistemological deductions the author draws from this "period of doubt": "It is not nature which imposes on [or dictates to] us the concepts of space and time, but we who impose them on nature"; "whatever is not thought, is pure nothing." These deductions are idealist deductions. The breakdown of the most fundamental principles shows (such is Poincaré's trend of thought) that these principles are not copies, photographs of nature, not images of something external in relation to man's consciousness, but products of his consciousness. Poincaré does not develop these deductions consistently, nor is he essentially interested in the philosophical aspect of the question. . . .

2. "Matter Has Disappeared"

Such, literally, is the expression that may be encountered in the descriptions given by modern physicists of recent discoveries. For instance, L. Houllevigue, in his book *L'évolution des sciences,* entitles his chapter on the new theories of matter: "Does Matter Exist?" He says: "The atom dematerializes, matter disappears." To see how easily fundamental philosophical conclusions are drawn from this by the Machians, let us take Valentinov.* He

* See above, p. 64 for work referred to.—*Ed.*

writes: "The statement that the scientific explanation of the world can find a firm foundation *only* in materialism is nothing but a fiction, and what is more, an absurd fiction" (p. 67). He quotes as a destroyer of this absurd fiction Augusto Righi, the Italian physicist, who says that the electron theory "is not so much a theory of electricity as of matter; the new system simply puts electricity in the place of matter." Having quoted these words (p. 64), Mr. Valentinov exclaims: "Why does Righi permit himself to commit this offence against sacred matter? Is it perhaps because he is a solipsist, an idealist, a bourgeois criticist, an empirio-monist, or even something worse?"

This remark, which seems to Mr. Valentinov to annihilate the materialists by its sarcasm, only discloses his virgin innocence on the subject of philosophical materialism. Mr. Valentinov has no suspicion of the *real* connection between philosophical idealism and the "disappearance of matter." That "disappearance of matter" of which he speaks, in imitation of the modern physicists, has no relation to the epistemological distinction between materialism and idealism. . . .

Materialism and idealism differ in their respective answers to the question of the *source* of our knowledge and of the relation of knowledge (and of the "psychical" in general) to the *physical* world; while the question of the structure of matter, of atoms and electrons, is a question that concerns only this "physical world." When the physicists say that "matter is disappearing," they mean that hitherto science reduced its investigations of the physical world to three ultimate concepts: matter, electricity and ether; whereas now *only* the two latter remain. For it has become possible to reduce matter to electricity; the atom can be explained as resembling an infinitely small solar system, within which negative electrons move around a positive electron with a definite (and, as we have seen, enormously large) velocity. It is consequently possible to reduce the physical world from scores of elements to two or three elements (inasmuch as positive and negative electrons constitute "two essentially distinct kinds of matter," as the physicist Pellat says). Hence, natural science leads to the "*unity of matter*"—such is the real meaning of the statement regarding the disappearance of matter, its replacement by electricity, etc., which is leading so many people astray. "Matter is disappearing" means that the limit within which we have hitherto known matter is vanishing and that our knowledge is penetrating deeper; properties of matter are disappearing which formerly seemed absolute, immutable, and primary (impenetrability, inertia, mass, etc.) and which are now revealed to be relative and characteristic only of certain states of matter. For the *sole* "property" of matter with whose recognition philosophical materialism is bound up is the property of *being an objective reality,* of existing outside our mind.

The error of Machism in general, as of the Machian new physics, is that it ignores this basis of philosophical materialism and the distinction between metaphysical materialism and dialectical materialism. The recognition of immutable elements, "of the immutable substance of things," and so forth, is not materialism, but *metaphysical,* i.e., anti-dialectical, materialism. That is why J. Dietzgen emphasized that the "subject-matter of science is endless," that not only the infinite, but the "smallest atom" is immeasurable, unknowable to the end, *inexhaustible,* "for nature in all her parts has no beginning and no end" (*Kleinere philosophische Schriften,* pp. 229*f*). That is why Engels gave the example of the discovery of alizarin in coal tar and criticized *mechanical* materialism. In order to present the question in the only correct way, that is, from the dialectical materialist standpoint, we must ask: Do electrons, ether *and so on* exist as objective realities outside the human mind or not? The scientists will also have to answer this question unhesitatingly; and they do invariably answer it in the *affirmative,* just as they unhesitatingly recognize that nature existed prior to man and prior to organic matter. Thus, the question is decided in favor of materialism, for the concept matter, as we already stated, epistemologically implies *nothing but* objective reality existing independently of the human mind and reflected by it.

But dialectical materialism insists on the approximate, relative character of every scientific theory of the structure of matter and its properties; it insists on the absence of absolute boundaries in nature, on the transformation of moving matter from one state into another which, from one point of view, is to us apparently irreconcilable with it, and so forth. However bizarre from the standpoint of "common sense" the transformation of imponderable ether into ponderable matter and *vice versa* may appear, however "strange" may seem the absence of any other kind of mass in the electron save electromagnetic mass, however extraordinary may be the fact that the mechanical laws of motion are confined only to a single sphere of natural phenomena and are subordinated to the more profound laws of electromagnetic phenomena, and so forth—all this is but another *corroboration* of dialectical materialism. It is mainly because the physicists did not know dialectics that the new physics strayed into idealism. They combated metaphysical (in Engels', and not the positivist, i.e., Humean sense of the word) materialism and its one-sided "mechanism," and in so doing threw the baby out with the bathwater. Denying the immutability of the elements and the properties of matter known hitherto, they ended in denying matter, i.e., the objective reality of the physical world. Denying the absolute character of some of the most important and basic laws, they ended in denying all objective law in nature and in declaring that a law of nature is a mere convention, "a limitation of expectation," "a logical necessity," and so forth. Insisting on the approximate and relative character of our knowledge, they ended in denying the object independent of the mind and reflected approximately correctly and relatively truthfully by the mind. And so on, and so forth, without end.

The opinions expressed by Bogdanov in 1899 regarding "the immutable essence of things," the opinions of Valentinov and Yushkevich regarding "substance," and so forth—are similar fruits of ignorance of dialectics. From Engels' point of view, the only immutability is the reflection by the human mind (when there is a human mind) of an external world existing and developing independently of the mind. No other "immutability," no other "essence," no other "absolute substance," in the sense in which these concepts were depicted by the empty professorial philosophy, exist for Marx and Engels. The "essence" of things, or "substance," is *also* relative; it expresses only the degree of profundity of man's knowledge of objects; and while yesterday the profundity of this knowledge did not go beyond the atom, and today does not go beyond the electron and ether, dialectical materialism insists on the temporary, relative, approximate character of all these *milestones* in the knowledge of nature gained by the progressing science of man. The electron is as *inexhaustible* as the atom, nature is infinite, but it infinitely *exists*. And it is this sole categorical, this sole unconditional recognition of nature's *existence* outside the mind and perceptions of man that distinguishes dialectical materialism from relativist agnosticism and idealism. . . .

3. Is Motion Without Matter Conceivable?

The fact that philosophical idealism is attempting to make use of the new physics, or that idealist conclusions are being drawn from the latter, is due not to the discovery of new kinds of substance and force, of matter and motion, but to the fact that an attempt is being made to conceive motion without matter. And it is the essence of this attempt which our Machians fail to examine. They were unwilling to take account of Engels' statement that "motion without matter is *inconceivable.*" J. Dietzgen in 1869, in his *The Nature of Human Brain-Work,** expressed the same idea as Engels, although, it is true, not without his usual muddled attempts to "reconcile" materialism and idealism. Let us leave aside these attempts, which are to a large extent to be explained by the fact that Dietzgen is arguing against Büchner's non-dialectical materialism, and let us examine Dietzgen's own statements on the question under consideration. He says: "They [the idealists] want to have the general without the particular, mind without matter, force without substance, science without experience or material, the absolute without the relative" (p. 137). Thus the endeavor to divorce motion from matter, force from substance, Dietzgen associates with idealism, compares with the endeavor to divorce thought from the brain.

> "Liebig [Dietzgen continues] who is especially fond of straying from his inductive science into the field of speculation, says in the spirit of idealism: 'force cannot be seen' . . ." (pp. 138 *f.*). "The spiritualist or the idealist *believes* in the spiritual, *i.e.*, ghostlike and inexplicable, nature of force . . ." (p. 140). "The antithesis between force and matter is as old as the antithesis between idealism and materialism . . ." (p. 141). "Of course, there is no force without matter, no matter without force; forceless matter and matterless force are absurdities. If there are idealist natural scientists who believe in the immaterial existence of forces . . . on this point they are not natural scientists . . . but seers of ghosts" (p. 144).

We thus see that scientists who were prepared to grant that motion is conceivable without matter were to be encountered 40 years ago too, and that "on this point" Dietzgen declared them to be seers of ghosts. What, then, is the connection between idealism and the divorce of matter from motion, the separation of sub-

* Contained in *The Positive Outcome of Philosophy,* Kerr, Chicago, 1928. This translation varies somewhat from that given below.—*Ed.*

stance from force? Is it not "more economical," indeed, to conceive motion without matter?

Let us imagine a consistent idealist who holds that the entire world is his sensation, his idea, etc. (if we take "nobody's" sensation or idea, this changes only the variety of philosophical idealism but not its essence). The idealist would not even think of denying that the world is motion, i.e., the motion of my thoughts, ideas, sensations. The question as to *what* moves, the idealist will reject and regard as absurd: What is taking place is a change of my sensations, my ideas come and go, and nothing more. Outside me there is nothing. "It moves"—and that is all. It is impossible to conceive a more "economical" way of thinking. And no proofs, syllogisms, or definitions are capable of refuting the solipsist if he consistently adheres to his view.

The fundamental distinction between the materialist and the adherent of idealist philosophy consists in the fact that the sensation, perception, idea, and the mind of man generally, is regarded as an image of objective reality. The world is the movement of this objective reality reflected by our consciousness. To the movement of ideas, perceptions, etc., there corresponds the movement of matter outside me. The concept matter expresses nothing more than the objective reality which is given us in sensation. Therefore, to divorce motion from matter is equivalent to divorcing thought from objective reality, or to divorcing my sensations from the external world—in a word, it is to go over to idealism. The trick which is usually performed in denying matter, and in assuming motion without matter, consists in ignoring the relation of matter to thought. The question is presented as though this relation did not exist, but in reality it is introduced surreptitiously; at the beginning of the argument it remains unexpressed, but subsequently crops up more or less imperceptibly.

Matter has disappeared, they tell us, wishing from this to draw epistemological conclusions. But, we ask, has thought remained? If not, if with the disappearance of matter thought has also disappeared, if with the disappearance of the brain and nervous system ideas and sensations, too, have disappeared—then it follows that everything has disappeared. And your argument has disappeared as a sample of "thought" (or lack of thought)! But if it has remained, if it is assumed that with the disappearance of matter, thought (idea, sensation, etc.) does not disappear, then you have surreptitiously gone over to the standpoint of philosophical idealism. And this always happens with people who wish, for "economy's sake," to conceive of motion without matter, for *tacitly*, by the very fact that they continue to argue, they are acknowledging the existence of thought *after* the disappearance of matter. This means that a very simple, or a very complex philosophical idealism is taken as a basis; a very simple one, if it is a case of frank solipsism (*I* exist, and the world is only *my* sensation); a very complex one, if instead of the thought, ideas and sensations of a living person, a dead abstraction is posited, that is, nobody's thought, nobody's idea, nobody's sensation, but thought in general (the Absolute Idea, the Universal Will, etc.), sensation as an indeterminate "element," the "psychical," which is substituted for the whole of physical nature, etc., etc. Thousands of shades of varieties of philosophical idealism are possible and it is always possible to create a thousand-and-first shade; and to the author of this thousand-and-first little system (empirio-monism, for example) what distinguishes it from the rest may appear to be momentous. From the standpoint of materialism, however, these distinctions are absolutely unessential. What is essential is the point of departure. What is essential is that the attempt to *think* of motion without matter smuggles in *thought* divorced from matter—and that is philosophical idealism.

—LENIN, *Materialism and Empirio-Criticism* (1908), pp. 257–59, 265–69, 273–75.

PART THREE

DIALECTICS AND THE DIALECTICAL METHOD

Nothing is eternal but eternally changing, eternally moving matter and the laws according to which it moves and changes.
—ENGELS, *Dialectics of Nature* (1882), p. 24.

Introduction

IF MARXIST materialism has been misunderstood and misrepresented by the failure to differentiate it from previous forms of materialism, the dialectics of Marx and Engels has been similarly distorted by not being sufficiently distinguished from the dialectics of Hegel. The founders of Marxism, while ever acknowledging their debt to Hegel, and to Heraclitus too, took considerable pains to separate what they regarded as the "rational kernel" from the "mystical shell" of dialectics. The first five or six entries in this section should give the reader an idea of what is meant by "materialist" dialectics, as well as provide cautions against its misuse.

One idea that is constantly presented and reiterated in the following selections is that dialectics or the dialectical method (two sides of the same thing) is derived from our experience and knowledge of the objective world and the study of our own thought processes. This is emphasized against any view that it is a creation of pure thought which is then imposed upon the world of nature and society. Whatever Marx and Engels believed concerning dialectics, they were convinced that it was something they found inherent in the nature of things, not something they or anyone else invented in their heads.

A second idea concerning dialectics, emphasized in these passages, is that it is not a magic formula that solves problems automatically. Dialectics does not solve problems at all but *can help men* in the solution of problems. We might solve them the same way without ever having heard of dialectics, but Marx, Engels, and Lenin believed that with a consciousness of the laws or principles of dialectics we are better equipped to handle the subtleties, interrelations, contradictions, and complexities of the subject matter before us. Dialectics is no schema we can impose upon any area of reality; it is no substitute for the fullest gathering of facts and the most painstaking analysis of them. For Marx, the dialectical method was essentially the *method* for dealing with matter, that is, with any concrete, empirical subject matter (*see, e.g.,* Marx, *Letters to Kugelmann,* New York, 1934, p. 112).

It is unfortunate that because of their preoccupation with the writing and publication of *Capital,* neither Marx nor Engels was able to make a full-scale analysis of the dialectical method. Marx long planned a book on the dialectics of Hegel that would have constituted a thorough study of logic, as well as a methodology for history and the social sciences generally. Engels made notes for years with the aim of producing a book on the role of dialectics in the natural sciences. Neither of these works were ever written, but Engels' notes, together with a few completed sections, consisting of several hundred pages, were finally published in 1927 under the title, *Dialectics of Nature.* Lenin, similarly, seems to have been working on a serious and lengthy exposition of dialectics while in exile in Switzerland where he was deeply immersed in the study of Hegel and Aristotle. This work, foreshadowed in the posthumous *Philosophical Notebooks,* was interrupted by developments in Russia, his return there, and his subsequent leadership of the Russian Revolution.

The reader can readily see from the selections in this section, supplemented by those from Lenin in Appendix II, that Marxists believe dialectics essential and indispensable for correct thought and adequate scientific analysis in any area. The reader who is acquainted with contemporary developments in the sciences will find, indeed, that many dialectical principles have become an integral part of scientific thinking, even though expressed in other terms, such as "principle of polarity," "integrative levels," etc.

Marxists recognize that there is still considerable "unfinished business" concerning the precise meaning of the categories of dialectics and their sphere of application. What is the relation of dialectics to formal logic? What is the meaning of law in dialectics and what are the dialectical laws? What does "contradiction" mean, and does it mean the same thing in different areas of reality and thought? These and other questions are being examined today, more than ever before, by Marxist philosophers and scientists.

[1]

"ALL THAT IS REAL IS RATIONAL"— THE REVOLUTIONARY SIDE OF HEGELIAN PHILOSOPHY

No philosophical proposition has earned more gratitude from narrow-minded governments and wrath from equally narrow-minded liberals than Hegel's famous statement: "All that is real is rational: and all that is rational is real." That was tangibly a sanctification of things that be, a philosophical benediction bestowed upon despotism, police government, Star Chamber proceedings and censorship. That is how Frederick William III and his subjects understood it. But according to Hegel everything that exists is certainly not also *real,* without further qualification. For Hegel the attribute of reality belongs only to that which at the same time is necessary: "The reality proves itself to be the necessary in the course of its development."...

Now, according to Hegel, reality is, however, in no way an attribute of any given state of affairs, social or political, in all circumstances and for all time. On the contrary. The Roman Republic was real, but so was the Roman Empire which superseded it. In 1789 the French monarchy had become so unreal, that is to say, it had been so robbed of all necessity, so non-rational, that it had to be destroyed by the great revolution—of which Hegel always speaks with the greatest enthusiasm. In this case the monarchy was the unreal and the revolution was the real. And so, in the course of development, all that was previously real becomes unreal, loses its necessity, its right of existence, its rationality. And in the place of moribund reality comes a new reality capable of living—peacefully if the old has enough intelligence to go to its death without a struggle; forcibly if it resists this necessity. Thus the Hegelian proposition turns into its opposite through Hegelian dialectics itself: All that is real in the sphere of human history becomes irrational in the process of time and is therefore irrational already by its destination, is tainted beforehand with irrationality, and everything which is rational in the minds of men is destined to become real, however much it may contradict the apparent reality of existing conditions. In accordance with all the rules of the Hegelian method of thought, the proposition of the rationality of everything which is real resolves itself into the other proposition: All that exists has this much value, that it perishes.*

But precisely here lay the true significance and the revolutionary character of the Hegelian philosophy (to which, as the close of the whole movement since Kant, we must here confine ourselves), that it once and for all dealt the deathblow to the finality of all products of human thought and action. Truth, the cognition of which is the business of philosophy, became in the hands of Hegel no longer an aggregate of finished dogmatic statements, which once discovered, had merely to be learned by heart. Truth lay now in the process of cognition itself, in the long historical development of science, which mounts from lower to ever higher levels of knowledge without ever reaching, by discovering so-called absolute truth, a point at which it can proceed no further and where it would have nothing more to do than to fold its hands and admire the absolute truth to which it had attained. And what holds good for the realm of philosophic knowledge holds good also for that of every other kind of knowledge and also for practical affairs. Just as knowledge is unable to reach a perfected termination in a perfect, ideal condition of humanity, so is history unable to do so; a perfect society, a perfect "state," are things which can only exist in imagination. On the contrary, all successive historical situations are only transitory stages in the endless course of development of human society from the lower to the higher. Each stage is necessary, and therefore justified for the time and conditions to which it owes its origin. But in the newer and higher conditions which gradually develop in its own bosom, each loses its validity and justification. It must give way to a higher form which will also in its turn decay and perish. Just

* The words of Mephistopheles in Goethe's *Faust*: *"Alles, was besteht, ist wert, dass es zugrunde geht."—Ed.*

as the bourgeoisie by large-scale industry, competition, and the world market dissolves in practice all stable, time-honored institutions, so this dialectical philosophy dissolves all conceptions of final, absolute truth, and of a final absolute state of humanity corresponding to it. For it nothing is final, absolute, sacred. It reveals the transitory character of everything and in everything; nothing can endure before it except the uninterrupted process of becoming and of passing away, of endless ascendancy from the lower to the higher. And dialectical philosophy itself is nothing more than the mere reflection of this process in the thinking brain. It has, of course, also a conservative side: It recognizes that definite stages of knowledge and society are justified for their time and circumstances; but only so far. The conservatism of this mode of outlook is relative; its revolutionary character is absolute —the only absolute it admits.

—ENGELS, *Ludwig Feuerbach* (1888), pp. 10–12.

[2]

MARXIST DIALECTICS THE OPPOSITE OF HEGEL'S

My dialectic method is not only different from the Hegelian, but is its direct opposite. To Hegel, the life process of the human brain, i.e., the process of thinking, which, under the name of "the Idea," he even transforms into an independent subject, is the demiurge of the real world, and the real world is only the external, phenomenal form of "the Idea." With me, on the contrary, the ideal is nothing else than the material world reflected by the human mind, and translated into forms of thought.

The mystifying side of Hegelian dialectic I criticized nearly 30 years ago,* at a time when it was still the fashion. But just as I was working at the first volume of *Das Kapital*, it was the good pleasure of the peevish, arrogant, mediocre *Epigonoi* who now talk large in cultured Germany, to treat Hegel in the same way as the brave Moses Mendelssohn in Lessing's time treated Spinoza, i.e., as a "dead dog." I therefore openly avowed myself the pupil of that mighty thinker, and even here and there, in the chapter

* Marx is referring to several works written in 1844, selections from which are contained in Appendix I.—*Ed.*

on the theory of value, coquetted with the modes of expression peculiar to him. The mystification which dialectic suffers in Hegel's hands, by no means prevents him from being the first to present its general form of working in a comprehensive and conscious manner. With him it is standing on its head. It must be turned right side up again, if you would discover the rational kernel within the mystical shell.

In its mystified form, dialectic became the fashion in Germany, because it seemed to transfigure and to glorify the existing state of things. In its rational form it is a scandal and abomination to bourgeoisdom and its doctrinaire professors, because it includes in its comprehension and affirmative recognition of the existing state of things, at the same time also, the recognition of the negation of that state, of its inevitable breaking up; because it regards every historically developed social form as in fluid movement, and therefore takes into account its transient nature not less than its momentary existence; because it lets nothing impose upon it, and is in its essence critical and revolutionary.

The contradictions inherent in the movement of capitalist society impress themselves upon the practical bourgeois most strikingly in the changes of the periodic cycle, through which modern industry runs, and whose crowning point is the universal crisis. That crisis is once again approaching, although as yet but in its preliminary stage; and by the universality of its theatre and the intensity of its action it will drum dialectics even into the heads of the mushroom-upstarts of the new, holy Prusso-German empire.

—MARX, *Capital*, vol. I, Preface to Second Edition (1873), pp. xxx *f*.

[3]

FROM HEGELIAN TO MATERIALIST DIALECTICS

A. THE ROLE OF THE NATURAL SCIENCES

According to Hegel, dialectics is the self-development of the concept. The absolute concept does not only exist—where unknown—from eternity, it is also the actual living soul of the whole existing world. It develops into itself through all the preliminary stages which are treated at length in the *Logic* and which are all included in it. Then it "alienates" itself by changing into nature, where, without consciousness of itself, disguised as the necessity of nature, it goes through a new development and finally comes again to self-consciousness in man. This self-consciousness then elaborates itself again in history from the crude form until finally the absolute concept again comes to itself completely in the Hegelian philosophy. According to Hegel, therefore, the dialectical development apparent in nature and history, i.e., the causal interconnection of the progressive movement from the lower to the higher, which asserts itself through all zig-zag movements and temporary setbacks, is only a miserable copy of the self-movement of the concept going on from eternity, no one knows where, but at all events independently of any thinking human brain. This ideological reversal had to be done away with. We comprehended the concepts in our heads once more materialistically—as images of real things instead of regarding the real things as images of this or that stage of development of the absolute concept. Thus dialectics reduced itself to the science of the general laws of motion—both of the external world and of human thought—two sets of laws which are identical in substance, but differ in their expression in so far as the human mind can apply them consciously, while in nature and also up to now for the most part in human history, these laws assert themselves unconsciously in the form of external necessity in the midst of an endless series of seeming accidents. Thereby the dialectic of the concept itself became merely the conscious reflex of the dialectical motion of the real world and the dialectic of Hegel was placed upon its head; or rather, turned off its head, on which it was standing before, and placed upon its feet again. And this materialist dialectic which for years has been our best working tool and our sharpest weapon was, remarkably enough, discovered not only by us, but also independently of us and even of Hegel by a German worker, Joseph Dietzgen.

In this way, however, the revolutionary side of Hegelian philosophy was again taken up and at the same time freed from the idealist trammels which in Hegel's hands had prevented its consistent execution. The great basic thought that the world is not to be comprehended as a complex of ready-made *things*, but as a complex of *processes*, in which the things apparently stable no less than their mind-images in our heads, the concepts, go through an uninterrupted change of coming into being and passing away, in which, in spite of all seeming accidents and of all temporary retrogression, a progressive development asserts itself in the end—this great fundamental thought has, especially since the time of Hegel, so thoroughly permeated ordinary consciousness that in this generality it is scarcely ever contradicted. But to acknowledge this fundamental thought in words and to apply it in reality in detail to each domain of investigation are two different things. If, however, investigation always proceeds from this standpoint, the demand for final solutions and eternal truths ceases once for all; one is always conscious of the necessary limitation of all acquired knowledge, of the fact that it is conditioned by the circumstances in which it was acquired. On the other hand, one no longer permits oneself to be imposed upon by the antitheses, insuperable for the still common old metaphysics, between true and false, good and bad, identical and different, necessary and accidental. One knows that these antitheses have only a relative validity; that that which is recognized now as true has also its latent false side which will later manifest itself, just as that which is now regarded as false has also its true side by virtue of which it could previously have been regarded as true. One knows that what is maintained to be necessary is composed of sheer accidents and that the so-called accidental is the form behind which necessity hides itself, and so on.

The old method of investigation and thought which Hegel calls "metaphysical," which preferred to investigate *things* as given, as fixed and stable, a method the relics of which still strongly haunt people's minds, had a good deal of historical justification in its day. It was necessary first to examine things before it was possible to examine processes. One had first to know what a particular thing was before one could observe the changes going on in connection with it. And such was the case with natural science. The old metaphysics which accepted things as finished objects arose from a natural science which investigated dead and living things as finished objects. But when this investigation had progressed so far that it became possible to take the decisive step forward of transition to the systematic investigation of the changes which these things undergo in nature itself, then the last hour of the old metaphysics sounded in the realm of philosophy also. And in fact, while natural science up to the end of the last century was predominantly a *collecting* science, a science of finished things, in our century it is essentially a *classifying* science, a science of the processes, of the origin and development of these things and of the inter-connection which binds all these natural processes into one great whole. Physiology, which investigates the processes occurring in plant and animal organisms; embryology, which deals with the development of individual organisms from germ to maturity; geology, which investigates the gradual formation of the earth's surface—all these are the offspring of our century.

But, above all, there are three great discoveries which had enabled our knowledge of the inter-connection of natural processes to advance by leaps and bounds: First, the discovery of the cell as the unit from whose multiplication and differentiation the whole plant and animal body develops—so that not only is the development and growth of all higher organisms recognized to proceed according to a single general law, but also, in the capacity of the cell to change, the way is pointed out by which organisms can change their species and thus go through a more than individual development. Second, the transformation of energy, which has demonstrated that all the so-called forces operative in the first instance in inorganic nature—mechanical force and its complement, so-called potential energy, heat, radiation (light or radiant heat), electricity, magnetism, and chemical energy—are different forms of manifestation of universal motion, which pass into one another in definite proportions so that in place of a certain quantity of the one which disappears, a certain quantity of another makes its appearance and thus the whole motion of nature is reduced to this incessant process of transformation from one form into another. Finally, the proof which Darwin first developed in connected form that the stock of organic products of nature surrounding us today, including mankind, is the result of a long process of evolution from a few original unicellular germs, and that these again have arisen from protoplasm or albumen which came into existence by chemical means.

Thanks to these three great discoveries and the other immense advances in natural science, we have now arrived at the point where we can demonstrate as a whole the inter-connection between the processes in nature not only in particular spheres but also in the inter-connection of these particular spheres themselves, and so can present in an approximately systematic form a comprehensive view of the inter-connection in nature by means of the facts provided by empirical natural science itself. To furnish this comprehensive view was formerly the task of so-called natural philosophy. It could do this only by putting in place of the real but as yet unknown inter-connections ideal and imaginary ones, filling out the missing facts by figments of the mind and bridging the actual gaps merely in imagination. In the course of this procedure it conceived many brilliant ideas and foreshadowed many later discoveries, but it also produced a considerable amount of nonsense, which indeed could not have been otherwise. Today, when one needs to comprehend the results of natural scientific investigation only dialectically, that is, in the sense of their own inter-connections, in order to arrive at a "system of nature" sufficient for our time; when the dialectical character of this interconnection is forcing itself against their will even into the metaphysically trained minds of the natural scientists, today this natural philosophy is finally disposed of. Every attempt at resurrecting it would be not only superfluous but a *step backwards.*

—ENGELS, *Ludwig Feuerbach* (1888), pp. 43–47.

B. THE ROLE OF MARX'S POLITICAL ECONOMY

Since Hegel's death hardly any attempt has been made to develop a science in its own inner inter-connection. The official Hegelian school had appropriated from the dialectics of the master only the manipulation of the simplest tricks, which it applied to anything and everything often with ludicrous clumsiness. For it, the whole inheritance of Hegel was limited to a mere pattern by the help of which every theme could be correctly devised, and to a compilation of words and turns of speech which had no other purpose than to turn up at the right time when thought and positive knowledge failed. Thus it came about that, as a Bonn professor said, these Hegelians understood nothing about anything, but could write about everything. Its worth was in accordance. Meanwhile, these gentlemen were, in spite of their self-complacency, so conscious of their weakness that they avoided big problems as much as possible. The old pedantic science held the field by its superiority in positive knowledge. And when Feuerbach also gave notice that he was quitting the field of speculative conceptions, Hegelianism quietly fell asleep; and it seemed as if the old metaphysics, with its fixed categories, had begun to reign anew in science. . . .

Here, therefore, was another problem to be solved, one which had nothing to do with political economy as such. How was science to be treated? On the one hand there was the Hegelian dialectics in the wholly abstract, "speculative" form in which Hegel had bequeathed it; on the other hand there was the ordinary, essentially metaphysical Wolffian* method which had again become fashionable and in which the bourgeois economists had written their fat, disjointed tomes. This latter method had been so annihilated theoretically by Kant and particularly by Hegel that only laziness and the lack of any *simple* alternative method could make possible its continued existence in practice. On the other hand the Hegelian method was absolutely unusable in its *available* form. It was essentially idealistic, and the problem here was that of developing a world outlook more materialistic than any previously advanced. The Hegelian method started out from pure thinking and here one had to start from stubborn facts. A method which, according to its own admission, "came from nothing, through nothing, to nothing," was in this form completely out of place here.

Nevertheless, of all the available logical material, it was the only thing which could be used at least as a starting point. It had never been criticized, never overcome. Not one of the opponents of the great dialectician had been able to make a breach in its proud structure; it fell into oblivion, because the Hegelian school had not the slightest notion what to do with it. It was, therefore, above all necessary to subject the Hegelian method to thoroughgoing criticism.

What distinguishes Hegel's mode of thought from that of all other philosophers was the enormous historical sense upon which it was based. Abstract and idealist though it was in form, yet the development of his thoughts always proceeded in line with the development of world history and the latter was really meant to be only the test of the former. If, thereby, the real relation was inverted and put on its head, nevertheless its real content entered everywhere into the philosophy, all the more so since Hegel—in contrast to his disciples—did not parade ignorance, but was one of the best intellects of all time. He was the first who attempted to show an evolution, and inner coherence, in history; and while today much in his *Philosophy of History* may seem peculiar to us, yet the grandeur of the basis of his fundamental

* See Christian Wolff in Biographical Index.—*Ed.*

outlook is admirable even today, whether one makes comparison with his predecessors, or with anyone since his time who has taken the liberty of reflecting in general about history. Everywhere, in his *Phenomenology, Aesthetics, History of Philosophy,* this magnificent conception of history penetrates, and everywhere this material is treated historically, in a definite even if abstractly distorted inter-connection with history.

This epoch-making conception of history was the direct theoretical prerequisite for the new materialist outlook, and thereby provided a connecting point for the logical method. Since this forgotten dialectics had led to such results even from the standpoint of "pure thinking," and had, in addition, so easily settled accounts with all preceding logic and metaphysics, in any case there must have been something more to it than sophistry and hair-splitting. But the criticism of this method, which all officially recognized philosophy had fought shy of and still does, was no trifle.

Marx was, and is, the only one who could undertake the work of extracting from the Hegelian logic the kernel which comprised Hegel's real discoveries in this sphere, and to construct the dialectical method divested of its idealistic trappings, in the simple shape in which it becomes the only true form of development of thought.

The working out of the method which forms the foundation of Marx's *Critique of Political Economy* we consider a result of hardly less importance than the basic materialistic outlook itself.

The criticism of economics, even according to the method employed, could still be exercised in two ways—historically or logically. Since in history, as in its literary reflection, development as a whole proceeds from the most simple to the most complex relations, the historical development of the literature of political economy provided a natural guiding thread with which criticism could link up and the economic categories as a whole would thereby appear in the same sequence as in the logical development. This form apparently has the advantage of greater clearness, since indeed it is the *actual* development that is followed, but as a matter of fact it would thereby at most become more popular. History often proceeds by jumps and zigzags and it would in this way have to be followed everywhere, whereby not only would much material of minor importance have to be incorporated but there would be many interruptions of the chain of thought. Furthermore, the history of economics could not be written without that of bourgeois society and this would make the task endless, since all preliminary work is lacking. The logical method of treatment was, therefore, the only appropriate one. But this, as a matter of fact, is nothing else than the historical method, only divested of its historical form and disturbing fortuities. The chain of thought must begin with the same thing that this history begins with and its further course will be nothing but the mirror-image of the historical course in abstract and theoretically consistent form, a corrected mirror-image but corrected according to laws furnished by the real course of history itself, in that each factor can be considered at its ripest point of development, in its classic form.

In this method we proceed from the first and simplest relation that historically, and in fact, confronts us; therefore from the first economic relation to be found. We analyze this relation. Being a *relation* already implies that it has two sides *related to each other*. Each of these sides is considered by itself, which brings us to the way they behave to each other, their reciprocal interaction. Contradictions will result which demand a solution. But as we are not considering an abstract process of thought taking place solely in our heads, but a real happening which has actually taken place at some particular time, or is still taking place, these contradictions, too, will have developed in practice and will probably have found their solution. We shall trace the nature of this solution, and shall discover that it has been brought about by the establishment of a new relation whose two opposite sides we now have to develop, and so on.

Political economy begins with *commodities,* begins with the moment when products are exchanged for one another—whether by individuals or by primitive communities. The product that appears in exchange is a commodity. It is, however, a commodity solely because a *relation* between two persons or communities attaches to the *thing,* the product, the relation between producer and consumer who are here no longer united in the same person. Here we have an example of a peculiar fact, which runs through the whole of economics and which has caused utter confusion in the minds of the bourgeois economists: Economics deals not with things but with relations between persons and in the last resort between classes; these relations are, however, always *attached to things* and *appear as things.* This inter-connection, which in isolated cases, it is true, has dawned upon particular economists, was first discovered by Marx as obtaining for all political economy, whereby he made the most difficult questions so simple and clear that now even the bourgeois economists will be able to grasp them.

If now we consider commodities from their various aspects, commodities in their complete development, and not as they first laboriously develop in the primitive barter between two primitive communities, they present themselves to us from the two points of view of use value and exchange value, and here we at once enter the sphere of economic dispute. Anyone who would like to have a striking illustration of the fact that the German dialectical method in its present state of elaboration is at least as superior to the old, shallow, garrulous metaphysical method as the railway is to the means of transport of the Middle Ages, should read in Adam Smith or any other reputable official economist what a torment exchange value and use value were to these gentlemen, how difficult it was for them to keep them properly apart and to comprehend each in its peculiar distinctness, and should then compare the simple, clear treatment by Marx. . . .

It is seen that with this method the logical development is by no means compelled to keep to the purely abstract sphere. On the contrary, this method requires historical illustrations, continual contact with reality. Such proofs are accordingly introduced in great variety, with references to the actual course of history at different stages of social development as well as to the economic literature in which the clear working out of the determinations of economic relations is pursued from the beginning. The criticism of individual, more or less one-sided or confused modes of conception is then in essence already given in the logical development itself and can be briefly formulated.

—ENGELS, "Review of Marx's Critique of Political Economy" (1859), in *Ludwig Feuerbach,* Appendix, pp. 75–81.

[*For a further statement on the importance of Hegel's Logic for Marxian economics, see Lenin: Appendix II, 18.*—Ed.]

[4]

SCIENTIFIC VERSUS SCHEMATIC USE OF DIALECTICS

[*Lenin is discussing here a "refutation" of materialism and especially historical materialism by the subjective sociologist, N. Mikhailovsky. Mikhailovsky had argued that Marx could prove his case only by a reliance on the "unquestionableness of the dialectical process" as developed by Hegel.*—Ed.]

And so, the materialists rest their case on the "unquestionableness" of the dialectical process! In other words, they base their sociological theories on Hegelian triads. Here we have the stereotyped accusation that Marxism is Hegelian dialectics which one thought had already been worn sufficiently threadbare by Marx's bourgeois critics. Unable to bring anything against the doctrine itself, these gentlemen fastened on Marx's method of expression and attacked the origin of the theory, thinking thereby to undermine the theory itself. And Mr. Mikhailovsky makes no bones about resorting to similar methods. He uses a chapter from Engels' *Anti-Dühring* as a pretext. Replying to Dühring, who had attacked Marx's dialectics, Engels says that Marx never even thought of "proving" anything by means of Hegelian triads, that Marx only studied and investigated the real process, and that he regarded the conformity of a theory to reality as its only criterion. If, however, it sometimes transpired that the development of any particular social phenomenon conformed with the Hegelian scheme, namely, thesis—negation—negation of the negation, there is nothing at all surprising in this, for it is no rare thing in nature generally. And Engels proceeds to cite examples from the field of natural history (the development of a seed) and from the social field—for instance, that first there was primitive communism, then private property, and then the capitalist socialization of labor; or that first there was primitive materialism, then idealism, and then scientific materialism, and so forth. It is clear to everybody that the main burden of Engels' argument is that materialists must depict the historical process correctly and accurately, and that insistence on dialectics, the selection of examples which demonstrate the correctness of the triad, is nothing but a relic of the Hegelianism out of which scientific Socialism has grown, a relic of its method of expression.* And, indeed, once it has been categorically declared that to attempt to "prove" anything by triads is absurd, and that nobody even thought of doing so, what significance can examples of "dialectical" processes have? Is it not obvious that they merely point to the origin of the doctrine, and nothing more? Mr. Mikhailovsky himself feels this when he says that the theory should not be blamed for its origin. But in order to discern in Engels' arguments something more than the origin of the theory, it was obviously necessary to prove that the materialists had settled at least one historical "problem" by means of triads, and not on the basis of the appropriate facts. Did Mr. Mikhailovsky attempt to prove this? Not a bit of it. On the contrary, he was himself obliged to admit that "Marx filled the empty dialectical scheme with a factual content to such an extent" that "it could be removed from this content like a lid from a bowl without anything being changed" (as to the exception which Mr. Mikhailovsky makes here—regarding the future—we shall deal with it below). If that is so, why is Mr. Mikhailovsky so eagerly concerned with this lid that changes nothing? What is the point of asserting that the materialists "rest" their case on the unquestionableness of the dialectical process? Why, when he is combating this lid, does he declare that he is combating one of the "pillars" of scientific socialism, which is a direct untruth?

I shall not, of course, examine how Mr. Mikhailovsky analyzes the examples of triads, because, I repeat, this has no connection whatever either with scientific materialism or with Russian Marxism. But the interesting question arises: What grounds did Mr. Mikhailovsky have for so distorting the attitude of Marxists to dialectics? Twofold grounds: Firstly, Mr. Mikhailovsky heard something, but did not quite grasp what it was all about; secondly, Mr. Mikhailovsky performed another piece of juggling (or, rather, borrowed it from Dühring).

* Marx, in a letter to Engels in 1858, said of Lassalle "the fellow is proposing to present political economy in the Hegelian manner in his second great work. He will learn to his cost that to bring a science by criticism to the point where it can be dialectically presented is an altogether different thing from applying an abstract ready-made system of logic to mere inklings of such a system." (Marx and Engels, *Selected Correspondence*, p. 105.)

As to the first point, when reading Marxist literature Mr. Mikhailovsky constantly came across the phrases "the dialectical method" in social science, "dialectical thought," again in the sphere of social questions, "which is alone in question," and so forth. In his simplicity of heart (it were well if it were only simplicity) he took it for granted that this method consists in solving all sociological problems in accordance with the laws of the Hegelian triad. If he had been just a little more attentive to the matter in hand he could not but have become convinced of the stupidity of this notion. What Marx and Engels called the dialectical method—in contradistinction to the metaphysical method—is nothing more or less than the scientific method in sociology, which consists in regarding society as a living organism in a constant state of development (and not as something mechanically concatenated and therefore permitting any arbitrary combination of individual social elements), the study of which requires an objective analysis of the relations of production that constitute the given social formation and an investigation of its laws of functioning and development. We shall endeavor below to illustrate the relation between the dialectical method and the metaphysical method (to which concept the subjective method in sociology undoubtedly belongs) by an example taken from Mr. Mikhailovsky's own arguments. For the present we shall only observe that anyone who reads the definition and description of the dialectical method given either by Engels (in the polemic against Dühring: *Socialism, Utopian and Scientific*) or by Marx (various remarks in *Capital,* in the Postscript to its second edition, and in *The Poverty of Philosophy*), will see that the Hegelian triads are not even mentioned, and that it all amounts to regarding social evolution as a natural-historical process of development of social-economic formations.

—LENIN, "What the 'Friends of the People' Are" (1894), *Selected Works,* vol. XI, pp. 442–45.

[5]

DIALECTICS AND NATURAL SCIENCE

Marx and I were pretty well the only people to rescue conscious dialectics from German idealist philosophy and apply it in the materialist conception of nature and history. But a knowledge of mathematics and natural science is essential to a conception of nature which is dialectical and at the same time materialist. Marx was well versed in mathematics,* but we could only partially, intermittently and sporadically keep up with the natural sciences. For this reason, when I retired from business and transferred my home to London, thus enabling myself to give the necessary time to it, I went through as complete as possible a "molting," as Liebig calls it, in mathematics and the natural sciences, and spent the best part of eight years on it. I was right in the middle of this "molting" process when I had occasion to turn my attention to Herr Dühring's so-called natural philosophy. It is therefore only too natural that in dealing with this subject I was often unable to find the correct technical expression, and in general moved with a certain clumsiness in the field of theoretical natural science. On the other hand, my knowledge that I was still insecure in this field made me cautious, and I cannot be charged with real blunders in relation to the facts known at that time or with the incorrect presentations of recognized theories. In this connection there was only one unrecognized genius of a mathematician who complained in a letter to Marx that I had made a wanton attack upon the honor of $\sqrt{-1}$.

It goes without saying that my recapitulation of mathematics and the natural sciences was undertaken in order to convince myself in detail—of which in general I was not in doubt—that amid the welter of innumerable changes taking place in nature, the same dialectical laws of motion are in operation as those which in history govern the apparent fortuitousness of events; the same laws as those which similarly form the thread running through the history of the development of human thought and gradually rise to consciousness in the mind of man; the laws which Hegel

* See, for example, Dirk J. Struik, "Marx and Mathematics," *Science and Society*, vol. XII. No. 1, Winter, 1948.—*Ed.*

first developed in all-embracing but mystical form, and which we made it our aim to strip of this mystic form and to bring clearly before the mind in their complete simplicity and universality. It went without saying that the old natural philosophy—in spite of its real value and the many fruitful seeds it contains—was unable to satisfy us.*

As is more fully brought out in this book, natural philosophy, particularly in the Hegelian form, was lacking in that it did not recognize any development of nature in time, any "succession," but only "juxtaposition." This was on the one hand grounded in the Hegelian system itself, which ascribed historical evolution only to the "spirit," but on the other hand was also due to the whole state of the natural sciences at that period. In this Hegel fell far behind Kant, whose nebular theory had already indicated the origin of the solar system, and whose discovery of the retardation of the earth's rotation by the tides had already also proclaimed its extinction. And finally, to me there could be no question of building the laws of dialectics into nature, but of discovering them in it and evolving them from it. . . .

It may be, however, that the advance of theoretical natural science will make my work to a great extent or even altogether superfluous. For the revolution which is being forced on theoretical natural science by the mere need to set in order the purely empirical discoveries, great masses of which are now being piled up, is of such a kind that it must bring the dialectical character of natural events more and more to the consciousness even of those empiricists who are most opposed to it. The old rigid

* It is much easier, along with the unthinking mob *à la* Karl Vogt, to assail the old natural philosophy than to appreciate its historical significance. It contains a great deal of nonsense and phantasy, but not more than the contemporary unphilosophical theories of the empirical natural scientists and that there was also in it much that was sensible and rational is beginning to be perceived now that the theory of evolution is becoming widespread. Haeckel, for example, was fully justified in recognizing the merits of Treviranus and Oken. In his primordial slime and primordial vesicle Oken put forward as biological postulates what were in fact subsequently discovered as protoplasm and cell. As far as Hegel is concerned, in many respects he is head and shoulders above his empiricist contemporaries, who thought that they had explained all unexplained phenomena when they had endowed them with some power—the power of gravity, the power of buoyancy, the power of electrical contact, etc., or where this would not do, with some unknown substance—the substance of light, of warmth, of electricity, etc. . . . The natural philosophers stand in the same relation to consciously dialectical natural science as the utopians to modern communism.

antitheses, the sharp, impassable dividing lines are more and more disappearing. Since even the last "pure" gases have been liquefied, and since it has been proved that a body can be brought into a condition in which the liquid and the gaseous forms cannot be distinguished from each other, the physical states have lost the last relics of their former absolute character. With the thesis of the kinetic theory of gases, that in perfect gases at equal temperature the squares of the speeds with which the individual gas molecules move are in inverse ratio to their molecular weight, heat also takes its place directly among the forms of motion which can be immediately measured as such. Although ten years ago the great basic law of motion, then recently discovered, was as yet conceived merely as a law of the *conservation* of energy, as the mere expression of the indestructibility and uncreatability of motion, that is, merely in its quantitative aspect, this narrow, negative conception is being more and more supplanted by the positive idea of the *transformation* of energy, in which for the first time the qualitative content of the process comes into its own, and the last vestige of a creator external to the world is obliterated. That the quantity of motion (so-called energy) remains unaltered when it is transformed from kinetic energy (so-called mechanical force) into electricity, heat, potential energy, etc., and *vice versa,* no longer needs to be preached as something new; it serves as the already secured basis for the investigation, which is now of much greater significance, into the process of transformation itself, the great basic process, knowledge of which comprises all knowledge of nature. And since biology has been pursued in the light of the theory of evolution, in the domain of organic nature one fixed boundary line of classification after another has been swept away. The almost unclassifiable intermediate links are growing daily more numerous; closer investigation throws organisms out of one class into another, and distinguishing characteristics which had become almost articles of faith are losing their absolute validity; we now have mammals that lay eggs, and if the report is confirmed, also birds that walk on all-fours. Years ago Virchow was compelled, following on the discovery of the cell, to dissolve the unity of the individual animal being into a federation of cell-states—a theory which was progressive rather than scientific and dialectical—and now the conception of animal (therefore also human) individuality is becoming far more complex owing to the discovery of the ameba-like white blood corpuscles which creep about within the bodies of the higher animals. It is however precisely the polar antagonisms put forward as irreconcilable and insoluble, the forcibly fixed lines of demarcation and distinctions between classes, which have given modern theoretical natural science its restricted and metaphysical character. The recognition that these antagonisms and distinctions are in fact to be found in nature, but only with relative validity, and that on the other hand their imagined rigidity and absoluteness have been introduced into nature only by our minds—this recognition is the kernel of the dialectical conception of nature. It is possible to reach this standpoint because the accumulating facts of natural science compel us to do so; but we reach it more easily if we approach the dialectical character of these facts equipped with the consciousness of the laws of dialectical thought. In any case natural science has now advanced so far that it can no longer escape the dialectical synthesis. But it will make this process easier for itself if it does not lose sight of the fact that the results in which its experiences are summarized are concepts; but that the art of working with concepts is not inborn and also is not given with ordinary everyday consciousness, but requires real thought, and that this thought similarly has a long empirical history, not more and not less than empirical natural science. Only by learning to assimilate the results of the development of philosophy during the past two and a half thousand years will it be able to rid itself on the one hand of any isolated natural philosophy standing apart from it, outside it and above it, and on the other hand also of its own limited method of thought, which was its inheritance from English empiricism.

—ENGELS, *Anti-Dühring*, 1885 Preface, pp. 15–19.

[6]

DIALECTICS AND FORMAL LOGIC

A. THE LAW OF IDENTITY

The law of identity in the old metaphysical sense is the fundamental law of the old outlook: a = a. Each thing is equal to itself. Everything was permanent, the solar system, stars, organisms. This law has been refuted by natural science bit by bit in each separate case, but theoretically it still prevails and is still put forward by the supporters of the old in opposition to the new: A thing cannot simultaneously be itself and something else. And yet the fact that true, concrete identity includes difference, change, has recently been shown in detail by natural science. Abstract identity, like all metaphysical categories, suffices for *everyday* use, where small-scale conditions or brief periods of time are in question; the limits within which it is usable differ in almost every case and are determined by the nature of the object. For a planetary system, where for ordinary astronomical calculation the ellipse can be taken as the basic form without committing errors in practice, they are much wider than for an insect that completes its metamorphosis in a few weeks. (Give other examples, *e.g.*, alteration of species, which is reckoned in periods of many thousands of years.) For natural science in its comprehensive role, however, even in each single branch, abstract identity is totally insufficient, and although on the whole it has now been abolished in practice, theoretically it still dominates people's minds, and most natural scientists imagine that identity and difference are irreconcilable opposites, instead of one-sided poles the truth of which lies only in their reciprocal action, in the inclusion of difference *within* identity.

—ENGELS, *Dialectics of Nature* (1882), pp. 182*f*.

B. DEFINITION: ECLECTIC AND DIALECTIC

Comrade Bukharin talks about "logical" grounds. The whole of his argument shows that he—perhaps unconsciously—holds the point of view of formal, or scholastic, logic and not of dialectical, or Marxist, logic. In order to explain what I mean, I shall start with the very simple example which Comrade Bukharin himself has given. During the discussion on December 30 * he said:

> "Comrades, perhaps the controversy that is going on here is making the following impression upon many of you: Two men meet and ask each other, What is the glass that is standing on the rostrum? One says: 'It is a glass cylinder, and he who says it is not, let him be anathematized.' The other says: 'A glass is a drinking vessel, and he who says it is not, let him be anathematized!' "

As the reader will see, Bukharin wanted, with the aid of this example, to explain to me in a popular manner the harmfulness

* 1920, at a Moscow conference on the trade unions.—*Ed.*

of one-sidedness. I gratefully accept this explanation, and in order to prove my gratitude with deeds I will reciprocate by giving a popular explanation of what eclecticism is, as distinct from dialectics.

A glass is undoubtedly a glass cylinder and a drinking vessel. But a glass not only has these two properties, or qualities, or sides, but an infinite number of other properties, qualities, sides, interrelations and "mediations" with the rest of the world. A glass is a heavy object which may be used as a missile. A glass may serve as a paperweight, as a jar to keep a captive butterfly in, a glass may have value as an object with an artistic engraving or design, quite apart from the fact that it can be used as a drinking vessel, that it is made of glass, that its form is cylindrical, or not quite so, and so on and so forth.

To proceed. If I now need a glass as a drinking vessel it is not at all important for me to know whether its form is completely cylindrical and whether it is really made of glass; what is important is that its bottom shall not be cracked, that it should not cut my lips when I drink from it, etc. If I need a glass, not for drinking purposes, but for some purpose that any glass cylinder could serve, then even a glass with a cracked bottom, or even with no bottom at all, would do.

Formal logic, to which schools confine themselves (and to which, with modifications, the lower forms should confine themselves), takes formal definitions, and is guided exclusively by what is most customary, or most often noted. If in this two or more different definitions are combined quite casually (a glass cylinder and a drinking vessel), we get an eclectic definition which points to various sides of the object and nothing more.

Dialectical logic demands that we go further. In the first place, in order really to know an object we must embrace, study, all its sides, all connections and "mediations." We shall never achieve this completely, but the demand for all-sidedness is a safeguard against mistakes and rigidity. Secondly, dialectical logic demands that we take an object in its development, its "self-movement" (as Hegel sometimes puts it), in its changes. In relation to a glass this is not clear at once, but even a glass does not remain unchanged, particularly the purpose of the glass, its use, its *connections* with the surrounding world. Thirdly, the whole of human experience should enter the full "definition" of an object as a criterion of the truth and as a practical index of the object's connection with what man requires. Fourthly, dialectical logic teaches that "there is no abstract truth, truth is always concrete," as the late Plekhanov was fond of saying after Hegel. . . .

Of course, I have not exhausted the concept of dialectical logic, but I think what I have said is sufficient for the time being.

—LENIN, "Once Again on the Trade Unions" (1921), *Selected Works,* vol. IX, pp. 65*f*.

[7]

CONTRADICTIONS IN REALITY

[It is said] that contradiction = absurdity, and therefore cannot be found in the real world. People who in other respects show a fair degree of common sense may regard this statement as having the same self-evident validity as the statement that a straight line cannot be a curve and a curve cannot be straight. But, regardless of all protests made by common sense, the differential calculus assumes that under certain circumstances straight lines and curves are nevertheless identical, and with this assumption reaches results which common sense, insisting on the absurdity of straight lines being identical with curves, can never attain. And in view of the important role which the so-called dialectics of contradiction has played in philosophy from the time of the earliest Greeks up to the present, even a stronger opponent than Herr Dühring should have felt obliged to attack it with other arguments besides one assertion and a good many abusive epithets.

So long as we consider things as static and lifeless, each one by itself, alongside of and after each other, it is true that we do not run up against any contradictions in them. We find certain qualities which are partly common to, partly diverse from, and even contradictory to each other, but which in this case are distributed among different objects and therefore contain no contradiction. Within the limits of this sphere of thought we can get along on the basis of the usual metaphysical mode of thought. But the position is quite different as soon as we consider things in their motion, their change, their life, their reciprocal influence on one another. Then we immediately become involved in contradictions. Motion itself is a contradiction; even simple mechanical change of place can only come about through a body at one and the same moment of time being both in one place and in another place, being in one and the same place and also not in it. And the continuous assertion and simultaneous solution of this contradiction is precisely what motion is.

Here, therefore, we have a contradiction which "is objectively present in things and processes themselves and so to speak appears in corporeal form." And what has Herr Dühring to say about it? He asserts that up to the present there is absolutely "no bridge, in rational mechanics, from the strictly static to the dynamic." The reader can now at last see what is hiding behind this favorite phrase of Herr Dühring's—it is nothing but this: The mind which thinks metaphysically is absolutely unable to pass from the idea of rest to the idea of motion, because the contradiction pointed out above blocks its path. To it, motion is simply incomprehensible because it is a contradiction. And in asserting the incomprehensibility of motion, it thereby against its will admits the existence of this contradiction, and in so doing admits the objective presence of a contradiction in things and processes themselves, a contradiction which is moreover an actual force.

And if simple mechanical change of place contains a contradiction, this is even more true of the higher forms of motion of matter, and especially of organic life and its development. We saw above that life consists just precisely in this—that a living thing is at each moment itself and yet something else. Life is therefore also a contradiction which is present in things and processes themselves, and which constantly asserts and solves itself; and as soon as the contradiction ceases, life too comes to an end, and death steps in. We likewise saw that in the sphere of thought also we could not avoid contradictions, and that for example the contradiction between man's inherently unlimited faculty of knowledge and its actual realization in men who are limited by their external conditions and limited also in their intellectual faculties finds its solution in what is, for us at least, and from a practical standpoint, an endless succession of generations, in infinite progress. . . .

In its operations with variable magnitudes mathematics itself enters the field of dialectics, and it is significant that it was a dialectical philosopher, Descartes, who first introduced this advance in mathematics. The relation between the mathematics of variable and the mathematics of constant magnitudes is in general the same as the relation of dialectical to metaphysical thought. But this does not prevent the great mass of mathematicians from recognizing dialectics only in the sphere of mathematics, and a good many of them from continuing to work in the old, limited metaphysical way with methods that have been obtained dialectically.

—ENGELS, *Anti-Dühring* (1878), pp. 132–34.

[8]

CONTRADICTIONS: CHANCE AND NECESSITY

Another contradiction in which metaphysics is entangled is that of chance and necessity. What can be more sharply contradictory than these two thought determinations? How is it possible that both are identical, that the accidental is necessary, and the necessary is also accidental? Common sense, and with it the great majority of natural scientists, treats necessity and chance as determinations that exclude one another once for all. A thing, a circumstance, a process is either accidental or necessary, but not both. Hence both exist side by side in nature; nature contains all sorts of objects and processes, of which some are accidental, the others necessary, and it is only a matter of not confusing the two sorts with one another. Thus, for instance, one assumes the decisive specific characters to be necessary, other differences between individuals of the same species being termed accidental, and this holds good for crystals as it does for plants and animals. Then again the lower group becomes accidental in relation to the higher, so that it is declared to be a matter of chance how many different species are included in the genus *Felis* or *Agnus,* or how many genera and orders there are in a class, and how many individuals of each of these species exist, or how many different species of animals occur in a given region, or what in general the fauna and flora are like. And then it is declared that the necessary is the sole thing of scientific interest and that the accidental is a matter of indifference to science. That is to say: What can be brought under laws, hence what one *knows,* is interesting; what cannot be brought under laws, and therefore what one does not know, is a matter of indifference and can be ignored. Thereby all science comes to an end, for it has to investigate precisely that which we do *not* know. It means to say: What can be brought under general laws is regarded as necessary, and what cannot be so brought as accidental. Anyone can see that this is the same sort of science as that which proclaims natural what it can explain, and ascribes what it cannot explain to supernatural causes; whether I term the cause of the inexplicable, chance, or whether I term it God, is a matter of complete indifference as far as the thing itself is concerned. Both are only expressions which say: I do not know, and therefore do not belong to science. The latter ceases where the requisite connection is wanting.

In opposition to this view there is determinism, which has passed from French materialism into natural science, and which tries to dispose of chance by denying it altogether. According to this conception only simple, direct necessity prevails in nature. That a particular pea pod contains five peas and not four or six, that a particular dog's tail is five inches long and not a whit longer or shorter, that this year a particular clover flower was fertilized by a bee and another not, and indeed by precisely one particular bee and at a particular time, that a particular wind-blown dandelion seed has sprouted and another not, that last night I was bitten by a flea at four o'clock in the morning, and not at three or five o'clock, and on the right shoulder and not on the left calf—these are all facts which have been produced by an irrevocable concatenation of cause and effect, by an unshatterable necessity of such a nature indeed that the gaseous sphere, from which the solar system was derived, was already so constituted that these events had to happen thus and not otherwise. With this kind of necessity we likewise do not get away from the theological conception of nature. Whether with Augustine and Calvin we call it the eternal decree of God, or Kismet as the Turks do, or whether we call it necessity, is all pretty much the same for science. There is no question of tracing the chain of causation in any of these cases; so we are just as wise in one as in another, the so-called necessity remains an empty phrase, and with it—chance also remains what it was before. As long as we are not able to show on what the number of peas in the pod depends, it remains just a matter of chance, and the assertion that the case was foreseen already in the primordial constitution of the solar system does not get us a step further. Still more. A science which was to set about the task of following back the *casus* of this individual pea pod in its causal concatenation would be no longer science but pure trifling; for this same pea pod alone has in addition innumerable other individual, accidental-seeming qualities—shade of color, thickness, hardness of the pod, size of the peas, not to speak of the individual peculiarities revealed by the microscope. The one pea pod, therefore, would already provide more causal connections for following up than all the botanists in the world could solve.

Hence chance is not here explained by necessity, but rather necessity is degraded to the production of what is merely accidental. If the fact that a particular pea pod contains six peas, and not five or seven, is of the same order as the law of motion of the solar system, or the law of the transformation of energy, then as a matter of fact chance is not elevated into necessity, but rather necessity degraded into chance. Furthermore, however much the diversity of the organic and inorganic species and individuals existing side by side in a given area may be asserted to be based on irrefragable necessity, for the separate species and individuals it remains what it was before, a matter of chance. For the individual animal it is a matter of chance, where it happens to be born, what medium it finds for living, what enemies and how many of them threaten it. For the mother plant it is a matter of chance whither the wind scatters its seeds, and, for the daughter plant, where the seed finds soil for germination; and to assure us that here also everything rests on irrefragable necessity is a poor consolation. The jumbling together of natural objects in a given region, nay more, in the whole world, for all the primordial determination from eternity, remains what it was before—a matter of chance.

In contrast to both conceptions, Hegel came forward with the hitherto quite unheard-of propositions that the accidental has a cause because it is accidental, and just as much also has no cause because it is accidental; that the accidental is necessary, that necessity determines itself as chance, and, on the other hand, this chance is rather absolute necessity (*Logic*, II, pp. 173–86 : *Actuality*). Natural science has simply ignored these propositions as paradoxical trifling, as self-contradictory nonsense, and, as regards theory, has persisted on the one hand in the barrenness of thought of Wolffian metaphysics, according to which a thing is either accidental *or* necessary, but not both at once; or, on the other hand, in the hardly less thoughtless mechanical determinism which by a phrase denies chance in general only to recognize it in practice in each particular case.

While natural science continued to think in this way, what *did it do* in the person of Darwin?

Darwin, in his epoch-making work, set out from the widest existing basis of chance. Precisely the infinite, accidental differences between individuals within a single species, differences which become accentuated until they break through the character of the species, and whose immediate causes even can be demonstrated only in extremely few cases, compelled him to question the previous basis of all regularity in biology, *viz,* the concept of species in its previous metaphysical rigidity and unchangeability. Without the concept of species, however, all science was nothing. All its branches needed the concept of species as basis—human anatomy and comparative anatomy; embryology, zoology, palæontology, botany, etc.—what were they without the concept of species? All their results were not only put in question but directly suspended. Chance overthrows necessity, as conceived hitherto (the material of chance occurrences which had accumulated in the meantime smothered and shattered the old idea of necessity). The previous idea of necessity breaks down. To retain it means dictatorially to impose on nature as a law a human arbitrary determination that is in contradiction to itself and to reality, it means to deny thereby all inner necessity in living nature, it means generally to proclaim the chaotic kingdom of chance to be the sole law of living nature.

—ENGELS, *Dialectics of Nature* (1882), pp. 230–34.

[9]

THE LAWS OF DIALECTICS

It is . . . from the history of nature and human society that the laws of dialectics are abstracted. For they are nothing but the most general laws of these two aspects of historical development, as well as of thought itself. And indeed they can be reduced in the main to three:

The law of the transformation of quantity into quality and *vice versa;*

The law of the interpenetration of opposites;
The law of the negation of the negation.

All three are developed by Hegel in his idealist fashion as mere laws of *thought:* the first, in the first part of his *Logic,* in the *Doctrine of Being;* the second fills the whole of the second and by far the most important part of his *Logic,* the *Doctrine of Essence;* finally the third figures as the fundamental law for the construction of the whole system. The mistake lies in the fact that these laws are foisted on nature and history as laws of thought, and not deduced from them. This is the source of the whole forced and often outrageous treatment; the universe, willy-nilly, is made out to be arranged in accordance with a system of thought which itself is only the product of a definite stage of evolution of human thought. If we turn the thing round, then everything becomes simple, and the dialectical laws that look so extremely mysterious in idealist philosophy at once become simple and clear as noonday.

Moreover, anyone who is even only slightly acquainted with his Hegel will be aware that in hundreds of passages Hegel is capable of giving the most striking individual illustrations from nature and history of the dialectical laws.

We are not concerned here with writing a handbook of dialectics, but only with showing that the dialectical laws are really laws of development of nature, and therefore are valid also for theoretical natural science. Hence we cannot go into the interconnections of these laws with one another.

—Engels, *Dialectics of Nature* (1882), pp. 26*f.*

[*For a summary of the essential elements of dialectics, see Lenin: Appendix II, 32.*—Ed.]

[10]

THE INTERACTION OF QUANTITY AND QUALITY

A. In the Natural Sciences

The law of the transformation of quantity into quality and *vice versa.* For our purpose, we could express this by saying that in nature, in a manner exactly fixed for each individual case, qualitative changes can only occur by the quantitative addition or subtraction of matter or motion (so-called energy).

All qualitative differences in nature rest on differences of chemical composition or on different quantities or forms of motion (energy) or, as is almost always the case, on both. Hence it is impossible to alter the quality of a body without addition or subtraction of matter or motion, i.e., without quantitative alteration of the body concerned. In this form, therefore, Hegel's mysterious principle appears not only quite rational but even rather obvious.

It is surely hardly necessary to point out that the various allotropic and aggregational states of bodies, because they depend on various groupings of the molecules depend on greater or lesser quantities of motion communicated to the bodies.

But what is the position in regard to change of form of motion, or so-called energy? If we change heat into mechanical motion or *vice versa,* is not the quality altered while the quantity remains the same? Quite correct. But it is with change of form of motion as with Heine's vices; anyone can be virtuous by himself, for vices two are always necessary. Change of form of motion is always a process that takes place between at least two bodies, of which one loses a definite quantity of motion of one quality (*e.g., heat*), while the other gains a corresponding quantity of motion of another quality (mechanical motion, electricity, chemical decomposition). Here, therefore, quantity and quality mutually correspond to each other. So far it has not been found possible to convert motion from one form to another inside a single isolated body.

We are concerned here in the first place with non-living bodies; the same law holds for living bodies, but it operates under very complex conditions and at present quantitative measurement is still often impossible for us.

If we imagine any non-living body cut up into smaller and smaller portions, at first no qualitative change occurs. But this has a limit: If we succeed, as by evaporation, in obtaining the separate molecules in the free state, then it is true that we can usually divide these still further, yet only with a complete change of quality. The molecule is decomposed into its separate atoms, which have quite different properties from those of the molecule. In the case of molecules composed of various chemical elements, atoms or molecules of these elements themselves make their appearance in the place of the compound molecule; in the case of molecules of elements, the free atoms appear, which exert quite distinct qualitative effects: the free atoms of nascent oxygen are easily able to effect what the atoms of atmospheric oxygen, bound together in the molecule, can never achieve.

But the molecule is also qualitatively different from the mass of the body to which it belongs. It can carry out movements independently of this mass and while the latter remains apparently at rest, *e.g.*, heat oscillations; by means of a change of position and of connection with neighboring molecules it can change the body into an allotrope or a different state of aggregation.

Thus we see that the purely quantitative operation of division has a limit at which it becomes transformed into a qualitative difference: The mass consists solely of molecules, but it is something essentially different from the molecule, just as the latter is different from the atom. It is this difference that is the basis for the separation of mechanics, as the science of heavenly and terrestrial masses, from physics, as the mechanics of the molecule, and from chemistry, as the physics of the atom.

In mechanics, no qualities occur; at most, states, such as equilibrium, motion, potential energy, which all depend on measurable transference of motion and are themselves capable of quantitative expression. Hence, in so far as qualitative change takes place here, it is determined by a corresponding quantitative change.

In physics, bodies are treated as chemically unalterable or indifferent; we have to do with changes of their molecular states and with the change of form of the motion which in all cases, at least on one of the two sides, brings the molecule into play. Here every change is a transformation of quantity into quality, a consequence of the quantitative change of the quantity of motion of one form or another that is inherent in the body or communicated to it. "Thus the temperature of water is, in the first place, a point of no consequence in respect of its liquidity: still with the increase or diminution of the temperature of the liquid water, there comes a point where this state of cohesion suffers a qualitative change, and the water is converted into steam or ice." [Hegel, *The Logic of Hegel,* trans. W. Wallace, p. 202.] Similarly, a definite minimum current strength is required to cause the platinum wire of an electric incandescent lamp to glow; and every metal has its temperature of incandescence and fusion, every liquid its definite freezing and boiling point at a given pressure—in so far as our means allow us to produce the temperature required; finally also every gas has its critical point at which it can be liquefied by pressure and cooling. In short, the so-called physical constants are for the most part nothing but designations of the nodal points at which quantitative addition or subtraction of motion produces qualitative alteration in the state of the body concerned at which, therefore, quantity is transformed into quality.

The sphere, however, in which the law of nature discovered by Hegel celebrates its most important triumphs is that of chemistry. Chemistry can be termed the science of the qualitative changes of bodies as a result of changed quantitative composition. . . .

In biology, as in the history of human society, the same law holds good at every step, but we prefer to dwell here on examples from the exact sciences, since here the quantities are accurately measurable and traceable.

Probably the same gentlemen who up to now have decried the transformation of quantity into quality as mysticism and incomprehensible transcendentalism will now declare that it is indeed something quite self-evident, trivial, and commonplace, which they have long employed, and so they have been taught nothing new. But to have formulated for the first time in its universally valid form a general law of development of nature, society, and thought, will always remain an act of historic importance. And if these gentlemen have for years caused quantity and quality to be transformed into one another, without knowing what they did, then they will have to console themselves with Molière's Monsieur Jourdain who had spoken prose all his life without having the slightest inkling of it.

—ENGELS, *Dialectics of Nature* (1882), pp. 27–30; 33*f.*

B. IN THE SOCIAL SCIENCES

"What a comical effect is produced by the reference to the confused and foggy Hegelian conception that quantity changes into quality, and that therefore an advance, when it reaches a certain size, becomes capital by this mere quantitative increase!"

In this "purged" presentation by Herr Dühring it certainly looks curious enough. But let us see how it looks in the original, in Marx. On page 294,* Marx, on the basis of the previous

* *Capital,* Vol. I, Ch. XI.

examination of constant and variable capital and surplus value, draws the conclusion that "not every sum of money, or of value, is at pleasure transformable into capital. To effect this transformation, in fact, a certain minimum of money or of exchange-value must be presupposed in the hands of the individual possessor of money or commodities."

He then takes as an example the case of a laborer in any branch of industry, who works eight hours for himself—that is, in producing the value of his wages—and the following four hours for the capitalist, in producing surplus value, which immediately flows into the pocket of the capitalist. In this case a capitalist would have to dispose of a sum of value sufficient to enable him to provide two laborers with raw materials, instruments of labor, and wages, in order to appropriate enough surplus value every day to enable him to live on it even as well as one of his laborers. And as the aim of capitalist production is not mere subsistence but the increase of wealth, our man with his two laborers would still not be a capitalist. Now in order that he may live twice as well as an ordinary laborer, and besides turn half of the surplus value produced again into capital, he would have to be able to employ eight laborers, that is, he would have to dispose of four times the sum of value assumed above. And it is only after this, and in the course of still further explanations elucidating and establishing the fact that not every petty sum of value is enough to be transformable into capital, but that the minimum sum required varies with each period of development and each branch of industry, it is only then that Marx observes: "Here, as in natural science, is shown the correctness of the law discovered by Hegel (in his *Logic*), that merely quantitative differences beyond a certain point pass into qualitative changes."

And now let the reader admire the higher and nobler style, by virtue of which Herr Dühring attributes to Marx the opposite of what he really said. Marx says: The fact that a sum of value can only be transformed into capital when it has reached a certain size, varying according to the circumstances, but in each case with a definite minimum—this fact is a *proof of the correctness* of the Hegelian law. Herr Dühring makes him say: *Because,* according to the Hegelian law, quantity changes into quality, "*therefore*" "an advance, when it reaches a certain size, becomes capital." That is to say, the very opposite.

In connection with Herr Dühring's putting Darwin on trial we have already got to know his habit, "in the interests of complete truth" and because of his "duty to the public which is outside the exclusive professional circle," of citing passages incorrectly. It becomes more and more evident that this habit is an inner necessity of the philosophy of reality, and it is certainly a very "summary treatment." Not to mention the fact that Herr Dühring further makes Marx speak of any kind of "advance" whatsoever, whereas Marx only refers to an advance made in the form of raw materials, instruments of labor, and wages; and that in doing this Herr Dühring succeeds in making Marx speak pure nonsense. And then he has the cheek to describe as *comic* the nonsense which he has himself fabricated. Just as he built up a fantastic image of Darwin in order to try out his strength against it, so here he builds up a fantastic image of Marx. It is indeed a "historical treatment in the grand style"!

We have already seen earlier, in regard to world schematism, that in connection with this Hegelian nodal line of measure-relations—in which quantitative change suddenly produces, at certain points, a qualitative difference—Herr Dühring had a little accident; in a weak moment he himself recognized and made use of this principle. We gave there one of the best-known examples —that of the change of the state of water, which under normal atmospheric pressure changes at 0° C. from the liquid into the solid state, and at 100° C. from the liquid into the gaseous state, so that at both these turning points the merely quantitative change of temperature brings about a qualitative change in the condition of the water.

In proof of this law we might have cited hundreds of other similar facts from nature as well as from human society. Thus, for example, the whole of Part IV of Marx's *Capital—Production of Relative Surplus Value—Co-operation, Division of Labor and Manufacture, Machinery and Large Scale Industry*—deals with innumerable cases in which quantitative change alters the quality, and also qualitative change alters the quantity, of the things under consideration; in which therefore, to use the expression which is so hated by Herr Dühring, quantity is transformed into quality and *vice versa.* As for example the fact that the co-operation of a number of people, the fusion of many forces into one single force, to use Marx's phrase, creates a "new power," which is essentially different from the sum of its individual powers. . . .

In conclusion we shall call one more witness for the transformation of quantity into quality, namely—Napoleon. He makes the following reference to the fights between the French cavalry, who were bad riders but disciplined, and the Mamelukes, who were undoubtedly the best horsemen of their time for single combat, but lacked discipline: "Two Mamelukes were undoubtedly more than a match for three Frenchmen: 100 Mamelukes were equal to 100 Frenchmen; 300 Frenchmen could generally beat 300 Mamelukes, and 1,000 Frenchmen invariably defeated 1,500 Mamelukes." Just as with Marx a definite, though varying, minimum sum of exchange value was necessary to make possible its transformation into capital, so with Napoleon a detachment of cavalry had to be of a definite minimum number in order to make it possible for the force of discipline, embodied in closed order and planned application, to manifest itself and rise superior even to greater numbers of irregular cavalry, in spite of the latter being better mounted, more skillful horsemen and fighters, and at least as brave as the former. But what does this prove as against Herr Dühring? Was not Napoleon miserably vanquished in his conflict with Europe? Did he not suffer defeat after defeat? And why? Simply as a result of his having introduced confused nebulous Hegelian conceptions into his cavalry tactics!

—ENGELS, *Anti-Dühring* (1878), pp. 136–39, 141.

C. In the Labor Process

Just as the offensive power of a squadron of cavalry, or the defensive power of a regiment of infantry, is essentially different from the sum of the offensive or defensive powers of the individual cavalry or infantry soldiers taken separately, so the sum total of the mechanical forces exerted by isolated workmen differs from the social force that is developed, when many hands take part simultaneously in one and the same undivided operation, such as raising a heavy weight, turning a winch, or removing an obstacle. In such cases the effect of the combined labor could either not be produced at all by isolated individual labor, or it could only be produced by a great expenditure of time, or on a very dwarfed scale. Not only have we here an increase in the productive power of the individual, by means of co-operation, but the creation of a new power, namely, the collective power of masses.

Apart from the new power that arises from the fusion of many forces into one single force, mere social contact begets in most industries an emulation and a stimulation of the animal spirits that heighten the efficiency of each individual workman. Hence it is that a dozen persons working together will, in their collective working day of 144 hours, produce far more than 12 isolated men each working 12 hours, or than one man who works 12 days in succession. The reason of this is that a man is, if not as Aristotle contends, a political, at all events a social animal.

—MARX, *Capital* (1867), vol. I, pp. 357*f*.

[11]

THE UNITY AND CONFLICT OF OPPOSITES

The splitting of a single whole and the cognition of its contradictory parts . . . is the *essence* (one of the "essentials," one of the principal, if not the principal, characteristics or features) of dialectics. That is precisely how Hegel, too, puts the matter (Aristotle in his *Metaphysics* continually *grapples* with it and *combats* Heraclitus and Heraclitean ideas).

The correctness of this aspect of the content of dialectics must be tested by the history of science. This aspect of dialectics usually receives inadequate attention (*e.g.*, Plekhanov); the identity of opposites is taken as the sum-total of *examples* ("for example, a seed," "for example, primitive communism." The same is true of Engels. But with him it is "in the interests of popularization . . .") and not as a *law of cognition* (*and* as a law of the objective world):

In mathematics: + and −. Differential and integral.

In mechanics: action and reaction.

In physics: positive and negative electricity.

In chemistry: the combination and dissociation of atoms.

In social science: the class struggle.

The identity of opposites (it would be more correct, perhaps, to say their "unity"—although the difference between the terms identity and unity is not particularly important here. In a certain sense both are correct) is the recognition (discovery) of the contradictory, *mutually exclusive,* opposite tendencies in *all* phenomena and processes of nature (*including* mind and society). The condition for the knowledge of all processes of the world in their "*self-movement,*" in their spontaneous development, in their real life, is the knowledge of them as a unity of opposites. Development is the "struggle" of opposites. The two basic (or two possible? or two historically observable?) conceptions of development (evolution) are: Development as decrease and increase, as repetition, *and* development as a unity of opposites (the division of a unity into mutually exclusive opposites and their reciprocal relation).

In the first conception of motion, *self*-movement, its *driving* force, its source, its motive, remains in the shade (or this source is made *external*—God, subject, etc.). In the second conception the chief attention is directed precisely to the knowledge of the *source* of "*self*"-movement.

The first conception is lifeless, pale and dry. The second is living. The second *alone* furnishes the key to the "self-movement" of everything existing; it alone furnishes the key to the "leaps," to the "break in continuity," to the "transformation into the opposite," to the destruction of the old and the emergence of the new.

The unity (coincidence, identity, equal action) of opposites is conditional, temporary, transitory, relative. The struggle of mutually exclusive opposites is absolute, just as development and motion are absolute.

N.B. The distinction between subjectivism (skepticism, sophistry, etc.) and dialectics, incidentally, is that in (objective) dialectics the difference between the relative and the absolute is itself relative. For objective dialectics there *is* an absolute even *within* the relative. For subjectivism and sophistry the relative is only relative and excludes the absolute.

In his *Capital,* Marx first analyzes the simplest, most ordinary and fundamental, most common and everyday *relation* of bourgeois (commodity) society, a relation that is encountered billions of times, *viz.,* the exchange of commodities. In this very simple phenomenon (in this "cell" of bourgeois society) analysis reveals *all* the contradictions (or the germs of *all* the contradictions) of modern society. The subsequent exposition shows us the development (*both* growth *and* movement) of these contradictions and of this society in the *summation* of its individual parts, from its beginning to its end.

Such must also be the method of exposition (or study) of dialectics in general (for with Marx the dialectics of bourgeois society is only a particular case of dialectics). To begin with what is the simplest, most common, etc., with *any proposition:* The leaves of a tree are green; John is a man; Fido is a dog, etc. Here already we have *dialectics* (as Hegel's genius recognized): the *individual is* the *universal* (*cf.* Aristotle's *Metaphysics, Bk. B, ch. 4* "For evidently . . . we could not suppose that there is a house [a house in general] besides the particular houses.") Consequently, the opposites (the individual is opposed to the universal) are identical: the individual exists only in the connection that leads to the universal. The universal exists only in the individual and through the individual. Every individual is (in one way or another) a universal. Every universal is (a fragment, or an aspect, or the essence of) an individual. Every universal only approximately comprises all the individual objects. Every individual enters incompletely into the universal, etc., etc.

Every individual is connected by thousands of transitions with other *kinds* of individuals (things, phenomena, processes), etc. *Here already* we have the elements, the germs, the concepts of *necessity,* of objective connection in nature, etc. Here already we have the contingent and the necessary, the phenomenon and the essence; for when we say: John is a man, Fido is a dog, *this* is a leaf of a tree, etc., we *disregard* a number of attributes as *contingent;* we separate the essence from the appearance, and counterpose the one to the other.

Thus in *any* proposition we can (and must) disclose as in a "nucleus" ("cell") the germs of *all* the elements of dialectics, and thereby show that dialectics is a property of all human knowledge in general. And natural science shows us (and here again it must be demonstrated in *any* simple instance) objective nature with the same qualities, the transformation of the individual into the universal, of the contingent into the necessary, transitions, modulations, and the reciprocal connections of opposites. Dialectics *is* the theory of knowledge of (Hegel and) Marxism. This is the "aspect" of the matter (it is not "an aspect" but the *essence* of the matter) to which Plekhanov, not to speak of other Marxists, paid no attention.

—LENIN, "On the Question of Dialectics" (1915), *Philosophical Notebooks,* pp. 359–63.

[12]

THE NEGATION OF THE NEGATION

What role does the negation of the negation play in Marx? On page 786 * and the following pages he sets out the conclusions which he draws from the preceding fifty pages of economic and historical investigation into the so-called primitive accumulation of capital. Before the capitalist era, at least in England, petty industry existed on the basis of the private property of the laborer in his means of production. The so-called primitive accumulation of capital consisted in this case in the expropriation of these immediate producers, that is, in the dissolution of private property based on the labor of its owner. This was possible because the petty industry referred to above is compatible only with a system of production, and a society, moving within narrow and primitive bounds, and at a certain stage of its development it brings forth the material agencies for its own annihilation. This annihilation, the transformation of the individual and scattered means of production into socially concentrated ones, forms the pre-history of capital. As soon as the laborers are turned into proletarians, their means of labor into capital, as soon as the capitalist mode of production stands on its own feet, the further socialization of labor and further transformation of the land and other means of production, and therefore the further expropriation of private proprietors, takes a new form.

"That which is now to be expropriated is no longer the laborer working for himself, but the capitalist exploiting many laborers. This expropriation is accomplished by the action of the immanent laws of capitalistic production itself, by the centralization of capital. One capitalist always kills many. Hand in hand with this centralization, or this expropriation of many capitalists by few, develop, on an ever extending scale, the co-operative form of the labor process, the conscious technical application of science, the methodical cultivation of the soil, the transformation of the instruments of labor into instruments of labor only usable in common, the economizing of all means of production by their use as the means of production of combined, socialized labor, . . . Along with the constantly diminishing number of the magnates

* *Capital,* Vol. I, Ch. XXXII.

of capital, who usurp and monopolize all advantages of this process of transformation, grows the mass of misery, oppression, slavery, degradation, exploitation; but with this too grows the revolt of the working class, a class always increasing in numbers, and disciplined, united, organized by the very mechanism of the process of capitalist production itself. The monopoly of capital becomes a fetter upon the mode of production, which has sprung up and flourished along with, and under it. Centralization of the means of production and socialization of labor at last reach a point where they become incompatible with their capitalist integument. This integument is burst asunder. The knell of capitalist private property sounds. The expropriators are expropriated." *

And now I ask the reader: Where are the dialectical frills and mazes and intellectual arabesques; where the mixed and misconceived ideas as a result of which everything is all one in the end; where the dialectical miracles for his faithful followers; where the mysterious dialectical rubbish and the contortions based on the Hegelian Logos doctrine, without which Marx, according to Herr Dühring, is quite unable to accomplish his development? Marx merely shows from history, and in this passage states in a summarized form, that just as the former petty industry necessarily, through its own development, created the conditions of its annihilation, *i.e.*, of the expropriation of the small proprietors, so now the capitalist mode of production has likewise itself created the material conditions which will annihilate it. The process is a historical one, and if it is at the same time a dialectical process, this is not Marx's fault, however annoying it may be for Herr Dühring.

It is only at this point, after Marx has completed his proof on the basis of historical and economic facts, that he proceeds: "The capitalist mode of appropriation, the result of the capitalist mode of production, produces capitalist private property. This is the first negation of individual private property, as founded on the labor of the proprietor. But capitalist production begets, with the inexorability of a law of Nature, its own negation. It is the negation of the negation"—and so on (as quoted above).

In characterizing the process as the negation of the negation, therefore, Marx does not dream of attempting to prove by this that the process was historically necessary. On the contrary; after

* *Ibid.*, pp. 788 *f.*

he has proved from history that in fact the process has partially already occurred, and partially must occur in the future, he then also characterizes it as a process which develops in accordance with a definite dialectical law. That is all. It is therefore once again a pure distortion of the facts by Herr Dühring, when he declares that the negation of the negation has to serve as the midwife to deliver the future from the womb of the past, or that Marx wants anyone to allow himself to be convinced of the necessity of the common ownership of land and capital (which is itself a Dühringian corporeal contradiction) on the basis of the negation of the negation. . . .

It is the same, too, in history. All civilized peoples begin with the common ownership of the land. With all peoples who have passed a certain primitive stage, in the course of the development of agriculture this common ownership becomes a fetter on production. It is abolished, negated, and after a long or shorter series of intermediate stages is transformed into private property. But at a higher stage of agricultural development, brought about by private property in land itself, private property in turn becomes a fetter on production as is the case today, both with small and large landownership. The demand that it also should be negated, that it should once again be transformed into common property, necessarily arises. But this demand does not mean the restoration of the old original common ownership, but the institution of a far higher and more developed form of possession in common which, far from being a hindrance to production, on the contrary for the first time frees production from all fetters and gives it the possibility of making full use of modern chemical discoveries and mechanical inventions. . . .

What therefore is the negation of the negation? An extremely general—and for this reason extremely comprehensive and important—law of development of nature, history and thought; a law which, as we have seen, holds good in the animal and plant kingdoms, in geology, in mathematics, in history and in philosophy—a law which even Herr Dühring, in spite of all his struggles and resistance, has unwittingly and in his own way to follow. It is obvious that in describing any evolutionary process as the negation of the negation I do not say anything concerning the *particular* process of development, for example, of the grain of barley from germination to the death of the fruit-bearing plant. For, as the integral calculus also is a negation of the negation, if

I said anything of the sort I should only be making the nonsensical statement that the life process of a barley plant was the integral calculus or for that matter that it was socialism. That, however, is what the metaphysicians are constantly trying to impute to dialectics. When I say that all these processes are the negation of the negation, I bring them all together under this one law of motion, and for this very reason I leave out of account the peculiarities of each separate individual process. Dialectics is nothing more than the science of the general laws of motion and development of nature, human society, and thought.

But someone may object: The negation that has taken place in this case is not a real negation; I negate a grain of barley also when I grind it down, an insect when I crush it underfoot, or the positive magnitude *a* when I cancel it, and so on. Or I negate the sentence, the rose is a rose, when I say: The rose is not a rose; and what do I get if I then negate the negation and say, but after all the rose is a rose?—These objections are in fact the chief arguments put forward by the metaphysicians against dialectics, and they are eminently worthy of the narrow-mindedness of this mode of thought. Negation in dialectics does not mean simply saying no, or declaring that something does not exist, or destroying it in any way one likes. Long ago Spinoza said: *Omnis determinatio est negatio*—every limitation or determination is at the same time a negation. And further; the kind of negation is here determined in the first place by the general, and secondly by the particular, nature of the process. I must not only negate, but also in turn sublate the negation. I must therefore so construct the first negation that the second remains or becomes possible. In what way? This depends on the particular nature of each individual case. If I grind a grain of barley, or crush an insect, it is true I have carried out the first part of the action, but I have made the second part impossible. Each class of things therefore has its appropriate form of being negated in such a way that it gives rise to a development, and it is just the same with each class of conceptions and ideas. The infinitesimal calculus involves a form of negation which is different from that used in the formation of positive powers from negative roots. This has to be learnt, like everything else. The mere knowledge that the barley plant and the infinitesimal calculus are both governed by the negation of the negation does not enable me either to grow barley successfully or to use the calculus; just as little as the mere knowledge of the laws of the determination of sound by the thickness of strings enables me to play the violin.

But it is clear that in a negation of the negation which consists of the childish pastime of alternately writing and cancelling *a,* or of alternately declaring that a rose is a rose and that it is not a rose, nothing comes out of it but the stupidity of the person who adopts such a tedious procedure. And yet the metaphysicians try to tell us that this is the right way to carry out the negation of the negation, if we ever want to do such a thing.

Once again, therefore, it is no one but Herr Dühring who is mystifying us when he asserts that the negation of the negation is a stupid analogy invented by Hegel, borrowed from the sphere of religion and based on the story of the fall of man and redemption. Men thought dialectically long before they knew what dialectics was, just as they spoke prose long before the term prose existed. The law of the negation of the negation, which is unconsciously operative in nature and history, and until it has been recognized, also in our heads, was only clearly formulated for the first time by Hegel. And if Herr Dühring wants to use it himself on the quiet and it is only the name which he cannot stand, let him find a better name. But if his aim is to expel the process itself from thought, we must ask him to be so good as first to banish it from nature and history and to invent a mathematical system in which $-a \times -a$ is not $+a^2$ and in which the differential and integral calculus are prohibited under severe penalties.

ENGELS, *Anti-Dühring* (1878), pp. 145–47, 151, 154–56.

[*Lenin makes a distinction between genuine and eclectic negation. See Appendix II, 33.*—Ed.]

PART FOUR

THEORY OF KNOWLEDGE AND THE PHILOSOPHY OF SCIENCE

The question whether objective truth can be attributed to human thinking is not a question of theory but is a practical question. In practice man must prove the truth . . . of his thinking.

—MARX, *Theses on Feuerbach,* II (1845).

All science would be superfluous, if the appearance, the form, and the nature of things were wholly identical.

—MARX, *Capital,* vol. III (1894), p. 951.

It is . . . paradox that the earth moves round the sun, and that water consists of two highly inflammable gases. Scientific truth is always paradox, if judged by everyday experience, which catches only the delusive appearance of things.

—MARX, *Value, Price and Profit* (1865), p. 37.

Introduction

WHILE IT is known and accepted that Marxism has a philosophy, little notice has been paid to the fact that it has a distinctive theory of knowledge. Engels suggested frequently that philosophy had to be a methodology—that is, logic and dialectics —*and* a theory of science. Actually, the heart of the philosophy of dialectical materialism is simply the insistence that the sciences in their historical development provide the only means there are for knowing and controlling the world we live in. It is the affirmation that only empirically derived data, organized through man's power to form concepts, and tested in practice, can acquaint us with the nature of things.

Many English-speaking students of Marxism are troubled by statements that appear to be anti-empirical. Marx and Engels criticized, for example, Newton and Darwin, not because of their conclusions, but in terms of their method. This has to be understood against the European background which for two centuries was torn between the proponents of "rationalism" and those of "empiricism," with rationalism dominating the continent and empiricism the British Isles. Some of the materials in this section clearly show that Marx and Engels were trying to resolve this difficulty by finding a "dialectical" solution. They could be neither empiricists nor rationalists. The heart of their position lies, as is shown in the quotations that head this section, in the belief that we need and develop science because things are not what they appear to be, and that in turn we can only learn what things really are by the most scrupulous investigation of their appearances and by testing our theories in practical situations.

Marxism is often regarded as being rigid, inflexible, dogmatic, absolutist. It may have been treated as such in different places and times, but the fact is that Marx, Engels, and Lenin had a theory that was viable and flexible, running counter to all forms of dogmatism. Knowledge or science is to them a never-ending process that achieves some truth concerning the nature of things, gets closer and closer to "absolute truth"—without ever reaching it—and thus moves towards an ever closer approximation to reality. It must be noted that Lenin, in the passages on truth given here, makes it clear that he is not defining truth in the formal logical sense which limits it to a property of judgments, such as "this is water," or "water is H_2O." Rather, he is defining truth as the objective content of such judgments, the objective reality by virtue of which alone such judgments can be true. The central issue of the Lenin excerpts presented here is whether "truth" is *discovered* or *invented* by men.

The final selections of this part, after discussions of what is now known as the "sociology of science" and of the indispensability of a philosophy of some kind for all scientists, deal with the function of concepts and abstractions. Enormous work on these questions has gone on in professional philosophy in the years since these passages were written. The editors believe that these selections show how Marx, Engels, and Lenin, on the basis of their rejection of both rationalism and empiricism as one-sided, and in the light of the highest developments of the sciences of their day, raised and answered these questions with extraordinary philosophical acumen. Only a dialectical synthesis, they believed, could resolve such age-old problems as the relation of the empirical and the rational, the concrete and the abstract, the fact and the concept, the relative and the absolute, and the relatively fixed amidst the flux. For them, the sciences could develop only to the extent that such a synthesis was achieved.

[1]

THREE PROPOSITIONS OF THE MARXIST THEORY OF KNOWLEDGE

(1) Things exist independently of our consciousness, independently of our perceptions, outside of us, for it is beyond doubt that alizarin existed in coal tar yesterday and it is equally beyond doubt that yesterday we knew nothing of the existence of this alizarin and received no sensations from it.

(2) There is definitely no difference in principle between the phenomenon and the thing-in-itself, and there can be no such difference. The only difference is between what is known and what is not yet known. And philosophical inventions of specific boundaries between the one and the other, inventions to the effect that the thing-in-itself is "beyond" phenomena (Kant), or that we can or must fence ourselves off by some philosophical partition from the problem of a world which in one part or another is still unknown but which exists outside us (Hume)—all this is the sheerest nonsense, evasion, invention.

(3) In the theory of knowledge, as in every other branch of science, we must think dialectically, that is, we must not regard our knowledge as ready-made and unalterable, but must determine how *knowledge* emerges from *ignorance,* how incomplete, inexact knowledge becomes more complete and more exact.

Once we accept the point of view that human knowledge develops from ignorance, we shall find millions of examples of it just as simple as the discovery of alizarin in coal tar, millions of observations not only in the history of science and technology but in the everyday life of each and every one of us that illustrate the transformation of "things-in-themselves" into "things-for-us," the appearance of "phenomena" when our sense-organs experience a jolt from external objects, the disappearance of "phenomena" when some obstacle prevents the action upon our sense-organs of an object which we know to exist. The sole and unavoidable deduction to be made from this—a deduction which all of us make in everyday practice and which materialism deliberately places at the foundation of its epistemology—is that outside us, and independently of us, there exist objects, things, and bodies and that our perceptions are images of the external world.

—LENIN, *Materialism and Empirio-Criticism* (1908), pp. 99*f*.

[2]

HOW DO WE KNOW OBJECTIVE REALITY?

"In what relation do our thoughts about the world surrounding us stand to this world itself?

"Is our thinking capable of the cognition of the real world?

"Are we able in our ideas and notions of the real world to produce a correct reflection of reality?" (Engels, see Part Two [1]).

Our agnostic* admits that all our knowledge is based upon the information imparted to us by our senses. But, he adds, how do we know that our senses give us correct representations of the objects we perceive through them? And he proceeds to inform us that, whenever he speaks of objects or their qualities, he does in reality not mean these objects and qualities, of which he cannot know anything for certain, but merely the impressions which they have produced on his senses. Now, this line of reasoning seems undoubtedly hard to beat by mere argumentation. But before there was argumentation, there was action. *Im Anfang war die Tat.* [In the beginning was the deed—GOETHE] And

* In general, the position attributed here to the agnostic corresponds with that of 20th century pragmatists and logical positivists.—*Ed.*

human action had solved the difficulty long before human ingenuity invented it. The proof of the pudding is in the eating. From the moment we turn to our own use these objects, according to the qualities we perceive in them, we put to an infallible test the correctness or otherwise of our sense perceptions. If these perceptions have been wrong, then our estimate of the use to which an object can be turned must also be wrong, and our attempt must fail. But if we succeed in accomplishing our aim, if we find that the object does agree with our idea of it, and does answer the purpose we intended it for, then that is positive proof that our perceptions of it and of its qualities, *so far,* agree with reality outside ourselves. And whenever we find ourselves face to face with a failure, then we generally are not long in making out the cause that made us fail; we find that the perception upon which we acted was either incomplete and superficial, or combined with the result of other perceptions in a way not warranted by them—what we call defective reasoning. So long as we take care to train and to use our senses properly, and to keep our action within the limits prescribed by perceptions properly made and properly used, so long we shall find that the result of our action proves the conformity of our perceptions with the objective nature of the things perceived. Not in one single instance, so far, have we been led to the conclusion that our sense perceptions, scientifically controlled, induce in our minds ideas respecting the outer world that are, by their very nature, at variance with reality, or that there is an inherent incompatibility between the outer world and our sense perceptions of it.

But then come the Neo-Kantian agnostics and say: We may correctly perceive the qualities of a thing, but we cannot by any sensible or mental process grasp the thing-in-itself. This "thing-in-itself" is beyond our ken. To this Hegel, long since, has replied: If you know all the qualities of a thing, you know the thing itself; nothing remains but the fact that the said thing exists without us; and when your senses have taught you that fact, you have grasped the last remnant of the thing-in-itself, Kant's celebrated unknowable *Ding an sich.* To which it may be added, that in Kant's time our knowledge of natural objects was indeed so fragmentary that he might well suspect, behind the little we knew about each of them, a mysterious "thing-in-itself." But one after another these ungraspable things have been grasped, analyzed, and, what is more, *reproduced* by the giant progress of science; and what we can produce, we certainly cannot consider as unknowable. To the chemistry of the first half of this century organic substances were such mysterious objects; now we learn to build them up one after another from their chemical elements without the aid of organic processes. Modern chemists declare that as soon as the chemical constitution of no matter what body is known, it can be built up from its elements. We are still far from knowing the constitution of the highest organic substances, albuminous bodies; but there is no reason why we should not, if only after centuries, arrive at that knowledge and, armed with it, produce artificial albumen. But if we arrive at that, we shall at the same time have produced organic life, for life, from its lowest to its highest forms, is but the normal mode of existence of albuminous bodies.

As soon, however, as our agnostic has made these formal mental reservations, he talks and acts as the rank materialist he at bottom is. He may say that, as far as *we* know, matter and motion, or as it is now called, energy, can neither be created nor destroyed, but that we have no proof of their not having been created at some time or other. But if you try to use this admission against him in any particular case, he will quickly put you out of court. If he admits the possibility of spiritualism *in abstracto,* he will have none of it *in concreto.* As far as we know and can know, he will tell you there is no Creator and no Ruler of the universe; as far as we are concerned, matter and energy can neither be created nor annihilated; for us, mind is a mode of energy, a function of the brain; all we know is that the material world is governed by immutable laws, and so forth. Thus, as far as he is a scientific man, as far as he *knows* anything, he is a materialist; outside his science, in spheres about which he knows nothing, he translates his ignorance into Greek and calls it agnosticism.

—ENGELS, *Socialism, Utopian and Scientific,* intro. to Eng. ed. (1892), pp. 13–15.

[3]

THE "THING-IN-ITSELF"

A. No "Thing-in-Itself" for Science

The number and succession of hypotheses supplanting one another—given the lack of logical and dialectical education among scientists—easily gives rise to the idea that we cannot know the *essence* of things. This is not peculiar to natural science since all human knowledge develops in a curve which twists many times; and in the historical sciences also, including philosophy, theories displace one another, from which, however, nobody concludes that formal logic, for instance, is nonsense. The last form of this outlook is the "thing-in-itself." In the first place, this assertion that we cannot know the thing-in-itself passes out of science into fantasy. In the second place, it does not add a word to our scientific knowledge, for if we cannot occupy ourselves with things, they do not exist for us. And, thirdly, it is a mere phrase and is never applied. Taken in the abstract it sounds quite sensible. But suppose one applies it. What would one think of a zoologist who said: A dog *seems* to have four legs, but we do not know whether in reality it has four million legs or none at all? Or of a mathematician who first of all defines a triangle as having three sides, and then declares that he does not know whether it might not have 25? That 2 × 2 *seems* to be 4? But scientists take care not to apply the phrase "the thing-in-itself" in natural science, they permit themselves this only in passing into philosophy. This is the best proof how little seriously they take it and of what little value it is itself. If they did take it seriously, what would be the good of investigating anything? Taken historically the thing would have a certain meaning; we can only know under the conditions of our epoch and *as far as these reach.*

—ENGELS, *Dialectics of Nature* (1882), pp. 159*f.*

[*For Hegel's strictures on the "thing-in-itself" and Lenin's comments, see Appendix II, 5.*—Ed.]

B. THE KNOWABILITY OF THE "THING-IN-ITSELF"

The development of consciousness in each human individual and the development of the collective knowledge of humanity at large presents us at every step with examples of the transformation of the unknown "thing-in-itself" into the known "thing-for-us," of the transformation of blind, unknown necessity, "necessity-in-itself," into the known "necessity-for-us." Epistemologically, there is no difference whatever between these two transformations, for the basic point of view in both cases is the same, *viz.*, materialistic, the recognition of the objective reality of the external world and of the laws of external nature, and of the fact that this world and these laws are fully knowable to man but can never be known to him *with finality*. We do not know the necessity of nature in the phenomena of the weather, and to that extent we are inevitably—slaves of the weather. But while we *do not know this necessity, we do know that it exists.* Whence this knowledge? From the very source whence comes the knowledge that things exist outside our mind and independently of it, namely, from the development of our knowledge, which provides millions of examples to every individual of knowledge replacing ignorance when an object acts upon our sense organs, and conversely of ignorance replacing knowledge when the possibility of such action is eliminated.

—LENIN, *Materialism and Empirio-Criticism* (1908), pp. 191*f.*

[4]

WHAT IS OBJECTIVE TRUTH?

Bogdanov declares: "As I understand it, Marxism contains a denial of the unconditional objectivity of any truth whatsoever, the denial of all eternal truths." [He] agrees to recognize "objective truth only within the limits of a given epoch."

Two questions are obviously confused here:

(1) Is there such a thing as objective truth, that is, can human ideas have a content that does not depend on a subject, that does not depend either on a human being or on humanity?

(2) If so, can human ideas, which give expression to objective truth, express it all at one time, as a whole, unconditionally, absolutely, or only approximately, relatively? This second question is a question of the relation of absolute to relative truth.

" . . . The criterion of objective truth," writes Bogdanov a little further on, "in Beltov's* sense, does not exist: truth is an ideological form, an organizing form of human experience. . . ."

Neither "Beltov's sense"—for it is a question of one of the fundamental philosophical problems and not of Beltov—nor the *criterion* of truth—which must be treated separately, without confounding it with the question of whether objective truth *exists*—

* Beltov was one of the pen-names of George V. Plekhanov.—*Ed.*

has anything to do with the case here. Bogdanov's negative answer to the latter question is clear: If truth is *only* an ideological form, then there can be no truth independent of the subject, of humanity, for neither Bogdanov nor we know any other ideology but human ideology. And Bogdanov's negative answer emerges still more clearly from the second half of his statement: If truth is a form of human experience, then there can be no truth independent of humanity; there can be no objective truth.

Bogdanov's denial of objective truth is agnosticism and subjectivism. . . . Natural science leaves no room for doubt that its assertion that the earth existed prior to man is a truth. This is entirely compatible with the materialist theory of knowledge; the existence of the thing reflected independent of the reflector (the independence of the external world from the mind) is a fundamental tenet of materialism. The assertion made by science that the earth existed prior to man is an objective truth. This proposition of natural science is incompatible with the philosophy of the Machians and with their doctrine of truth: If truth is an organizing form of human experience, then the assertion of the earth's existence *outside* human experience cannot be true.

But that is not all. If truth is only an organizing form of human experience, then the teaching, say, of Catholicism is also true. For there is not the slightest doubt that Catholicism is an "organizing form of human experience." Bogdanov himself senses the crying falsity of his theory and it is extremely interesting to watch how he attempts to extricate himself from the swamp into which he has fallen.

"The basis of objectivity [we read in Book I of *Empirio-Monism*] must lie in the sphere of *collective* experience. . . . The objective character of the physical world consists in the fact that it exists not for me personally, but for everybody [that is not true! It exists independently of everybody!], and has a definite meaning for everybody, the same, I am convinced, as for me. The objectivity of the physical series is its *universal significance*" (Bogdanov's italics). . . . "In general, the physical world is socially co-ordinated, socially harmonized, in a word, *socially organized experience*" (Bogdanov's italics).

We shall not repeat that this is a fundamentally untrue, idealist definition, that the physical world exists independently of humanity and of human experience, that the physical world existed at a time when no "sociality" and no "organization" of human experience was possible, and so forth. We shall now stop to expose the Machian philosophy from another aspect. Objectivity is so defined that religious doctrines, which undoubtedly possess a "universal significance," acceptance, and so forth, come under the definition. But listen to Bogdanov again:

"We remind the reader once more that 'objective' experience is by no means the same as 'social' experience. . . . Social experience is far from being altogether socially organized and contains various contradictions, so that certain of its parts do not agree with others. Sprites and hobgoblins may exist in the sphere of social experience of a given people or of a given group of people—for example, the peasantry; but they need not therefore be included under socially organized or objective experience, for they do not harmonize with the rest of collective experience and do not fit in with its organizing forms, for example, with the chain of causality."

Of course it is very gratifying that Bogdanov himself "does not include" the social experience in respect to sprites and hobgoblins under objective experience. But this well-meant amendment in the spirit of anti-fideism by no means corrects the fundamental error of Bogdanov's whole position. Bogdanov's definition of objectivity and of the physical world completely falls to the ground, since the religious doctrine has "universal significance" to a greater degree than the scientific doctrine; the greater part of mankind clings to the former doctrine to this day. Catholicism has been "socially organized, harmonized and co-ordinated" by centuries of development; it "*fits in*" with the "chain of causality" in the most indisputable manner; for religions did not originate without cause, it is not by accident that they retain their hold over the masses under modern conditions, and that professors of philosophy adapt themselves to them quite "lawfully." If this undoubtedly "universally significant" and undoubtedly highly organized social and religious experience does "not harmonize" with the "experience" of science, it is because there is a fundamental difference between the two, which Bogdanov obliterated when he rejected objective truth. And however much Bogdanov tries to "correct" himself by saying that fideism, or clericalism, does not harmonize with science, the undeniable fact remains that Bogdanov's denial of objective truth completely "harmonizes" with fideism. Contemporary fideism does not reject science; all it rejects is the "exaggerated claims" of science, to wit, its claim to objective truth. If objective truth exists (as the materialists think), if natural science, reflecting the outer world in human "experience," is alone capable of giving us objective truth, then all fideism is absolutely refuted. But if there is no objective truth, if truth (including scientific truth) is only an organizing form of human experience, then this in itself is an admission of the fundamental premise of clericalism, the door is thrown open for it, and a place is cleared for the "organizing forms" of religious experience.

The question arises, does this denial of objective truth belong personally to Bogdanov, who refuses to own himself a Machian, or does it follow from the fundamental teachings of Mach and Avenarius? The second is the only possible answer to the question. If only sensation exists in the world (Avenarius in 1876), if bodies are complexes of sensations (Mach, in the *Analysis of Sensations*), then we are obviously confronted with a philosophical subjectivism which inevitably leads to the denial of objective truth. And if sensations are called "elements" which in one connection give rise to the physical and in another to the psychical, this, as we have seen, only confuses but does not reject the fundamental point of departure of empirio-criticism. Avenarius and Mach recognize sensations as the source of our knowledge. Consequently, they adopt the standpoint of empiricism (all knowledge derives from experience) or sensationalism (all knowledge derives from sensations). But this standpoint gives rise to the difference between the fundamental philosophical trends, idealism and materialism, and does not eliminate that difference, no matter in what "new" verbal garb ("elements") you clothe it. Both the solipsist, that is, the subjective idealist, and the materialist may regard sensations as the source of our knowledge. Both Berkeley and Diderot started from Locke. The first premise of the theory of knowledge undoubtedly is that the sole source of our knowledge is sensation. Having recognized the first premise, Mach confuses the second important premise, i.e., regarding the objective reality that is given to man in his sensations, or that forms the source of man's sensations. Starting from sensations, one may follow the line of subjectivism, which leads to solipsism ("bodies are complexes or combinations of sensations"), or the line of objectivism, which leads to materialism (sensations are images of objects, of the external world). For the first point of view, i.e., agnosticism, or, pushed a little further, subjective idealism, there can be no objective truth. For the second point of view, i.e., materialism, the recognition of objective truth is essential. This old philosophical question of the two trends, or rather, of the two possible deductions from the premises of empiricism and sensationalism, is not solved by Mach, it is not eliminated or overcome by him, but is *muddled* by verbal trickery with the word "element," and the like. Bogdanov's denial of objective truth is an inevitable consequence of Machism as a whole, and not a deviation from it.

Engels in his *Ludwig Feuerbach* calls Hume and Kant philosophers "who question the possibility of any cognition (or at least of an exhaustive cognition) of the world." Engels, therefore, lays stress on what is common both to Hume and Kant, and not on what divides them. Engels states further that "what is decisive in the refutation of this [Humean and Kantian] view has already been said by Hegel." In this connection it seems to me not uninteresting to note that Hegel, declaring *materialism* to be "a consistent system of empiricism," wrote:

"Generally speaking, Empiricism finds the truth in the outward world; and even if it allows a super-sensible world, it holds knowledge of that world to be impossible, and would restrict us to the province of sense-perception. This doctrine when systematically carried out produces what has been latterly termed Materialism. Materialism of this stamp looks upon matter, *qua* matter, as the genuine objective world." [Hegel, *The Logic of Hegel* (the *Encyclopedia Logic*) trans. W. Wallace, p. 81.—*Ed.*].

All knowledge comes from experience, from sensation, from perception. That is true. But the question arises, does *objective reality* "belong to perception," i.e., is it the source of perception? If you answer yes, you are a materialist. If you answer no, you are inconsistent and will inevitably arrive at subjectivism, or agnosticism, irrespective of whether you deny the knowability of the thing-in-itself, or the objectivity of time, space and causality (with Kant), or whether you do not even permit the thought of a thing-in-itself (with Hume). The inconsistency of your empiricism, of your philosophy of experience, will in that case lie in the fact that you deny the objective content of experience, the objective truth of experimental knowledge.

Those who hold to the line of Kant and Hume (Mach and Avenarius included, in so far as they are not pure Berkeleians) call us, the materialists, "metaphysicians" because we recognize objective reality which is given us in experience, because we recognize an objective source of our sensations independent of man. We materialists follow Engels in calling the Kantians and Humeans *agnostics,* because they deny objective reality as the source of our sensations. . . . Hence the denial of objective truth by the agnostic, and the tolerance—the philistine, cowardly tolerance—of the dogmas regarding sprites, hobgoblins, Catholic saints, and the like. Mach and Avenarius, pretentiously resorting to a "new" terminology, a supposedly "new" point of view, repeat, in fact, although in a confused and muddled way, the reply of the agnostic: On the one hand, bodies are complexes of sensations (pure subjectivism, pure Berkeleianism); on the other hand, if we rechristen our sensations "elements," we may think of them as existing independently of our sense organs!

The Machians love to assert that they are philosophers who completely trust the evidence of our sense organs, who regard the world as actually being what it seems to us to be, full of sounds, colors, etc., whereas to the materialists, they say, the world is dead, devoid of sound and color, and in its reality different from what it seems to be, and so forth. . . . But, in fact, the Machians are subjectivists and agnostics, for they *do not sufficiently* trust the evidence of our sense organs and are inconsistent in their sensationalism. They do not recognize objective reality, independent of humanity, as the source of our sensations. They do not regard sensations as the true copy of this objective reality, thereby directly conflicting with natural science and throwing the door open for fideism. On the contrary, for the materialist the world is richer, livelier, more varied than it actually seems, for with each step in the development of science new aspects are discovered. For the materialist, sensations are images of the ultimate and sole objective reality, ultimate not in the sense that it has already been explored to the end, but in the sense that there is not and cannot be any other. This view irrevocably closes the door not only to every species of fideism, but also to that professorial scholasticism which, while not regarding objective reality as the source of our sensations, "deduces" the concept of the objective by means of such artificial verbal constructions as universal significance, socially-organized, and so on and so forth, and which is unable, and frequently unwilling, to separate objective truth from belief in sprites and hobgoblins.

The Machians contemptuously shrug their shoulders at the "antiquated" views of the "dogmatists," the materialists, who still cling to the concept *matter,* which supposedly has been refuted by "recent science" and "recent positivism." We shall speak separately of the new theories of physics on the structure of matter. But it is absolutely unpardonable to confound, as the Machians do, any particular theory of the structure of matter with the epistemological category, to confound the problem of the new properties of new aspects of matter (electrons for example) with the old problem of the theory of knowledge, with the problem of the sources of our knowledge, the existence of objective truth, etc. We are told that Mach "discovered the world-elements": red, green, hard, soft, loud, long, etc. We ask, is a man given objective reality when he sees something red or feels something hard, etc., or not? This hoary philosophical query is confused by Mach. If you hold that it is not given, you, together with Mach, inevitably sink to subjectivism and agnosticism and deservedly fall into the embrace of the immanentists, i.e., the philosophical Menshikovs. If you hold that it is given, a philosophical concept is needed for this objective reality, and this concept has been worked out long, long ago. This concept is *matter*. Matter is a philosophical category designating the objective reality which is given to man by his sensations, and which is copied, photographed and reflected by our sensations, while existing independently of them. Therefore, to say that such a concept can become antiquated is *childish talk,* a senseless repetition of the arguments of fashionable *reactionary* philosophy. Could the struggle between materialism and idealism, the struggle between the tendencies or lines of Plato and Democritus in philosophy, the struggle between religion and science, the denial of objective truth and its assertion, the struggle between the adherents of supersensible knowledge and its adversaries have become antiquated during the two thousand years of the development of philosophy?

Acceptance or rejection of the concept matter is a question of the confidence man places in the evidence of his sense organs, a question of the source of our knowledge, a question which has been asked and debated from the very inception of philosophy, which may be disguised in a thousand different garbs by professorial clowns, but which can no more become antiquated than the question whether the source of human cognition is sight and touch, hearing and smell. To regard our sensations as images of the external world, to recognize objective truth, to hold the materialist theory of knowledge—these are all one and the same thing.

—LENIN, *Materialism and Empirio-Criticism* (1928), pp. 120–29.

[5]

TRUTH: RELATIVE AND ABSOLUTE

Is human thought sovereign? Before we can answer yes or no we must first enquire: What is human thought? Is it the thought of the individual human being? No. But it exists only as the individual thought of many billions of past, present and future men. If then, I say that the total thought of all these human beings, including future ones, which is embraced in my idea, is *sovereign,* able to know the world as it exists, if only mankind lasts long enough and in so far as no limits are imposed on its knowledge by its perceptive organs or the objects to be known, then I am saying something which is pretty banal and, in addition, pretty barren. For the most valuable result from it would be that it should make us extremely distrustful of our present knowledge, inasmuch as in all probability we are but little beyond the beginning of human history, and the generations which will put *us* right are likely to be far more numerous than those whose knowledge we—often enough with a considerable degree of contempt—are in a position to correct. . . .

In other words, the sovereignty of thought is realized in a number of extremely unsovereignly thinking human beings; the knowledge which has an unconditional claim to truth is realized in a number of relative errors; neither the one nor the other can be fully realized except through an endless eternity of human existence.

Here once again we find the same contradiction as we found above, between the character of human thought, necessarily conceived as absolute, and its reality in individual human beings with their extremely limited thought. This is a contradiction which can only be solved in the infinite progression, or what is for us, at least from a practical standpoint, the endless succession, of generations of mankind. In this sense human thought is just as much sovereign as not sovereign, and its capacity for knowledge just as much unlimited as limited. It is sovereign and unlimited in its disposition, its vocation, its possibilities, and its historical goal; it is not sovereign and it is limited in its individual expression and in its realization at each particular moment.

It is just the same with eternal truths. If mankind ever reached the stage at which it could only work with eternal truths, with conclusions of thought which possess sovereign validity and an unconditional claim to truth, it would then have reached the point where the infinity of the intellectual world, both in its actuality and in its potentiality, had been exhausted, and this would mean that the famous miracle of the infinite series which has been counted would have been performed.

But in spite of all this, are there any truths which are so securely based that any doubt of them seems to us to amount to insanity? That twice two makes four, that the three angles of a triangle are equal to two right angles, that Paris is in France, that a man who gets no food dies of hunger, and so forth? Are there then nevertheless *eternal* truths, final and ultimate truths?

Certainly there are. We can divide the whole realm of knowledge in the traditional way into three great departments. The first includes all sciences which are concerned with inanimate nature and are to a greater or less degree susceptible of mathematical treatment—mathematics, astronomy, mechanics, physics, chemistry. If it gives anyone any pleasure to use mighty words for very simple things, it can be asserted that *certain* results obtained by these sciences are eternal truths, final and ultimate truths; for which reason these sciences are also known as the *exact* sciences. But very far from all their results have this validity. With the introduction of variable magnitudes and the extension of their variability to the infinitely small and infinitely large, mathematics, in other respects so strictly moral, fell from grace; it ate of the tree of knowledge, which opened up to it a career of most colossal achievements, but at the same time a path of error. The virgin state of absolute validity and irrefutable certainty of everything mathematical was gone forever; mathematics entered the realm of controversy, and we have reached the point where most people differentiate and integrate not because they understand what they are doing but from pure faith, because up to now it has always come out right. Things are even worse with astronomy and mechanics, and in physics and chemistry we are surrounded by hypotheses as by a swarm of bees. And it must of necessity be so. In physics we are dealing with the motion of molecules, in chemistry with the formation of molecules out of atoms, and if the interference of light waves is not a myth, we have absolutely no prospect of ever seeing these interesting objects with our own eyes. As time goes on, final and ultimate truths become remarkably rare in this field.

We are even worse off for them in geology, which by its nature is concerned chiefly with events which took place not only in our absence but in the absence of any human being whatever. The winning of final and absolute truths in this field is therefore a very troublesome business, and the crop is extremely meager.

The second department of science is the one which covers the investigation of living organisms. In this field there is such a multitude of reciprocal relations and causalities that not only does the solution of each question give rise to a host of other questions, but each separate problem can usually only be solved piecemeal, through a series of investigations which often requires centuries to complete; and even then the need for a systematic presentation of the interrelations makes it necessary again and again to surround the final and ultimate truths with a luxuriant growth of hypotheses. What a long series of intermediaries from Galen to Malpighi was necessary for correctly establishing such a simple matter as the circulation of the blood in mammals, how slight is our knowledge of the origin of blood corpuscles, and how numerous are the missing links even today, for example, in our attempts to bring the symptoms of a disease into some rational relationship with its causes! And often enough discoveries, such as that of the cell, are made which compel us to revise completely all formerly established final and ultimate truths in the realm of biology, and to put whole piles of them on the scrap heap once and for all. Anyone who wants to establish really pure and immutable truths in this science will therefore have to be content with such platitudes as, all men are mortal, all female mammals have lacteal glands, and the like; he will not even be able to assert that the higher mammals digest with their stomach and intestines and not with their heads, for the nervous activity which is centralized in the head is indispensable to digestion.

But eternal truths are in an even worse plight in the third, the historical group of sciences. The subjects investigated by these in their historical sequence and in their present forms are the conditions of human life, social relationships, forms of law and the state, with their ideal superstructure of philosophy, religion, art, etc. In organic nature we are at least dealing with a succession of phenomena which, so far as our immediate observation is concerned, recur with fair regularity between very wide limits. Organic species have on the whole remained unchanged since the time of Aristotle. In social history, however, the repetition of conditions is the exception and not the rule, once we pass beyond the primitive stage of man, the so-called Stone Age; and when such repetitions occur, they never arise under exactly similar conditions—as for example the existence of an original common ownership of the land among all civilized peoples, and the way in which this came to an end. In the realm of human history our knowledge is therefore even more backward than in the realm of biology. Furthermore, when by way of exception the inner connection between the social and political forms of existence in an epoch come to be recognized, this as a rule only occurs when these forms are already out of date and are nearing extinction. Therefore, knowledge is here essentially relative, inasmuch as it is limited to the perception of relationships and consequences of certain social and state forms which exist only at a particular epoch and among particular people and are of their very nature transitory. Anyone therefore who sets out on this field to hunt down final and ultimate truths, truths which are pure and absolutely immutable, will bring home but little, apart from platitudes and commonplaces of the sorriest kind—for example, that generally speaking man cannot live except by labor; that up to the present mankind for the most part has been divided into rulers and ruled; that Napoleon died on May 5, 1821, and so on. . . .

We might have made mention above of the sciences which investigate the laws of human thought, i.e., logic and dialectics. In these, however, we do not fare any better as regards eternal truths. Herr Dühring declares that dialectics proper is pure nonsense, and the many books which have been and in the future will be written on logic provide abundant proof that also in this science final and ultimate truths are much more sparsely sown than is commonly believed.

For that matter, there is absolutely no need to be alarmed at the fact that the stage of knowledge which we have now reached is as little final as all that have preceded it. It already embraces a vast mass of facts and requires very great specialization of study on the part of anyone who wants to become an expert in any particular science. But a man who applies the measure of pure, immutable, final and ultimate truth to knowledge which, by the very nature of its object, must either remain relative for long successions of generations and be completed only step by step, or which, as in cosmogony, geology and the history of man, must always remain defective and incomplete because of the faultiness of the historical material—such a man only proves thereby his own ignorance and perversity, even if the real background to his pretensions is not, as it is in this case, his claim to personal infallibility. Truth and error, like all concepts which are expressed in polar opposites, have absolute validity only in an extremely limited field, as we have just seen, and as even Herr Dühring would realize if he had any acquaintance with the first elements of dialectics, which deal precisely with the inadequacy of all polar opposites. As soon as we apply the antithesis between truth and error outside of that narrow field which has been referred to above it becomes relative and therefore unserviceable for exact scientific modes of expression; and if we attempt to apply it as absolutely valid outside that field we then really find ourselves beaten; both poles of the antithesis become transformed into their opposites, truth becomes error and error truth. Let us take as an example the well-known Boyle's law, by which, if the temperature remains constant, the volume of gases varies inversely with the pressure to which they are subjected. Regnault found that this law did not hold good in certain cases. Had he been a philosopher of reality he would have had to say: Boyle's law is mutable, and is therefore not a pure truth, therefore it is not a truth at all, therefore it is an error. But had he done this he would have committed an error far greater than the one that was contained in Boyle's law; his grain of truth would have been lost sight of in a sandhill of error; he would have distorted his originally correct conclusion into an error compared with which Boyle's law, along with the little particle of error that clings to it, would have seemed like truth. But Regnault, being a man of science, did not indulge in such childishness, but continued his investigations and discovered that Boyle's law is in general only approximately correct, and in particular loses its validity in the case of gases which can be liquefied by pressure, as soon as the pressure approaches the point at which liquefaction begins. Boyle's law therefore was proved to be correct only within definite limits. But is it absolutely and finally true even within those limits? No physicist would assert that this was so. He would say that it holds good within certain limits of pressure and temperature and for certain gases; and even within these more restricted limits he would not exclude the possibility of a still narrower limitation or altered formulation as the result of future investigations. This is how things stand with final and ultimate truths in physics for example. Really scientific works therefore as a rule avoid such dogmatic and moral expressions as error and truth, while these expressions meet us everywhere in works such as the "philosophy of reality," in which empty phrase-mongering attempts to impose on us as the sovereign result of sovereign thought.

—ENGELS, *Anti-Dühring* (1878), pp. 96–103.

[6]

RELATIVITY OF KNOWLEDGE VERSUS RELATIVISM

A. CONDITIONAL VERSUS UNCONDITIONAL TRUTH

From the standpoint of modern materialism, i.e., Marxism, the *limits* of approximation of our knowledge to the objective, absolute truth are historically conditional, but the existence of such truth is *unconditional,* and the fact that we are approaching nearer to it is also unconditional. The contours of the picture are historically conditional, but the fact that this picture depicts an objectively existing model is unconditional. When and under what circumstances we reached, in our knowledge of the essential nature of things, the discovery of alizarin in coal tar or the discovery of electrons in the atom is historically conditional; but that every such discovery is an advance of "absolutely objective knowledge" is unconditional. In a word, every ideology is historically conditional, but it is unconditionally true that to every scientific ideology (as distinct, for instance, from religious ideology), there corresponds an objective truth, absolute nature. You will say that this distinction between relative and absolute truth is indefinite. And I shall reply: Yes, it is sufficiently "indefinite" to prevent science from becoming a dogma in the bad sense of the term, from becoming something dead, frozen, ossified; but it is at the same time sufficiently "definite" to enable us to dissociate ourselves in the most emphatic and irrevocable manner from fideism and agnosticism, from philosophical idealism and the sophistry of the followers of Hume and Kant. Here is a boundary which you have not noticed, and not having noticed it, you have fallen into the swamp of reactionary philosophy. It is the boundary between dialectical materialism and relativism. . . .

To make relativism the basis of the theory of knowledge is inevitably to condemn oneself either to absolute skepticism, agnosticism, and sophistry, or to subjectivism. Relativism as the basis of the theory of knowledge is not only the recognition of the relativity of our knowledge, but also a denial of any objective measure or model existing independently of humanity to which our relative knowledge approximates. From the standpoint of naked relativism one can justify any sophistry; one may regard as "conditional" whether Napoleon died on May 5, 1821, or not; one may declare the admission, alongside of scientific ideology ("convenient" in one respect), of religious ideology (very "convenient" in another respect) a mere "convenience" for man or humanity, and so forth.

Dialectics—as Hegel in his time explained—*contains* an element of relativism, of negation, of skepticism, but *is not reducible* to relativism. The materialist dialectics of Marx and Engels certainly does contain relativism, but is not reducible to relativism, that is, it recognizes the relativity of all our knowledge, not in the sense of the denial of objective truth, but in the sense of the historically conditional nature of the limits of the approximation of our knowledge of this truth.*

Bogdanov writes in italics: "*Consistent Marxism does not admit such dogmatism and such static concepts*" as eternal truths. This is a muddle. If the world is eternally moving and developing matter (as the Marxists think), reflected by the developing human consciousness, what is there "static" here? The point at issue is not the immutable essence of things, or an immutable consciousness, but the *correspondence* between the consciousness which reflects nature and the nature which is reflected by consciousness. In connection with this question, and this question alone, the term "dogmatism" has a specific, characteristic, philosophical flavor: it is a favorite word used by the idealists and the agnostics *against* the materialists, as we have already seen in the case of the fairly "old" materialist, Feuerbach. The objections brought

* For further development of this point see Lenin, Appendix II, Nos. 24–26, 33–34.—*Ed.*

against materialism from the standpoint of the celebrated "recent positivism" are just such ancient trash.

—LENIN, *Materialism and Empirio-Criticism* (1908), pp. 134–36.

B. RELATIVISM AND DIALECTICS

The question of the relation between relativism and dialectics plays perhaps the most important part in explaining the theoretical misadventures of Machism. Take Rey, for instance, who like all European positivists has no conception whatever of Marxian dialectics. He employs the word dialectics exclusively in the sense of idealist philosophical speculation. As a result, although he feels that the new physics has gone astray on the question of relativism, he nevertheless flounders helplessly and attempts to differentiate between moderate and immoderate relativism. Of course, "immoderate relativism . . . logically, if not in practice, borders on actual skepticism," but there is no "immoderate" relativism, you see, in Poincaré. Just fancy, one can, like an apothecary, weigh out a little more or a little less relativism and thus correct Machism!

As a matter of fact, the only theoretically correct formulation of the question of relativism is given in the dialectical materialism of Marx and Engels, and ignorance of it is *bound* to lead from relativism to philosophical idealism. Incidentally, the failure to understand this fact is enough to render Mr. Berman's absurd book, *Dialectics in the Light of the Modern Theory of Knowledge,* utterly valueless. Mr. Berman repeats the ancient nonsense about dialectics, which he has entirely failed to understand. We have already seen that *all* the Machians, *at every step,* reveal a similar lack of understanding of the theory of knowledge.

All the old truths of physics, including those which were regarded as firmly established and incontestable, have proven to be relative truth—*hence,* there can be no objective truth independent of mankind. Such is the argument not only of the Machians, but of the "physical" idealists in general. That absolute truth results from the sum-total of relative truths in the course of their development; that relative truths represent relatively faithful reflections of an object existing independently of man; that these reflections become more and more faithful; that every scientific truth, notwithstanding its relative nature, contains an element of absolute truth—all these propositions, which are obvious to anyone who has thought over Engels' *Anti-Dühring,* are for the "modern" theory of knowledge a book with seven seals.

Such works as Duhem's *Theory of Physics,* or Stallo's *The Concepts and Theories of Modern Physics,* which Mach particularly recommends, show very clearly that these "physical" idealists attach the most significance to the proof of the relativity of our knowledge, and that they are in reality vacillating between idealism and dialectical materialism. Both authors, who belong to different periods, and who approach the question from different points of view (Duhem's specialty is physics, in which field he has worked for twenty years; Stallo was an erstwhile orthodox Hegelian who grew ashamed of his own book on natural philosophy, written in 1848 in the old Hegelian spirit), energetically combat the atomistic-mechanical conception of nature. They point to the narrowness of this conception, to the impossibility of accepting it as the limit of our knowledge, to the petrification of many of the ideas of writers who hold this conception. And it is indeed undeniable that the *old* materialism did suffer from such a defect; Engels reproached the earlier materialists for their failure to appreciate the relativity of all scientific theories, for their ignorance of dialectics, and for their exaggeration of the mechanical point of view. But Engels (unlike Stallo) was able to discard Hegelian idealism and *to grasp* the great and true kernel of Hegelian dialectics. Engels rejected the old metaphysical materialism for *dialectical* materialism, and not for relativism that sinks into subjectivism.

—LENIN, *Materialism and Empirio-Criticism* (1908), pp. 318–20.

[7]

THE CATEGORY OF CAUSALITY

A. OUR KNOWLEDGE OF CAUSALITY

Causality.—The first thing that strikes us in considering matter in motion is the interconnection of the individual motions of separate bodies, their *being determined* by one another. But not only do we find that a particular motion is followed by another, we find also that we can evoke a particular motion by setting up the conditions in which it takes place in nature, indeed that we can produce motions which do not occur at all in nature (industry), at least not in this way, and that we can give these motions a predetermined direction and extent. *In this way,* by the *activity of human beings,* the idea of *causality* becomes established, the idea that one motion is the *cause* of another. True, the regular sequence of certain natural phenomena can by itself give rise to the idea of causality—the heat and light that come with the sun; but this affords no proof, and to that extent Hume's skepticism was correct in saying that a regular *post hoc* [after this] can never establish a *propter hoc* [because of this]. But the activity of human beings *forms the test* of causality. If we bring the sun's rays to a focus by means of a lens and make them act like the rays of an ordinary fire, we thereby prove that the heat comes from the sun. If we bring together in a rifle the priming, the explosive charge, and the bullet and then fire it, we count upon the effect known in advance from previous experience, because we can follow in all its details the whole process of ignition, combustion, explosion by the sudden conversion into gas and pressure of the gas on the bullet. And here the skeptic cannot even say that because of previous experience it does not follow that it will be the same next time. For, as a matter of fact, it does sometimes happen that it is *not* the same, that the priming or the gunpowder fails to work, that the barrel bursts, etc. But it is precisely this which *proves* causality instead of refuting it, because we can find out the cause of each such deviation from the rule by appropriate investigation—chemical decomposition of the priming, dampness, etc., of the gunpowder, defect in the barrel, etc., etc., so that here the test of causality is so to say a *double* one.

Natural science, like philosophy, has hitherto entirely neglected the influence of men's activity on their thought; both know only nature on the one hand and thought on the other. But it is precisely *the alteration of nature by men,* not solely nature as such, which is the most essential and immediate basis of human thought, and it is in the measure that man has learned to change nature that his intelligence has increased. The naturalistic conception of history, as found, for instance, to a greater or lesser extent in Draper and other scientists, as if nature exclusively reacts on man, and natural conditions everywhere exclusively determined his historical development, is therefore one-sided and forgets that man also reacts on nature, changing it and creating new conditions of existence for himself. There is damned little left of "nature" as it was in Germany at the time when the Germanic peoples immigrated into it. The earth's surface, climate, vegetation, fauna, and the human beings themselves have continually changed, and all this owing to human activity, while the changes of nature in Germany which have occurred in the process of time without human interference are incalculably small.

—ENGELS, *Dialectics of Nature* (1872–1882), pp. 170–72.

[*For Hegel's notion of causality and Lenin's elaboration, see Appendix II, 15.*—Ed.]

B. CAUSALITY A REFLECTION OF OBJECTIVE REALITY

The question of causality is particularly important in determining the philosophical line of any new "ism," and we must therefore dwell on it in some detail.

Let us begin with an exposition of the materialist theory of knowledge on this point. . . .

Feuerbach recognizes objective law in nature and objective causality, which are reflected only with approximate fidelity by human ideas of order, law and so forth. With Feuerbach the recognition of objective law in nature is inseparably connected with the recognition of the objective reality of the external world, of objects, bodies, things, reflected by our mind. Feuerbach's views are consistently materialistic. All other views, or rather, any other philosophical line on the question of causality, the denial of objective law, causality and necessity in nature, are justly regarded by Feuerbach as belonging to the fideist trend. For it is, indeed, clear that the subjectivist line on the question of causality, the deduction of the order and necessity of nature not from the external objective world, but from consciousness, reason, logic, and so forth, not only cuts human reason off from nature, not only opposes the former to the latter, but makes nature a *part* of reason, instead of regarding reason as a part of nature. The subjectivist line in the question of causality is philosophical idealism (varieties of which are the theories of causality of Hume and Kant), i.e., fideism, more or less weakened and diluted. The recognition of objective law in nature and the recognition that this law is reflected with approximate fidelity in the mind of man is materialism.

As regards Engels, he had, if I am not mistaken, no occasion to contrast his materialist view with other trends on the particular question of causality. He had no need to do so, since he had definitely dissociated himself from all the agnostics on the more fundamental question of the objective reality of the external world in general. But to anyone who has read his philosophical works at all attentively it must be clear that Engels does not admit even the shadow of a doubt as to the existence of objective law, order, causality, and necessity in nature. We shall confine ourselves to a few examples. In the first section of *Anti-Dühring* Engels says: "In order to understand these details [of the general picture of the world phenomena], we must detach them from their natural or historical connections, and examine each one separately, as to its nature, its special causes and effects, etc." (p. 27). That this natural connection, the connection between natural phenomena, exists objectively, is obvious. Engels particularly emphasizes the dialectical view of cause and effect:

> "It is just the same with cause and effect; these are conceptions which only have validity in their application to a particular case as such, but when we consider the particular case in its general connection with the world as a whole they merge and dissolve in the conception of universal action and interaction, in which causes and effects are constantly changing places, and what is now or here an effect becomes there or then a cause, and *vice versa*" (p. 29).

Hence, the human conception of cause and effect always somewhat simplifies the objective connection of the phenomena of nature, reflecting it only approximately, artificially isolating one or another aspect of a single world process. If we find that the laws of thought correspond with the laws of nature, says Engels, this becomes quite conceivable when we take into account that reason and consciousness are "products of the human brain and man himself a product of nature." Of course, "the products of the human brain, being in the last analysis also products of nature, do not contradict the rest of nature but are in correspondence with it" (p. 45). There is no doubt that there exists a natural, objective relation between the phenomena of the world. Engels constantly speaks of the "laws of nature," of the "necessities of nature" (*Naturnotwendigkeiten*), without considering it necessary to explain the generally known propositions of materialism.

In *Ludwig Feuerbach* also we read that

"the general laws of motion—both of the external world and of human thought—[are] two sets of laws which are identical in substance but differ in their expression in so far as the human mind can apply them consciously, while in nature and also up to now for the most part in human history, these laws assert themselves unconsciously in the form of external necessity in the midst of an endless series of seeming accidents" (*op. cit.*, p. 44).

And Engels reproaches the old natural philosophy for having replaced "the real but as yet unknown inter-connections" (of the phenomena of nature) by "ideal and imaginary ones" (p. 47). Engels' recognition of objective law, causality and necessity in nature is absolutely clear, as is his emphasis on the relative character of our, i.e., man's approximate reflections of this law in various concepts. . . .

The really important epistemological question that divides the philosophical trends is not the degree of precision attained by our descriptions of causal connections, or whether these descriptions can be expressed in exact mathematical formulae, but whether the source of our knowledge of these connections is objective natural law or properties of our mind, its innate faculty of apprehending certain *a priori* truths, and so forth. This is what so irrevocably divides the materialists Feuerbach, Marx, and Engels from the agnostics (Humeans) Avenarius and Mach.

—LENIN, *Materialism and Empirio-Criticism* (1908), pp. 152–57, 159*f*.

[8]

MODERN SCIENCE: FROM A STATIC TO A DYNAMIC WORLD-VIEW

The first breach in this petrified outlook on nature * was made not by a natural scientist but by a philosopher. In 1755 appeared Kant's *Allgemeine Naturgeschichte und Theorie des Himmels* [*General Natural History and Theory of the Heavens*]. The ques-

* In the preceding pages Engels discussed the rise and development of early modern science. He showed, however, that with all its gigantic advances and revolutionary achievements, it still looked upon the world "as something ossified, something immutable," and for the most part "something that had been created at one stroke."—*Ed.*

tion of the first impulse was abolished; the earth and the whole solar system appeared as something that had *come into being* in the course of time. If the great majority of the natural scientists had had a little less of the repugnance to thinking that Newton expressed in the warning: "Physics, beware of metaphysics!," they would have been compelled from this single brilliant discovery of Kant's to draw conclusions that would have spared them endless deviations and immeasurable amounts of time and labor wasted in false directions. For Kant's discovery contained the point of departure for all further progress. If the earth were something that had come into being, then its present geological, geographical, and climatic state, and its plants and animals likewise, must be something that had come into being; it must have had a history not only of co-existence in space but also of succession in time. If at once further investigations had been resolutely pursued in this direction, natural science would now be considerably further advanced than it is. But what good could come of philosophy? Kant's work remained without immediate results, until many years later Laplace and Herschel expounded its contents and gave them a deeper foundation, thereby gradually bringing the "nebular hypothesis" into favor. Further discoveries finally brought it victory; the most important of these were: the proper motion of the fixed stars; the demonstration of a resistant medium in universal space; the proof furnished by spectral analysis of the chemical identity of the matter of the universe, and the existence of such glowing nebular masses as Kant had postulated.

It is, however, permissible to doubt whether the majority of natural scientists would so soon have become conscious of the contradiction of a changing earth that bore immutable organisms, had not the dawning conception that nature does not just *exist,* but *comes into being* and *passes away,* derived support from another quarter. Geology arose and pointed out, not only the terrestrial strata formed one after another and deposited one upon another, but also the shells and skeletons of extinct animals and the trunks, leaves, and fruits of no longer existing plants contained in these strata. It had finally to be acknowledged that not only the earth as a whole but also its present surface and the plants and animals living on it possessed a history in time. At first the acknowledgment occurred reluctantly enough. Cuvier's theory of the revolutions of the earth was revolutionary in phrase and reactionary in substance. In place of a single divine creation, he put a whole series of repeated acts of creation, making the miracle an essential natural agent. Lyell first brought sense into geology by substituting for the sudden revolutions due to the moods of the creator the gradual effects of a slow transformation of the earth.*

Lyell's theory was even more incompatible than any of its predecessors with the assumption of constant organic species. Gradual transformation of the earth's surface and of all conditions of life led directly to gradual transformation of the organisms and their adaptation to the changing environment, to the mutability of species. But tradition is a power not only in the Catholic Church but also in natural science. For years, Lyell himself did not see the contradiction, and his pupils still less. This is only to be explained by the division of labor that had meanwhile become dominant in natural science, which more or less restricted each person to his special sphere, there being only a few whom it did not rob of a comprehensive view.

Meanwhile physics had made mighty advances, the results of which were summed up almost simultaneously by three different persons in the year 1842, an epoch-making year for this branch of natural investigation. Mayer in Heilbronn and Joule in Manchester demonstrated the transformation of heat into mechanical energy and of mechanical energy into heat. The determination of the mechanical equivalent of heat put this result beyond question. Simultaneously, by simply working up the separate physical results already arrived at, Grove—not a natural scientist by profession, but an English lawyer—proved that all so-called physical energy, mechanical energy, heat, light, electricity, magnetism, indeed even so-called chemical energy, become transformed into one another under definite conditions without any loss of energy occurring, and so proved *post factum* along physical lines Descartes' principle that the quantity of motion present in the world is constant. With that the special physical energies, the as it were immutable "species" of physics, were resolved into variously differentiated forms of the motion of matter, convertible into one another according to definite laws. The fortuitousness of

* The defect of Lyell's view—at least in its first form—lay in conceiving the forces at work on the earth as constant, both in quality and quantity. The cooling of the earth does not exist for him; the earth does not develop in a definite direction but merely changes in an inconsequent fortuitous manner.

the existence of a number of physical energies was abolished from science by the proof of their inter-connections and transitions. Physics, like astronomy before it, had arrived at a result that necessarily pointed to the eternal cycle of matter in motion as the ultimate reality.

The wonderfully rapid development of chemistry, since Lavoisier, and especially since Dalton, attacked the old ideas of nature from another aspect. The preparation by inorganic means of compounds that hitherto had been produced only in the living organism proved that the laws of chemistry have the same validity for organic as for inorganic bodies, and to a large extent bridged the gulf between inorganic and organic nature, a gulf that even Kant regarded as forever impassable.

Finally, in the sphere of biological research also the scientific journeys and expeditions that had been systematically organized since the middle of the previous century, the more thorough exploration of the European colonies in all parts of the world by specialists living there, and further the progress of paleontology, anatomy, and physiology in general, particularly since the systematic use of the microscope and the discovery of the cell, had accumulated so much material that the application of the comparative method became possible and at the same time indispensable. On the one hand the conditions of life of the various floras and faunas were determined by means of comparative physical geography; on the other hand the various organisms were compared with one another according to their homologous organs, and this not only in the adult condition but at all stages of development. The more deeply and exactly this research was carried on, the more did the rigid system of an immutable, fixed organic nature crumble away at its touch. Not only did the separate species of plants and animals become more and more inextricably intermingled, but animals turned up, such as *Amphioxus* * and *Lepidosiren,* † that made a mockery of all previous classification, and finally organisms were encountered of which it was not possible to say whether they belonged to the plant or animal kingdom. More and more the gaps in the paleontological record were filled up, compelling even the most reluctant to

* *Amphioxus.* A headless marine animal with some of the characteristics of a fish, but much more primitive.—*Ed.*

† *Lepidosiren.* One of the lungfish which can breathe air for months on end. —*Ed.*

acknowledge the striking parallelism between the evolutionary history of the organic world as a whole and that of the individual organism, the Ariadne's thread that was to lead the way out of the labyrinth in which botany and zoology appeared to have become more and more deeply lost. It was characteristic that, almost simultaneously with Kant's attack on the eternity of the solar system, C. F. Wolff in 1759 launched the first attack on the fixity of species and proclaimed the theory of descent. But what in his case was still only a brilliant anticipation took firm shape in the hands of Oken, Lamarck, Baer, and was victoriously carried through by Darwin in 1859, exactly a hundred years later. Almost simultaneously it was established that protoplasm and the cell, which had already been shown to be the ultimate morphological constituents of all organisms, occurred independently as the lowest forms of organic life. This not only reduced the gulf between inorganic and organic nature to a minimum but removed one of the most essential difficulties that had previously stood in the way of the theory of descent of organisms. The new conception of nature was complete in its main features; all rigidity was dissolved, all fixity dissipated, all particularity that had been regarded as eternal became transient, the whole of nature shown as moving in eternal flux and cyclical course.

Thus we have once again returned to the point of view of the great founders of Greek philosophy, the view that the whole of nature, from the smallest element to the greatest, from grains of sand to suns, from protista* to men, has its existence in eternal coming into being and passing away, in ceaseless flux, in unresting motion and change, only with the essential difference that what for the Greeks was a brilliant intuition, is in our case the result of strictly scientific research in accordance with experience, and hence also it emerges in a much more definite and clear form. It is true that the empirical proof of this motion is not wholly free from gaps, but these are insignificant in comparison with what has already been firmly established, and with each year they become more and more filled up. And how could the proof in detail be otherwise than defective when one bears in mind that the most essential branches of science—trans-planetary astronomy, chemistry, geology—have a scientific existence of barely a hundred years, and the comparative method in physiology one of barely

* *Protista.* Single-celled animals and plants such as Paramecium, Ameba, Bacillus.—*Ed.*

fifty years, and that the basic form of almost all organic development, the cell, is a discovery not yet forty years old?

—ENGELS, *Dialectics of Nature* (1882), pp. 8–14.

[9]

ROLE OF PRODUCTION IN THE DEVELOPMENT OF THE SCIENCES

The successive development of the separate branches of natural science should be studied. First of all, *astronomy,* which, if only on account of the seasons, was absolutely indispensable for pastoral and agricultural peoples. Astronomy can only develop with the aid of *mathematics.* Hence this also had to be tackled. Further, at a certain stage of agriculture and in certain regions (raising of water for irrigation in Egypt), and especially with the origin of towns, big building operations, and the development of handicrafts—*mechanics.* This was soon needed also for *navigation* and *war.* Moreover, it requires the aid of mathematics and so promotes the latter's development. Thus, from the very beginning the origin and development of the sciences has been determined by production.

Throughout antiquity, scientific investigation proper remained restricted to these three branches, and indeed in the form of exact, systematic research it occurs for the first time in the post-classical period (the Alexandrines, Archimedes, etc.). In physics and chemistry, which were as yet hardly separated in men's minds (theory of the elements, absence of the idea of a chemical element), in botany, zoology, human and animal anatomy, it had only been possible until then to collect facts and arrange them as systematically as possible. Physiology was sheer guesswork, as soon as one went beyond the most tangible things—e.g., digestion and excretion—and it could not be otherwise when even the circulation of the blood was not known. At the end of the period, chemistry makes its appearance in its primitive form of alchemy.

If, after the dark night of the Middle Ages was over, the sciences suddenly arose anew with undreamt-of force, developing at a miraculous rate, once again we owe this miracle to—production. In the first place, following the Crusades, industry developed enormously and brought to light a quantity of new mechanical (weaving, clock-making, milling), chemical (dyeing, metallurgy, alcohol), and physical (lenses) facts, and this not only gave enormous material for observation, but also itself provided quite other means for experimenting than previously existed, and allowed the construction of *new* instruments; it can be said that really systematic experimental science had now become possible for the first time. Secondly, the whole of West and Middle Europe, including Poland, now developed in a connected fashion, even though Italy was still at the head in virtue of its old-inherited civilization. Thirdly, geographical discoveries—made purely on behalf of gain and, therefore, in the last resort, of production—opened up an infinite and hitherto inaccessible amount of material of a meteorological, zoological, botanical, and physiological (human) bearing. Fourthly, there was the *printing press.**

—ENGELS, *Dialectics of Nature* (1882), pp. 214*f*.

[10]

NATURAL SCIENTISTS AND PHILOSOPHY

A. WHY SCIENTISTS NEED A PHILOSOPHY

Natural scientists believe that they free themselves from philosophy by ignoring it or abusing it. They cannot, however, make any headway without thought, and for thought they need thought determinations. But they take these categories unreflectingly from the common consciousness of so-called educated persons, which is dominated by the relics of long obsolete philosophies, or from the little bit of philosophy compulsorily listened to at the university (which is not only fragmentary, but also a medley of views of people belonging to the most varied and usually the worst schools), or from uncritical and unsystematic reading of philosophical writings of all kinds. Hence they are no less in bondage to philosophy, but unfortunately in most cases to the worst philosophy, and those who abuse philosophy most are slaves to precisely the worst vulgarized relics of the worst philosophers.

—ENGELS, *ibid.*, pp. 183 *f*.

* Compare *The German Ideology*, p. 36: "Even this 'pure' natural science is provided with an aim, as with its material, only through trade and commerce, through the sensuous activity of men."—*Ed.*

B. From Metaphysics to Positive Science

Natural scientists may adopt whatever attitude they please, they will still be under the domination of philosophy. It is only a question whether they want to be dominated by a bad, fashionable philosophy or by a form of theoretical thought which rests on acquaintance with the history of thought and its achievements.

"Physics, beware of metaphysics," is quite right, but in a contrary sense.

Natural scientists allow philosophy to prolong a pseudo-existence by making shift with the dregs of the old metaphysics. Only when natural and historical science has adopted dialectics will all the philosophical rubbish—outside the pure theory of thought—be superfluous, disappearing in positive science.

—Engels, *ibid.*, pp. 243*f*.

C. Necessity of Dialectics for Scientists

The dialectics of the brain is only the reflection of the forms of motion of the real world, both of nature and of history. Until the end of the last century, indeed until 1830, natural scientists could manage pretty well with the old metaphysics, because real science did not go beyond mechanics—terrestrial and cosmic. Nevertheless, confusion had already been introduced by higher mathematics, which regards the eternal truth of lower mathematics as a superseded point of view, often asserting the contrary, and putting forward propositions which appear sheer nonsense to the lower mathematician. The rigid categories disappeared here; mathematics arrived at a field where even such simple relations as those of mere abstract quantity, bad infinity, assumed a completely dialectical form and compelled the mathematicians to become dialectical, unconsciously and against their will. There is nothing more comical than the twistings, subterfuges, and expedients employed by the mathematicians to solve this contradiction, to reconcile higher and lower mathematics, to make clear to their understanding that what they had arrived at as an undeniable result is not sheer nonsense, and in general rationally to explain the starting point, method, and result of the mathematics of the infinite.

Now, however, everything is quite different. Chemistry, the abstract divisibility of physical things, bad infinity—atomistics. Physiology—the cell (the organic process of development, both of the individual and of species, by differentiation, the most striking test of rational dialectics), and finally the identity of the forces of nature and their mutual convertibility, which put an end to all fixity of categories. Nevertheless, the bulk of natural scientists are still held fast in the old metaphysical categories and helpless when these modern facts, which so to say prove the dialectics in nature, have to be rationally explained and brought into relation with one another. And here *thinking* is necessary; atoms and molecules, etc., cannot be observed under the microscope, but only by the process of thought. Compare the chemists (except for Schorlemmer, who is acquainted with Hegel) and Virchow's cellular pathology, where in the end the helplessness has to be concealed by general phrases. Dialectics divested of mysticism becomes an absolute necessity for natural science, which has forsaken the field where rigid categories sufficed, as it were the lower mathematics of logic, its everyday weapons. Philosophy takes its revenge posthumously on natural science for the latter having deserted it; and yet the scientists could have seen even from the successes in natural science achieved by philosophy that the latter possessed something that was superior to them in their own special sphere.

—ENGELS, *ibid.*, pp. 153–55.

[11]

SCIENCE VERSUS METAPHYSICS

Mr. Mikhailovsky accuses Marx of not having "examined (sic!) all the known theories of the historical process." . . . Of what did nine-tenths of these theories consist? Of purely *a priori*, dogmatic, abstract constructions, such as: What is society? What is progress? and so on. (I purposely take examples which are dear to the heart and mind of Mr. Mikhailovsky.) Why, these theories are useless because of the very thing to which they owe their existence, they are useless because of their basic methods, because of their utter and unrelieved metaphysics.

To begin by asking what is society and what is progress, is to begin from the very end. Whence are you to get your concept of society and progress in general when you have not studied a single social formation in particular, when you have been unable even to establish this concept, when you have been unable even to undertake a serious factual investigation, an objective analysis of social relations of any kind? That is the most obvious earmark of metaphysics, with which every science began; as long as people were unable to make a study of the facts, they always invented *a priori* general theories, which were always sterile. The metaphysical chemist who was still unable to investigate real chemical processes would invent a theory about the force of chemical affinity. The metaphysical biologist would talk about the nature of life and the vital force. The metaphysical psychologist would reason about the nature of the soul. The method itself was an absurd one. You cannot argue about the soul without having explained the psychical processes in particular; here progress must consist in abandoning general theories and philosophical constructions about the nature of the soul, and in being able to put the study of facts which characterize any particular psychical process on a scientific footing. And therefore Mr. Mikhailovsky's accusation is exactly as though a metaphysical psychologist, who all his life has been writing "inquiries" into the nature of the soul (without knowing precisely the explanation of a single psychical phenomenon, even the simplest), were to accuse a scientific psychologist of not having examined all the known theories of the soul. He, the scientific psychologist, discarded all philosophical theories of the soul and set about making a direct study of the material substratum of psychical phenomena—the nervous processes—and gave, let us say, an analysis and explanation of such and such psychological processes. And our metaphysical psychologist reads this work and praises it; the description of the processes and the study of the facts, he says, are good. But he is not satisfied. "Pardon me," he exclaims excitedly, hearing people around him speak of the absolutely new conception of psychology given by this scientist, of his special method of scientific psychology: "Pardon me," the philosopher cries heatedly, "in what work is this method expounded? Why, this work contains only 'facts.' It does not even hint at an examination of 'all the known philosophical theories of the soul.' This is not the corresponding work by any means!"

In the same way, of course, *Capital* is also not the corresponding work for a metaphysical sociologist who does not observe the sterility of *a priori* discussions about the nature of society and who does not understand that such methods, instead of studying and explaining, only serve to foist on the concept society either the bourgeois ideas of a British shopkeeper or the philistine socialist ideals of a Russian democrat—and nothing more. That is why all these philosophico-historical theories arose and burst like soap bubbles, being at best but a symptom of the social ideas and relations of their time, and not advancing one iota man's "understanding" of even a few, but real, social relations (and not such as "correspond to human nature"). The gigantic forward stride which Marx made in this respect consisted precisely in the fact that he discarded all these discussions about society and progress in general and gave a "scientific" analysis of "one" society and of "one" progress—capitalist society and capitalist progress. And Mr. Mikhailovsky condemns him for having begun from the beginning and not from the end, for having begun with an analysis of the facts and not with final conclusions, with a study of partial, historically determined social relations and not with general theories about the nature of social relations in general! And he asks: Where is the corresponding work? O, sapient subjective sociologist!

—LENIN, "What the 'Friends of the People' Are" (1894), *Selected Works,* vol. XI, pp. 423–25.

[12]

INSEPARABILITY OF INDUCTION AND DEDUCTION

A. FALLIBILITY OF INDUCTION

To the Pan-Inductionists.—With all the induction in the world we would never have got to the point of becoming clear about the *process* of induction. Only the *analysis* of this process could accomplish this. Induction and deduction belong together as necessarily as synthesis and analysis. Instead of one-sidedly raising one to the heavens at the cost of the other, one should seek to apply each of them in its place, and that can only be done by bearing in mind that they belong together, that each completes the other. According to the inductionists, induction would be an infallible method. It is so little so that its apparently surest results are everyday overthrown by new discoveries. Light corpuscles, caloric, were results of induction. Where are they now? Induction taught us that all vertebrates have a central nervous system differentiated into brain and spinal cord, and that the spinal cord is enclosed in cartilaginous or bony vertebrae—whence indeed the name is derived. Then *Amphioxus* was revealed as a vertebrate with an undifferentiated central nervous strand and *without* vertebrae. Induction established that fishes are those vertebrates which throughout life breathe exclusively by means of gills. Then animals come to light whose fish character is almost universally recognized, but which, besides gills, have also well-developed lungs, and it turns out that every fish carries a potential lung in the swim bladder. Only by audacious application of the theory of evolution did Haeckel rescue the inductionists, who were feeling quite comfortable in these contradictions. If induction were really so infallible, whence come the rapid successive revolutions in classification of the organic world? They are the most characteristic product of induction, and yet they annihilate one another.

—ENGELS, *Dialectics of Nature* [1882], pp. 204*f*.

B. INDUCTION AND ANALYSIS

A striking example of how little induction can claim to be the sole or even the predominant form of scientific discovery occurs in thermodynamics; the steam engine provided the most striking proof that one can impart heat and obtain mechanical motion. One hundred thousand steam engines do not prove this more than one, but only more and more forced the physicists into the necessity of providing an explanation. Sadi Carnot was the first seriously to set about the task. But not by induction. He studied the steam engine, analyzed it, and found that in it the process which mattered does not appear *in pure form* but is concealed by all sorts of subsidiary processes. He did away with these subsidiary circumstances that have no bearing on the essential process, and constructed an ideal steam engine (or gas engine), which it is true is as little capable of being realized as, for instance, a geometrical line or surface, but in its way performs the same service as these mathematical abstractions—it presents the process in a pure, independent, and unadulterated form. And he came right up against the mechanical equivalent of heat (see the significance of his function C), which he only failed to discover and see because he believed in *caloric*. Here also proof of the damage done by false theories.

—ENGELS, *ibid.*, 213*f*.

C. INDUCTION: CLASSIFICATION AND EVOLUTION

It is also characteristic of the thinking capacity of our natural scientists that Haeckel fanatically champions induction at the very moment when the *results* of induction—the systems of classification—are everywhere put in question (*Limulus,* * a spider; *Ascidia,* † a vertebrate or chordate, the *Dipnoi,* ‡ however, being fishes, in opposition to all original definitions of amphibia) and daily new facts are being discovered which overthrow the *entire* previous classification by induction. What a beautiful confirmation of Hegel's thesis that the inductive conclusion is essentially a problematic one! Indeed, even the whole classification of organisms has been taken away from induction owing to the theory of evolution, and referred back to "deduction," to heredity—one species being literally *deduced* from another by heredity—and it is impossible to prove the theory of evolution by induction alone, since it is quite anti-inductive. The concepts with which induction operates—species, genus, class—have been rendered fluid by the theory of evolution and so have become *relative;* but one cannot use relative concepts for induction.

—ENGELS, *ibid.*, p. 226.

[13]

THE FUNCTION OF CONCEPTS: TO REFLECT REALITY

[You] absorb yourself to such a degree in details, without always, as it seems to me, paying attention to the connection as a whole, that you degrade the law of value to a fiction, a neces-

* The king-crab, shown by Marx's friend Ray Lankester to be an arachnid, *i.e.*, related to the spiders and scorpions, though not, of course, exactly a spider.—*Ed.*

† A see-squirt. Though the adult is sessile, the larva resembles a tadpole.—*Ed.*

‡ Lungfishes.—*Ed.*

sary fiction, rather as Kant makes the existence of God a postulate of the practical reason.

The reproaches you make against the law of value apply to *all* concepts, regarded from the standpoint of reality. The identity of thought and being, to express myself in Hegelian fashion, everywhere coincides with your example of the circle and the polygon. Or the two of them, the concept of a thing and its reality, run side by side like two asymptotes, always approaching each other yet never meeting. This difference between the two is the very difference which prevents the concept from being directly and immediately reality and reality from being immediately its own concept. But although a concept has the essential nature of a concept and cannot therefore *prima facie* directly coincide with reality, from which it must first be abstracted, it is still something more than a fiction, unless you are going to declare all the results of thought fictions because reality has to go a long way round before it corresponds to them, and even then only corresponds to them with asymptotic approximation.

Is it any different with the general rate of profit? At each moment it only exists approximately. If it were for once realized in two undertakings down to the last dot on the *i*, if both resulted in *exactly the same rate of profit* in a given year, that would be pure accident; in reality the rates of profit vary from business to business and from year to year according to different circumstances, and the general rate only exists as an average of many businesses and a series of years. But if we were to demand that the rate of profit—say 14.876934 . . .—should be exactly similar in every business and every year down to the 100th decimal place, on pain of degradation to fiction, we should be grossly misunderstanding the nature of the rate of profit and of economic laws in general—none of them has any reality except as approximation, tendency, average, and not as *immediate* reality. This is due partly to the fact that their action clashes with the simultaneous action of other laws, but partly to their own nature as concepts.

Or take the law of wages, the realization of the value of labor power, which is only realized as an average, and even that not always, and which varies in every locality, even in every branch, according to the customary standard of life. Or ground rent, representing a superprofit above the general rate, derived from monopoly over a force of nature. There too there is by no means a direct coincidence between real superprofit and real rent, but only an average approximation.

It is exactly the same with the law of value and the distribution of the surplus value by means of the rate of profit.

Both only attain their most complete approximate realization on the presupposition that capitalist production has been everywhere completely established, society reduced to the modern classes of landowners, capitalists (industrialists and merchants) and workers—all intermediate stages, however, having been got rid of. This does not exist even in England and never will exist—we shall not let it get so far as that.

Did feudalism ever correspond to its concept? Founded in the kingdom of the West Franks, further developed in Normandy by the Norwegian conquerors, its formation continued by the French Norsemen in England and Southern Italy, it came nearest to its concept—in Jerusalem, in the kingdom of a day, which in the *Assises de Jerusalem** left behind it the most classic expression of the feudal order. Was this order therefore a fiction because it only achieved a short-lived existence in full classical form in Palestine, and even that mostly only—on paper?

Or are the concepts which prevail in the natural sciences fictions because they by no means always coincide with reality? From the moment we accept the theory of evolution all our concepts of organic life correspond only approximately to reality. Otherwise there would be no change; on the day when concepts and reality completely coincide in the organic world development comes to an end. The concept fish includes a life in water and breathing through gills; how are you going to get from fish to amphibian without breaking through this concept? And it has been broken through and we know a whole series of fish which have developed their air bladders further into lungs and can breathe air. How, without bringing one or both concepts into conflict with reality, are you going to get from the egg-laying reptile to the mammal, which gives birth to living young? And in reality we have in the monotremata a whole sub-class of egg-laying mammals—in 1843, I saw the eggs of the duck-bill in Manchester and with arrogant narrow-mindedness mocked at such stupidity—as if a mammal could lay eggs—and now it has

* *Assises de Jerusalem:* The statute book of Godfrey of Bouillon for the kingdom of Jerusalem in the 11th century.—*Ed.*

been proved! So do not behave to the conceptions of value in the way I had later to beg the duck-bill's pardon for!

—ENGELS, Letter to Conrad Schmidt (1895), MARX and ENGELS, *Selected Correspondence*, pp. 527–30.

[*For the process of the coinciding of thought and reality, in Lenin's view, see Appendix II, 24, 25, 26, 28.*—Ed.]

[14]

CONCEPTS, TERMINOLOGY, AND THE GROWTH OF SCIENCE

Every new aspect of a science involves a revolution in the technical terms of that science. This is best shown by chemistry, where the whole of the terminology is radically changed about once in 20 years, and where you will hardly find a single organic compound that has not gone through a whole series of different names. Political economy has generally been content to take, just as they were, the terms of commercial and industrial life, and to operate with them, entirely failing to see that by so doing, it confined itself within the narrow circle of ideas expressed by those terms. Thus, though perfectly aware that both profits and rent are but sub-divisions, fragments of that unpaid part of the product which the laborer has to supply to his employer (its first appropriator, though not its ultimate exclusive owner), yet even classical political economy never went beyond the received notions of profits and rent, never examined this unpaid part of the product (called by Marx surplus product) in its integrity as a whole, and therefore never arrived at a clear comprehension, either of its origin and nature, or of the laws that regulate the subsequent distribution of its value. Similarly all industry, not agricultural or handicraft, is indiscriminately comprised in the term, manufacture, and thereby the distinction is obliterated between two great and essentially different periods of economic history—the period of manufacture proper, based on the division of manual labor, and the period of modern industry based on machinery. It is, however, self-evident that a theory which views modern capitalist production as a mere passing stage in the economic history of mankind, must make use of terms different from those habitual to writers who look upon that form of production as imperishable and final.

—ENGELS, Preface to 1st Eng. trans. of *Capital* (1886), pp. xi *f*.

[15]

DEFINITIONS, ABSTRACTIONS, AND REALITY

A. DIALECTICS AND DEFINITIONS

He [one of Marx's German critics.—*Ed.*] starts out from the mistaken assumption that Marx wishes to define where he is only analyzing, or that one may look in Marx's work at all for fixed and universally applicable definitions. It is a matter of course that when things and their mutual interrelations are conceived, not as fixed, but as changing, that their mental images, the ideas concerning them, are likewise subject to change and transformation; that they cannot be sealed up in rigid definitions, but must be developed in the historical or logical process of their formation.

—ENGELS, Preface to Marx's *Capital,* vol. III (1894), p. 24.

B. LIMITATIONS OF DEFINITION

Our definition of life is naturally very inadequate, inasmuch as, far from including *all* the phenomena of life, it has to be limited to those which are the most common and the simplest. From a scientific standpoint all definitions are of little value. In order to gain a really exhaustive knowledge of what life is, we should have to go through all the forms in which it appears, from the lowest up to the highest. But for ordinary usage, however, such definitions are very convenient and in places cannot well be dispensed with; moreover, they can do no harm, provided their inevitable deficiencies are not forgotten.

—ENGELS, *Anti-Dühring,* (1878), p. 96.

C. ALL "LAWS" AN APPROXIMATION

Such a general rate of surplus-value—as a tendency, like all other economic laws—has been assumed by us for the sake of theoretical simplification. But in reality it is an actual premise of the capitalist mode of production, although it is more or less obstructed by practical frictions causing more or less considerable differences locally, such as the settlement laws for English farm laborers. But in theory it is the custom to assume that the laws of capitalist production evolve in their pure form. In reality, however, there is always but an approximation. Still, this approximation is so much greater to the extent that the capitalist mode of production is normally developed, and to the extent that its adulteration and amalgamation with remains of former economic conditions is outgrown.

—MARX, *Capital,* vol. III, p. 206.

D. THE CONCRETE AND ABSTRACT ILLUSTRATED*

When we consider a given country from a politico-economic standpoint, we begin with its population, then analyze the latter according to its subdivisions into classes, location in city, country, or by the sea, occupation in different branches of production; then we study its exports and imports, annual production and consumption, prices of commodities, etc. It seems to be the correct procedure to commence with the real and concrete aspect of conditions as they are; in the case of political economy, to commence with population which is the basis and the author of the entire productive activity of society. Yet, on closer consideration it proves to be wrong. Population is an abstraction, if we leave out, e.g., the classes of which it consists. These classes, again, are but an empty word, unless we know what are the elements on which they are based, such as wage labor, capital, etc. These imply, in their turn, exchange, division of labor, prices, etc. Capital, e.g., does not mean anything without wage labor, value, money, price, etc. If we start out, therefore, with population, we do so with a chaotic conception of the whole, and by closer analysis we will gradually arrive at simpler ideas; thus we shall proceed from the imaginary concrete to less and less complex abstractions, until we get at the simplest conception. This once attained, we might start on our return journey until we would finally come back to population, but this time not as a chaotic notion of an integral whole, but as a rich aggregate of many conceptions and relations.

—MARX, *Critique of Political Economy* (1859), pp. 292*f.*

* For another statement of the relation of the concrete and abstract see Lenin, Appendix II, No. 16.—*Ed.*

PART FIVE

THE MATERIALIST INTERPRETATION OF HISTORY

Mankind must first of all eat and drink, have shelter and clothing, before it can pursue politics, science, religion, art, etc.

—ENGELS, "Speech at the Graveside of Karl MARX" (1883), *Selected Works,* vol. I, p. 16.

Technology discloses man's mode of dealing with nature, the process of production by which he sustains his life, and thereby also lays bare the mode of formation of his social relations, and of the mental conceptions that flow from them.

—MARX, *Capital* (1867), vol. I, p. 367n.

Introduction

THE MATERIALIST interpretation of history, commonly known as historical materialism, is defined as the application of dialectical materialism to the study of the evolution of human societies. It affirms that, just as there are objective laws of nature, so are there objective laws of history; that consequently a science of history is possible. It holds, however, that such a science is possible provided that: (1) We acknowledge the existence of objective laws in history; (2) we proceed on the basis that these laws can be discovered; (3) we attain the data necessary for the understanding of the way these laws operate, and (4) we apply these laws in any given historical area without subjectivism or schematism.

Marxism rejects as obscurantist all notions that would reduce history to a succession of unique, unpredictable events, occasioned by the conflicting wills of men. It holds that this is a shallow approach, confining itself to surface appearances. Marxism affirms that there are human wills and that the clash of these wills plays a great role in historical development. But it asks, what determines this clash of wills? Not to ask this question is to beg it. Hegel, indeed, had asked this question but gave an objective idealist answer which Marx finally rejected on the ground that it was mystical, nonobjective, and *a priori*. Marx's search for an answer led him to the conclusion that the will and the passions of men could be explained only by an investigation of the underlying driving forces of social development.

These driving forces are, in the last analysis, society's productive powers and the relationship of man to man in the process of obtaining the necessities of life. In this process contradictions arise, first of all, of an economic character. These contradictions are the basis for the class struggle which, according to Marxism, is the real key to the understanding of the course of human history.

A concise statement of the Marxist position was given by Lenin: "That in any given society the strivings of some of its members conflict with the striving of others, that social life is full of contradictions, that history discloses a struggle between nations and societies as well as within nations and societies, and, in addition, an alternation of periods of revolution and reaction, peace and war, stagnation and rapid progress or decline—are facts that are generally known. Marxism provides the clue which enables us to discover the laws governing this seeming labyrinth and chaos, namely, the theory of the class struggle. Only a study of the ensemble of strivings of all the members of a given society can lead to a scientific definition of the results of these strivings. And the source of the conflict of strivings lies in the differences in the position and mode of life of the *classes* into which each society is divided." (*Teachings of Karl Marx,* pp. 16 *f.*)

From this it follows, according to Marxism, that not only the immediate strivings of men, but also the political and legal institutions of society, together with the ethical, philosophical, and religious aspects of social life, can be explained fundamentally as the expressions of a conflict between classes which in turn is rooted in the contradictions that arise in the mode of production itself.

Thus historical materialism stresses the need always to distinguish between that which is primary and that which is secondary or derived, between that which *seems* to be and that which *is* determining in social life.

Thinkers before Marx had discovered the class struggle. But Marx went beyond them in asserting that the class struggle itself had its source in the very process of man's labor activity and he held that this activity resulted historically in the transition from a communal non-class society to societies divided into classes. He further believed that the development of the productive forces by capitalism would of necessity lead to a classless society, preceded by a transition period whose political form would be the dictatorship of the proletariat.

This section is so arranged that the reader will find here the major problems that come within the purview of historical materialism. Some of these are: The relationship of social being and social consciousness; the structure of society and the superstructure; the productive forces and the relations of production; the role of ideology; classes and class consciousness.

The reader will, we believe, see that the formulations of Marx, Engels, and Lenin contain shadings and subtleties, and were by no means intended to supply final answers. These men rejected easy, simple solutions. In their examination of history they stressed the extreme complexity confronting those who would *seriously* undertake to apply the dialectical materialist method to any given area of social development. It was for this reason, for example, that Marx heaped scorn on those who used historical materialism "as an excuse for *not* studying history." It was in reference to this procedure by so-called disciples that caused Marx to exclaim, "All I know is that I am not a Marxist."

Not included here, for want of space, are selections from the historical writing of Marx, Engels, and Lenin. Marx's "first attempt to explain a section of contemporary history with the aid of his materialist conception, on the basis of the given economic situation" (Engels) was his *Class Struggles in France, 1848–50*. His *Eighteenth Brumaire of Louis Bonaparte* (1852) covering the same period, is a classic in the writing of contemporary history: almost as empirical as a journalist could desire and yet with the depth of the theoretical historian. His *Civil War in France* (1870–71), consisting of three addresses written in the name of the General Council of the International Working Men's Association (the First International) covers the Franco-German war and the Paris Commune in a comparable way. Marx wrote numerous articles on various aspects of the history of Spain, of India, and of Ireland. His writings on the struggles between Russia and England over control of the Middle East, centering about the Crimean War, were later collected and published as *The Eastern Question.* His writings, together with those of Engels, brought together under the title, *The Civil War in the United States,* even today afford valuable insights to historians because of their analyses of the forces at work in that war.

Engels worked on sections of German history, as represented by his *The Peasant War in Germany* (1850), a study of the class struggles of the Reformation period, and his *Revolution and Counter-Revolution in Germany* (1851–52), consisting originally of articles published in the *New York Daily Tribune* concerning the abortive German Revolution of 1848 and its aftermath through 1852.

Lenin's use of the basic principles of historical materialism can be seen in his *The Development of Capitalism in Russia* (1897). Here he employs Marxist methodology in the analysis of a vast amount of statistical and documentary data in order to explain Russian economic development and to chart its future course.

These writings still stand as exemplars of the application of historical materialism to specific historical events and as general guidelines to historians concerning what they need to look for to attain adequate explanatory depth and breadth. The reader of these works will learn how difficult it is to write what Marx and Engels thought was "scientific" history. Nothing can be left out, and at the same time focus must always be kept on the important, the dynamic, the essential and most fundamental aspects of an ever-changing situation.

[1]

MODE OF PRODUCTION: THE BASIS OF SOCIAL LIFE

A. The Law of Social Development

The first work undertaken for the solution of the question that troubled me, was a critical revision of Hegel's "Philosophy of Law"; the introduction to that work appeared in the *Deutsch-Französischen Jahrbücher,* published in Paris in 1844. I was led by my studies to the conclusion that legal relations as well as forms of state could neither be understood by themselves, nor explained by the so-called general progress of the human mind, but that they are rooted in the material conditions of life, which are summed up by Hegel after the fashion of the English and French of the 18th century under the name "civil society"; the anatomy of that civil society is to be sought in political economy. The study of the latter which I had taken up in Paris, I continued at Brussels whither I emigrated on account of an order of expulsion issued by Mr. Guizot. The general conclusion at which I arrived and which, once reached, continued to serve as the leading thread in my studies, may be briefly summed up as follows: In the social production which men carry on they enter into definite relations that are indispensable and independent of their will; these relations of production correspond to a definite stage of development of their material powers of production. The sum total of these relations of production constitutes the economic structure of society—the real foundation, on which rise legal and political superstructures and to which correspond definite forms of social consciousness. The mode of production in material life determines the general character of the social, political, and spiritual processes of life. It is not the consciousness of men that determines their existence, but, on the contrary, their social existence determines their consciousness. At a certain stage of their development, the material forces of production in society come in conflict with the existing relations of production, or—what is but a legal expression for the same thing—with the property relations within which they had been at work before. From forms of development of the forces of production these relations turn into their fetters. Then comes the period of social revolution.* With the change of the economic foundation the entire immense superstructure is more or less rapidly transformed. In considering such transformtions the distinction should always be made between the material transformation of the economic conditions of production which can be determined with the precision of natural science, and the legal, political, religious, aesthetic, or philosophic—in short ideological forms in which men become conscious of this conflict and fight it out. Just as our opinion of an individual is not based on what he thinks of himself, so can we not judge of such a period of transformation by its own consciousness; on the contrary, this consciousness must rather be explained from the contradictions of material life, from the existing conflict beween the social forces of production and the relations of production. No social order ever disappears before all the productive forces, for which there is room in it, have been developed; and new higher relations of production never appear before the material conditions of their existence have matured in the womb of the old society. Therefore, mankind always takes up only such problems as it can solve; since, looking at the matter more closely, we will always find that the problem itself arises only when the material conditions necessary for its solution already exist or are at least in the process of formation. In broad outlines we can designate the Asiatic, the ancient, the feudal, and the modern bourgeois methods of production as so many epochs in the progress of the economic formation of society. The bourgeois relations of production are the last antagonistic form of the social process of production—antagonistic not in the sense of individual antagonism, but of one arising from conditions surrounding the life of individuals in society; at the same time the productive forces developing in the womb of bourgeois society create the material conditions for the solution of that antagonism. This social formation constitutes, therefore, the closing chapter of the prehistoric stage of human society.

—MARX, *Critique of Political Economy* (1859), pp. 10–13.

B. Man's Thought Corresponds to His Social Relations

Economic categories are only the theoretical expressions, the abstractions of the social relations of production. . . .

M. Proudhon the economist understands very well that men

* Compare Marx, *Capital,* vol. III. p. 1030.—*Ed.*

make cloth, linen, or silk materials in definite relations of production. But what he has not understood is that these definite social relations are just as much produced by men as linen, flax, etc. Social relations are closely bound up with productive forces. In acquiring new productive forces men change their mode of production; and in changing their mode of production, in changing the way of earning their living, they change all their social relations. The hand mill gives you society with the feudal lord; the steam mill, society with the industrial capitalist.

The same men who establish their social relations in conformity with their material productivity, produce also principles, ideas and categories, in conformity with their social relations.

Thus these ideas, these categories, are as little eternal as the relations they express. They are *historical and transitory products.*

There is a continual movement of growth in productive forces, of destruction in social relations, of formation in ideas; the only immutable thing is the abstraction of movement—*mors immortalis* [eternal death].

—MARX, *Poverty of Philosophy* (1847), pp. 109*f.*

[2]

WHAT MARX DISCOVERED

A. THE MATERIAL BASIS OF SOCIETY

Just as Darwin discovered the law of evolution in organic nature,* so Marx discovered the law of evolution in human history: he discovered the simple fact, hitherto concealed by an overgrowth of ideology, that mankind must first of all eat and drink, have shelter and clothing, before it can pursue politics, science, religion, art, etc., and that therefore the production of the immediate material means of subsistence and consequently the degree of economic development attained by a given people or during a given epoch, form the foundation upon which the state institutions, the legal conceptions, the art and even the

* Marx himself said of Darwin's *Origin of Species,* which appeared in 1859, the same year as Marx's *Critique of Political Economy:* "Darwin's book is very important and serves me as a basis in natural science for the class struggle in history."—*Ed.*

religious ideas of the people concerned have been evolved, and in the light of which these things must therefore be explained, instead of *vice versa* as had hitherto been the case.*

—ENGELS, "Speech at the Graveside of Karl Marx" (1883), *Selected Works*, vol. I, p. 16.

B. How a Science of History Became Possible

The discovery of the materialist conception of history, or, more correctly, the consistent extension of materialism to the domain of social phenomena, obviated the two chief defects in earlier historical theories. For, in the first place, those theories, at best, examined only the ideological motives of the historical activity of human beings without investigating the origin of these ideological motives, or grasping the objective conformity to law in the development of the system of social relationships, or discerning the roots of these social relationships in the degree of development of material production. In the second place, the earlier historical theories ignored the activities of the *masses*, whereas historical materialism first made it possible to study with scientific accuracy the social conditions of the life of the masses and the changes in these conditions. At best, pre-Marxist "sociology" and historiography gave an accumulation of raw facts collected at random, and a description of separate sides of the historic process. Examining the *totality* of all the opposing tendencies, reducing them to precisely definable conditions in the mode of life and the method of production of the various *classes* of society, discarding subjectivism and free will in the choice of various "leading" ideas or in their interpretation, showing how all the ideas and all the various tendencies, without exception, have their roots in the condition of the material forces of production, Marxism pointed the way to a comprehensive, an all-embracing study of the rise, development, and decay of socio-economic structures. People make their own history; but what determines their motives, that is, the motives of people in the mass; what gives rise to the clash of conflicting ideas and endeavors; what is the sum total of all these clashes among the whole mass of human societies; what are the objective conditions for the production of the material means of life that form the basis of all the historical activity of man; what is the law of the

* For another summary statement by Engels of the materialist conception of history, see *Anti-Dühring*, p.292.—*Ed.*

development of these conditions—to all these matters Marx directed attention, pointing out the way to a scientific study of history as a unified and true-to-law process despite its being extremely variegated and contradictory.

—LENIN, *The Teachings of Karl Marx* (1914), p. 16.

[3]

THE SOCIAL NATURE OF CONSCIOUSNESS

Men are the producers of their conceptions, ideas, etc.—real, active men, as they are conditioned by a definite development of their productive forces and of the intercourse corresponding to these, up to its furthest forms. Consciousness can never be anything else than conscious existence, and the existence of men is their actual life process. If in all ideology men and their circumstances appear upside down as in a *camera obscura,** this phenomenon arises just as much from their historical life process as the inversion of objects on the retina does from their physical life process.

In direct contrast to German philosophy which descends from heaven to earth, here we ascend from earth to heaven. That is to say, we do not set out from what men say, imagine, conceive, nor from men as narrated, thought of, imagined, conceived, in order to arrive at men in the flesh. We set out from real, active men, and on the basis of their real life process we demonstrate the development of the ideological reflexes and echoes of this life process. The phantoms formed in the human brain are also, necessarily, sublimates of their material life process, which is empirically verifiable and bound to material premises. Morality, religion, metaphysics, all the rest of ideology and their corresponding forms of consciousness, thus no longer retain the semblance of independence. They have no history, no development; but men, developing their material production and their material intercourse, alter, along with this their real existence, their thinking and the products of their thinking. Life is not determined by consciousness, but consciousness by life. In the

* An instrument that projected, by means of mirrors, an inverted image of a scene on a plane surface.—*Ed.*

first method of approach the starting point is consciousness taken as the living individual; in the second it is the real living individuals themselves, as they are in actual life, and consciousness is considered solely as *their* consciousness.

This method of approach is not devoid of premises. It starts out from the real premises and does not abandon them for a moment. Its premises are men, not in any fantastic isolation or abstract definition, but in their actual, empirically perceptible process of development under definite conditions. As soon as this active life process is described, history ceases to be a collection of dead facts as it is with the empiricists (themselves still abstract), or an imagined activity of imagined subjects, as with the idealists.

Where speculation ends—in real life—there real, positive science begins; the representation of the practical activity, of the practical process of development of men. Empty talk about consciousness ceases, and real knowledge has to take its place. When reality is depicted, philosophy as an independent branch of activity loses its medium of existence. At the best its place can only be taken by a summing-up of the most general results, abstractions which arise from the observation of the historical development of men. Viewed apart from real history, these abstractions have in themselves no value whatsoever. They can only serve to facilitate the arrangement of historical material, to indicate the sequence of its separate strata. But they by no means afford a recipe or schema, as does philosophy, for neatly trimming the epochs of history.

—MARX and ENGELS, *The German Ideology* (1846), pp. 13–15.

[4]

SCIENTIFIC VERSUS SPECULATIVE HISTORY

The philosophy of history, of law, of religion, etc., has consisted in the substitution of an inter-connection fabricated in the mind of the philosopher for the actual inter-connection to be demonstrated in the events; and in the comprehension of history as a whole as well as in its separate parts, as the gradual realization of ideas—and, indeed, naturally always the pet ideas of the philosopher himself. According to this, history worked unconsciously but with necessity towards a certain pre-determined, ideal goal—as, for example, according to Hegel, towards the realization of his absolute idea—and the unalterable trend towards this absolute idea formed the inner inter-connection in the events of history. A new mysterious providence—unconscious or gradually coming into consciousness—was thus put in the place of the real, still unknown inter-connection. Here, therefore, just as in the realm of nature, it was necessary to do away with these fabricated, artificial inter-connections by the discovery of the real ones; a task which ultimately amounts to the discovery of the general laws of motion which assert themselves as the ruling ones in the history of human society.

In one point, however, the history of the development of society proves to be essentially different from that of nature. In nature—in so far as we ignore man's reactions upon nature—there are only blind unconscious agencies acting upon one another and out of whose interplay the general law comes into operation. Nothing of all that happens—whether in the innumerable apparent accidents observable upon the surface of things, or in the ultimate results which confirm the regularity underlying these accidents—is attained as a consciously desired aim. In the history of society, on the other hand, the actors are all endowed with consciousness, are men acting with deliberation or passion, working towards definite goals; nothing happens without a conscious purpose, without an intended aim. But this distinction, important as it is for historical investigation, particularly of single epochs and events, cannot alter the fact that the course of history is governed by inner general laws. For here, also, on the whole, in spite of the consciously desired aims of all individuals, accident apparently reigns on the surface. That which is willed happens but rarely; in the majority of instances the numerous desired ends cross and conflict with one another, or these ends themselves are from the outset incapable of realization or the means of attaining them are insufficient. Thus the conflict of innumerable individual wills and individual actions in the domain of history produces a state of affairs entirely analogous to that in the realm of unconscious nature. The ends of the actions are intended, but the results which actually follow from these actions are not intended; or when they do seem to correspond to the end intended, they ultimately have consequences quite other than those intended.

Historical events thus appear on the whole to be likewise governed by chance. But where on the surface accident holds sway, there actually it is always governed by inner, hidden laws and it is only a matter of discovering these laws.

Men make their own history, whatever its outcome may be, in that each person follows his own consciously desired end, and it is precisely the resultant of these many wills operating in different directions and of their manifold effects upon the outer world that constitutes history. Thus it is also a question of what the many individuals desire. The will is determined by passion or deliberation. But the levers which immediately determine passion or deliberation are of very different kinds. Partly they may be external objects, partly ideal motives, ambition, "enthusiasm for truth and justice," personal hatred or even purely individual whims of all kinds. But, on the one hand, we have seen that the many individual wills active in history for the most part produce results quite other than those they intended—often quite the opposite; their motives therefore in relation to the total result are likewise of only secondary significance. On the other hand, the further question arises: What driving forces in turn stand behind these motives? What are the historical causes which transform themselves into these motives in the brains of the actors?

The old materialism never put this question to itself. Its conception of history, in so far as it has one at all, is therefore essentially pragmatic; it judges everything according to the motives of the action; it divides men in their historical activity into noble and ignoble and then finds that as a rule the noble are defrauded and the ignoble are victorious. Hence it follows for the old materialism that nothing very edifying is to be got from the study of history, and for us that in the realm of history the old materialism becomes untrue to itself because it takes the ideal driving forces which operate there as ultimate causes, instead of investigating what is behind them, what are the driving forces of these driving forces. The inconsistency does not lie in the fact that *ideal* driving forces are recognized, but in the investigation not being carried further back behind these into their motive causes. On the other hand, philosophy of history, particularly as represented by Hegel, recognizes that the ostensible and also the really operating motives of men who figure in history are by no means the ultimate causes of historical events; that behind these motives are other moving forces, which have to be discovered.

But it does not seek these forces in history itself, it imports them rather from outside, from out of philosophical ideology, into history. Hegel, for example, instead of explaining the history of ancient Greece out of its own inner inter-connections, simply maintains that it is nothing more than the working out of "types of beautiful individuality," the realization of a "work of art" as such. He says much in this connection about the old Greeks that is fine and profound but that does not prevent us today from refusing to be put off with such an explanation, which is a mere manner of speech.

When, therefore, it is a question of investigating the driving forces which—consciously or unconsciously, and indeed very often unconsciously—lie behind the motives of men in their historical actions and which constitute the real ultimate driving forces of history, then it is not a question so much of the motives of single individuals, however eminent, as of those motives which set in motion great masses, whole peoples, and again whole classes of the people in each people; and here, too, not the transient flaring up of a straw-fire which quickly dies down, but a lasting action resulting in a great historical transformation. To ascertain the driving causes which here in the minds of acting masses and their leaders—the so-called great men—are reflected as conscious motives, clearly or unclearly, directly or in ideological, even glorified form—that is the only path which can put us on the track of the laws holding sway both in history as a whole, and at particular periods and in particular lands. Everything which sets men in motion must go through their minds; but what form it will take in the mind will depend very much upon the circumstances. The workers have by no means become reconciled to capitalist machine-industry, even though they no longer simply break the machines to pieces as they still did in 1848 on the Rhine.

But while in all earlier periods the investigation of these driving causes of history was almost impossible—on account of the complicated and concealed inter-connections between them and their effects—our present period has so far simplified these inter-connections that the riddle could be solved. Since the establishment of large-scale industry, i.e., at least since the peace of Europe in 1815, it has been no longer a secret to any man in England that the whole political struggle there has turned on the claims to supremacy of two classes: the landed aristocracy and the middle class. In France, with the return of the Bourbons, the same fact was perceived; the historians of the Restoration period, from Thierry to Guizot, Mignet and Thiers, speak of it everywhere as the key to the understanding of all French history since the Middle Ages. And since 1830 the working class, the proletariat, has been recognized in both countries as a third competitor for power. Conditions had become so simplified that one would have had to close one's eyes deliberately not to see in the fight of these three great classes and in the conflict of their interests the driving force of modern history—at least in the two most advanced countries.

But how did these classes come into existence? If it was possible at first glance still to ascribe the origin of the great, formerly feudal landed property—at least in the first instance—to political causes, to taking possession by force, this could no longer be done in regard to the bourgeoisie and the proletariat. Here the origin and development of two great classes was seen to lie clearly and palpably in purely economic causes. And it was just as clear that in the struggle between landed property and the bourgeoisie, no less than in the struggle between the bourgeoisie and the proletariat, it was a question in the first instance of economic interests, to the furtherance of which political power was intended to serve merely as a means. Bourgeoisie and proletariat both arose in consequence of a transformation of the economic conditions, more precisely, of the mode of production. . . .

In modern history at least it is therefore proved that all political struggles are class struggles, and all class struggles for emancipation in the last resort, despite their necessarily political form —for every class struggle is a political struggle—turn ultimately on the question of economic emancipation. Therefore, here at least the state—the political order—is the subordinate, and civil society—the realm of economic relations—the decisive element. The traditional conception, to which Hegel, too, pays homage, saw in the state the determining element, and in civil society the element determined by it. Appearances correspond to this. As all the driving forces of the actions of any individual person must pass through his brain, and transform themselves into motives of his will in order to set him into action, so also all the needs of civil society—no matter which class happens to be the ruling one —must pass through the will of the state in order to secure general validity in the form of laws. That is the formal aspect of the matter—the one which is self-evident. The question arises, however, what is the content of this merely formal *will*—of the individual as well as of the state—and whence is this content derived? Why is just this intended and not something else? If we enquire into this we discover that in modern history the will of the state is, on the whole, determined by the changing needs of civil society, by the supremacy of this or that class, in the last resort, by the development of the productive forces and relations of exchange.

—ENGELS, *Ludwig Feuerbach* (1888), pp. 47–53.

[5]

THREE CRITERIA FOR A SCIENTIFIC SOCIOLOGY

Marx's basic idea that the development of the economic formation of society is a process of natural history cuts the ground from under this childish morality which lays claim to the title of sociology.* By what method did Marx arrive at this basic idea? He arrived at it by selecting from the various spheres of social life the economic sphere, by selecting from all social relations the "production relations," as being the basic and prime relations that determine all other relations. . . .

This idea of materialism in sociology was in itself a piece of genius. Naturally, "*for the time being*" it was only an hypothesis, but it was the first hypothesis to create the possibility of a strictly scientific approach to historical and social problems. Hitherto, being unable to descend to such simple and primary relations as the relations of production, the sociologists proceeded directly to investigate and study the political and legal forms. They stumbled on the fact that these forms arise out of certain ideas held by men in the period in question—and there they stopped. It appeared as if social relations were established by man consciously. But this deduction, which was fully expressed in the idea of the [Rousseau's] *Contrat Social* (traces of

* Lenin is here carrying on a polemic against the Russian sociologist, N. Mikhailovsky, who defined the task of sociology as follows: "to ascertain the social conditions under which any particular requirement of human nature is satisfied."—*Ed.*

which are very noticeable in all systems of utopian socialism), was in complete contradiction to all historical observations. Never has it been the case, nor is it the case now, that the members of society are aware of the sum-total of the social relations in which they live as something definite, integral, as something pervaded by some principle. On the contrary, the mass of people adapt themselves to these relations unconsciously, and are unaware of them as specific historical social relations; so much so, in fact, that the explanation, for instance, of the relations of exchange, under which people have lived for centuries, was discovered only in very recent times. Materialism has removed this contradiction by carrying the analysis deeper, to the very origin of these social ideas of man; and its conclusion that the course of ideas depends on the course of things is the only deduction compatible with scientific psychology.

Moreover, this hypothesis was the first to elevate sociology to the level of a science from yet another aspect. Hitherto, sociologists had found difficulty in distinguishing in the complex network of social phenomena which phenomena were important and which unimportant (that is the root of subjectivism in sociology) and had been unable to discover any objective criterion for such a distinction. Materialism provided an absolutely objective criterion by singling out the "relations of production" as the structure of society, and by making it possible to apply to these relations that general scientific criterion of repetition whose applicability to sociology the subjectivists denied. As long as they confined themselves to ideological social relations (i.e., such as, before taking shape, pass through man's consciousness—we are, of course, referring all the time to the consciousness of "social relations" and no others) they were unable to observe repetition and order in the social phenomena of the various countries, and their science was at best only a description of these phenomena, a collection of raw material. The analysis of material social relations (i.e., such as take shape without passing through man's consciousness; when exchanging products men enter into relations of production without even realizing that social relations of production are involved in the act) made it at once possible to observe repetition and order and to generalize the systems of the various countries so as to arrive at the single fundamental concept: the "formation of society." It was this generalization that alone made it possible to proceed from the description of social phenomena (and their evaluation from the standpoint of an ideal) to their strictly scientific analysis, which, let us say by way of example, selects "what" distinguishes one capitalist country from another and investigates "what" is common to all of them.

Thirdly and finally, another reason why this hypothesis was the first to make a "scientific" sociology possible was that the reduction of social relations to relations of production, and the latter to the level of forces of production, provided a firm basis for the conception that the development of the formations of society is a process of natural history. And it goes without saying that without such a view there can be no social science. (For instance, the subjectivists, although they admitted that historical phenomena conform to law, were incapable of regarding the evolution of historical phenomena as a process of natural history precisely because they confined themselves to the social ideas and aims of man and were unable to reduce these ideas and aims to material social relations.) . . .

Just as Darwin put an end to the view that the species of animals and plants are unconnected among themselves, fortuitous, "created by God" and immutable, and was the first to put biology on an absolutely scientific basis by establishing the mutability and succession of species, so Marx put an end to the view that society is a mechanical aggregation of individuals, which will tolerate any kind of modification at the will of the powers that be (or, what amounts to the same thing, at the will of society and the government) and which arises and changes in a fortuitous way, and was the first to put sociology on a scientific footing by establishing the concept of the economic formation of society as the sum-total of the given relations of production and by establishing the fact that the development of these formations is a process of natural history.

Now—since the appearance of *Capital*—the materialist conception of history is no longer a hypothesis, but a scientifically demonstrated proposition. And as long as no other attempt is made to give a scientific explanation of the functioning and development of any social formation—social formation, and not the customs and habits of any country or people, or even class, etc.—an attempt which would be just as capable as materialism of introducing order into the "pertinent facts" and of presenting a living picture of a given formation and at the same time of explaining it in a strictly scientific way, until then the materialist conception of history will be synonymous with social science. Materialism is not "primarily a scientific conception of history," as Mr. Mikhailovsky thinks, but the only scientific conception of history.

—LENIN, *What the 'Friends of the People' Are* (1894), *Selected Works,* vol. XI, pp. 417–22.

[6]

CLASSES AND IDEOLOGY

The ideas of the ruling class are in every epoch the ruling ideas; i.e. the class, which is the ruling material force of society, is at the same time its ruling intellectual force. The class which has the means of material production at its disposal, has control at the same time over the means of mental production, so that thereby, generally speaking, the ideas of those who lack the means of mental production are subject to it. The ruling ideas are nothing more than the ideal expression of the dominant material relationships, the dominant material relationships grasped as ideas; hence of the relationships which make the one class the ruling one, therefore the ideas of its dominance. The individuals composing the ruling class possess among other things consciousness, and therefore think. In so far, therefore, as they rule as a class and determine the extent and compass of an epoch, it is self-evident that they do this in their whole range, hence among other things rule also as thinkers, as producers of ideas, and regulate the production and distribution of the ideas of their age; thus their ideas are the ruling ideas of the epoch. For instance, in an age and in a country where royal power, aristocracy, and bourgeoisie are contending for mastery and where, therefore, mastery is shared, the doctrine of the separation of powers proves to be the dominant idea and is expressed as an "eternal law." The division of labor, which we saw above as one of the chief forces of history up till now, manifests itself also in the ruling class as the division of mental and material labor, so that inside this class one part appears as the thinkers of the class (its active, conceptive ideologists, who make the perfecting of the illusion of the class about itself their chief source of livelihood), while the others' attitude to these ideas and illusions is more passive and receptive, because they are in reality the active members of this class and have less time to make up illusions and ideas about themselves. Within this class this cleavage can even develop into a certain opposition and hostility between the two parts, which, however, in the case of a practical collision, in which the class itself is endangered, automatically comes to nothing, in which case there also vanishes the semblance that the ruling ideas were not the ideas of the ruling class and had a power distinct from the power of this class. The existence of revolutionary ideas in a particular period presupposes the existence of a revolutionary class; about the premises for the latter sufficient has already been said above.

If now in considering the course of history we detach the ideas of the ruling class from the ruling class itself and attribute to them an independent existence, if we confine ourselves to saying that these or those ideas were dominant, without bothering ourselves about the conditions of production and the producers of these ideas, if we then ignore the individuals and world conditions which are the source of the ideas, we can say, for instance, that during the time that the aristocracy was dominant, the concepts honor, loyalty, etc., were dominant, during the dominance of the bourgeoisie the concepts freedom, equality, etc. The ruling class itself on the whole imagines this to be so. This conception of history, which is common to all historians, particularly since the 18th century, will necessarily come up against the phenomenon that increasingly abstract ideas hold sway, i.e., ideas which increasingly take on the form of universality. For each new class which puts itself in the place of one ruling before it, is compelled, merely in order to carry through its aim, to represent its interest as the common interest of all the members of society, put in an ideal form; it will give its ideas the form of universality, and represent them as the only rational, universally valid ones. The class making a revolution appears from the very start, merely because it is opposed to a *class,* not as a class but as the representative of the whole of society; it appears as the whole mass of society confronting the one ruling class. It can do this because, to start with, its interest really is more connected with the common interest of all other non-ruling classes, because under the pressure of conditions its interest has not yet been able to develop as the particular interest of a particular class. Its victory, therefore, benefits also many individuals of the other classes which are not winning a dominant position, but only in so far as it now puts these individuals in a position to raise themselves into the ruling class. When the French bourgeoisie overthrew the power of the aristocracy, it thereby made it possible for many proletarians to raise themselves above the proletariat, but only in so far as they became bourgeois. Every new class, therefore, achieves its hegemony only on a broader basis than that of the class ruling previously, in return for which the opposition of the non-ruling class against the new ruling class later develops all the more sharply and profoundly. Both these things determine the fact that the struggle to be waged against this new ruling class, in its turn, aims at a more decided and radical negation of the previous conditions of society than could all previous classes which sought to rule.

This whole semblance, that the rule of a certain class is only the rule of certain ideas, comes to a natural end, of course, as soon as society ceases at last to be organized in the form of class rule, that is to say as soon as it is no longer necessary to represent a particular interest as general or "the general interest" as ruling.

—MARX and ENGELS, *The German Ideology* (1846), pp. 39–41.

[7]

THE ROLE OF ECONOMIC CONDITIONS, OF THE SUPERSTRUCTURE, AND OF CHANCE

(1) What we understand by the economic conditions which we regard as the determining basis of the history of society are the methods by which human beings in a given society produce their means of subsistence and exchange the products among themselves (in so far as division of labor exists). Thus the *entire technique* of production and transport is here included. According to our conception this technique also determines the method of exchange and, further, the division of products, and with it, after the dissolution of tribal society, the division into classes also and hence the relations of lordship and servitude and with them the state, politics, law, etc. Under economic conditions are

further included the geographical basis on which they operate and those remnants of earlier stages of economic development which have actually been transmitted and have survived—often only through tradition or the force of inertia; also of course the external milieu which surrounds this form of society.

If, as you say, technique largely depends on the state of science, science depends far more still on the *state* and the *requirements* of technique. If society has a technical need, that helps science forward more than ten universities. The whole of hydrostatics (Torricelli, etc.) was called forth by the necessity for regulating the mountain streams of Italy in the 16th and 17th centuries. We have only known anything reasonable about electricity since its technical applicability was discovered. But unfortunately it has become the custom in Germany to write the history of the sciences as if they had fallen from the skies.

(2) We regard economic conditions as the factor which ultimately determines historical development. But race is itself an economic factor. Here, however, two points must not be overlooked:

(*a*) Political, juridical, philosophical, religious, literary, artistic, etc., development is based on economic development. But all these react upon one another and also upon the economic base. It is not that the economic position is the *cause and alone active*, while everything else only has a passive effect. There is, rather, interaction on the basis of the economic necessity, which *ultimately* always asserts itself. The state, for instance, exercises an influence by tariffs, free trade, good or bad fiscal system; and even the deadly inanition and impotence of the German petty bourgeois, arising from the miserable economic position of Germany from 1640 to 1830 and expressing itself at first in pietism, then in sentimentality and cringing servility to princes and nobles, was not without economic effect. It was one of the greatest hindrances to recovery and was not shaken until the revolutionary and Napoleonic wars made the chronic misery an acute one. So it is not, as people try here and there conveniently to imagine, that the economic position produces an automatic effect. Men make their history themselves, only in given surroundings which condition it and on the basis of actual relations already existing, among which the economic relations, however much they may be influenced by the other political and ideological ones, are still ultimately the decisive ones, forming the red thread which runs through them and alone leads to understanding.

(*b*) Men make their history themselves, but not as yet with a collective will or according to a collective plan or even in a definitely defined, given society. Their efforts clash, and for that very reason all such societies are governed by *necessity,* which is supplemented by and appears under the forms of *accident.* The necessity which here asserts itself amidst all accident is again ultimately economic necessity. This is where the so-called great men come in for treatment. That such and such a man and precisely that man arises at that particular time in that given country is of course pure accident. But cut him out and there will be a demand for a substitute, and this substitute will be found, good or bad, but in the long run he will be found. That Napoleon, just that particular Corsican, should have been the military dictator whom the French Republic, exhausted by its own war, had rendered necessary, was an accident; but that, if a Napoleon had been lacking, another would have filled the place, is proved by the fact that the man has always been found as soon as he became necessary: Caesar, Augustus, Cromwell, etc. While Marx discovered the materialist conception of history, Thierry, Mignet, Guizot, and all the English historians up to 1850 are the proof that it was being striven for, and the discovery of the same conception by Morgan proves that the time was ripe for it and that indeed it *had* to be discovered.

So with all the other accidents, and apparent accidents, of history. The further the particular sphere which we are investigating is removed from the economic sphere and approaches that of pure abstract ideology, the more shall we find it exhibiting accidents in its development, the more will its curve run in a zigzag. So also you will find that the axis of this curve will approach more and more nearly parallel to the axis of the curve of economic development the longer the period considered and the wider the field dealt with. . . .

—ENGELS, Letter to Heinz Starkenburg (1894), MARX and ENGELS, *Selected Correspondence,* pp. 516–18.

[8]

THE ECONOMIC ELEMENT NOT THE ONLY DETERMINING ONE

According to the materialist conception of history the determining element in history is *ultimately* the production and reproduction in real life. More than this neither Marx nor I have ever asserted. If therefore somebody twists this into the statement that the economic element is the *only* determining one, he transforms it into a meaningless, abstract and absurd phrase. The economic situation is the basis, but the various elements of the superstructure—political forms of the class struggle and its consequences, constitutions established by the victorious class after a successful battle, etc.—forms of law—and then even the reflexes of all these actual struggles in the brains of the combatants: political, legal, philosophical theories, religious ideas and their further development into systems of dogma—also exercise their influence upon the course of the historical struggles and in many cases preponderate in determining their *form*. There is an interaction of all these elements, in which, amid all the endless *host* of accidents (*i.e.*, of things and events whose inner connection is so remote or so impossible to prove that we regard it as absent and can neglect it), the economic movement finally asserts itself as necessary. Otherwise the application of the theory to any period of history one chose would be easier than the solution of a simple equation of the first degree.

We make our own history, but in the first place under very definite presuppositions and conditions. Among these the economic ones are finally decisive. But the political, etc., ones and indeed even the traditions which haunt human minds, also play a part, although not the decisive one. The Prussian state arose and developed from historical, ultimately from economic causes. But it could scarcely be maintained without pedantry that among the many small states of North Germany, Brandenburg was specifically determined by economic necessity to become the great power embodying the economic, linguistic and, after the reformation, also the religious differences between north and south, and not by other elements as well (above all by its entanglement with Poland, owing to the possession of Prussia, and hence with international, political relations—which were indeed also decisive in the formation of the Austrian dynastic power). Without making oneself ridiculous it would be difficult to succeed in explaining in terms of economics the existence of every small state in Germany, past and present, or the origin of the High German consonant mutations, which the geographical wall of partition formed by the mountains from the Sudetic range to the Taunus extended to a regular division throughout Germany.

In the second place, however, history makes itself in such a way that the final result always arises from conflicts between many individual wills, of which each again has been made what it is by a host of particular conditions of life. Thus there are innumerable intersecting forces, an infinite series of parallelograms of forces which give rise to one resultant—the historical event. This again may itself be viewed as the product of a power which, taken as a whole, works *unconsciously* and without volition. For what each individual wills is obstructed by everyone else, and what emerges is something that no one willed. Thus past history proceeds in the manner of a natural process and is also essentially subject to the same laws of movement. But from the fact that individual wills—of which each desires what he is impelled to by his physical constitution and external, in the last resort economic, circumstances (either his own personal circumstances or those of society in general)—do not attain what they want, but are merged into a collective mean, a common resultant, it must not be concluded that their value = 0. On the contrary, each contributes to the resultant and is to this degree involved in it.

I would ask you to study this theory further from its original sources and not at second-hand, it is really much easier. Marx hardly wrote anything in which it did not play a part. But especially *The Eighteenth Brumaire of Louis Bonaparte* is a most excellent example of its application. There are also many allusions in *Capital.* Then I may also direct you to my writings: *Herr E. Dühring's Revolution in Science* and *Ludwig Feuerbach and the Outcome of Classical German Philosophy,* in which I have given the most detailed account of historical materialism which, so far as I know, exists.

Marx and I are ourselves partly to blame for the fact that younger writers sometimes lay more stress on the economic side than is due to it. We had to emphasize this main principle in opposition to our adversaries, who denied it, and we had not always the time, the place or the opportunity to allow the other elements involved in the interaction to come into their rights. But when it was a case of presenting a section of history, that is, of a practical application, the thing was different and there no error was possible. Unfortunately, however, it happens only too often that people think they have fully understood a theory and can apply it without more ado from the moment they have mastered its main principles, and those even not always correctly. And I cannot exempt many of the more recent "Marxists" from this reproach, for the most wonderful rubbish has been produced from this quarter too.

—ENGELS, Letter to Joseph Bloch (1890), MARX and ENGELS, *Selected Correspondence,* pp. 475–77.

[9]

INTERACTION OF ECONOMIC CONDITIONS, INSTITUTIONS, AND IDEOLOGY

Society gives rise to certain common functions which it cannot dispense with. The persons selected for these functions form a new branch of the division of labor *within society*. This gives them particular interests, distinct too from the interests of those who gave them their office; they make themselves independent of the latter and—the state is in being. And now the development is the same as it was with commodity trade and later with money trade; the new independent power, while having in the main to follow the movement of production, also, owing to its inward independence (the relative independence originally transferred to it and gradually further developed) reacts in its turn upon the conditions and course of production. It is the interaction of two unequal forces; on one hand the economic movement, on the other the new political power, which strives for as much independence as possible, and which, having once been established, is also endowed with a movement of its own. On the whole, the economic movement gets its way, but it has also to suffer reactions from the political movement which it established and endowed with relative independence itself, from the movement of the state power on the one hand and of the opposition simultaneously engendered on the other. Just as the movement of the industrial market is, in the main and with the reservations already indicated, reflected in the money market and, of course, in inverted form, so the struggle between the classes already existing and already in conflict with one another is reflected in the struggle between government and opposition, but also in inverted form, no longer directly but indirectly, not as a class struggle but as a fight for political principles, and so distorted that it has taken us thousands of years to get behind it again.

The reaction of the state power upon economic development can be one of three kinds: It can run in the same direction, and then development is more rapid; it can oppose the line of development, in which case nowadays state power in every great nation will go to pieces in the long run; or it can cut off the economic development from certain paths, and impose on it certain others. This case ultimately reduces itself to one of the two previous ones. But it is obvious that in cases two and three the political power can do great damage to the economic development and result in the squandering of great masses of energy and material.

Then there is also the case of the conquest and brutal destruction of economic resources, by which, in certain circumstances, a whole local or national economic development could formerly be ruined. Nowadays such a case usually has the opposite effect, at least among great nations; in the long run the defeated power often gains more economically, politically and morally than the victor.

It is similar with law. As soon as the new division of labor which creates professional lawyers becomes necessary, another new and independent sphere is opened up which, for all its general dependence on production and trade, still has its own capacity for reacting upon these spheres as well. In a modern state, law must not only correspond to the general economic position and be its expression, but must also be an expression which is *consistent in itself,* and which does not, owing to inner contradictions, look glaringly inconsistent. And in order to achieve this, the faithful reflection of economic conditions is more and more infringed upon. All the more so the more rarely it happens that a code of law is the blunt, unmitigated, unadulterated expression of the domination of a class—this in itself would already offend the "conception of justice." Even in the Code Napoleon the pure logical conception of justice held by the revolutionary bourgeoisie of 1792–96 is already adulterated in many ways, and in so far as it is embodied there has daily to undergo all sorts of attenuation owing to the rising power of the proletariat. Which does not prevent the Code Napoleon from being the statute book which serves as a basis for every new code of law in every part of the world. Thus to a great extent the course of the "development of law" only consists, first, in the attempt to do away with the contradictions arising from the direct translation of economic relations into legal principles, and to establish a harmonious system of law, and, then, in the repeated breaches made in this system by the influence and pressure of further economic development, which involves it in further contradictions (I am only speaking here of civil law for the moment).

The reflection of economic relations as legal principles is necessarily also a topsy turvy one; it happens without the person who is acting being conscious of it; the jurist imagines he is operating with *a priori* principles, whereas they are really only economic reflexes; so everything is upside down. And it seems to me obvious that this inversion, which, so long as it remains unrecognized, forms what we call *ideological conception,* reacts in its turn upon the economic basis and may, within certain limits, modify it. The basis of the law of inheritance—assuming that the stages reached in the development of the family are equal—is an economic one. But it would be difficult to prove, for instance, that the absolute liberty of the testator in England and the severe restrictions imposed upon him in France are only due in every detail to economic causes. Both react back, however, on the economic sphere to a very considerable extent, because they influence the division of property.

As to the realms of ideology which soar still higher in the air, religion, philosophy, etc., these have a prehistoric stock, found already in existence and taken over in the historic period, of what we should today call bunk. These various false conceptions of nature, of man's own being, of spirits, magic forces, etc., have for the most part only a negative economic basis; but the low economic development of the prehistoric period is supplemented and also partially conditioned and even caused by the false conceptions of nature. And even though economic necessity was the main driving force of the progressive knowledge of nature and becomes ever more so, it would surely be pedantic to try and find economic causes for all this primitive nonsense. The history of science is the history of the gradual clearing away of this nonsense or of its replacement by fresh but already less absurd nonsense. The people who deal with this belong in their turn to special spheres in the division of labor and appear to themselves to be working in an independent field. And in so far as they form an independent group within the social division of labor, in so far do their productions, including their errors, react back as an influence upon the whole development of society, even on its economic development. But all the same they themselves remain under the dominating influence of economic development. In philosophy, for instance, this can be most readily proved in the bourgeois period. Hobbes was the first modern materialist (in the 18th-century sense) but he was an absolutist in a period when absolute monarchy was at its height throughout the whole of Europe and when the fight of absolute monarchy versus the people was beginning in England. Locke, both in religion and politics, was the child of the class compromise of 1688. The English deists and their more consistent successors, the French materialists, were the true philosophers of the bourgeoisie, the French even of the bourgeois revolution. The German petty bourgeois runs through German philosophy from Kant to Hegel, sometimes positively and sometimes negatively. But the philosophy of every epoch, since it is a definite sphere in the division of labor, has as its presupposition certain definite intellectual material handed down to it by its predecessors, from which it takes its start. And that is why economically backward countries can still play first fiddle in philosophy: France in the 18th century compared with England, on whose philosophy the French based themselves, and later Germany in comparison with both. But the philosophy both of France and Germany and the general blossoming of literature at that time were also the result of a rising economic development. I consider the ultimate supremacy of economic development established in these spheres too, but it comes to pass within conditions imposed by the particular sphere itself: In philosophy, for instance, through the operation of economic influences (which again generally only act under political, etc., disguises) upon the existing philosophic material handed down by predecessors. Here economy creates nothing absolutely new (*a novo*), but it determines the way in which the existing material of thought is altered and further developed, and that too for the most part indirectly, for it is the political, legal, and moral reflexes which exercise the greatest direct influence upon philosophy.

About religion I have said the most necessary things in the last section on Feuerbach.*

If therefore Barth supposes that we deny any and every reaction of the political, etc., reflexes of the economic movement upon the movement itself, he is simply tilting at windmills. He has only got to look at Marx's *Eighteenth Brumaire,* which deals almost exclusively with the *particular* part played by political struggles and events; of course, within their *general* dependence upon economic conditions. Or *Capital,* the section on the working day, for instance, where legislation, which is surely a political act, has such a trenchant effect. Or the section on the history of the bourgeoisie (Chapter XXIV). Or why do we fight for the political dictatorship of the proletariat if political power is economically impotent? Force (that is, state power) is also an economic power.

But I have no time to criticize the book now. I must first get Vol. III [of Marx's *Capital*—Ed.] out and besides I think too that Bernstein, for instance, could deal with it quite effectively.

What these gentlemen all lack is dialectic. They never see anything but here cause and there effect. That this is a hollow abstraction, that such metaphysical polar opposites only exist in the real world during crises, while the whole vast process proceeds in the form of interaction (though of very unequal forces, the economic movement being by far the strongest, most elemental and most decisive) and that here everything is relative and nothing is absolute—this they never begin to see. Hegel has never existed for them.

—ENGELS, Letter to Conrad Schmidt (1890), MARX and ENGELS, *Selected Correspondence,* pp. 480–84.

* See *Ludwig Feuerbach,* pp. 65–69.—*Ed.*

[10]

HOW MAN MAKES HIS OWN HISTORY: CONTRADICTION BETWEEN HIS AIMS AND RESULTS

The specialization of the hand—this implies the *tool,* and the tool implies specific human activity, the transforming reaction of man on nature, production. Animals in the narrower sense also have tools, but only as limbs of their bodies—the ant, the bee, the beaver; animals also produce, but their productive effect on surrounding nature in relation to the latter amounts to nothing at all. Man alone has succeeded in impressing his stamp on nature, not only by shifting the plant and animal world from one place to another, but also by so altering the aspect and climate of his dwelling place, and even the plants and animals themselves, that the consequences of his activity can disappear only with the general extinction of the terrestrial globe. And he has accomplished this primarily and essentially by means of *the hand.* Even the steam engine, so far his most powerful tool for the transformation of nature, depends, because it is a tool, in the last resort on the hand. But step by step with the development of the hand went that of the brain; first of all consciousness of the conditions for separate practically useful actions, and later, among the more favored peoples and arising from the preceding, insight into the natural laws governing them. And with the rapidly growing knowledge of the laws of nature the means for reacting on nature also grew; the hand alone would never have achieved the steam engine if the brain of man had not attained a correlative development with it, and parallel to it, and partly owing to it.

With men we enter *history*. Animals also have a history, that of their derivation and gradual evolution to their present position. This history, however, is made for them, and in so far as they themselves take part in it, this occurs without their knowledge or desire. On the other hand, the more that human beings become removed from animals in the narrower sense of the word, the more they make their own history consciously, the less becomes the influence of unforeseen effects and uncontrolled forces on this history, and the more accurately does the historical result correspond to the aim laid down in advance. If, however, we apply this measure to human history, to that of even the most developed peoples of the present day, we find that there still exists here a colossal disproportion between the proposed aims and the results arrived at, that unforeseen effects predominate, and that the uncontrolled forces are far more powerful than those set into motion according to plan. And this cannot be otherwise as long as the most essential historical activity of men, the one which has raised them from bestiality to humanity and which forms the material foundation of all their other activities, namely the production of their requirements of life, that is today social production, is above all subject to the interplay of unintended effects from uncontrolled forces and achieves its desired end only by way of exception and, much more frequently, the exact opposite. In the most advanced industrial countries we have subdued the forces of nature and pressed them into the service of mankind; we have thereby infinitely multiplied production, so that a child now produces more than 100 adults previously did. And what is the result? Increasing overwork and increasing misery of the masses, and every ten years a great collapse. Darwin did not know what a bitter satire he wrote on mankind, and especially on his countrymen, when he showed that free competition, the struggle for existence, which the economists celebrate as the highest historical achievement, is the normal state of the *animal kingdom.* Only conscious organization of social production, in which production and distribution are carried on in a planned way, can lift mankind above the rest of the animal world as regards the social aspect, in the same way that production in general has done this for men in their aspect as species. Historical evolution makes such an organization daily more indispensable, but also with every day more possible. From it will date a new epoch of history, in which mankind itself, and with mankind all branches of its activity, and especially natural science, will experience an advance that will put everything preceding it in the deepest shade.

—ENGELS, *Dialectics of Nature* (1882), pp. 17–20.

[11]

HISTORY AND IDEOLOGY

A. Three Ways of Making Speculative History

Once the ruling ideas have been separated from the ruling individuals and, above all, from the relationships which result from a given stage of the mode of production, and in this way the conclusion has been reached that history is always under the sway of ideas, it is very easy to abstract from these various ideas "the idea," "*die Idee,*" etc., as the dominant force in history, and thus to understand all these separate ideas and concepts as "forms of self-determination" on the part of *the* concept developing in history. It follows then naturally, too, that all the relationships of men can be derived from the concept of man, man as conceived, the essence of man, *Man*. This has been done by the speculative philosophers. Hegel himself confesses at the end of *The Philosophy of History* that he "has considered the progress of *the concept* only" and has represented in history "the true theodicy." Now one can go back again to the "producers of the concept," to the theoreticians, ideologists and philosophers, and one comes then to the conclusion that the philosophers, the thinkers as such, have at all times been dominant in history, a conclusion, as we see, already expressed by Hegel. The whole trick of proving the hegemony of the spirit in history (hierarchy, Stirner calls it) is thus confined to the following three tricks.

1. One must separate the ideas of those ruling for empirical reasons, under empirical conditions and as empirical individuals, from these actual rulers, and thus recognize the rule of ideas or illusions in history.

2. One must bring an order into this rule of ideas, prove a mystical connection among the successive ruling ideas, which is managed by understanding them as "acts of self-determination on the part of the concept" (this is possible because by virtue of their empirical basis these ideas are really connected with one another and because, conceived as *mere* ideas, they become self-distinctions, distinctions made by thought).

3. To remove the mystical appearance of this "self-determining concept" it is changed into a person—"self-consciousness"—or, to appear thoroughly materialistic, into a series of persons, who

represent the "concept" in history, into the "thinkers," the "philosophers," the ideologists, who again are understood as the manufacturers of history, as "the council of guardians," as the rulers. Thus the whole body of materialistic elements has been removed from history and now full rein can be given to the speculative steed.

Whilst in ordinary life every shopkeeper is very well able to distinguish between what somebody professes to be and what he really is, our historians have not yet won even this trivial insight. They take every epoch at its word and believe that everything it says and imagines about itself is true.

This historical method which reigned in Germany (and especially the reason why), must be understood from its connection with the illusion of ideologists in general, e.g. the illusions of the jurists, politicians (of the practical statesmen among them, too), from the dogmatic dreamings and distortions of these fellows; this illusion is explained perfectly easily from their practical position in life, their job, and the division of labor.

—MARX AND ENGELS, *The German Ideology* (1846), pp. 42*f*.

B. THE NATURE OF IDEOLOGY

Ideology is a process accomplished by the so-called thinker consciously, indeed, but with a false consciousness. The real motives impelling him remain unknown to him, otherwise it would not be an ideological process at all. Hence he imagines false or apparent motives. Because it is a process of thought he derives both its form and its content from pure thought, either his own or that of his predecessors. He works with mere thought material which he accepts without examination as the product of thought, he does not investigate further for a more remote process independent of thought; indeed its origin seems obvious to him, because as all action is produced through the medium of thought it also appears to him to be ultimately based upon thought. The ideologist who deals with history (history is here simply meant to comprise all the spheres—political, juridical, philosophical, theological—belonging to society and not only to nature), the ideologist dealing with history then, possesses in every sphere of science material which has formed itself independently out of the thought of previous generations and has gone through an independent series of developments in the brains of these successive generations. True, external facts belonging to its own or other spheres may have exercised a codetermining influence on this development, but the tacit presupposition is that these facts themselves are also only the fruits of a process of thought, and so we still remain within that realm of pure thought which has successfully digested the hardest facts.

It is above all this appearance of an independent history of state constitutions, of systems of law, of ideological conceptions in every separate domain, which dazzles most people. If Luther and Calvin "overcome" the official Catholic religion, or Hegel "overcomes" Fichte and Kant, or if the constitutional Montesquieu is indirectly "overcome" by Rousseau with his "Social Contract," each of these events remains within the sphere of theology, philosophy or political science, represents a stage in the history of these particular spheres of thought and never passes outside the sphere of thought. And since the bourgeois illusion of the eternity and the finality of capitalist production has been added as well, even the victory of the physiocrats and Adam Smith over the mercantilists is accounted as a sheer victory of thought; not as the reflection in thought of changed economic facts but as the finally achieved correct understanding of actual conditions subsisting always and everywhere—in fact if Richard Coeur de Lion and Philip Augustus had introduced free trade instead of getting mixed up in the crusades we should have been spared 500 years of misery and stupidity.

This side of the matter, which I can only indicate here, we have all, I think, neglected more than it deserves. It is the old story—form is always neglected at first for content. As I say, I have done that too, and the mistake has always only struck me later. So I am not only far from reproaching you with this in any way, but as the older of the guilty parties I have no right to do so, on the contrary; but I would like all the same to draw your attention to this point for the future. Hanging together with this too is the fatuous notion of the ideologists that because we deny an independent historical development to the various ideological spheres which play a part in history we also deny them any effect upon history. The basis of this is the common undialectical conception of cause and effect as rigidly opposite poles, the total disregarding of interaction; these gentlemen often almost deliberately forget that once an historic element has been brought into the world by other elements, ultimately by economic facts, it also reacts in its turn and may react on its environment and even on its own causes.

—ENGELS, Letter to F. Mehring (1893), MARX and ENGELS, *Selected Correspondence,* pp. 511*f*.

[12]

SOCIETY, CIVILIZATION, AND THE STATE

The state is . . . by no means a power imposed on society from without; just as little is it "the reality of the moral idea," "the image and the reality of reason," as Hegel maintains. Rather, it is a product of society at a particular stage of development; it is the admission that this society has involved itself in insoluble self-contradiction and is cleft into irreconcilable antagonisms which it is powerless to exorcise. But in order that these antagonisms, classes with conflicting economic interests, shall not consume themselves and society in fruitless struggle, a power, apparently standing above society, has become necessary to moderate the conflict and keep it within the grounds of "order"; and this power, arisen out of society, but placing itself above it and increasingly alienating itself from it, is the state. . . .

As the state arose from the need to keep class antagonisms in check, but also arose in the thick of the fight between the classes, it is normally the state of the most powerful, economically ruling class, which by its means becomes also the politically ruling class, and so acquires new means of holding down and exploiting the oppressed class. The ancient state was, above all, the state of the slaveowners for holding down the slaves, just as the feudal state was the organ of the nobility for holding down the peasant serfs and bondsmen, and the modern representative state is the instrument for exploiting wage-labor by capital. Exceptional periods, however, occur when the warring classes are so nearly equal in forces that the state power, as apparent mediator, acquires for the moment a certain independence in relation to both. This applies to the absolute monarchy of the 17th and 18th centuries, which balances the nobility and the bourgeoisie against one another; and to the Bonapartism of the First and particularly of the Second French Empire, which played off the proletariat against the bourgeoisie and the bourgeoisie against the proletariat. . . .

The state, therefore, has not existed from all eternity. There have been societies which have managed without it, which had no notion of the state or state power. At a definite stage of economic development, which necessarily involved the cleavage of society into classes, the state became a necessity because of this cleavage. We are now rapidly approaching a stage in the development of production at which the existence of these classes has not only ceased to be a necessity, but becomes a positive hindrance to production. They will fall as inevitably as they once arose. The state inevitably falls with them. The society which organizes production anew on the basis of free and equal association of the producers will put the whole state machinery where it will then belong—into the museum of antiquities, next to the spinning wheel and the bronze ax. . . .

The binding force of civilized society is the state, which in all the typical periods is exclusively the state of the ruling class, and in all cases essentially a machine for keeping down the oppressed and exploited class. Other marks of civilization are: on the one hand, the permanent antithesis between town and country as the basis of the entire division of social labor; on the other hand, the introduction of the bequest, by which the property holder is able to dispose of his property even after his death. This institution, which was a direct blow at the old gentile constitution, was unknown in Athens until the time of Solon; in Rome it was introduced very early, but we do not know when. Among the Germans it was introduced by the priests in order that the honest German might without hindrance bequeath his property to the Church.

With this fundamental constitution, civilization has accomplished things for which the old gentile society was totally unfitted. But it accomplished them by playing on the most sordid instincts and passions of man, and by developing them at the expense of all his other faculties. Naked greed has been the moving spirit of civilization from the first day of its existence to the present time; wealth, more wealth and wealth again; wealth, not for society, but for this miserable individual, was its sole and determining aim. If, in the pursuit of this aim, the increasing development of science and repeated periods of the fullest blooming of art fell into its lap, it was only because without them the full realization of the attributes of wealth would have been impossible in our time.

Since the exploitation of one class by another is the basis of civilization, its whole development moves in a continuous contradiction. Every advance in the sphere of production is at the same time a retrogression in the conditions of the oppressed class, that is, of the great majority. What is a boon for one is bane for another; the emancipation of one class always means the oppression of another class. The most striking proof of this is furnished by the introduction of machinery, the effects of which are well known today. And while among barbarians, as we have seen, hardly any distinction could be made between rights and duties, civilization makes the difference and contradiction between these two plain even to the dullest mind by giving one class nearly all the rights and assigning to the other class nearly all the duties.

But this is not what ought to be. What is good for the ruling class should be good for the whole of society, with which the ruling class identifies itself. That is why the more civilization advances, the more it is compelled to cover the evils it necessarily creates with the cloak of love, to excuse them, or to deny their existence; in short, to introduce conventional hypocrisy—unknown both in previous forms of society and in the earliest stages of civilization—that culminates in the declaration: The exploiting class exploits the oppressed class solely in the interest of the exploited class itself; and if the latter fails to recognize this, and even becomes rebellious, it thereby shows the worst ingratitude to its benefactors, the exploiters.

—ENGELS, *The Origin of the Family, Private Property and the State* (1884), pp. 155–62.

[13]

A SUMMARY STATEMENT: HISTORICAL MATERIALISM THE BASIS OF MODERN SOCIALISM

The materialist conception of history starts from the principle that production, and with production the exchange of its products, is the basis of every social order; that in every society which has appeared in history the distribution of the products, and with it the division of society into classes or estates, is determined by what is produced and how it is produced, and how the product is exchanged. According to this conception, the ultimate causes of all social changes and political revolutions are to be sought, not in the minds of men, in their increasing insight into eternal truth and justice, but in changes in the mode of production and exchange; they are to be sought not in the *philosophy* but in the *economics* of the epoch concerned. The growing realization that existing social institutions are irrational and unjust, that reason has become nonsense and good deeds a scourge is only a sign that changes have been taking place quietly in the methods of production and forms of exchange with which the social order, adapted to previous economic conditions, is no longer in accord. This also involves that the means through which the abuses that have been revealed can be got rid of must likewise be present, in more or less developed form, in the altered conditions of productions. These means are not to be *invented* by the mind, but *discovered* by means of the mind in the existing material facts of production.

Where then, on this basis, does modern socialism stand?

The existing social order, as is now fairly generally admitted, is the creation of the present ruling class, the bourgeoisie. The mode of production peculiar to the bourgeoisie—called, since Marx, the capitalist mode of production—was incompatible with the local privileges and privileges of birth as well as with the reciprocal personal ties of the feudal system; the bourgeoisie shattered the feudal system, and on its ruins established the bourgeois social order, the realm of free competition, freedom of movement, equal rights for commodity owners, and all the other bourgeois glories. The capitalist mode of production could now develop freely. From the time when steam and the new tool-making machinery had begun to transform the former manufacture into large-scale industry, the productive forces evolved under bourgeois direction developed at a pace that was previously unknown and to an unprecedented degree. But just as manufacture, and the handicraft industry which had been further developed under its influence, had previously come into conflict with the feudal fetters of the guilds, so large-scale industry, as it develops more fully, comes into conflict with the barriers within which the capitalist mode of production holds it confined. The new forces of production have already outgrown the bourgeois form of using them; and this conflict between productive forces and mode of production is not a conflict which has risen in men's heads, as for example the conflict between original sin and divine justice; but it exists in the facts, objectively, outside of us, independently of the will or purpose even of the men who brought it about. Modern socialism is nothing but the reflex in thought of this actual conflict, its ideal reflection in the minds first of the class which is directly suffering under it—the working class. . . .

[The] solution can only consist in the recognition in practice of the social nature of the modern productive forces, in bringing, therefore, the mode of production, appropriation, and exchange into accord with the social character of the means of production. And this can only be brought about by society, openly and without deviation, taking possession of the productive forces which have outgrown all control other than that of society itself. Thereby the social character of the means of production and of the products—which today operates against the producers themselves, periodically breaking through the mode of production and exchange and enforcing itself only as a blind law of nature, violently and destructively—is quite consciously asserted by the producers, and is transformed from a cause of disorder and periodic collapse into the most powerful lever of production itself.

The forces operating in society work exactly like the forces operating in nature—blindly, violently, destructively, so long as we do not understand them and fail to take them into account. But when once we have recognized them and understood how they work, their direction and their effects, the gradual subjection of them to our will and the use of them for the attainment of our aims depend entirely upon ourselves. And this is quite especially true of the mighty productive forces of the present day. So long as we obstinately refuse to understand their nature and their character—and the capitalist mode of production and its defenders set themselves against any such attempt—so long do these forces operate in spite of us, against us, and so long do they control us, as we have shown in detail. But once their nature is grasped, in the hands of the producers working in association they can be transformed from demoniac masters into willing servants. It is the difference between the destructive force of electricity in the lightning of a thunderstorm and the tamed electricity of the telegraph and the arc light; the difference between a conflagration and fire in the service of man. This treatment of the productive forces of the present day, on the basis of their real nature at last recognized by society, opens the way to the replacement of the anarchy of social production by a socially planned regulation of production in accordance with the needs both of society as a whole and of each individual. The capitalist mode of appropriation, in which the product enslaves first the producer, and then also the appropriator, will thereby be replaced by the mode of appropriation of the products based on the nature of the modern means of production themselves; on the one hand direct social appropriation as a means to the maintenance and extension of production, and on the other hand direct individual appropriation as a means to life and pleasure. . . .

Since the emergence in history of the capitalist mode of production, the taking over of all means of production by society has often been dreamed of by individuals as well as by whole sects, more or less vaguely and as an ideal of the future. But it could only become possible, it could only become a historical necessity, when the material conditions for its realization had come into existence. Like every other social advance, it becomes realizable not through the perception that the existence of classes is in contradiction with justice, equality, etc., not through the mere will to abolish these classes, but through certain new economic conditions. The division of society into an exploiting and an exploited class, a ruling and an oppressed class, was the necessary outcome of the low development of production hitherto. So long as the sum of social labor yielded a product which only slightly exceeded what was necessary for the bare existence of all; so long, therefore, as all or almost all the time of the great majority of the members of society was absorbed in labor, so long was society necessarily divided into classes. Alongside of this great majority exclusively absorbed in labor there developed a class, freed from direct productive labor, which managed the general business of society; the direction of labor, affairs of state, justice, science, art, and so forth. It is therefore the law of the division of labor which lies at the root of the division into classes. But this does not mean that this division into classes was not established by violence and robbery, by deception and fraud, or that the ruling class, once in the saddle, has ever failed to strengthen its domination at the cost of the working class and to convert its social management into the exploitation of the masses.

But if, on these grounds, the division into classes has a certain historical justification, it has this only for a given period of time, for given social conditions. It was based on the insufficiency of production; it will be swept away by the full development of the modern productive forces. And in fact the abolition of social classes has as its presupposition a stage of historical development at which the existence not merely of some particular ruling class or other but of any ruling class at all, that is to say, of class difference itself, has become an anachronism, is out of date. It therefore presupposes that the development of production has reached a level at which the appropriation of means of production and of products, and with these, of political supremacy, the monopoly of education and intellectual leadership by a special class of society, has become not only superfluous but also economically, politically and intellectually a hindrance to development.

This point has now been reached. Their political and intellectual bankruptcy is hardly still a secret to the bourgeoisie themselves, and their economic bankruptcy recurs regularly every ten years. In each crisis society is smothered under the weight of its own productive forces and products of which it can make no use, and stands helpless in face of the absurd contradiction that the producers have nothing to consume because there are no consumers. The expanding force of the means of production bursts asunder the bonds imposed upon them by the capitalist mode of production. Their release from these bonds is the sole condition necessary for an unbroken and constantly more rapidly progressing development of the productive forces, and therewith of a practically limitless growth of production itself. Nor is this all. The appropriation by society of the means of production puts an end not only to the artificial restraints on production which exist today, but also to the positive waste and destruction of productive forces and products which is now the inevitable accompaniment of production and reaches its zenith in crises. Further, it sets free for society as a whole a mass of means of production and products by putting an end to the senseless luxury and extravagance of the present ruling class and its political representatives. The possibility of securing for every member of society, through social production, an existence which is not only fully sufficient from a material standpoint and becoming richer from day to day, but also guarantees to them the completely unrestricted development and exercise of their physical and mental faculties—this possibility now exists for the first time, but it *does exist.*

The seizure of the means of production by society puts an end to commodity production, and therewith to the domination of the product over the producer. Anarchy in social production is replaced by conscious organization on a planned basis. The struggle for individual existence comes to an end. And at this point, in a certain sense, man finally cuts himself off from the animal world, leaves the conditions of animal existence behind him and enters conditions which are really human. The conditions of existence forming man's environment, which up to now have dominated man, at this point pass under the domination and control of man, who now for the first time becomes the real conscious master of nature, because and in so far as he has become master of his own social organization. The laws of his own social activity, which have hitherto confronted him as external, dominating laws of nature, will then be applied by man with complete understanding, and hence will be dominated by man. Men's own social organization which has hitherto stood in opposition to them as if arbitrarily decreed by nature and history, will then become the voluntary act of men themselves. The objective, external forces which have hitherto dominated history, will then pass under the control of men themselves. It is only from this point that men, with full consciousness, will fashion their own history; it is only from this point that the social causes set in motion by men will have, predominantly and in constantly increasing measure, the effects willed by men. It is humanity's leap from the realm of necessity into the realm of freedom.

To carry through this world-emancipating act is the historical mission of the modern proletariat. And it is the task of scientific socialism, the theoretical expression of the proletarian movement, to establish the historical conditions and, with these, the nature of this act, and thus to bring to the consciousness of the now oppressed class the conditions and nature of the act which it is its destiny to accomplish.

—ENGELS, *Anti-Dühring* (1878), pp. 292*f;* 305–10.

PART SIX

RELIGION

All religion . . . is nothing but the fantastic reflection in men's minds of those forces which control their daily life.

—ENGELS, *Anti-Dühring* (1878), p. 344.

Introduction

FEW ASPECTS of Marxist thought have been more consistently misunderstood and distorted than its position on religion. It is as if Marx and Engels together, in all their lives, had said nothing more on the score than "Religion is the opium of the people," and that Marxists ever since have confined themselves to repeating this phrase. The fact is that while Marx was probably not the first to say it, others since, independently, have said the same thing. Four years after Marx wrote the involved and richly textured passage in which this phrase occurs, Charles Kingsley, a Canon of the Church of England, said that the Bible was used as an "opium dose for keeping beasts of burden patient while they were being overloaded."

The following passages reveal something of the complexity of the historical, social, and psychological levels on which Marx, Engels, and Lenin discussed religion. They had a certain sympathy for the atheism of the 18th century French *philosophes,* combined with considerable intellectual disdain for what they called the "bourgeois atheism" of the 19th century. There is nothing coarse-grained in their analyses. Religion is seen as a many-faceted reflection of the real world, including deep-seated human needs for security, consolation, and beauty. They do not want to take away from people the solace, comfort or beauty that religion brings into their lives. They do want to do away with the need for this particular *form* of achieving these satisfactions by abolishing the conditions that require the "illusions" religion offers.

The second leading idea found in these selections is that religious beliefs are not merely illusory; they stand in the way of man's mastering both nature and his social relations in the interests of a better and fuller life. If religion is used by exploiting classes as an "opium dose" to make working people accept their teachings and the authority of the clergy, then, ipso facto, it is inextricably intertwined with the class struggle. These passages should make it clear that the founders of Marxism did not believe they brought religion into the class struggle; they found it there. They were convinced, in fact, that the major conflicts in the history of religion were themselves forms of the class struggle.

This approach in no way overlooks the complex role religion has played in great social struggles. They saw, for example, in the origins of Christianity the role of the mass revolts that marked the decay of the Roman world. In the rise of Islam they called attention to the internal struggles between the Bedouins and the townspeople, the liberation of the Arabian peninsula from the Abyssinians, the desire to reestablish long dormant trade routes, and the awakening of an Arabian national consciousness. Similarly, their view of the Protestant Reformation was one of a vast complex of class struggles, taking place in different ways in various countries, but summed up in the sentence: "The ineradicability of the Protestant heresy corresponded to the invincibility of the rising bourgeoisie." (Engels, *Feuerbach,* p. 57*f*.)

The Lenin selections further develop the dialectics of religion and the class struggle by emphasizing that although religion may retard the struggle for socialism, the opposition to religion must always be subordinated to the long-range interests of the proletariat. On the other hand, workers and peasants and intellectuals who are religious and believe in socialism must not be estranged because of their religious beliefs. These beliefs can themselves, in certain circumstances, become powerful revolutionary forces. Not only in the class struggle but under socialism, Lenin believed, religious freedom must be maintained.

As will be easily seen in the following materials, Marxism

differs from the atheism of "metaphysical" materialism by not ascribing all evil to religion and all good to atheism. It is able to avoid this pitfall, as well as that of ascribing all that is good in the world to religion, by refusing to regard religion as existing by itself, independent of the driving forces of society and history. Marxism does not blame the Crusades on *religion,* nor the persecution of such Copernicans as Bruno and Galileo. Neither does it credit *religion* with giving us morality and the "brotherhood of man." It regards all these things, good and bad, as natural manifestations of social forces and movements expressing themselves in religious terms because religion has been the dominant form of ideology throughout almost all recorded history. Progressive and reactionary ideas, the vested interests of a ruling class or the demands of a submerged class, equally presented themselves in men's minds, so long as men conceived the world in spiritualist terms, in religious guise. The recognition of this important truth avoids making religion a "thing-in-itself." Marxism holds that the student of religion must seek its roots, its varied forms, and its constant changes and developments, not in the unfolding of a "divine idea," nor in the nature of man (Feuerbach), but in the concrete conditions of life, the forces of production, and the accompanying forms of social organization, the family, the state, and so on.

Marx and Engels wrote an enormous body of material on religion, especially during the middle 1840's when religion was a central issue among German intellectuals, with Ludwig Feuerbach's critique of Christianity, Bruno Bauer's studies of the origins of Christianity, and David Strauss' *Life of Jesus* being discussed intensively. Frequent suggestions of this occur in *Appendix I* as part of the materials from their formative period. Some of the selections in this section date from the same years but are nevertheless sufficiently clear to the modern reader to stand by themselves.

[1]

RELIGION "THE OPIUM OF THE PEOPLE"

The basis of irreligious criticism is: Man makes religion, religion does not make man. In other words, religion is the self-consciousness and self-feeling of man who has either not yet found himself or has already lost himself again. But man is no abstract being squatting outside the world. Man is the world of man, the state, society. This state, this society, produce religion, a reversed world-consciousness, because they are a reversed world. Religion is the general theory of that world, its encyclopedic compendium, its logic in a popular form, its spiritualistic point d'honneur, its enthusiasm, its moral sanction, its solemn completion, its universal ground for consolation and justification. It is the fantastic realization of the human essence because the human essence has no true reality. The struggle against religion is therefore mediately the fight against the other world, of which religion is the spiritual aroma.

Religious distress is at the same time the expression of real distress and the protest against real distress. Religion is the sigh of the oppressed creature, the heart of a heartless world, just as it is the spirit of a spiritless situation. It is the opium of the people.

The abolition of religion as the illusory happiness of the people is required for their real happiness. The demand to give up the illusions about its condition is the demand to give up a condition which needs illusions. The criticism of religion is therefore in embryo the criticism of the vale of woe, the halo of which is religion.

Criticism has plucked the imaginary flowers from the chain not so that man will wear the chain without any fantasy or consolation but so that he will shake off the chain and cull the living flower. The criticism of religion disillusions man to make him think and act and shape his reality like a man who has been disillusioned and has come to reason, so that he will revolve round himself and therefore round his true sun. Religion is only the illusory sun which revolves round man as long as he does not revolve round himself.

The task of history, therefore, once the world beyond the truth has disappeared, is to establish the truth of this world. The immediate task of philosophy, which is at the service of history, once the saintly form of human self-alienation has been unmasked, is to unmask self-alienation in its unholy forms. Thus the criticism of heaven turns into the criticism of the earth, the criticism of religion into the criticism of right and the criticism of theology into the criticism of politics.

—Marx, "Introduction to the Critique of Hegel's Philosophy of Right" (1844), Marx and Engels, *On Religion*, pp. 41*f*.

[2]

THE RELIGIOUS WORLD: THE REFLEX OF THE REAL WORLD

A. Religious Sentiment a Social Product

Feuerbach starts out from the fact of religious self-alienation, the duplication of the world into a religious, imaginary world and a real one. His work consists in the dissolution of the religious world into its secular basis. He overlooks the fact that after completing this work, the chief thing still remains to be done. For the fact that the secular foundation lifts itself above itself and establishes itself in the clouds as an independent realm is only to be explained by the self-cleavage and self-contradictoriness of this secular basis. The latter must itself, therefore, first be understood in its contradiction and then, by the removal of the contradiction, revolutionized in practice. Thus, for instance, once the earthly family is discovered to be the secret of the holy family, the former must then itself be theoretically criticized and radically changed in practice.

Feuerbach resolves the religious essence into the human.* But the human essence is no abstraction inherent in each single individual. In its reality it is the *ensemble* of the social relations.

Feuerbach, who does not attempt the criticism of this real essence, is consequently compelled:

1. To abstract from the historical process and to fix the religious sentiment as something for itself and to presuppose an abstract—*isolated*—human individual.

2. The human essence, therefore, can with him be comprehended only as "genus," as a dumb internal generality which merely *naturally* unites the many individuals.

Feuerbach, consequently, does not see that the "religious sentiment" is itself a *social product*, and that the abstract individual whom he analyzes belongs in reality to a particular form of society.

—Marx, "Theses on Feuerbach," IV, VI, VII (1845). [See Appendix I for all eleven theses.]

* In his "*Essence of Christianity*."—*Ed.*

B. When Will Religion Vanish?

The religious world is but the reflex of the real world. And for a society based upon the production of commodities, in which the producers in general enter into social relations with one another by treating their products as commodities and values, whereby they reduce their individual private labor to the standard of homogeneous human labor—for such a society, Christianity with its *cultus* of abstract man, more especially in its bourgeois developments, Protestantism, Deism, etc., is the most fitting form of religion. In the ancient Asiatic and other ancient modes of production, we find that the conversion of products into commodities, and therefore the conversion of men into producers of commodities, holds a subordinate place, which, however, increases in importance as the primitive communities approach nearer and nearer to their dissolution. Trading nations, properly so called, exist in the ancient world only in its interstices, like the gods of Epicurus in the Intermundia, or like Jews in the pores of Polish society. These ancient social organisms of production are, as compared with bourgeois society, extremely simple and transparent. But they are founded either on the immature development of man individually, who has not yet severed the umbilical cord that unites him with his fellow men in a primitive tribal community, or upon direct relations of subjection. They can arise and exist only when the development of the productive power of labor has not risen beyond a low stage, and when, therefore, the social relations within the sphere of material life, between man and man, and between man and nature, are correspondingly narrow. This narrowness is reflected in the ancient worship of nature, and in the other elements of the popular religions. The religious reflex of the real world can, in any case, only then finally vanish, when the practical relations of everyday life offer to man none but perfectly intelligible and reasonable relations with regard to his fellowmen and to nature.

The life process of society, which is based on the process of material production, does not strip off its mystical veil until it is treated as production by freely associated men, and is consciously regulated by them in accordance with a settled plan. This, however, demands for society a certain material groundwork or set of conditions of existence which in their turn are the spontaneous product of a long and painful process of development.

—Marx, *Capital,* vol. I (1867), pp. 51*f*.

C. The Religious Reflex: From Natural to Social Forces

All religion, however, is nothing but the fantastic reflection in men's minds of those external forces which control their daily life, a reflection in which the terrestrial forces assume the form of supernatural forces. In the beginnings of history it was the forces of nature which were at first so reflected, and in the course of further evolution they underwent the most manifold and varied personifications among the various peoples. Comparative mythology has traced back this first process, at least in the case of the Indo-European nations, to its origin in the Indian Vedas, and has shown its detailed evolution among the Indians, Persians, Greeks, Romans, Germans and, so far as material is available, also among the Celts, Lithuanians, and Slavs. But it is not long before, side by side with the forces of nature, social forces begin to be active; forces which present themselves to man as equally extraneous and at first equally inexplicable, dominating them with the same apparent necessity, as the forces of nature themselves. The fantastic personifications, which at first only reflected the mysterious forces of nature, at this point acquire social attributes, become representatives of the forces of history. At a still further stage of evolution, all the natural and social attributes of the innumerable gods are transferred to one almighty God, who himself once more is only the reflex of the abstract man. Such was the origin of monotheism, which was historically the last product of the vulgarized philosophy of the later Greeks and found its incarnation in the exclusively national god of the Jews, Jehovah. In this convenient, handy and readily adaptable form, religion can continue to exist as the immediate, that is, the sentimental form of men's relation to the extraneous natural and social forces which dominate them, so long as men remain under the control of these forces. We have already seen, more than once, that in existing bourgeois society men are dominated by the economic conditions created by themselves, by the means of production which they themselves have produced, as if by an extraneous force. The actual basis of religious reflex action therefore continues to exist, and with it the religious reflex itself. And although bourgeois political economy has given a certain insight into the causal basis of this domination by extraneous forces, this makes no essential difference. Bourgeois economics can neither prevent crises in general, nor protect the individual capitalists from losses, bad debts and bankruptcy, nor secure the individual workers against unemployment and destitution. It is still true that man proposes and God (that is, the extraneous force of the capitalist mode of production) disposes. Mere knowledge, even if it went much further and deeper than that of bourgeois economic science, is not enough to bring social forces under the control of society. What is above all necessary for this, is a social *act*. And when this act has been accomplished, when society, by taking possession of all means of production and using them on a planned basis, has freed itself and all its members from the bondage in which they are at present held by these means of production which they themselves have produced but which now confront them as an irresistible extraneous force; when therefore man no longer merely proposes, but also disposes—only then will the last extraneous force which is still reflected in religion vanish; and with it will also vanish the religious reflection itself, for the simple reason that then there will be nothing left to reflect.*

—ENGELS, *Anti-Dühring* (1878), pp. 344–46.

[3]

FEUERBACH'S IDEALIST APPROACH TO RELIGION

The real idealism of Feuerbach becomes evident as soon as we come to his philosophy of religion and ethics. He by no means wishes to abolish religion; he wants to perfect it. Philosophy itself must be absorbed in religion. "The periods of humanity are distinguished only by religious changes. A historical movement is fundamental only when it is rooted in the hearts of men. The heart is not a form of religion, so that the latter should exist also in the heart; the heart is the essence of religion."

* Dühring had said that a "socialitarian system, rightly conceived, *has* therefore . . . *to abolish* all the paraphernalia of religious magic, and therewith all the essential elements of religious cults." Engels replied to this at the close of the passage above: "Herr Dühring, however, cannot wait until religion dies this natural death. . . he incites his gendarmes of the future to attack religion, and thereby helps it to martyrdom and a prolonged lease of life" (*ibid.*, p. 346).—*Ed.*

According to Feuerbach, religion is the relation based on the affections, the relation based on the heart, between man and man, which until now has sought its truth in a fantastic reflection of reality—in the fantastic reflection of human qualities through the medium of one or many gods. But now it finds its truth directly and without any intermediary in the love between the "I" and the "Thou." Thus, finally, with Feuerbach sex love becomes one of the highest forms, if not the highest form, of the practice of his religion. . . .

Feuerbach's idealism consists here in this: He does not simply accept mutual relations based on reciprocal inclination between human beings, such as sex love, friendship, compassion, self-sacrifice, etc., as what they are in themselves—without associating them with any particular religion which to him, too, belongs to the past; but instead he asserts that they will come to their full realization for the first time as soon as they are consecrated by the name of religion. The chief thing for him is not that these purely human relations exist, but that they shall be conceived of as the new, true religion. They are to have full value only after they have been marked with a religious stamp. Religion is derived from *religare* and meant originally "a bond." Therefore, every bond between two men is a religion. Such etymological tricks are the last resource of idealist philosophy. Not what the word has meant according to the historical development of its actual use, but what it ought to mean according to its derivation is what counts. And so sex love and the intercourse between the sexes is apotheosized to a "religion," merely in order that the word religion, which is so dear to idealistic memories, may not disappear from the language. The Parisian reformers of the type of Louis Blanc used to speak in precisely the same way in the 'forties. They likewise could conceive of a man without religion only as a monster, and used to say: "*Donc, l'athéisme c'est votre religion!*" [Well, then, atheism is your religion!] If Feuerbach wishes to establish a true religion upon the basis of an essentially materialist conception of nature, that is the same as regarding modern chemistry as true alchemy. . . .

Feuerbach's assertion that "the periods of human development are distinguished only by religious changes" is decidedly false. Great historical turning points have been *accompanied* by religious changes only so far as the three world religions which have existed up to the present—Buddhism, Christianity and Islam—

are concerned. The old primitive tribal and national religions did not proselytize and lost all their power of resistance as soon as the independence of the tribe or people was lost. For the Germans it was sufficient to have simple contact with the decaying Roman Empire and with its newly adopted Christian world religion which fitted its economic, political and ideological conditions. Only with these more or less artificially created world religions, particularly Christianity and Islam, do we find that general historical movements acquire a religious imprint. Even in regard to Christianity the religious stamp in revolutions of really universal significance is restricted to the first stages of the struggle for the emancipation of the bourgeoisie—from the 13th to the 17th centuries—and is to be accounted for not as Feuerbach thinks by the hearts of men and their religious needs but by the entire previous history of the Middle Ages which knew no other form of ideology than religion and theology. But when the bourgeoisie of the 18th century was strengthened enough likewise to possess an ideology of its own, suited to its own class standpoint, it made its great and conclusive revolution, the French, appealing exclusively to juristic and political ideas, and troubling itself with religion only in so far as this stood in its way. But it never occurred to it to put a new religion in place of the old. Everyone knows how Robespierre failed in his attempt.

The possibility of purely human sentiments in the intercourse with other human beings has nowadays been sufficiently curtailed by the society in which we live, which is based upon class antagonism and class rule. We have therefore no reason to curtail it still more by exalting these sentiments to a religion. And similarly the understanding of the great historical class struggles has already been sufficiently obscured by current historiography, particularly in Germany, so that there is also no need for us to make such an understanding totally impossible by transforming the history of these struggles into a mere appendix of ecclesiastical history.

—ENGELS, *Ludwig Feuerbach* (1888), pp. 33–36.

[4]

HUMANISM VERSUS PANTHEISM: ON THOMAS CARLYLE

The English have no pantheism, instead merely skepticism; the outcome of all English philosophizing is the doubting of reason, the admitted inability to resolve the contradictions to which one is driven in the end, and as a result of this on the one hand a falling back on faith, on the other the surrender to mere practice without further bothering one's self over metaphysics and such things. Carlyle is, therefore, quite a "phenomenon" in England with his pantheism derived from German writings: a phenomenon rather incomprehensible to the practical and skeptical English. People gaze at him, talk of "German mysticism," of strained English; others maintain there is in the end Something behind it, his English is of course unusual but still beautiful, he is a prophet, etc.—but no one really knows what to make of it all.

For us Germans who know the presuppositions for Carlyle's viewpoint, the matter is clear enough. Survivals of Tory romanticism, along with humanitarian views from Goethe on the one hand, and from skeptical-empirical England on the other—these factors are sufficient for us to deduce Carlyle's whole view of the world. Carlyle, like all pantheists, has not yet come out beyond the inner contradiction, and Carlyle's dualism is the worse for the fact that he knows, of course, German literature but not its necessary complement, German philosophy. So all his views are immediate, intuitive, more like Schelling than like Hegel. With Schelling—that is the old Schelling, not the Schelling of revelation—Carlyle has actually a great many points of contact; with Strauss, whose viewpoint is likewise pantheistic, he coincides in the "cult of heroes" or the "cult of genius."...

Carlyle bewails the emptiness and shallowness of the age, the inner corruption of all social institutions. The complaint is just, but mere bewailing gets nowhere; in order to do away with the evil, the cause of it must be discovered; and if Carlyle had done this he would have found that this emptiness and shallowness, this "lack of soul," this irreligion and this "atheism" have their basis in religion itself. Religion is essentially the emptying of man and nature of all content, the transferring of this content to the phantom of a distant God who then in his turn graciously allows something from his abundance to come to human beings and to nature. So long, then, as the belief in this distant phantom is strong and living, so long does man in this roundabout way arrive at some kind of content. The strong faith of the Middle Ages lent, in this way, a significant energy to the whole epoch, but this energy came not from outside but lay already in the nature of man even though still unrecognized, still undeveloped. Faith became gradually weak, religion crumbled before the rising civilization, but still man did not yet see that he had worshipped and deified his own being as a strange being. In this unconscious and at the same time unbelieving state, man can have no substance; he must doubt truth, reason and nature, and this hollowness and lack of content, the doubting of the enduring facts of the universe will continue so long as mankind does not understand that the Being which it has honored as God, was his own not yet understood Being, until—but what! shall I copy from Feuerbach?

The emptiness has been there a very long time, for religion is man's act of digging himself out; and you are amazed that now after the purple which concealed it has faded, after the haze which veiled it has died away, it now steps into daylight and frightens you?

Carlyle complains further—this is the immediate result of the foregoing—over the age of hypocrisy and falsehood. Of course, the hollowness and distress must still be veiled and held upright by draperies, decorated walls, and fishbone splints! We even understand the hypocrisy of the present world state of Christianity; the struggle against it, our release from it and the release of the world from it are at the end of our single job; but because through the development of philosophy we have come to recognize this hypocrisy, and because we lead the struggle scientifically, the essence of this hypocrisy is no longer so strange and mysterious as it still is, at least for Carlyle. This hypocrisy we trace also back to the religion of which the first word is a falsehood—or does religion not begin by showing us something human and declaring that it is something superhuman, divine? But because we know that all this lying and hypocrisy follows from religion, that the religious hypocrisy, theology, is the great original of all other lies and hypocrisy, we are justified in spreading the word theology over the whole falsehood and hypocrisy of the present time as was first done by Feuerbach and B. Bauer. Carlyle may read their writings if he wishes to know whence comes the immorality which taints all our relationships.

A new religion, a pantheistic hero worship, worship of labor might be founded or must be awaited! Impossible; all possibilities of religion are exhausted; after Christianity, after the absolute, that is, abstract religion, after "religion as such" no other form of religion can still arise. Carlyle himself realizes that Catholic, Protestant, or whatever other Christianity moves irresistibly toward extinction; if he knew the nature of Christianity, he would realize that after it no other religion is still possible. Not even pantheism! Pantheism is itself still—according to its own premisses—an inseparable result of Christianity, at least the modern pantheism of Spinoza, Schelling, Hegel, and even of Carlyle! The trouble of providing evidence for this has again been spared me by Feuerbach.

As I have said, the responsibility therefore rests upon us to fight against the superficiality, the inner emptiness, the intellectual death, the untruthfulness of the age; against all these things we carry on a war of life and death, just as did Carlyle, and we have far greater probability of success than he had, because we know what we want. We want to raise up atheism as Carlyle pictures it, while we give man the substance which he has lost through religion; not as a divine but as a human content, and the whole restitution consists simply in the awakening of self-consciousness. We wish to get everything out of the way which offers itself as supernatural and superhuman, and thereby remove untruthfulness; for the pretense of the human and natural to desire to be superhuman, supernatural, is the root of all untruth and falsehood. Therefore we have once for all declared war on religion and religious conceptions, and are quite indifferent whether they call us atheists or anything else. But if Carlyle's pantheistic definition of atheism were correct, not we but our Christian opponents would be the true atheists. It does not occur to us to grasp the "eternal inner facts of the Universe"; on the contrary, we have for the first time truly established them while we emphasized their eternal quality and protected them from the almighty will of an essentially contradictory God. It does not occur to us to call "the world, Man and his life, a lie"; on the contrary, our Christian opponents are guilty of this immorality, when they make the world and man dependent upon the favor of a God who actually was produced only as man saw himself reflected in the desert of his own undeveloped consciousness. It does not occur to us to doubt or to despise the "revelation of history"; history is our one and all and is more highly regarded by us than by any other, earlier, philosophical school, more highly even than by Hegel to whom in the end it was to serve only as the test of his logical mathematical problems. The scorn of history, the disregard for the development of mankind is entirely on the other side; it is rather the Christians who with the setting forth of a separate "history of the kingdom of God" deny all inner significance to actual history and appropriate this significance only for their partisan, abstract and even also fictional history which, by the perfecting of the human race in their Christ, has history reaching an imaginary goal, breaking it off in the midst of its course, and now compelled as a result to picture the following 1800 years as barren folly and sheer emptiness. We reclaim the content of history; but we see in history not the revelation of "God," but of man and only of man.

In order to see the grandeur of the human being, to recognize the development of the race in history, its ceaseless progress, its always certain victory over the unreason of the individual, its conquest of all that is apparently superhuman, its difficult but successful struggle with nature, even to the final achievement of the free human self-consciousness, with insight into the unity of man with nature and the free spontaneous creation of a new world based on purely humane and moral conditions of living—we have no need, in order to recognize all this in its greatness, to summon first the abstraction of a "God" and ascribe to it all that is beautiful, great, sublime, and truly human; we do not need this by-path, we need not first set the stamp of "divine" on that which is truly human in order to be assured of its greatness and splendor. On the contrary, the more "divine," the more unhuman something is, the less shall we be able to wonder at it. Only the human origin of the content of all religions preserves for them here and there still some claim to respect; only the consciousness that even the wildest superstition contains at bottom the eternal decisions of the human race, even if in so twisted and distorted a form, only this consciousness saves the history of religion, and especially of the Middle Ages from complete rejection and eternal oblivion which would otherwise certainly be the fate of these "godly" stories. The more "godly," the more unhuman, the more animal; and the "godly" Middle Ages certainly produced the perfection of human bestiality, bondage, *jus primae noctis* [right of the first night], etc. The god*lessness* of our age, of which Carlyle complains so much, is actually its god*fullness*. From this it becomes also clear why I have given the human being as the answer to the riddle of the Sphinx. The question has always been, hitherto, What is God? and German philosophy has solved the question thus: God is Man. Man has only to know himself, to measure all conditions of life against himself, to judge according to his being, to arrange the world in a truly human way according to the needs of his nature—then he has solved the riddle of our time. Not in distant regions that do not exist; not out beyond time and space; not through a "God" immanent in the world or set over against it is truth to be found, but much nearer, in the human being's own breast. The human being's own nature is much more glorious and sublime than the imaginary nature of all possible "Gods," which are after all only the more or less unclear and distorted image of the human being himself. So if Carlyle (after Ben Jonson) says man has lost his soul and now begins to notice the lack of it, the correct statement for this would be: Man has in religion lost his own existence, he has renounced his humanity, and now is aware (since through the progress of history religion has begun to totter) of its emptiness and lack of content. But there is no other salvation for him, he can once more win his humanity, his essence only through a basic overcoming of all religious assumptions and a decisive, honest return not to "God," but to himself.

All this is to be found also in Goethe, the "prophet," and he who has open eyes can read it there. Goethe did not like to have anything to do with "God"; the word made him uncomfortable, he felt himself at home in that which is human, and this humanity, this emancipation of art from the chains of religion, constitutes exactly Goethe's greatness. Neither the Ancients, nor Shakespeare can compare with him in this respect. But this complete humanity, this surmounting of religious dualism can be grasped in its full historic significance only by one to whom the other side of the German national development—philosophy—is not alien. What Goethe was able for the first time to express directly, in a certain sense, at least, "as a prophet," is developed and established in the latest German philosophy. Carlyle also brings certain hypotheses which must in logical sequence lead to the viewpoint developed above. Pantheism is itself only the last preliminary step to the free human approach. History which Carlyle sets up as the genuine "revelation," actually contains only that which is human, and only by violent distortion can its substance be removed from humanity and placed to the credit of a "God." The labor, the free activity, in which Carlyle likewise sees a "cult," is again a purely human affair and can also only in a violent manner be brought into connection with "God." Why continually press into the foreground a word that, at best, expresses only the endlessness of uncertainty and further maintains the appearance of dualism? A word that in itself is a declaration of the nothingness of nature and humanity?

So much for the inner religious side of the Carlyle viewpoint. Judgment of the outer, political-social is directly tied to it; Carlyle has still enough religion to remain in a condition of bondage; pantheism always recognizes something higher than man as such. Therefore his desire for a "genuine aristocracy," for "heroes"; as if these heroes might at best be something more than human beings. If he could have grasped man as man in his whole boundless essence, so he would not have arrived at the idea of separating humanity in two groups, sheep and goats, ruling and ruled, aristocrats and mob, gentlemen and blockheads; he would have found the correct social placing of talent not in forcible ruling but in stimulating and leading. Talent has to persuade the masses of the truth of its ideas, and will then no longer have to complain about the carrying out of these ideas which will follow as a matter of course. Humanity makes its way through democracy, in truth, not in order to arrive at last at the point from which it started. What further Carlyle says about democracy leaves little more to be desired, if we except that lack of clarity (just noted) about the goal, the purpose of modern democracy. Democracy is of course only a transition, but not to a new improved aristocracy, but to genuine human freedom; just as the irreligion of the age will lead at last to complete emancipation from all that is religious, superhuman and supernatural, but not to their better re-establishment.

—ENGELS, "Review of Thomas Carlyle's *Past and Present*" (*Deutsch-Franzöische Jahrbücher,* 1844), MARX and ENGELS, *Werke,* Berlin, 1958, vol. I, pp. 542–48.

[5]

THE DECAY OF RELIGIOUS AUTHORITY

From the period of the Protestant Reformation, the upper classes in every European nation, whether it remained Catholic or adopted Protestantism, and especially the statesmen, lawyers, and diplomatists, began to unfasten themselves individually from all religious belief, and become free-thinkers so-called. This intellectual movement in the higher circles manifested itself without reserve in France from the time of Louis XIV, resulting in the universal predilection for what was denominated philosophy during the 18th century. But when Voltaire found residence in France no longer safe, not because of his opinions, nor because he had given oral expression to them, but because he had communicated them by his writings to the whole reading public, he betook himself to England and testified that he found the *salons* of high life in London still "freer" than those of Paris. Indeed, the men and women of the court of Charles II, Bolingbroke, the Walpoles, Hume, Gibbon, and Charles Fox, are names which all suggest a prevalent unbelief in religious dogmas, and a general adhesion to the philosophy of that age on the part of the upper classes, statesmen, and politicians of England. This may be called, by way of distinction, the era of aristocratic revolt against ecclesiastical authority. Comte, in one short sentence, has characterized this situation:

"From the opening of the revolutionary period in the 16th century this system of hypocrisy has been more and more elaborated in practice, *permitting the emancipation of all minds of a certain bearing*, on the tacit condition that they should aid in protracting the submission of the masses. This was eminently the policy of the Jesuits."

This brings us down to the period of the French Revolution, when the masses, firstly of France, and afterwards of all Western Europe, along with a desire for political and social freedom, began to entertain an ever-growing aversion from religious dogma. The total abolition of Christianity, as a recognized institution of State, by the French Republican Convention of 1793, and since then the gradual repeal in Western Europe, wherever the popular voice has had power, of religious tests and political and civil disabilities of the same character, together with the Italian movement of 1848, sufficiently announce the well-known direction of the popular mind in Europe. We are still witnesses of this epoch, which may be characterized as the era of democratic revolt against ecclesiastical authority.

But this very movement among the masses since the French Revolution, bound up as it was with the movement for social equality, brought about a violent reaction in favor of church authority in high quarters. Nobility and clergy, lords temporal and lords spiritual, found themselves equally threatened by the popular movement, and it naturally came to pass that the upper classes of Europe threw aside their skepticism in public life and made an outward alliance with the State churches and their systems. This reaction was most apparent in France, first under Bonaparte, and during the Restoration under the elder branch of the Bourbons, but it was not less the case with the rest of Western Europe. In our own day we have seen renewed on a smaller scale this patching up of an alliance, offensive and defensive, between the upper classes and the ecclesiastical interest. Since the epoch of 1830 the statesmen had begun to manifest anew a spirit of independence towards ecclesiastical control, but the events of 1848 threw them back into the arms of Mother Church. Again France gave the clearest exemplification of this phenomenon. In 1849, when the terror of the Democratic deluge was at its height, Messrs. Thiers, De Hauranne, and the Universitarians (who had passed for Atheists with the clergy), were unanimous in supporting that admirably qualified "savior of religion," M. Bonaparte, in his project for the violent restoration of the Pope of Rome, while the Whig Ministry of Protestant England, at whose head was a member of the ultra-Protestant family of Russell, were warm in their approval of the same expedition. This religious restoration by such processes was indeed only redeemed from universal ridicule by the extremely critical posture of affairs which, for the moment, in the interest of "order" did not allow the public men of Europe to indulge in the sense of the ludicrous.

But the submission of the classes of leading social influence to ecclesiastical control, which was hollow and hypocritical at the beginning of this century after the Revolution of 1792, has been far more precarious and superficial since 1848, and is only acknowledged by those classes so far as it suits their immediate political interest. The humiliating position of utter dependence which the ecclesiastical power sustains toward the temporal arm of government has been made fully manifest since 1848. The Pope indebted to the French Government for his present tenure of the chair of St. Peter; the French clergy, for the sake of their salaries, blessing trees of liberty and proclaiming the sovereignty of the people, and afterwards canonizing the present Emperor of France as the chosen instrument of God and the savior of religion, their old proper doctrines of legitimacy, and the divine right of kings being in each case laid aside with the downfall of the corresponding political *régime;* the Anglican clergy, whose *ex officio* head is a temporal Queen, dependent for promotion on the recommendation of the Prime Minister, now generally a Liberal, and looking for favors and support against popular encroachment to Parliament, in which the Liberal element is ever on the increase, constitute an *ensemble* from which it would be absurd to expect acts of pure ecclesiastical independence, except in the normally impossible case of an overwhelming popular support to fall back upon.

—MARX, Editorial, *New York Daily Tribune,* Oct. 24, 1854

[6]

GOD AND NATURAL SCIENCE

God is nowhere treated worse than by natural scientists, who believe in him. Materialists simply explain the *facts,* without making use of such phrases, they do this first when importunate pious believers try to force God upon them, and then they answer curtly, either like Laplace: *Sire, je n'avais pas, etc.,** or more rudely in the manner of the Dutch merchants who, when German commercial travellers press their shoddy goods on them, are accustomed to turn them away with the words: *Ik kan die zaken niet gebruiken* [I have no use for the things], and that is the end of the matter. But what God has had to suffer at the hands of his defenders! In the history of modern natural science,

* When Napoleon asked him why God did not appear in his "System of the World," he is reputed to have answered, "But Sir, I find no need of that hypothesis."—*Ed.*

God is treated by his defenders as Frederick William III was treated by his generals and officials in the campaign of Jena. One division of the army after another lowers its weapons, one fortress after another capitulates before the march of science, until at last the whole infinite realm of nature is conquered by science, and there is no place left in it for the Creator. Newton still allowed Him the "first impulse" but forbade Him any further interference in his solar system. Father Secchi bows Him out of the solar system altogether, with all canonical honors it is true, but none the less categorically for all that, and he only allows Him a creative act as regards the primordial nebula. And so in all spheres. In biology, His last great Don Quixote, Agassiz, even ascribes positive nonsense to Him; He is supposed to have created not only the actual animals but also abstract animals, the fish as such! And finally Tyndall totally forbids Him any entry into nature and relegates him to the world of emotional processes, only admitting Him because, after all, there must be somebody who knows more about all these things (nature) than J. Tyndall! What a distance from the old God—the Creator of heaven and earth, the maintainer of all things—without whom not a hair can fall from the head!

Tyndall's emotional need proves nothing. The Chevalier des Grieux also had an emotional need to love and possess Manon Lescaut, who sold herself and him over and over again; for her sake he became a card-sharper and pimp, and if Tyndall wants to reproach him, he replies with his "emotional need!"

God = *nescio* [to be ignorant]; but *ignorantia non est argumentum* [ignorance is not an argument] (Spinoza).

—ENGELS, *Dialectics of Nature* (1882), pp. 176–78.

[7]

RELIGION AND THE CLASS STRUGGLE

A. How Marxists Fight Religion

Marxism is materialism. As such, it is as relentlessly hostile to religion as was the materialism of the Encyclopedists of the 18th century or the materialism of Feuerbach. This is beyond doubt. But the dialectical materialism of Marx and Engels goes further than the Encyclopedists and Feuerbach by applying the materialist philosophy to the field of history, to the field of the social sciences. We must combat religion—that is the rudiment of *all* materialism, and consequently of Marxism. But Marxism is not a materialism which stops at rudiments. Marxism goes further. It says: We must *know how* to combat religion, and in order to do so we must explain the source of faith and religion among the masses *materialistically*. The fight against religion must not be confined to abstract ideological preaching or reduced to such preaching. The fight must be linked up with the concrete practical work of the class movement, which aims at eliminating the social roots of religion. Why does religion retain its hold over the backward sections of the urban proletariat, over the broad sections of the semi-proletariat, and over the peasant mass? Because of the ignorance of the people, replies the bourgeois progressivist, the radical, and the bourgeois materialist. And so, down with religion and long live atheism!—the dissemination of atheist views is our chief task. The Marxist says that this is not true, that it is a superficial view and narrow, bourgeois culturism. This view does not profoundly enough explain the roots of religion; it explains them not materialistically but idealistically. In modern capitalist countries these roots are mainly *social*. The deepest root of religion today is the social oppression of the working masses and their apparently complete helplessness in face of the blind forces of capitalism, which every day and every hour inflicts upon ordinary working people the most horrible suffering and the most savage torment, a thousand times more severe than those inflicted by extraordinary events, such as wars, earthquakes, etc. "Fear created the gods." Fear of the blind force of capital—blind because it cannot be foreseen by the masses of the people—a force which at every step in life threatens to inflict, and does inflict, on the proletarian and small owner "sudden," "unexpected," "accidental" destruction, ruin, pauperism, prostitution, and death from starvation—such is *the root* of modern religion which the materialist must bear in mind first and foremost if he does not want to remain an infant-school materialist. No educational book can eradicate religion from the minds of the masses, who are crushed by the grinding toil of capitalism and who are at the mercy of the blind destructive forces of capitalism, until these masses themselves learn to fight this *root* of religion, *the rule of capital* in all its forms, in a united, organized, planned and conscious way.

—LENIN, "The Attitude of the Worker's Party Towards Religion" (1909), *Selected Works*, vol. XI, pp. 666*f*.

B. SOCIALISM, ATHEISM, AND RELIGIOUS FREEDOM

Religion is one of the forms of spiritual oppression that everywhere weighs on the masses of the people, who are crushed by perpetual toil for the benefit of others, and by want and isolation. The impotence of the exploited classes in the struggle against the exploiters engenders faith in a better life beyond the grave just as inevitably as the impotence of the savage in his struggle against nature engenders faith in gods, devils, miracles and so forth. To him who toils and suffers want all his life religion teaches humility and patience on earth, consoling him with the hope of reward in heaven. And to those who live on the labor of others religion teaches charity on earth, offering them a very cheap justification for their whole existence as exploiters and selling them at a suitable price tickets for admission to heavenly bliss. Religion is the opium of the people. Religion is a kind of spiritual gin in which the slaves of capital drown their human shape and their claims to any decent human life.

But a slave who has realized his slavery and has risen up to fight for his emancipation is already only half a slave. The present-day class-conscious worker, trained by large-scale factory industry and educated by urban life, rejects religious superstitions with contempt, leaves heaven to the priests and the bourgeois hypocrites and fights for a better life here on earth. The modern proletariat is coming over to Socialism, which enlists science in the struggle against religious obscurity and emancipates the workers from belief in a life hereafter by welding them together for a real fight for a better life on earth.

Religion should be declared a private affair—these are the words in which the attitude of Socialists to religion is customarily expressed. But the meaning of these words must be precisely defined so as to leave no room for misunderstanding. We demand that religion should be a private affair as far as the state is concerned, but under no circumstances can we regard religion as a private affair as far as our own party is concerned. The state must not be concerned with religion, religious societies should have no connection with the state power. Everybody must be absolutely free to profess any religion he pleases or not to believe in any religion at all, that is, to be an atheist, as every Socialist usually is. No distinction whatever between citizens, as regards their rights, depending upon their religious beliefs can be tolerated. Every reference to the belief of citizens must be unconditionally expunged from all official documents. There must be absolutely no subsidies to a state church, no grants of government funds to church and religious societies, which must become associations absolutely free and independent of the state, associations of citizens holding the same ideas. Only the complete fulfilment of these demands can put an end to the disgraceful and accursed past, when the church was in feudal dependence on the state and the Russian citizens were in feudal dependence on the state church, when medieval, inquisitorial laws existed and were enforced (laws which to this day remain on our criminal statute books), laws which prosecuted people for their faith or lack of faith, which did violence to the conscience of man, which associated government posts and government incomes with the distribution of the state-clerical gin. The complete separation of the church from the state—that is the demand which the Socialist proletariat makes of the modern state and the modern church. . . .

Religion is not a private affair in relation to the party of the Socialist proletariat. Our party is a league of class-conscious and advanced fighters for the emancipation of the working class. Such a league must not be indifferent to unenlightenment, ignorance, and obscurantism in the form of religious beliefs. We demand the complete separation of the church from the state in order to combat religious darkness with a purely ideological, and exclusively ideological, weapon, our printed and oral propaganda. One reason why we have founded our league, the Russian Social-Democratic Labor Party, is just to wage such a fight against all religious stultification of the workers. For us therefore the ideological fight is not a private affair but a general affair of the party and the proletariat.

If that is so, why do we not declare in our program that we are atheists? Why do we not refuse Christians and those who believe in God admission to our party?

The reply to this question should serve to explain a very important difference between the bourgeois-democratic and the Social-Democratic attitude towards religion.

Our program is entirely based on the scientific, that is, the materialist world-outlook. The explanation of our program therefore necessarily includes an explanation of the true historical and economic roots of religious obscurantism. Our propaganda necessarily includes the propaganda of atheism; the publication of appropriate scientific literature, which the feudal-autocratic government has hitherto strictly prohibited and persecuted, must now constitute one of the branches of our party work. We shall now, apparently, have to follow the advice which Engels once gave the German Socialists, namely, to translate and widely disseminate the literature of the French enlighteners and atheists of the 18th century.

But in this connection we must not under any circumstances fall into the abstract and idealist error of arguing the religious question from the standpoint of "reason," apart from the class struggle—as is not infrequently done by bourgeois radical democrats. It would be absurd to think that in a society which is based on the endless oppression and stultification of the working class masses religious prejudices can be dispelled merely by preaching. It would be bourgeois narrow-mindedness to forget that the yoke of religion on mankind is only a product and reflection of the economic yoke in society. No books or sermons can enlighten the proletariat if it is not enlightened by its own struggle against the dark forces of capitalism. Unity in this truly revolutionary struggle of the oppressed class for the creation of a paradise on earth is more important to us than unity of opinion among the proletarians about a paradise in heaven.

That is why we do not and must not proclaim our atheism in our program; that is why we do not and must not forbid proletarians who still cherish certain relics of the old superstitions to approach our party. We shall always preach a scientific outlook, it is essential for us to combat the inconsistency of "Christians"; but this does not mean that the religious question must be given a prominence which it does not deserve, that we must consent to a division of the forces of the truly revolutionary economic and political struggle for the sake of unimportant opinions or ravings which are rapidly losing all political significance and are being rapidly cast on to the scrap heap by the very course of economic development.

—LENIN, "Socialism and Religion" (1905), *Selected Works,* vol. XI, pp. 658–62.

PART SEVEN

ETHICS

In place of the old bourgeois society, with its classes and class antagonisms, we shall have an association in which the free development of each is the condition for the free development of all.

—MARX and ENGELS, *Communist Manifesto* (1848), p. 31.

Introduction

MARXISM HAS been accused both of having no ethics and of allowing ethical considerations to direct and color its economic and political theories. Marx, Engels, and Lenin wrote little on ethical theory, yet moral judgments and ethical theories are ever implicit in their writings.

Marxism believes that it constitutes *the* scientific approach to society and at the same time it readily acknowledges that it has an ethics—a theory of good and bad, right and wrong, progress and reaction. Marx and Engels, in the mid-1840's, held that the only way out of utopian socialism was to transform the grounds for socialism from moral judgments to a scientific analysis of capitalism and socio-economic history generally. They objected to the moral position of the utopians not because it was "moral" but because it was not scientifically grounded.

Engels sought to explain this problem forty years later in his preface to the first German edition of Marx's *Poverty of Philosophy* (pp. 12–13). If we say that it is unjust under the laws of bourgeois economics that the greatest part of the product does not belong to the workers who produce it, we say nothing about economics but merely express our moral sentiments. That is why, he continued, Marx "never based his communist demands upon this [moral sentiments], but upon the inevitable collapse of the capitalist mode of production. . . ." Marx was examining, in short, not the "immorality" of capitalism but its inherent contradictions which would bring it to an end. His purpose in *Capital* was not to pass judgment on surplus value as evil, but to point out that it consists of unpaid labor—something he believed to be a simple economic fact.

The question immediately arises whether the two realms of morals and economics ever meet. It may be wrong, Engels admits, from a strictly scientific economic point of view to speak of the workers' unjust share under capitalism. "But," he argued, "what formally may be economically incorrect, may all the same be correct from the point of view of world history." And he added, "If the moral consciousness of the mass declares an economic fact to be unjust, as it has done in the case of slavery or serf labor, that is a proof that the fact itself has been outlived, that other economic facts have made their appearance, owing to which the former has become unbearable and untenable. Therefore, a very true economic content may be concealed behind the formal economic incorrectness."

Only in the historical process, Marxists believe, can the unity of ethical judgments and scientific analyses be found. Hence they refuse to condemn capitalism and praise socialism solely on ethical grounds, even though they are firmly convinced that socialism is morally superior. Different economic forms do not succeed one another for ethical reasons but because they are more or less successful in carrying on the business of life—of producing and distributing the means of subsistence. And, while ethical judgments change through definite causes in historical development, the only sound basis for enlightened ethical judgments must be found in scientific analyses of nature, man, and his social relations.

Some of the leading ideas in this section are: The idea of justice, "eternal justice," does not regulate the production of commodities, but is derived from the mode of production; it is the real needs and interests of the proletariat that impel it in the struggle against capitalism, not the ideas of justice or right although such ideas become powerful forces when the masses become convinced they suffer injustice and wrong. There are no eternal moral truths and there is no absolute universal good. Capitalist ethics, like that of all other ruling classes, necessarily identifies its class interest with universal good; all ethical notions and systems have a specific historical origin and are relative to particular forms of society. Communist ethics is the highest possible ethics at this period of historical development because it represents the needs and interests of that class alone which can raise society to a higher level through the elimination of capitalist exploitation and the release of the developing forces of production from the fetters capitalist relations impose upon them.

To base ethics on the process of history, Marxists believe, is to derive ethics from its only possible source—the life of man in nature and society. And if that life reveals an ethical process towards ever greater freedom it is only because men necessarily seek to master nature and their social inter-relationships more effectively. Marxist ethics therefore sees "justice," the "good," and the "right," as developmental concepts in terms of man's relationship to nature and his historic struggle to make this relationship serve ever better his own evolving purposes.

There is, of course, no iron-clad guarantee that the process of transition from capitalism to communism will not have its moral ups and downs as well as its economic ones. The USSR has had its full share of both, but aberrations of right and perversions of justice in the case of socialism necessarily become hindrances that must be corrected if the society itself is to survive, much less develop.

Marxists, rather than ignoring ethics and morality, believe that they put it on a higher plane than have all previous societies. Ethical and moral considerations are involved in everyday matters in farm, factory, and office, and are not merely precepts reserved for use on the sabbath. The most advanced socialist countries, looking towards the transition to communism, recognize that not only a high level of production is required but a universally high ethical level as well. The widespread concept of "communist man" embraces many qualities, including willingness to work without economic compulsion, ability to place the public welfare ahead of limited individual interests, respect for the producers and the products of labor, the endeavor to develop one's talents and capacities to their fullest, not merely for personal satisfaction or prestige but as a means of advancing the material and cultural well-being of society as a whole. To most people in the capitalist world the idea that such men and women could exist is the dream of a utopian. For Marxists it is the logical and ethical outcome of a whole theory of society and history.

[1]

THE CLASS NATURE OF MORALITY

The conceptions of good and bad have varied so much from nation to nation and from age to age that they have often been in direct contradiction to each other. But all the same, someone may object, good is not bad and bad is not good; if good is confused with bad there is an end to all morality, and everyone can do and leave undone whatever he cares. . . . But the matter cannot be so simply disposed of. If it was such an easy business there would certainly be no dispute at all over good and bad; everyone would know what was good and what was bad. But how do things stand today? What morality is preached to us today? There is first Christian-feudal morality, inherited from past periods of faith; and this again has two main subdivisions, Catholic and Protestant moralities, each of which in turn has no lack of further subdivisions from the Jesuit-Catholic and Orthodox-Protestant to loose "advanced" moralities. Alongside of these we find the modern bourgeois morality and with it too the proletarian morality of the future, so that in the most advanced European countries alone the past, present, and future provide three great groups of moral theories which are in force simultaneously and alongside of one another. Which is then the true one? Not one of them, in the sense of having absolute validity; but certainly that morality which contains the maximum of durable elements is the one which, in the present, represents the overthrow of the present, represents the future—that is, the proletarian.

But when we see that the three classes of modern society, the feudal aristocracy, the bourgeoisie, and the proletariat, each have their special morality, we can only draw the conclusion that men, consciously or unconsciously, derive their moral ideas in the last resort from the practical relations on which their class position is based—from the economic relations in which they carry on production and exchange.

But nevertheless there is much that is common to the three moral theories mentioned above—is this not at least a portion of a morality which is externally fixed? These moral theories represent three different stages of the same historical development, and have therefore a common historical background, and for that reason alone they necessarily have much in common. Even more. In similar or approximately similar stages of economic development moral theories must of necessity be more or less in agreement. From the moment when private property in movable objects developed, in all societies in which this private property existed there must be this moral law in common: Thou shalt not steal. Does this law thereby become an eternal moral law? By no means. In a society in which the motive for stealing has been done away with, in which therefore at the very most only lunatics would ever steal, how the teacher of morals would be laughed at who tried solemnly to proclaim the eternal truth: Thou shalt not steal!

We therefore reject every attempt to impose on us any moral dogma whatsoever as an eternal, ultimate, and forever immutable moral law on the pretext that the moral world too has its permanent principles which transcend history and the differences between nations. We maintain on the contrary that all former moral theories are the product, in the last analysis, of the economic stage which society had reached at that particular epoch. And as society has hitherto moved in class antagonisms, morality was always a class morality; it has either justified the domination and the interests of the ruling class, or, as soon as the oppressed class has become powerful enough, it has represented the revolt against this domination and the future interests of the oppressed. That in this process there has on the whole been progress in morality, as in all other branches of human knowledge, cannot be doubted. But we have not yet passed beyond class morality. A really human morality which transcends class antagonisms and their legacies in thought becomes possible only at a stage of society which has not only overcome class contradictions but has even forgotten them in practical life. . . .

Our ideologist may turn and twist as he likes, but the historical reality which he cast out at the door comes in again at the window, and while he thinks he is framing a doctrine of morals and law for all times and for all worlds, he is in fact only making an image of the conservative or revolutionary tendencies of his time—an image which is distorted because it has been torn from its real basis and, like a reflection in a concave mirror, is standing on its head.

—ENGELS, *Anti-Dühring* (1878), pp. 103–105; 107.

[2]

FEUERBACH: LOVE AND THE PURSUIT OF HAPPINESS

[As concerns morality] Feuerbach's astonishing poverty when compared with Hegel again becomes striking. The latter's ethics or doctrine of moral conduct is the philosophy of law and embraces: (1) abstract right; (2) morality; (3) moral conduct under which again are comprised the family, civil society, and the state. Here the content is as realistic as the form is idealistic. Besides morality the whole sphere of law, economy, politics is here included. With Feuerbach it is just the reverse. In form he is realistic since he takes his start from man; but there is absolutely no mention of the world in which this man lives; hence this "man" remains always the same abstract man who occupied the field in his philosophy of religion. For this man is not born of woman; he issues, as from a chrysalis, from the God of the monotheistic religions. He therefore does not live in a real world historically created and historically determined. It is true he has intercourse with other men, but each one of them is, however, just as much an abstraction as he himself is. In his philosophy of religion we still had men and women, but in his ethics even this last distinction disappears altogether. Feuerbach, to be sure, at long intervals makes such statements as: "A man thinks differently in a palace and in a hut." "If because of hunger, of misery, you have no foodstuff in your body, you likewise have no stuff for morality in your head or heart." "Politics must become our religion," etc. But Feuerbach is absolutely incapable of achieving anything with these remarks. They remain purely figures of speech; and even Starcke* has to admit that for Feuerbach politics constituted an impassable frontier and the "science of society, sociology, was *terra incognita* to him. . . ."

What Feuerbach has to tell us about morals can, therefore, only be extremely meager. The urge towards happiness is innate in man, and must therefore form the basis of all morals. But the urge towards happiness is subject to a double correction. First, by the natural consequences of our action; after the debauch come the "blues," and habitual excess is followed by illness. Secondly, by its social consequences; if we do not respect the similar urge of other people towards happiness they will defend themselves, and so interfere with our own urge towards happiness.

Consequently, in order to satisfy our urge, we must be in a position to appreciate rightly the results of our conduct and must likewise allow others an equal right to seek happiness. Rational self-restraint with regard to ourselves, and love—again and again love!—in our intercourse with others—these are the basic laws of Feuerbach's morality; from them all others are derived. And neither the most talented utterances of Feuerbach nor the strongest eulogies of Starcke can hide the tenuity and superficiality of these few propositions.

Only very exceptionally, and in no case to his and other people's profit, can an individual satisfy his urge towards happiness by preoccupation with himself. Rather it requires preoccupation with the outside world, means to satisfy his needs, that is to say means of subsistence, an individual of the opposite sex, books, conversation, argument, activities, articles for use and working up. Feuerbach's morality either presupposes that these means and objects of satisfaction are given to every individual as a matter of course, or else it offers only inapplicable good advice and is therefore not worth a brass farthing to people who are without these means. And Feuerbach himself states this in dry words: "A man thinks differently in a palace and in a hut. If because of hunger, of misery, you have no foodstuff in your body you likewise have no stuff for morality in your head or heart."

Do matters fare any better in regard to the equal right of others to the pursuit of happiness? Feuerbach posed this claim

* Engels' *Ludwig Feuerbach* is a revised version of two articles he contributed to *Die Neue Zeit* in 1886 in which he made a critical analysis of C. N. Starcke's book, *Ludwig Feuerbach.—Ed.*

as absolute, as holding good in all times and circumstances. But since when has it been valid? Was there ever in antiquity between slaves and masters, or in the Middle Ages between serfs and barons, any talk about an equal right to the pursuit of happiness? Was not the urge towards happiness of the oppressed class sacrificed ruthlessly and "by right of law" to the interests of the ruling class? Yes, that was indeed immoral; nowadays, however, equality of rights is recognized—recognized in words, since the bourgeoisie, in its fight against feudalism and in the development of capitalist production, was compelled to abolish all privileges of estate, i.e., personal privileges, and to introduce the equality of all individuals before the law, first in the sphere of private law, then gradually also in the sphere of state law. But the urge towards happiness thrives only to a trivial extent on ideal rights. To the greatest extent of all it thrives on material means; and capitalist production takes care to ensure that the great majority of those with equal rights shall get only what is essential for bare existence. Capitalist production has therefore little more respect, if indeed any more, for the "equal right to the pursuit of happiness" of the majority than had slavery or serfdom. And are we better off in regard to the mental means to happiness, the educational means? . . .

But love!—yes, with Feuerbach, love is everywhere and at all times the wonder-working god who should help to surmount all difficulties of practical life—and that in a society which is split into classes with diametrically opposite interests. At this point the last relic of its revolutionary character disappears from the philosophy, leaving only the old cant: Love one another—fall into each other's arms regardless of distinctions of sex or estate—a universal orgy of reconciliation.

In short, the Feuerbachian theory of morals fares like all its predecessors. It is designed to suit all periods, all peoples, and all conditions, and precisely for that reason it is never and nowhere applicable. It remains, as regards the real world, as powerless as Kant's categorical imperative. In reality every class, even every profession, has its own morality, and even this it violates whenever it can do so with impunity. And "love," which is to unite all, manifests itself in wars, altercations, lawsuits, domestic broils, divorces and every possible exploitation of one by another.

Now how was it possible that the powerful impetus given by

Feuerbach turned out to be so unfruitful for himself? For the simple reason that Feuerbach himself never contrives to escape from the realm of abstraction—for which he has a deadly hatred —into that of living reality. He clings hard to nature and humanity; but nature and humanity remain always mere words with him. He is incapable of telling us anything definite either about real nature or real men. But from the abstract men of Feuerbach one arrives at real living men only when one considers them as participants in history. And that is what Feuerbach resisted, and therefore the year 1848, which he did not understand, signified for him merely the final break with the real world, retirement into solitude. The blame for this again chiefly falls on the conditions then obtaining in Germany, which condemned him to rot away miserably.

But the step which Feuerbach did not take nevertheless had to be taken. The cult of abstract man which formed the kernel of Feuerbach's new religion had to be replaced by the science of real men and of their historical development. This further development of Feuerbach's standpoint beyond Feuerbach himself was inaugurated by Marx in 1845 in *The Holy Family*.

—ENGELS, *Ludwig Feuerbach* (1888), pp. 36–41.

[3]

EVOLUTION OF THE IDEA OF EQUALITY

The idea that all men, as men, have something in common, and that they are therefore equal so far as these common characteristics go, is of course primeval. But the modern demand for equality is something entirely different from that; this consists rather in deducing from those common characteristics of humanity, from that equality of men as men, a claim to equal political or social status for all human beings, or at least for all citizens of a state or all members of a society. Before the original conception of relative equality could lead to the conclusion that men should have equal rights in the state and in society, before this conclusion could appear to be something even natural and self-evident, however, thousands of years had to pass and did pass. In the oldest primitive communities equality of rights existed at most for members of the community; women, slaves, and strangers were excluded from this equality as a matter of course. Among the Greeks and Romans the inequalities of men were of greater importance than any form of equality. It would necessarily have seemed idiotic to the ancients that Greeks and barbarians, freemen and slaves, citizens and dependents, Roman citizens and Roman subjects (to use a comprehensive term) should have a claim to equal political status. Under the Roman Empire all these distinctions gradually disappeared, except the distinction between freemen and slaves, and in this way there arose, for the freemen at least, that equality as between private individuals on the basis of which Roman law developed—the complete elaboration of law based on private property which we know. But so long as the distinction between freemen and slaves existed, there could be no talk of drawing legal conclusions from the fact of general equality *as men*; and we saw this again quite recently, in the slaveowning states of the North American Union.

Christianity knew only *one* point in which all men were equal—that all were equally born in original sin, which corresponded perfectly with its character as the religion of the slaves and the oppressed. Apart from this is recognized, at most, the equality of the elect, which however was only stressed at the very beginning. The traces of common ownership which are also found in the early stages of the new religion can be ascribed to the solidarity of a proscribed sect rather than to real equalitarian ideas. Within a very short time the establishment of the distinction between priests and laymen put an end even to this tendency to Christian equality. The overrunning of Western Europe by the Germans abolished for centuries all ideas of equality, through the gradual building up of a complicated social and political hierarchy such as had never before existed. But at the same time the invasion drew Western and Central Europe into the course of historical development, created for the first time a compact cultural area, and within this area also for the first time a system of predominantly national states exerting mutual influence on each other and mutually holding each other in check. Thereby it prepared the ground on which alone the question of the equal status of men, of the rights of man, could at a later period be raised.

The feudal Middle Ages also developed in its womb the class which was destined in the future course of its evolution to be the standard-bearer of the modern demand for equality, the bourgeoisie. Itself in its origin one of the "estates" of the feudal order, the bourgeoisie developed the predominantly handicraft industry and the exchange of products within feudal society to a relatively high level, when at the end of the 15th century the great maritime discoveries opened to it a new and more comprehensive career. Trade beyond the confines of Europe, which had previously been carried on only between Italy and the Levant, was now extended to America and India, and soon surpassed in importance both the mutual exchange between the various European countries and the internal trade within each separate country. American gold and silver flooded Europe and forced its way like a disintegrating element into every fissure, hole, and pore of feudal society. Handicraft industry could no longer satisfy the rising demand; in the leading industries of the most advanced countries it was replaced by manufacture.

But this mighty revolution in the economic conditions of life in society was not followed immediately by any corresponding change in its political structure. The state order remained feudal, while society became more and more bourgeois. Trade on a large scale, that is to say, international and, even more, world trade, requires free owners of commodities who are unrestricted in their movements and have equal rights as traders to exchange their commodities on the basis of laws that are equal for them all, at least in each separate place. The transition from handicraft to manufacture presupposes the existence of a number of free workers—free on the one hand from the fetters of the guild and on the other from the means whereby they could themselves utilize their labor power; workers who can contract with their employers for the hire of their labor power, and as parties to the contract have rights equal with his. And finally the equality and equal status of all human labor, because and in so far as it is *human* labor, found its unconscious but clearest expression in the law of value of modern bourgeois economics, according to which the value of a commodity is measured by the socially necessary labor embodied in it.* But where economic relations required freedom and equality of rights, the political system opposed them at every step with guild restrictions and special privileges. Local privileges, differential

* This tracing of the origin of the modern ideas of equality to the economic conditions of bourgeois society was first developed by Marx in *Capital*. [See, for example, vol. I, p. 69.—*Ed.*]

duties, exceptional laws of all kinds affected in trading not only foreigners or people living in the colonies, but often enough also whole categories of the nationals of each country; the privileges of the guilds everywhere and ever anew formed barriers to the path of development of manufacture. Nowhere was the path open and the chances equal for the bourgeois competitors—and yet this was the first and ever more pressing need.

The demand for liberation from feudal fetters and the establishment of equality of rights by the abolition of feudal inequalities was bound soon to assume wider dimensions from the moment when the economic advance of society first placed it on the order of the day. If it was raised in the interests of industry and trade, it was also necessary to demand the same equality of rights for the great mass of the peasantry who, in every degree of bondage from total serfdom upwards, were compelled to give the greater part of their labor time to their feudal lord without payment and in addition to render innumerable other dues to him and to the state. On the other hand, it was impossible to avoid the demand for the abolition also of feudal privileges, the freedom from taxation of the nobility, the political privileges of the various feudal estates. And as people were no longer living in a world empire such as the Roman Empire had been, but in a system of independent states dealing with each other on an equal footing and at approximately the same degree of bourgeois development, it was a matter of course that the demand for equality should assume a general character reaching out beyond the individual state, that freedom and equality should be proclaimed as *human rights*. And it is significant of the specifically bourgeois character of these human rights that the American Constitution, the first to recognize the rights of man, in the same breath confirmed the slavery of the colored races in America; class privileges were proscribed, race privileges sanctified.

As is well known, however, from the moment when, like a butterfly from the chrysalis, the bourgeoisie arose out of the burghers of the feudal period, when this "estate" of the Middle Ages developed into a class of modern society, it was always and inevitably accompanied by its shadow, the proletariat. And in the same way the bourgeois demand for equality was accompanied by the proletarian demand for equality. From the moment when the bourgeois demand for the abolition of class *privileges* was put forward, alongside of it appeared the proletarian demand for the abolition of the *classes themselves*—at first in religious form, basing itself on primitive Christianity, and later drawing support from the bourgeois equalitarian theories themselves. The proletarians took the bourgeoisie at their word: Equality must not be merely apparent, must not apply merely to the sphere of the state, but must also be real, must be extended to the social and economic sphere. And especially since the time when the French bourgeoisie, from the Great Revolution on, brought bourgeois equality to the forefront, the French proletariat has answered it blow for blow with the demand for social and economic equality, and equality has become the battle-cry particularly of the French proletariat.

The demand for equality in the mouth of the proletariat has therefore a double meaning. It is either—as was especially the case at the very start, for example in the peasants' war—the spontaneous reaction against the crying social inequalities, against the contrast of rich and poor, the feudal lords and their serfs, surfeit and starvation; as such it is the simple expression of the revolutionary instinct, and finds its justification in that, and indeed only in that. Or, on the other hand, the proletarian demand for equality has arisen as the reaction against the bourgeois demand for equality, drawing more or less correct and more far-reaching demands from this bourgeois demand, and serving as an agitational means in order to rouse the workers against the capitalists on the basis of the capitalists' own assertions; and in this case it stands and falls with bourgeois equality itself. In both cases the real content of the proletarian demand for equality is the demand for the *abolition of classes*. Any demand for equality which goes beyond that, of necessity passes into absurdity. We have given examples of this, and shall find enough additional ones later when we come to Herr Dühring's fantasies of the future.

The idea of equality, therefore, both in its bourgeois and in its proletarian form, is itself a historical product, the creation of which required definite historical conditions which in turn themselves presuppose a long previous historical development. It is therefore anything but an eternal truth. And if today it is taken for granted by the general public—in one sense or another—if, as Marx says, it "already possesses the fixity of a popular prejudice," this is not the consequence of its axiomatic truth, but the result of the general diffusion and the continued appropriateness of the ideas of the 18th century.

—Engels, *Anti-Dühring* (1878), pp. 113–18.

[4]

EQUALITY VERSUS EQUALITARIANISM

What we have to deal with here * is a communist society, not as if it had *developed on a basis of its own,* but on the contrary as *it emerges from capitalist society,* which is thus in every respect tainted economically, morally, and intellectually with the hereditary diseases of the old society from whose womb it is emerging. In this way the individual producer receives back again from society, with deductions, exactly what he gives. What he has given to society is his individual amount of labor. For example, the social working day consists of the sum of the individuals' hours of work. The individual working time of the individual producer is that part of the social working day contributed by him, his part thereof. He receives from society a voucher that he has contributed such and such a quantity of work (after deductions from his work for the common fund) and draws through this voucher on the social storehouse as much of the means of consumption as the same quantity of work costs. The same amount of work which he has given to society in one form, he receives back in another.

Here obviously the same principle prevails as that which regulates the exchange of commodities so far as this exchange is of equal values. Content and form are changed because under the changed conditions no one can contribute anything except his labor and, on the other hand, nothing can pass into the possession of individuals except individual objects of consumption. But, so far as the distribution of the latter among individual producers is concerned, the same principle prevails as in the exchange of commodity-equivalents, i.e. equal quantities of labor in one form are exchanged for equal quantities of labor in another form.

* In this selection Marx is criticizing a statement in the Gotha Program drawn up by a congress of German Socialists at Gotha in 1875. The program called for "'an equitable distribution of the proceeds of labor," on the grounds that "the whole proceeds of labor belong with equal rights to all members of society."—*Ed.*

The equal right is here still based on the same principle as bourgeois right, although principle and practice are no longer at daggers drawn, while the exchange of equivalents in commodity exchange only exists *for the average* and not for the individual case.

In spite of this advance, this *equal right* is still continually handicapped by bourgeois limitations. The right of the producers is *proportional* to the amount of labor they contribute; the equality consists in the fact that everything is measured by an *equal measure,* labor.

But one man will excel another physically or intellectually and so contributes in the same time more labor, or can labor for a longer time; and labor, to serve as a measure, must be defined by its duration or intensity, otherwise it ceases to be a standard measure. This *equal* right is an unequal right for unequal work. It recognizes no class differences because every worker ranks as a worker like his fellows, but it tacitly recognizes unequal individual endowment, and thus capacities for production, as natural privileges. It is therefore a right of inequality in its content, as in general is every right. Right can by its very nature only consist in the application of an equal standard; but unequal individuals (and they would not be different individuals if they were not unequal), are only measurable by an equal standard in so far as they can be brought under an equal observation, be regarded from one *definite* aspect only, *e.g.* in the case under review, they must be considered *only as workers* and nothing more be seen in them, everything else being ignored. Further, one worker is married, another single, one has more children than another and so on. Given an equal capacity for labor and thence an equal share in the funds for social consumption, the one will in practice receive more than the other, the one will be richer than the other and so forth. To avoid all these inconveniences, rights must be unequal instead of being equal.

But these deficiencies are unavoidable in the first phase of communist society when it is just emerging after prolonged birth-pangs from capitalist society. Right can never be higher than the economic structure and the cultural development of society conditioned by it.

In a higher phase of communist society, after the tyrannical subordination of individuals according to the distribution of labor and thereby also the distinction between manual and intellectual work, have disappeared, after labor has become not merely a means to live but is in itself the first necessity of living, after the powers of production have also increased and all the springs of co-operative wealth are gushing more freely together with the all-round development of the individual, then and then only can the narrow bourgeois horizon of rights be left far behind and society will inscribe on its banner: "From each according to his capacity, to each according to his need."

—MARX, *Critique of the Gotha Program* (1875), pp. 29–31.

[5]

EVOLUTION OF THE CONCEPT OF JUSTICE

At a certain, very primitive stage of the development of society, the need arises to coordinate under a common regulation the daily recurring acts of production, distribution, and exchange of products, to see to it that the individual subordinates himself to the common conditions of production and exchange. This regulation, which is at first custom, soon becomes *law*. With law, organs necessarily arise which are entrusted with its maintenance —public authority, the state. With further social development, law develops into a more or less comprehensive legal system. The more complicated this legal system becomes, the more its terminology becomes removed from that in which the usual economic conditions of the life of society are expressed. It appears as an independent element which derives the justification for its existence and the reason for its further development not out of the existing economic conditions, but out of its own inner logic, or, if you like, out of "the concept of will." People forget the derivation of their legal system from their economic conditions of life, just as they have forgotten their own derivation from the animal world.

With the development of the legal system into a complicated and comprehensive whole the necessity arises for a new social division of labor; an order of professional jurists develops and with these legal science comes into being. In its further development this science compares the legal systems of various peoples and various times, not as the expression of the given economic relationships, but as systems which find their justification in themselves. The comparison assumes something common to them all, and this the jurists find by summing up that which is more or less common to all these legal systems as *natural law*. However, the standard which is taken to determine what is natural law and what is not, is precisely the most abstract expression of law itself, namely *justice*.

From this point on, therefore, the development of law for the jurists, and for those who believe them uncritically, is nothing more than the striving to bring human conditions, so far as they are expressed in legal terms, into closer and closer conformity with the ideal of justice, *eternal* justice. And this justice is never anything but the ideologized, glorified expression of the existing economic relations, at times from the conservative side, at times from the revolutionary side. The justice of the Greeks and Romans held slavery to be just. The justice of the bourgeois of 1789 demanded the abolition of feudalism because it was unjust. For the Prussian *Junker* even the miserable *Kreisordnung* [legislation establishing distinct local authorities] is a violation of eternal justice. The conception of eternal justice therefore varies not only according to time and place, but also according to persons, and it belongs among those things of which Mühlberger correctly says, "everyone understands something different." While in everyday life, in view of the simplicity of the relations which come into question, expressions like right, wrong, justice, conception of justice, can be used without misunderstanding even in relation to social matters, they create, as we have seen, hopeless confusion in any scientific investigation of economic relations, in fact, much the same confusion as would be created in modern chemistry if the terminology of the phlogiston theory were to be retained. The confusion becomes still worse if one, like Proudhon, believes in this social phlogiston, "justice," or if one, like Mülberger, declares that the phlogiston theory no less than the oxygen theory is perfectly correct.

—ENGELS, *The Housing Question* (1872), pp. 91–93.

[6]

MARXISM AND "ABSOLUTE" JUSTICE

A. UNSCIENTIFIC NATURE OF "ETERNAL JUSTICE"

Proudhon begins by taking his ideal of justice, of "*justice éternelle,*" from the juridical relations that correspond to the production of commodities; thereby, it may be noted, he proves, to the consolation of all good citizens, that the production of commodities is a form of production as everlasting as justice. Then he turns round and seeks to reform the actual production of commodities, and the actual legal system corresponding thereto, in accordance with this ideal. What opinion should we have of a chemist, who, instead of studying the actual laws of the molecular changes in the composition and decomposition of matter, and on that foundation solving definite problems, claimed to regulate the composition and decomposition of matter by means of the "eternal ideas," of "*naturalité*" and "*affinité*?" Do we really know any more about "usury," when we say it contradicts "*justice éternelle,*" "*équité éternelle,*" "*mutualité éternelle,*" and other "*vérités éternelles*" than the fathers of the church did when they said it was incompatible with "*grâce éternelle,*" "*foi éternelle,*" and "*la volonté éternelle de Dieu*?"

—MARX, *Capital,* vol. I (1867), p. 96, note 2.

B. JUSTICE DETERMINED BY MODE OF PRODUCTION

To speak in such a case of natural justice, as Gilbart is doing ("That a man, who borrows money with the intention of making a profit on it, should give a portion of the profit to the lender, is a self-understood principle of natural justice." Gilbart, *The History and Principles of Banking,* London, 1834, p. 163.) is nonsense. The justice of the transactions between the agents of production rests on the fact that these transactions arise as natural consequences from the conditions of production. The juristic forms, in which these economic transactions appear as activities of the will of the parties concerned, as expressions of their common will and as contracts which may be enforced by law against some individual party, cannot determine their content, since they are only forms. They merely express this content. This content is just, whenever it corresponds, and is adequate, to the mode of production. It is unjust, whenever it contradicts that mode. Slavery on the basis of capitalist production is unjust; likewise fraud in the quality of commodities.

—MARX, *Capital*, vol. III (1894), p. 399.

[7]

THE MEANING OF FREEDOM

Hegel was the first to state correctly the relation between freedom and necessity. To him, freedom is the appreciation of necessity. "Necessity is *blind* only *in so far as it is not understood.*" Freedom does not consist in the dream of independence of natural laws, but in the knowledge of these laws, and in the possibility this gives of systematically making them work towards definite ends. This holds good in relation both to the laws of external nature and to those which govern the bodily and mental existence of men themselves—two classes of laws which we can separate from each other at most only in thought but not in reality. Freedom of the will therefore means nothing but the capacity to make decisions with real knowledge of the subject. Therefore the *freer* a man's judgment is in relation to a definite question, with so much the greater *necessity* is the content of this judgment determined; while the uncertainty, founded on ignorance, which seems to make an arbitrary choice among many different and conflicting possible decisions, shows by this precisely that it is not free, that it is controlled by the very object it should itself control. Freedom therefore consists in the control over ourselves and over external nature which is founded on knowledge of natural necessity; it is therefore necessarily a product of historical development.

The first men who separated themselves from the animal kingdom were in all essentials as unfree as the animals themselves, but each step forward in civilization was a step towards freedom. On the threshold of human history stands the discovery that mechanical motion can be transformed into heat—the production of fire by friction; at the close of the development so far gone through stands the discovery that heat can be transformed into mechanical motion—the steam engine. And, in spite of the gigantic and liberating revolution in the social world which the steam engine is carrying through—and which is not yet half completed—it is beyond question that the generation of fire by friction was of even greater effectiveness for the liberation of mankind. For the generation of fire by friction gave man for the first time control over one of the forces of nature, and thereby separated him for ever from the animal kingdom. The steam engine will never bring about such a mighty leap forward in human development, however important it may seem in our eyes as representing all those powerful productive forces dependent on it—forces which alone make possible a state of society in which there are no longer class distinctions or anxiety over the means of subsistence for the individual, and in which for the first time there can be talk of real human freedom and of an existence in harmony with the established laws of nature. But how young the whole of human history still is, and how ridiculous it would be to attempt to ascribe any absolute validity to our present views, is evident from the simple fact that all past history can be characterized as the history of the epoch from the practical discovery of the transformation of mechanical motion into heat up to that of the transformation of heat into mechanical motion.

—ENGELS, *Anti-Dühring* (1878), pp. 125*f*.

[8]

TWO REALMS OF FREEDOM AND THEIR MATERIAL PRECONDITIONS

We have seen that the capitalist process of production is a historically determined form of the social process of production in general. This process is on the one hand the process by which the material requirements of life are produced, and on the other hand a process which takes place under specific historical and economic conditions of production and which produces and reproduces these conditions of production themselves, and with them the human agents of this process, their material conditions of existence and their mutual relations, that is, their particular economic form of society. For the aggregate of these relations, in which the agents of this production live with regard to nature and to themselves, and in which they produce, is precisely their society, considered from the point of view of its economic structure. Like all its predecessors, the capitalist process of production takes place under definite material conditions, which are at the same time the bearers of definite social relations maintained towards one another by the individuals in the process of producing their life's requirements. These conditions and these relations are on the one hand prerequisites, on the other hand results and creations of the capitalist process of production. They are produced and reproduced by it. We have also seen that capital (the capitalist is merely capital personified and functions in the process of production as the agent of capital), in the social process of production corresponding to it, pumps a certain quantity of surplus labor out of the direct producer, or laborer. It extorts this surplus without returning an equivalent. This surplus labor always remains forced labor in essence, no matter how much it may seem to be the result of free contract. This surplus labor is represented by a surplus value, and this surplus value is materialized in a surplus product. It must always remain surplus labor in the sense that it is labor performed above the normal requirements of the producer. In the capitalist system as well as in the slave system, etc., it merely assumes an antagonistic form and is supplemented by the complete idleness of a portion of society. A certain quantity of surplus labor is required for the purpose of discounting accidents, and by the necessary and progressive expansion of the process of reproduction in keeping with the development of the needs and the advance of population, called accumulation from the point of view of the capitalist. It is one of the civilizing sides of capital that it enforces this surplus labor in a manner and under conditions which promote the development of the productive forces, of social conditions, and the creation of the elements for a new and higher formation better than did the preceding forms of slavery, serfdom, etc. Thus it leads on the one hand to a stage, in which the coercion and the monopolization of the social development (including its material and intellectual advantages) by a portion of society at the expense of the other portion are eliminated; on the other hand it creates the material requirements and the germ of conditions, which make it possible to combine this surplus labor in a higher form of society with a greater reduction of the time devoted to material labor. For, according to the development of the productive power of labor, surplus labor may be large in a small total labor day, and relatively small in a large total labor day. If the necessary labor time equals three, and the surplus labor three, then the total working day is equal to six, and the rate of surplus labor 100%. If the necessary labor is equal to nine, and the surplus labor three, then the total working day is 12 and the rate of surplus labor only 33⅓%. Furthermore, it depends upon the productivity of labor, how much use value shall be produced in a definite time, hence also in a definite surplus labor time. The actual wealth of society, and the possibility of a continued expansion of its process of reproduction, do not depend upon the duration of the surplus labor, but upon its productivity and upon the more or less fertile conditions of production, under which it is performed.

In fact, the realm of freedom does not commence until the point is passed where labor under the compulsion of necessity and of external utility is required. In the very nature of things it lies beyond the sphere of material production in the strict meaning of the term. Just as the savage must wrestle with nature, in order to satisfy his wants, in order to maintain his life and reproduce it, so civilized man has to do it, and he must do it in all forms of society and under all possible modes of production. With his development the realm of natural necessity expands, because his wants increase; but at the same time the forces of production increase, by which these wants are satisfied. The freedom in this field cannot consist of anything else but of the fact that socialized man, the associated producers, regulate their interchange with nature rationally, bring it under their common control, instead of being ruled by it as by some blind power; that they accomplish their task with the least expenditure of energy and under conditions most adequate to their human nature and most worthy of it. But it always remains a realm of necessity. Beyond it begins that development of human power, which is its own end, the true realm of freedom, which, however, can flourish only upon that realm of necessity as its basis. The shortening of the working day is its fundamental premise.*

—MARX, *Capital,* vol. III (1894), pp. 952–55.

* Compare the following, from *Theories of Surplus Value* (*Theorien über den Mehrwert,* Berlin 1923, vol. II, p. 334): "The worker himself appears in this [the bourgeois] conception as what he really is in capitalist production—a mere means of production; not as an end in himself and the goal of production."—*Ed.*

[9]

CLASSLESS SOCIETY: BASIS FOR REAL PERSONAL FREEDOM

The transformation, through the division of labor, of personal powers (relationships) into material powers, cannot be dispelled by dismissing the general idea of it from one's mind, but only by the action of individuals in again subjecting these material powers to themselves and abolishing the division of labor. This is not possible without the community. Only in community with others has each individual the means of cultivating his gifts in all directions; only in the community, therefore, is personal freedom possible. In the previous substitutes for the community, in the state, etc., personal freedom has existed only for the individuals who developed within the relationships of the ruling class, and only in so far as they were individuals of this class. The illusory community, in which individuals have up till now combined, always took on an independent existence in relation to them, and was at the same time, since it was the combination of one class over against another, not only a completely illusory community, but a new fetter as well. In the real community the individuals obtain their freedom in and through their association.

It follows from all we have been saying up till now that the communal relationship into which the individuals of a class entered, and which was determined by their common interests over against a third party, was always a community to which these individuals belonged only as average individuals, only in so far as they lived within the conditions of existence of their class—a relationship in which they participated not as individuals but as members of a class. With the community of revolutionary proletarians on the other hand, who take their conditions of existence and those of all members of society under their control, it is just the reverse; it is as individuals that the individuals participate in it. It is just this combination of individuals (assuming the advanced stage of modern productive forces, of course) which puts the conditions of the free development and movement of individuals under their control—conditions which were previously abandoned to chance and had won an independent existence over against the separate individuals just because of their separation as individuals, and because their combination had been determined by the division of labor, and through their separation had become a bond alien to them. Combination up till now (by no means an arbitrary one, such as is expounded for example in the *Contrat Social,* but a necessary one) was permitted only upon these conditions, within which the individuals were at the mercy of chance (compare, *e.g.* the formation of the North American State and the South American republics). This right to the undisturbed enjoyment, upon certain conditions, of fortuity and chance has up till now been called personal freedom; but these conditions are, of course, only the productive forces and forms of intercourse * at any particular time.

—MARX and ENGELS, *The German Ideology* (1846), pp. 74–75.

[10]

PROGRESS: FROM BLIND NECESSITY TO FREEDOM

The bourgeois period of history has to create the material basis of the new world—on the one hand universal intercourse founded upon the mutual dependency of mankind, and the means of that intercourse; on the other hand the development of the productive powers of man and the transformation of material production into a scientific domination of natural agencies. Bourgeois industry and commerce create these material conditions of a new world in the same way as geological revolutions have created the surface of the earth. When a great social revolution shall have mastered the results of the bourgeois epoch, the market of the world and the modern powers of production, and subjected them to the common control of the most advanced peoples, then only will human progress cease to resemble that Hindoo pagan idol, who would not drink the nectar but from the skulls of the slain.

—MARX, *New York Daily Tribune,* Aug. 8, 1853.

* Marx later changed this phrase into a more precise one, namely, the relations of production.—*Ed.*

[11]

THE NATURE OF COMMUNIST ETHICS

The whole object of training, educating, and teaching the youth of today should be to imbue them with communist ethics.

But is there such a thing as communist ethics? Is there such a thing as communist morality? Of course, there is. It is often made to appear that we have no ethics of our own; and very often the bourgeoisie accuse us Communists of repudiating all ethics. This is a method of shuffling concepts, of throwing dust in the eyes of the workers and peasants.

In what sense do we repudiate ethics and morality?

In the sense that it is preached by the bourgeoisie, who derived ethics from God's commandments. We, of course, say that we do not believe in God, and know perfectly well that the clergy, the landlords, and the bourgeoisie spoke in the name of God in pursuit of their own interests as exploiters. Or instead of deriving ethics from the commandments of morality, from the commandments of God, they derived them from idealist or semi-idealist phrases, which always amounted to something very similar to God's commandments.

We repudiate all morality derived from non-human and non-class concepts. We say that it is a deception, a fraud, a befogging of the minds of the workers and peasants in the interests of the landlords and capitalists.

We say that our morality is entirely subordinated to the interests of the class struggle of the proletariat. Our morality is derived from the interests of the class struggle of the proletariat.*

The old society was based on the oppression of the workers and peasants by the landlords and capitalists. We had to destroy this, we had to overthrow them; but to do so we had to create unity. No God will create such unity.

This unity could be created only by factories and workshops, only by the proletariat, trained and roused from its long slumber. Only when that class had been formed did the mass movement

* Lenin is here applying to ethics the position he held with regard to all areas of ideology. Compare, for example: "In a society torn by class antagonisms there can never be non-class or above-class ideology." (*What is to be Done?* p. 41.)—*Ed.*

begin which led to what we see now—the victory of the proletarian revolution in one of the weakest of countries, which for three years has been resisting the onslaught of the bourgeoisie of the whole world.

And we see that the proletarian revolution is growing all over the world. We now say, on the basis of experience, that only the proletariat could have created that compact force which has the following of the disunited and scattered peasantry and which has withstood all the onslaughts of the exploiters. Only this class can help the laboring masses to unite, rally their ranks and definitely uphold, definitely consolidate, and definitely build up communist society.

That is why we say that for us there is no such thing as morality apart from human society; it is a fraud. Morality for us is subordinated to the interests of the class struggle of the proletariat. . . .

We say: morality is what serves to destroy the old exploiting society and to unite all laboring people around the proletariat, which is creating a new, communist society.

Communist morality is the morality which serves this struggle, which unites the toilers against all exploitation, against all small property; for small property puts into the hands of one person what has been created by the labor of the whole of society.

The land in our country is common property.

But suppose I take a piece of this common property and grow on it twice as much grain as I need and profiteer on the surplus? Suppose I argue that the more starving people there are the more they will pay? Would I then be behaving like a Communist?

No, I would be behaving like an exploiter, like a proprietor. This must be combated.

If this is allowed to go on we shall slide back to the rule of the capitalists, to the rule of the bourgeoisie, as has more than once happened in earlier revolutions. And in order to prevent the restoration of the rule of the capitalists and the bourgeoisie we must not allow such things to happen, we must not allow individuals to enrich themselves at the expense of the rest, and all laboring people must unite with the proletariat and form a communist society.

This is the principal feature of the fundamental task of the League and of the organizations of the Communist youth.

The old society was based on the principle: Rob or be robbed, work for others or make others work for you, be a slaveowner or a slave. Naturally, people brought up in such a society imbibe with their mother's milk, so to speak, the psychology, the habit, the concept: You are either a slaveowner or a slave, or else a small owner, a small employee, a small official, an intellectual—in short, a man who thinks only of himself, and doesn't care a hang for anybody else.

If I work this plot of land, I don't care a hang for anybody else; if others starve, all the better, the more I will get for my grain. If I have a job as a doctor, engineer, teacher, or clerk, I don't care a hang for anybody else. Perhaps if I toady and please the powers that be I shall keep my job, and even get on in life and become a bourgeois. A Communist cannot have such a psychology and such sentiments.

When the workers and peasants proved that they were able by their own efforts to defend themselves and create a new society, a new communist schooling began, a schooling in the fight against the exploiters, a schooling in alliance with the proletariat against the self-seekers, against the psychology and habits which say: I seek my own profit and I don't care a hang for anything else. . . .

When people talk to us about morality, we say: For the Communist, morality lies entirely in this compact, united disciplined, and conscious mass struggle against the exploiters. We do not believe in an eternal morality, and we expose all the lying fables about morality.

Morality serves to help human society rise to a higher level and get rid of the exploitation of labor.

—Lenin, "Address at Congress of Russian Young Communist League" (1920), *The Young Generation,* pp. 36–41.

APPENDICES

APPENDIX I

THE FORMATIVE PERIOD

> Real Humanism *has no more dangerous enemy in Germany than* spiritualism *or* speculative idealism *which substitutes* "self-consciousness" *or the* "spirit" *for the* real individual man *and teaches with the evangelist "that the spirit quickeneth everything and that the flesh profiteth not."*
>
> —MARX and ENGELS, *The Holy Family* (1844), p. 15.

Introduction

IT WAS noted in the introduction to this volume that the writings of Marx and Engels, and especially those of Marx, during their formative period, are difficult for the present-day reader. Yet a whole mass of literature dealing with this period has emerged in the last 30 years or so with interpretations designed to show that Marx was an orthodox Hegelian, a pragmatist, or an existentialist. Some commentators maintain that pure Marxism can be found only in these early works, and that consequently the later works are, so to speak, renunciations of the genuine Marxist philosophy. We believe, however, that these writings—once the unusual terminology is grasped—reveal that Marx and Engels, in traversing a path from Hegelian idealism to dialectical materialism were creating the germinal notions of their mature revolutionary philosophical position.

Most of the concepts embodied in the strange terminology found here are derived from Hegel. "Alienation," "negativity," "objectification" are only a few among many such. But Marx uses these terms with a content all his own, and in doing so, criticizes Hegel for his "abstract" and "mystical" handling of these notions. Thus, although Marx was a student of Hegel—and he so maintained to the very end of his life—he was, even at the beginning of his concern with philosophy, a *critical* student—critical of Hegel's schematic dialectic; critical of Hegel's views on the state and society.

The same applies to their approach to the Young Hegelians of whom Marx and Engels for a time formed a part. With them and opposed to them at one and the same time, the founders of Marxism held views that were unorthodox. Even Feuerbach, who for a short time exerted a great influence on their thinking, was never accepted by Marx and Engels without serious qualification. Marx drew conclusions from Feuerbach's work which the latter was incapable of drawing. In a letter of praise to Feuerbach, for instance, Marx says: "In these works [*Philosophy of the Future* and *Essence of Faith*] you—consciously or otherwise, I cannot say—have given socialism a philosophical foundation and that is precisely how the Communists have understood them. Unity of man with man based on the real distinctions between men, the concept of the human race, transferred from the heavens of abstraction to real earth—what can this be but the concept of *society*!" Everything that is stated here as praiseworthy is in essence a critique. Feuerbach did not deal with the "real distinctions between men" nor did he have the "concept of *society*." In short, what Marx is saying is that Feuerbach should have proceeded to do with his notion of "man" what was most necessary, namely, to deal with men in the concrete as members of a concrete class-divided society.

During the period from 1841 to 1845 surveyed in this section, the writings of Marx and Engels were so voluminous that an entire book the size of this one would be required to give an adequate picture of the various stages or levels of their thought. The most the editors could attempt to do was to give samples of their evolving thought, revealing as far as possible their key problems, their adversaries—in many cases old friends and philosophical associates—and some of the highlights on the road to the development of mature Marxism.

Marx's philosophical thought during these years was considerably in advance of that of Engels. The latter, on the other hand, from his vantage-point in England after the end of 1842—learning the textile business in a Manchester factory of which his father was a partner—was considerably ahead of Marx in his knowledge of political economy. Engels had, however, moved in Hegelian circles in Berlin, was a "Young Hegelian," and had published an anonymous pamphlet against the philosopher Schelling who was trying to turn philosophy back from Hegel to romanticism and mysticism. Regardless of differences in background and experience, both these young men in their early twenties were deeply involved in the advanced philosophical thought of the Germany of their day and absorbed in the social, economic, and political struggles of a Europe moving rapidly towards the revolutions of 1848. Their thought developed in the give and take of polemics among an almost bewildering variety of socialist and communist groups and ideologies that were vying for dominance.

The writings contained herein reveal the growth of the thought of Marx and Engels on religion, the beginning of their criticism of both Hegel's dialectical idealism and Feuerbach's undialectical materialism, and their initial efforts to put the dialectic on a sound materialist foundation as an instrument both of philosophical analysis and of social criticism.

In a sense, Feuerbach did not belong to the Young Hegelians. These latter, especially the Bauer brothers (Bruno and Edgar), Max Stirner, and David Strauss, were idealists who represented, as Marx and Engels put it, the decomposition of the Hegelian School. To the extent, however, that Feuerbach glorified "Man" in the abstract and treated this abstraction as a living reality, he shared in the ideological processes of the Young Hegelians. This rendered it necessary for Marx and Engels to settle accounts with Feuerbach by including him among the ideologists who had to be combatted. Though very few people today read the writings of the Young Hegelians, their influence was considerable during this period and it appeared to Marx and Engels to be inimical to the task of inculcating in the proletariat an understanding of class relations and the revolutionary challenge then facing German society.

Feuerbach was the inspiration for the emergence of the so-called "true Socialists" who preached a religion of love as the solution of all social problems. Marx and Engels gave a concise characterization of this current of thought in both *The German Ideology* and the *Communist Manifesto*. The Bauer brothers developed, on the other hand, a theory to the effect that the critic was everything, the masses nothing. Marx, in the first instance, believed that such a theory was idealist and reactionary. In his eyes, Bruno Bauer was fighting every immediate demand of the masses on the specious ground that it was not revolutionary enough. For this reason, among others, Marx accused the Young Hegelians of being heroes of the revolutionary phrase, that is, of fighting against mere phrases instead of fighting the enemies of progress. In reality, Marx declared, they were the worst of conservatives, for their thinking left the world exactly as it was.

A most glaring example of this "revolutionary" approach appeared in the writings of Max Stirner, particularly *The Ego and His Own.* For Stirner, the whole world was revolutionized the moment one dismissed the world's problems from one's mind. All one had to do to get rid of the state, of religion, of poverty, etc., was to recognize that they were merely spooks, and to assert in the loudest possible tones that the only thing that counts is one's own ego. To Marx, this was nothing but prosaic bourgeois individualism transfigured by rodomontades about the infinite worth of the individual as such and the utter worthlessness of anything else.

Two questions loom large in the writings of Marx and Engels during this formative period. One is the criticism of all views that would make changed social relations the result of changed ideas. In a passage of *The German Ideology* not included here, they speak of Stirner's "pious" belief that the state would collapse if all its members walked out of it, and that money would lose its value if workers refused to receive it. This is, they say, "the old illusion that it depends only upon the good will of the people to change existing relations and that the existing relations are ideas." They added that philosophers, in making a profession or business of changing consciousness apart from conditions, are only expressing ideologically their impotence in relation to the world.

The second question Marx dealt with at length is that of "alienation," a concept derived in the first instance from Hegel's *Phenomenology of Mind.* But here it takes on a new content and a new concreteness. Alienation played its major role in Marx's thought during 1844, in writings that appeared only posthumously and for the first time in English in 1959 (*Economic and Philosophic Manuscripts of 1844*). The questions the reader has to ask concerning these selections are: What is alienation? Who is alienated from what? Why and how does alienation take place? In what ways can alienation be overcome and unity be restored?

The selections give the essence of this phase of Marx's thought; a phase which played an important role in his development and which was then not so much discarded as superseded. It is fashionable today to contrast the Marx of this romantic-philosophical-humanist period with the soberer later Marx of *Capital* and the First International. He, reputedly, had left philosophy behind for economics. The fact is, however, that the concept of "alienation" is not at all absent from Volume I of *Capital,* as can be seen, for example, in the discussion of the "fetishism of commodities," and is ever present in the theory of surplus value. Although the language changes significantly between these writings of the formative period and those that begin with the *Poverty of Philosophy* and the *Manifesto,* the reader can readily see that all these writings constitute a unified and homogeneous line of thought. Marx and Engels never repudiated the writings of this formative period, though they acknowledged some of their formal defects. They developed beyond them to the point where Engels could say concerning *The German Ideology* that, having settled "accounts with our erstwhile philosophic conscience . . . we abandoned the MSS to the gnawing criticism of mice all the more willingly since we had achieved our principal aim—our self-clarification."*

After this formative period the language of Marx and Engels changed along with the kinds of problems that confronted them. Having settled accounts with their former philosophic conscience and having achieved "self-clarification," they were able to pursue their goals without being hampered by unnecessary baggage from these years of struggle against the idealism of Hegel and the Young Hegelians. Nevertheless, the materials of this period are vital and warm even today to those willing to work through the outmoded language. They reveal, too, the rich humanist background from which scientific socialism emerged and the humanist premises upon which it developed.

* Although *The German Ideology* represents the emergence of mature Marxist thought the editors felt that its opening pages, on the Young Hegelians, provided a fitting conclusion to the selections in this part.—*Ed.*

[1]

ON THE PHILOSOPHY OF EPICURUS

The form of this treatise would be more strictly scientific on the one hand, and less pedantic in some points on the other, had it not been originally intended as a doctor's thesis. However, I am obliged through external causes to have it printed in its present form. Besides, I believe that in it I have solved a hitherto unsolved problem in the history of Greek philosophy.

Experts know that there are no preliminary works which could be useful in any way for the subject of this treatise. Up to this time there has been nothing but repetition of Cicero's and Plutarch's rigmarole. Gassendi, who freed Epicurus from the interdict laid on him by the Fathers of the Church and the whole of the Middle Ages—that age of materialized irrationalism—provides but one interesting point in his observations. He tries to conciliate his Catholic conscience with his heathen knowledge and Epicurus with the Church—an obviously futile effort. It is like throwing the habit of a Christian nun over the exuberant body of the Greek Lais.* It is more a case of Gassendi learning philosophy from Epicurus than being able to teach us about Epicurus's philosophy.

This treatise should be considered as a precursor to a larger work in which I shall expound in detail the cycle of the Epicurean, stoic, and skeptic philosophies in their connection with the whole of Greek speculation. The shortcomings of this treatise as to form and the like will be remedied in that work.

Hegel, on the whole, correctly defined the general features of the above-mentioned systems. But in the admirably extensive and daring plan of his *History of Philosophy*, from which we can date all history of philosophy, it was impossible, for one thing, to go into details and, for another, the great thinker's view of what he called speculation *par excellence* prevented him from acknowledging the higher importance of those systems for the history of Greek philosophy and for the Greek mind in general. These systems are the key to the true history of Greek philosophy. . . .

* A famous Greek courtesan of the late 5th century B.C. who was regarded as the most beautiful woman of her age.—*Ed.*

As long as philosophy still has a drop of blood left in its world-conquering, absolutely free heart, it will not cease to call to its opponents with Epicurus: "Not he who rejects the gods of the crowd is impious, but he who embraces the crowd's opinion of the gods." (Letter to Menokeus, Diogenes Laertius, *Lives of Eminent Philosophers,* Bk. x.)

Philosophy makes no secret of it. Prometheus's admission: "In sooth all gods I hate" (Aeschylus, *Prometheus Bound*) is its own admission, its own motto against all gods, heavenly and earthly, who do not acknowledge the consciousness of man as the supreme divinity. There must be no god on a level with it.

And to the wretched March hares who exult over the apparent deterioration of philosophy's social position it again answers, as Prometheus did to Hermes, the messenger of the gods: "I shall never exchange my fetters for slavish servility. 'Tis better to be chained to the rock than bound to the service of Zeus." (*Ibid.*)

Prometheus is the noblest of saints and martyrs in the calendar of philosophy.

—MARX, Foreword to Doctoral Thesis, *The Difference between the Natural Philosophy of Democritus and the Natural Philosophy of Epicurus* (1841), in MARX and ENGELS, *On Religion,* pp. 13–15.

[2]

RELIGION, PHILOSOPHY, AND THE PROLETARIAN REVOLUTION

Already as the resolute opponent of the previous form of *German* political consciousness the criticism of speculative philosophy of right strays, not into itself, but into *problems* which there is only one means of solving—*practice.*

It is asked: Can Germany attain a practice *à la hauteur des principes* [equal to its principles], i.e., a *revolution* which will raise it not only to the *official level* of the modern nations but to the *height of humanity* which will be the near future of those nations?

The weapon of criticism cannot, of course, replace criticism of the weapon, material force must be overthrown by material force; but theory also becomes a material force as soon as it has gripped the masses. Theory is capable of gripping the masses as soon as it demonstrates *ad hominem*,* and it demonstrates *ad hominem* as soon as it becomes radical. To be radical is to grasp the root of the matter. But for man the root is man himself. The evident proof of the radicalism of German theory, and hence of its practical energy, is that it proceeds from a resolute positive *abolition* of religion. The criticism of religion ends with the teaching that *man is the highest essence for man,* hence with the *categoric imperative to overthrow all relations* in which man is a debased, enslaved, abandoned, despicable essence, relations which cannot be better described than by the cry of a Frenchman when it was planned to introduce a tax on dogs: Poor dogs! They want to treat you as human beings!

Even historically, theoretical emancipation has specific practical significance for Germany. For Germany's *revolutionary* past is theoretical, it is the *Reformation.* As the revolution then began in the brain of the *monk,* so now it begins in the brain of the *philosopher.* . . .

It is not the *radical* revolution, not the *general human* emancipation which is a utopian dream for Germany, but rather the partial, the *merely* political revolution, the revolution which leaves the pillars of the house standing. On what is a partial, a merely political revolution based? On *part of civil society emancipating* itself and attaining *general* domination; on a definite class, proceeding from its *particular situation,* undertaking the general emancipation of society. This class emancipates the whole of society but only provided the whole of society is in the same situation as this class, *e.g.,* possesses money and education or can acquire them at will.

No class of civil society can play this role without arousing a moment of enthusiasm in itself and in the masses, a moment in which it fraternizes and merges with society in general, becomes confused with it and is perceived and acknowledged as its *general representative,* a moment in which its claims and rights are truly the claims and rights of society itself, a moment in which it is truly the social head and the social heart. Only in the name of the general rights of society can a particular class vindicate for itself general domination. For the storming of this emancipatory position, and hence for the political exploitation of all sections

* That is, appeals to their emotions.—*Ed.*

of society in the interests of its own section, revolutionary energy and spiritual self-feeling alone are not sufficient. For the *revolution of a nation* and the *emancipation of a particular class* of civil society to coincide, for *one* estate to be acknowledged as the estate of the whole society, all the defects of society must conversely be concentrated in another class, a particular estate must be the estate of the general stumbling-block, the incorporation of the general limitation, a particular social sphere must be recognized as the *notorious crime* of the whole of society, so that liberation from that sphere appears as general self-liberation. For *one* estate to be *par excellence* the estate of liberation, another estate must conversely be the obvious estate of oppression. The negative general significance of the French nobility and the French clergy determined the positive general significance of the nearest neighboring and opposed class of the *bourgeoisie*. . . .

In France it is enough for somebody to be something for him to want to be everything; in Germany nobody can be anything if he is not prepared to renounce everything. In France partial emancipation is the basis of universal emancipation; in Germany universal emancipation is the *conditio sine qua non* [the essential condition] of any partial emancipation. In France it is the reality of gradual liberation that must give birth to complete freedom, in Germany the impossibility of gradual liberation. In France every class of the nation is a *political idealist* and becomes aware of itself at first not as a particular class but as a representative of social requirements generally. The role of *emancipator* therefore passes in dramatic motion to the various classes of the French nation one after the other until it finally comes to the class which implements social freedom no longer with the provision of certain conditions lying outside man and yet created by human society, but rather organizes all conditions of human existence on the premises of social freedom. On the contrary, in Germany, where practical life is as spiritless as spiritual life is unpractical, no class in civil society has any need or capacity for general emancipation until it is forced by its *immediate* condition, by *material* necessity, by its *very chains*.

Where, then, is the *positive* possibility of a German emancipation?

Answer: In the formation of a class with *radical chains,* a class of civil society which is not a class of civil society, an estate which is the dissolution of all estates, a sphere which has a universal character by its universal suffering and claims no *particular right* because no *particular wrong* but *wrong generally* is perpetrated against it; which can invoke no *historical* but only its *human* title, which does not stand in any one-sided antithesis to the consequences but in all-around antithesis to the premises of German statehood; a sphere, finally, which cannot emancipate itself without emancipating itself from all other spheres of society and thereby emancipating all other spheres of society, which, in a word, is the *complete loss* of man and hence can win itself only through the *complete re-winning* of man. This dissolution of society as a particular estate is the *proletariat.*

The proletariat is beginning to appear in Germany as a result of the rising *industrial* movement. For it is not the *naturally arising* poor but the *artificially impoverished,* not the human masses mechanically oppressed by the gravity of society but the masses resulting from the *drastic dissolution* of society, mainly of the middle estate, that form the proletariat, although, as is easily understood, the naturally arising poor and the Christian-Germanic serfs gradually join its ranks.

By heralding the *dissolution of the hitherto existing world order* the proletariat merely proclaims the *secret of its own existence,* for it is the *factual* dissolution of that world order. By demanding the *negation of private property,* the proletariat merely raises to the rank of a *principle of society* what society has raised to the rank of *its* principle, what is already incorporated in *it* as the negative result of society without its own participation. The proletarian then finds himself possessing the same right in regard to the world which is coming into being as the *German king* in regard to the world which has come into being when he calls the people *his* people as he calls the horse *his* horse. By declaring the people his private property the king merely proclaims that the private owner is king.

As philosophy finds its *material* weapon in the proletariat, so the proletariat finds its *spiritual* weapon in philosophy. And once the lightning of thought has squarely struck this ingenuous soil of the people the emancipation of the *Germans* into *men* will be accomplished.

Let us sum up the result:

The only *practically* possible liberation of Germany is liberation from the point of view of *the* theory which proclaims man to be the highest essence of man. In Germany emancipation from the *Middle Ages* is possible only as emancipation from the *partial* victories over the Middle Ages as well. In Germany *no* kind of bondage can be shattered without *every* kind of bondage being shattered. The *fundamental* Germany cannot revolutionize without revolutionizing *from the foundation.* The *emancipation of the German* is *the emancipation of man.* The *head* of this emancipation is *philosophy,* its *heart* is the *proletariat.* Philosophy cannot be made a reality without the abolition of the proletariat, the proletariat cannot be abolished without philosophy being made a reality.

—MARX, "Contribution to the Critique of Hegel's Philosophy of Right" (1844) in MARX and ENGELS, *On Religion,* 50*f,* 53*f,* 56–58.

[3]

ON SETTLING ACCOUNTS WITH HEGELIAN PHILOSOPHY

A. THEOLOGY AND THE DECAY OF PHILOSOPHY

In contrast to the *critical theologians** of our day, I have deemed the concluding chapter of the present work—the settling of accounts with *Hegelian dialectic* and Hegelian philosophy as a whole—to be absolutely necessary, a task not yet performed. This *lack of thoroughness* is not accidental, since even the *critical* theologian remains a *theologian.* Hence, either he had to start from certain presuppositions of philosophy accepted as authoritative; or if in the process of criticism and as a result of other people's discoveries doubts about these philosophical presuppositions have arisen in him, he abandons them without vindication and in a cowardly fashion, *abstracts* from them, showing his servile dependence on these presuppositions and his resentment at this dependence merely in a negative, unconscious and sophistical manner. . . .

On close inspection *theological criticism*—genuinely progressive though it was at the inception of the movement—is seen

* The reference is to Bruno Bauer and a group of Hegelians around him. See below, sect. 4.—*Ed.*

in the final analysis to be nothing but the culmination and consequence of the old *philosophical,* and especially the *Hegelian, transcendentalism,* twisted into a *theological caricature.* This interesting example of the justice in history, which now assigns to theology, ever philosophy's spot of infection, the further role of portraying in itself the negative dissolution of philosophy—i.e., the process of its decay—this historical nemesis I shall demonstrate on another occasion.

—MARX, *Economic and Philosophic Manuscripts of 1844,* pp. 17–20.

B. HEGEL: THE PHILOSOPHER OF "ABSTRACT THINKING"

Hegel's *Encyclopedia,** beginning as it does with Logic, with *pure speculative thought,* and ending with *Absolute Knowledge*—with the self-consciousness, self-comprehending, philosophic or absolute (i.e., superhuman) abstract mind—is in its entirety nothing but the *display,* the self-objectification, of the *essence* of the philosophic mind, and the philosophic mind is nothing but the estranged mind of the world thinking within its self-estrangement—i.e., comprehending itself abstractly. *Logic* (mind's *coin of the realm,* the speculative or *thought-value* of man and nature—their essence grown totally indifferent to all real determinateness, and hence their unreal essence) is *alienated thinking,* and therefore thinking which abstracts from nature and from real man: *abstract* thinking. Then: *The externality of this abstract thinking . . . nature,* as it is for this abstract thinking. Nature is external to it—its self-loss; and it apprehends nature also in an external fashion, as abstract thinking—but as alienated abstract thinking. Finally, *Mind,* this thinking returning home to its own point of origin—the thinking which, as the anthropological, phenomenological, psychological, ethical, artistic and religious mind is not valid for itself, until ultimately it finds itself, and relates itself to itself, as *absolute* knowledge in the hence absolute, i.e., abstract mind, and so receives its conscious embodiment in a mode of being corresponding to it. For its real mode of being is *abstraction.*

There is a double error in Hegel.

* The reference is to Hegel's *Encyclopedia of the Philosophical Sciences,* a one volume work in three parts, only the first and third of which have appeared in English. William Wallace's translation of Pt. I, on logic, is quoted frequently in Appendix II.—*Ed.*

The first emerges most clearly in the *Phenomenology,* the Hegelian philosophy's place of origin. When, for instance, wealth, state power, etc., are understood by Hegel as entities estranged from the *human* being, this only happens in their form as thoughts. . . . They are thought-entities, and therefore merely an estrangement of *pure,* i.e., abstract, philosophical thinking. The whole process therefore ends with Absolute Knowledge. It is precisely abstract thought from which these objects are estranged and which they confront with their arrogation of reality. The *philosopher* sets up himself (that is, one who is himself an abstract form of estranged man) as the *measuring rod* of the estranged world. The whole *history of the alienation-process* and the whole *process of the retraction* of the alienation is therefore nothing but the *history of the production* of abstract (i.e., absolute) thought—of logical, speculative thought. The *estrangement,* which therefore forms the real interest of this alienation and of the transcendence of this alienation, is the opposition of *in itself* and *for itself, of consciousness* and *self-consciousness,* of *object* and *subject*—that is to say, it is the opposition, within thought itself, between abstract thinking and sensuous reality or real sensuousness. All other oppositions and movements of these oppositions are but the *semblance, the cloak, the exoteric* shape of these oppositions which alone matter, and which constitute the *meaning* of these other, profane oppositions. It is not the fact that the human being *objectifies himself inhumanly,* in opposition to himself, but the fact that he *objectifies himself* in *distinction* from and in *opposition* to abstract thinking, that is the posited essence of the estrangement and the thing to be superseded.

The appropriation of man's essential powers, which have become objects—indeed, alien objects—is thus in the *first place* only an *appropriation* occurring in *consciousness,* in *pure thought* —i.e., in *abstraction*: It is the appropriation of these objects as *thoughts* and as *movements of thought.* Consequently, despite its thoroughly negative and critical appearance and despite the criticism really contained in it, which often anticipates far later development, there is already latent in the *Phenomenology* as a germ, a potentiality, a secret, the uncritical positivism and the equally uncritical idealism of Hegel's later works—that philosophic dissolution and restoration of the existing empirical world. In the *second place*: The vindication of the objective world for man—for example, the realization that *sensuous* consciousness is not an *abstractly* sensuous consciousness but a *humanly* sensuous consciousness—that religion, wealth, etc., are but the estranged world of *human* objectification, of *man's* essential powers given over to work and that they are therefore but the *path* to the true *human* world—this appropriation or the insight into this process consequently appears in Hegel in this form, that *sense, religion,* state power, etc., are *spiritual* entities; for only *mind* is the *true* essence of man, and the true form of mind is thinking mind, the logical, speculative mind. The *humanness* of nature and of the nature begotten by history—the humanness of man's products—appears in the form that they are *products* of abstract mind and as such, therefore, phases of *mind—thought entities*. The *Phenomenology* is, therefore, an occult critique—still to itself obscure and mystifying criticism; but inasmuch as it keeps steadily in view man's *estrangement,* even though man appears only in the shape of mind, there lie concealed in it *all* the elements of criticism, already *prepared* and *elaborated* in a manner often rising far above the Hegelian standpoint. The "Unhappy Consciousness," the "Honest Consciousness," the struggle of the "Noble and Base Consciousness," etc., etc.,—these separate sections contain, but still in an estranged form, the *critical* elements of whole spheres such as religion, the state, civil life, etc. Just as *entities, objects,* appear as *thought-entities,* so the *subject* is always *consciousness* or *self-consciousness*; or rather the object appears only as *abstract* consciousness, man only as *self-consciousness*: The distinct forms of estrangement which make their appearance are, therefore, only various forms of consciousness and self-consciousness. Just as *in itself* abstract consciousness (the form in which the object is conceived) is merely a moment of distinction of self-consciousness, what appears as the result of the movement is the identity of self-consciousness with consciousness—absolute knowledge—the movement of abstract thought no longer directed outwards but going on now only within its own self; that is to say, the dialectic of pure thought is the result.

The outstanding thing in Hegel's *Phenomenology* and its final outcome—that is, the dialectic of negativity as the moving and generating principle—is thus first that Hegel conceives the self-genesis of man as a process, conceives objectification as loss of the object, as alienation, and as transcendence of this alienation; that he thus grasps the essence of *labor* and comprehends objective man—true, because real man—as the outcome of man's *own labor.* The *real,* active orientation of man to himself as a species being, or his manifestation as a real species being (i.e., as a human being), is only possible by his really bringing out of himself all the *powers* that are his as the *species* man—something which in turn is only possible through the totality of man's actions, as the result of history—is only possible by man's treating these generic powers as objects; and this, to begin with, is again only possible in the form of estrangement.

—Marx, *Economic and Philosophical Manuscripts of 1844,* pp. 148–51.

C. Hegel's Positive and Negative Sides

There can therefore no longer be any question about an act of accommodation on Hegel's part *vis-à-vis* religion, the state, etc., since this lie is *the* lie of his principle.

If I *know* religion as *alienated* human self-consciousness, then what I know in it as religion is not my self-consciousness, but my alienated self-consciousness confirmed in it. I therefore know my own self, the self-consciousness that belongs to its very nature, confirmed not in *religion* but rather in *annihilated* and *superseded* religion.

In Hegel, therefore, the negation of the negation is not the confirmation of the true essence, effected precisely through negation of the pseudo-essence. With him the negation of the negation is the confirmation of the pseudo-essence, or of the self-estranged essence in its denial; or it is the denial of this pseudo-essence as an objective being dwelling outside man and independent of him, and its transformation into the subject.

A peculiar role, therefore, is played by the act of *superseding* in which denial and preservation—denial and affirmation—are bound together.

Thus, for example, in Hegel's *Philosophy of Right,* Private Right superseded equals *Morality,* Morality superseded equals the *Family,* the Family superseded equals *Civil Society,* Civil Society superseded equals the *State,* the State superseded equals *World History.* In the *actual world* private right, morality, the family, civil society, the state, etc., remain in existence, only they have become *moments* of man—state of his existence and being

—which have no validity in isolation, but dissolve and engender one another, etc. They have become *moments of motion.*

In their actual existence this *mobile* nature of theirs is hidden. It first appears and is made manifest in thought, in philosophy. Hence my true religious existence is my existence in the *philosophy of religion*; my true political existence is my existence within the *philosophy of right;* my true natural existence, existence in the *philosophy of nature;* my true artistic existence, existence in the *philosophy of art*; my true *human* existence, my existence in *philosophy*. Likewise the true existence of religion, the state, nature, art, is the *philosophy* of religion, of nature, of the state and of art. If, however, the philosophy of religion, etc., is for me the sole true existence of religion, then, too, it is only as a *philosopher of religion* that I am truly religious, and so I deny *real* religious sentiment and the really *religious* man. But at the same time I *assert* them, in part within my own existence or within the alien existence which I oppose to them—for this *is* only their *philosophic* expression—and in part I assert them in their own original shape, for they have validity for me as merely the *apparent* other-being, as allegories, forms of their own true existence (i.e., of my *philosophical* existence) hidden under sensuous disguises. . . .

It is now time to lay hold of the *positive* aspects of the Hegelian dialectic within the realm of estrangement.

(a) *Annulling* as an objective movement of *retracting* the alienation *into self.* This is the insight, expressed within the estrangement, concerning the *appropriation* of the objective essence through the annulment of its estrangement; it is the estranged insight into the *real objectification* of man, into the real appropriation of his objective essence through the annihilation of the *estranged* character of the objective world, through the annulment of the objective world in its estranged mode of being—just as atheism, being the annulment of God, is the advent of theoretic humanism, and communism, as the annulment of private property, is the justification of real human life as man's possession and thus the advent of practical humanism (or just as atheism is humanism mediated with itself through the annulment of religion, whilst communism is humanism mediated with itself through the annulment of private property). Only through the annulment of this mediation—which is itself, however, a necessary premise—does positively self-deriving humanism, *positive humanism,* come into being.

But atheism and communism are no flight, no abstraction; they are not a losing of the objective world begotten by man—of man's essential powers given over to the realm of objectivity; they are not a returning in poverty to unnatural, primitive simplicity. On the contrary, they are but the first real coming-to-be, the realization become real for man, of man's essence—of the essence of man as something real.

Thus, by grasping the *positive* meaning of self-referred negation (if even again in estranged fashion) Hegel grasps man's self-estrangement, the alienation of man's essense, man's loss of objectivity and his loss of realness as finding of self, change of his nature, his objectification and realization. In short, within the sphere of abstraction, Hegel conceives labor as man's act of *self-genesis*—conceives man's relation to himself as an alien being and the manifesting of himself as an alien being to be the coming-to-be of *species-consciousness* and *species-life.* . . .

Hegel's positive achievement here, in his speculative logic, is that the *determinate concepts,* the universal *fixed thought-forms* in their independence *vis-à-vis* nature and mind are a necessary result of the general estrangement of the human essence and therefore also of human thought, and that Hegel has therefore brought these together and presented them as moments of the abstraction-process. For example, superseded Being is Essence, superseded Essence is Concept, the Concept superseded is . . . the Absolute Idea. But what, then, is the Absolute Idea? It supersedes its own self again, if it does not want to traverse once more from the beginning the whole act of abstraction, and to acquiesce in being a totality of abstractions or in being the self-comprehending abstraction. But abstraction comprehending itself as abstraction knows itself to be nothing; it must abandon itself—abandon abstraction—and so it arrives at an entity which is its exact contrary—at *nature.* Thus, the entire *Logic* is the demonstration that abstract thought is nothing in itself; that the Absolute Idea is nothing in itself; that only *Nature* is something.

But *nature* too, taken abstractly, for itself—nature fixed in isolation from man—is *nothing* for man. It goes without saying that the abstract thinker who has committed himself to intuiting, intuits nature abstractly. Just as nature lay enclosed in the thinker in the form of the absolute idea, in the form of a thought-entity—in a shape which is his and yet is esoteric and mysterious even to him—so what he has let go forth from himself in truth is only this *abstract nature,* only nature as a *thought-entity*—but with the significance now of being the other-being of thought, of being real, intuited nature—of being nature distinguished from abstract thought. Or, to talk a human language, the abstract thinker learns in his intuition of nature that the entities which he thought to create from nothing, from pure abstraction—the entities he believed he was producing in the divine dialectic as pure products of the labor of thought forever weaving in itself and never looking outward—are nothing else but *abstractions* from *characteristics of nature.* To him, therefore, the whole of nature merely repeats the logical abstractions in a sensuous, external form. He *analyzes* it and these abstractions over again. Thus, his intuition of nature is only the act of confirming his abstraction from the intuition of nature—is only the conscious repetition by him of the process of begetting his abstraction. . . .

—MARX, *Economic and Philosophical Manuscripts of 1844,* pp. 161–70.

[4]

BRUNO BAUER: A THEOLOGIAN FROM THE VERY BEGINNING

Herr Bauer, who carries through his own opposition to substance, his own philosophy of self-consciousness or of the Spirit in all domains, must consequently only have the figments of his own brain to deal with in all domains. In his hand Criticism is the instrument to sublimate into mere appearance and pure thought all that claims a finite material existence outside infinite self-consciousness. In the substance it is not the metaphysical illusion he combats but its worldly kernel, Nature; nature existing both outside man and as man's nature. Not to presume Substance in any domain—he still uses this language—means therefore for him not to recognize any being distinct from thought, any natural energy distinct from the spontaneity of the spirit, any human power of being distinct from reason, any passivity distinct from activity, any influence distinct from one's own action, any feeling or willing distinct from knowing, any heart distinct from the head, any object distinct from the subject, any practice distinct from theory, any man distinct from the critic, any real universality distinct from abstract generality, any *tu* distinct from the *ego*. Herr Bauer is therefore consistent when he goes on to identify himself with infinite self-consciousness, with the Spirit, that is, to replace these creations of his by their creator. He is just as consistent in rejecting as stubborn mass and matter the rest of the world which obstinately claims to be something distinct from what he, Herr Bauer, produced. And so he hopes:

> *It won't be long*
> *Till the end of bodies comes.*
> —Goethe's *Faust*

His own discontent that he has so far been unable to get at the something of "this clumsy world," he also construes quite consistently as self-discontent of the world; and the indignation of his Criticism over the development of mankind as massy indignation of mankind over his Criticism, over the spirit, over Herr Bruno Bauer and Company.

Herr Bauer was a theologian from the very beginning but no ordinary one: He was a Critical theologian or theological Critic. While still the extreme representative of old Hegelian orthodoxy, a speculative arranger of all religious and theological nonsense, he constantly proclaimed Criticism his private domain. At that time he called Strauss's criticism human criticism and expressly vindicated the right of divine criticism in opposition to it. He later stripped the great self-reliance or self-consciousness, which was the hidden kernel of that divinity, of its religious shell, made it self-existing as an independent being, and raised it, under the trade-mark "infinite Self-consciousness," to the rank of principle of criticism. Then he accomplished in his own movement the movement that the "Philosophy of Self-consciousness" goes through as the absolute act of life. He again abolished the "distinction" between "the product," infinite self-consciousness, and the producer himself, and acknowledged that infinite self-consciousness in his movement "was only he himself," and that therefore the movement of the universe first becomes true and real in his ideal self-movement. . . .

Returning to its starting-point, Absolute Criticism ended the speculative circular motion and thereby its own life's career. Its further movement is pure—soaring round within itself above all massy interest and hence void of any further interest for the mass.

—Marx and Engels, *The Holy Family* (1844), pp. 189–92.

[5]

ALIENATION

A. Private Property and Alienated Labor

Now, therefore, we have to grasp the essential connection between private property, avarice, and the separation of labor, capital, and landed property; between exchange and competition, value and the devaluation of men, monopoly and competition, etc.; the connection between this whole estrangement and the *money* system.

Do not let us go back to a fictitious primordial condition as the political economist does, when he tries to explain. Such a primordial condition explains nothing. He merely pushes the question away into a grey nebulous distance. He assumes in the form of fact, of an event, what he is supposed to deduce—namely, the necessary relationship between two things—between, for example, division of labor and exchange. Theology in the same way explains the origin of evil by the fall of man; that is, it assumes as a fact, in historical form, what has to be explained.

We proceed from an *actual* economic fact.

The worker becomes all the poorer the more wealth he produces, the more his production increases in power and range. The worker becomes an ever cheaper commodity the more commodities he creates. With the *increasing value* of the world of things proceeds in direct proportion the *devaluation* of the world of men. Labor produces not only commodities: it produces itself and the worker as a *commodity*—and does so in the proportion in which it produces commodities generally.

This fact expresses merely that the object which labor produces—labor's product—confronts it as *something alien*, as a *power independent* of the producer. The product of labor is labor which has been congealed in an object, which has become material; it is the *objectification* of labor. Labor's realization is its objectification. In the conditions dealt with by political economy this realization of labor appears as *loss of reality* for the workers; objectification as *loss of the object* and *object-bondage;* appropriation as *estrangement,* as *alienation* [Entäusserung].*

So much does labor's realization appear as loss of reality that the worker loses reality to the point of starving to death. So much does objectification appear as loss of the object that the worker is robbed of the objects most necessary not only for his life but for his work. Indeed, labor itself becomes an object which he can get hold of only with the greatest effort and with the most irregular interruptions. So much does the appropriation of the object appear as estrangement that the more objects the worker produces the fewer can he possess and the more he falls under the dominion of his product, capital.

All these consequences are contained in the definition that the worker is related to the *product of his labor* as to an *alien* object. For on this premise it is clear that the more the worker spends himself, the more powerful the alien objective world becomes which he creates over against himself, the poorer he himself—his inner world—becomes, the less belongs to him as his own. It is the same in religion. The more man puts into God, the less he retains in himself. The worker puts his life into the object; but now his life no longer belongs to him but to the object. Hence, the greater this activity, the greater is the worker's lack of objects. Whatever the product of his labor is, he is not. Therefore the greater this product, the less is he himself. The *alienation* of the worker in his product means not only that his labor becomes an object, an *external* existence, but that it exists *outside him,* independently, as something alien to him, and that it becomes a power on its own confronting him; it means that the life which he has conferred on the object confronts him as something hostile and alien.

Let us now look more closely at the *objectification,* at the production of the worker; and therein at the *estrangement,* the *loss* of the object, his product.

The worker can create nothing without *nature,* without the *sensuous external world.* It is the material on which his labor

* For a later statement of this idea see Marx, *Capital,* vol. I, section 4, "The Fetishism of Commodities and the Secret thereof."—*Ed.*

is manifested, in which it is active, from which and by means of which it produces.

But just as nature provides labor with the *means of life* in the sense that labor cannot *live* without objects on which to operate, on the other hand, it also provides the *means of life* in the more restricted sense—i.e., the means for the physical subsistence of the *worker* himself.

Thus the more the worker by his labor *appropriates* the external world, sensuous nature, the more he deprives himself of *means of life* in the double respect: first, that the sensuous external world more and more ceases to be an object belonging to his labor—to be his labor's *means of life;* and secondly, that it more and more ceases to be *means of life* in the immediate sense, means for the physical subsistence of the worker.

Thus in this double respect the worker becomes a slave of his object, first, in that he receives an *object of labor,* i.e., in that he receives *work;* and secondly, in that he receives *means of subsistence.* Therefore, it enables him to exist, first, as a *worker;* and, second, as a *physical subject.* The extremity of this bondage is that it is only as a *worker* that he continues to maintain himself as a *physical subject,* and that it is only as a *physical subject* that he is a *worker. . . .*

What, then, constitutes the alienation of labor?

First, the fact that labor is *external* to the worker, i.e., it does not belong to his essential being; that in his work, therefore, he does not affirm himself but denies himself, does not feel content but unhappy, does not develop freely his physical and mental energy but mortifies his body and ruins his mind. The worker therefore only feels himself outside his work, and in his work feels outside himself. He is at home when he is not working, and when he is working he is not at home. His labor is therefore not voluntary, but coerced; it is *forced labor.* It is therefore not the satisfaction of a need; it is merely a *means* to satisfy needs external to it. Its alien character emerges clearly in the fact that as soon as no physical or other compulsion exists, labor is shunned like the plague. External labor, labor in which man alienates himself, is a labor of self-sacrifice, of mortification. Lastly, the external character of labor for the worker appears in the fact that it is not his own, but someone else's, that it does not belong to him, that in it he belongs, not to himself, but to another. Just as in religion the spontaneous activity of the human imagination, of the human brain and the human heart, operates independently of the individual—that is, operates on him as an alien, divine or diabolical activity—in the same way the worker's activity is not his spontaneous activity. It belongs to another; it is the loss of his self.

As a result, therefore, man (the worker) no longer feels himself to be freely active in any but his animal functions—eating, drinking, procreating, or at most in his dwelling and in dressing-up, etc.; and in his human functions he no longer feels himself to be anything but an animal. What is animal becomes human and what is human becomes animal.

Certainly eating, drinking, procreating, etc., are also genuinely human functions. But in the abstraction which separates them from the sphere of all other human activity and turns them into sole and ultimate ends, they are animal.

We have considered the act of estranging practical human activity, labor, in two of its aspects. (1) The relation of the worker to the *product of labor* as an alien object exercising power over him. This relation is at the same time the relation to the sensuous external world, to the objects of nature as an alien world antagonistically opposed to him. (2) The relation of labor to the *act of production* within the *labor* process. This relation is the relation of the worker to his own activity as an alien activity not belonging to him; it is activity as suffering, strength as weakness, begetting as emasculating. The worker's *own* physical and mental energy, his personal life or what is life other than activity—as an activity which is turned against him, neither depends on nor belongs to him.* Here we have *self-estrangement,* as we had previously the estrangement of the *thing.* . . .

The animal is immediately identical with its life-activity. It does not distinguish itself from it. It is *its life-activity.* Man makes his life-activity itself the object of his will and of his consciousness. He has conscious life-activity. It is not a determination with

* This idea of man's alienation from himself in the labor process is restated by Marx in *Capital,* where he says that under capitalism "the laborer exists for the process of production, and not the process of production for the laborer. . . ." (vol. I, p. 536). The same thought recurs in his *Theories of Surplus Value:* "The worker himself appears in this—the bourgeois conception —as what he really is in capitalist production—a mere means of production; not as an end in himself and the goal of production." (*Theorien über den Mehrwert,* ed. K. Kautsky, Stuttgart 1905–10, vol. II, p. 334.) See also above, Part seven, No. 8.—*Ed.*

which he directly merges. Conscious life-activity directly distinguishes man from animal life-activity. It is just because of this that he is a species being. Or it is only because he is a species being that he is a Conscious Being, i.e., that his own life is an object for him. Only because of that is his activity free activity. Estranged labor reverses this relationship, so that it is just because man is a conscious being that he makes his life-activity, his *essential* being, a mere means to his *existence.*

In creating an *objective world* by his practical activity, in *working-up* inorganic nature, man proves himself a conscious species being, i.e., as a being that treats the species as its own essential being, or that treats itself as a species being. Admittedly, animals also produce. They build themselves nests, dwellings, like the bees, beavers, ants, etc. But an animal only produces what it immediately needs for itself or its young. It produces one-sidedly, whilst man produces universally. It produces only under the dominion of immediate physical need, whilst man produces even when he is free from physical need and only truly produces in freedom therefrom. An animal produces only itself, whilst man reproduces the whole of nature. An animal's product belongs immediately to its physical body, whilst man freely confronts his product. An animal forms things in accordance with the standard and the need of the species to which it belongs, whilst man knows how to produce in accordance with the standard of every species, and knows how to apply everywhere the inherent standard to the object. Man therefore also forms things in accordance with the laws of beauty.*

It is just in the working-up of the objective world, therefore, that man first really proves himself to be a *species being.* This production is his active species life. Through and because of this production, nature appears as *his* work and his reality. The object of labor is, therefore, the *objectification of man's species life;* for he duplicates himself not only, as in consciousness, intellectually, but also actively, in reality, and therefore he contemplates himself in a world that he has created. In tearing away from man the object of his production, therefore, estranged labor tears from him his *species life,* his real species objectivity, and transforms his advantage over animals into the disadvantage that his inorganic body, nature, is taken from him.

* For the further development of some of the thoughts in this paragraph see *Capital,* vol. I, pp. 156–60, and p. 319.—*Ed.*

Similarly, in degrading spontaneous activity, free activity, to a means, estranged labor makes man's species life a means to his physical existence.

The consciousness which man has of his species is thus transformed by estrangement in such a way that the species life becomes for him a means.

Estranged labor turns thus:

Man's species being, both nature and his spiritual species property, into a being *alien* to him, into a *means* to his *individual existence.* It estranges man's own body from him, as it does external nature and his spiritual essence, his *human* being.

An immediate consequence of the fact that man is estranged from the product of his labor, from his life-activity, from his species being is the *estrangement of man* from *man.* If a man is confronted by himself, he is confronted by the *other* man. What applies to a man's relation to his work, to the product of his labor and to himself, also holds of a man's relation to the other man, and to the other man's labor and object of labor.

In fact, the proposition that man's species nature is estranged from him means that one man is estranged from the other, as each of them is from man's essential nature.

The estrangement of man, and in fact every relationship in which man stands to himself, is first realized and expressed in the relationship in which a man stands to other men.

Hence within the relationship of estranged labor each man views the other in accordance with the standard and the position in which he finds himself as a worker.

We took our departure from a fact of political economy—the estrangement of the worker and his production. We have formulated the concept of this fact—*estranged, alienated* labor. We have analyzed this concept—hence analyzing merely a fact of political economy.

Let us now see, further, how in real life the concept of estranged, alienated labor must express and present itself.

If the product of labor is alien to me, if it confronts me as an alien power, to whom, then, does it belong?

If my own activity does not belong to me, if it is an alien, a coerced activity, to whom, then, does it belong?

To a being *other* than me.

Who is this being?

The *gods?* To be sure, in the earliest times the principal production (for example, the building of temples, etc., in Egypt, India, and Mexico) appears to be in the service of the gods, and the product belongs to the gods. However, the gods on their own were never the lords of labor. No more was *nature*. And what a contradiction it would be if, the more man subjugated nature by his labor and the more the miracles of the gods were rendered superfluous by the miracles of industry, the more men were to renounce the joy of production and the enjoyment of the produce in favor of these powers.

The *alien* being, to whom labor and the produce of labor belongs, in whose service labor is done and for whose benefit the produce of labor is provided, can only be *man* himself.

If the product of labor does not belong to the worker, if it confronts him as an alien power, this can only be because it belongs to some *other man than the worker*. If the worker's activity is a torment to him, to another it must be *delight* and his life's joy. Not the gods, not nature, but only man himself can be this alien power over man.

We must bear in mind the above-stated proposition that man's relation to himself only becomes *objective* and *real* for him through his relation to the other man. Thus, if the product of his labor, his labor *objectified*, is for him an *alien*, hostile, powerful object independent of him, then his position towards it is such that someone else is master of this object, someone who is alien, hostile, powerful, and independent of him. If his own activity is to him an unfree activity, then he is treating it as activity performed in the service, under the dominion, the coercion, and the yoke of another man.

Every self-estrangement of man from himself and from nature appears in the relation in which he places himself and nature to men other than and differentiated from himself. For this reason religious self-estrangement necessarily appears in the relationship of the layman to the priest, or again to a mediator, etc., since we are here dealing with the intellectual world. In the real practical world self-estrangement can only become manifest through the real practical relationship to other men. The medium through which estrangement takes place is itself *practical*. Thus through estranged labor man not only engenders his relationship to the object and to the act of production as to powers that are alien and hostile to him; he also engenders the relationship in which other men stand to his production and to his product, and the relationship in which he stands to these other men. Just as he begets his own production as the loss of his reality, as his punishment; just as he begets his own product as a loss, as a product not belonging to him; so he begets the dominion over production and over the product of the one who does not produce. Just as he estranges from himself his own activity, so he confers to the stranger activity which is not his own.

Till now we have only considered this relationship from the standpoint of the worker. Later we shall be considering it also from the standpoint of the non-worker.

Through *estranged, alienated labor,* then, the worker produces the relationship to this labor of a man alien to labor and standing outside it. The relationship of the worker to labor engenders the relation to it of the capitalist, or whatever one chooses to call the master of labor. *Private property* is thus the product, the result, the necessary consequence, of *alienated labor,* of the external relation of the worker to nature and to himself.

Private property thus results by analysis from the concept of *alienated labor*—i.e., of *alienated man,* of estranged labor, of estranged life, of *estranged* man.

True, it is as a result of the *movement of private property* that we have obtained the concept of *alienated labor* (*of alienated life*) from political economy. But on analysis of this concept it becomes clear that though private property appears to be the source, the cause of alienated labor, it is really its consequence, just as the gods *in the beginning* are not the cause but the effect of man's intellectual confusion. Later this relationship becomes reciprocal.

Only at the very culmination of the development of private property does this, its secret, re-emerge, namely, that on the one hand it is the *product* of alienated labor, and that secondly it is the *means* by which labor alienates itself, the *realization of this alienation.*

—Marx, *Economic and Philosophic Manuscripts of 1844,* pp. 68–81.

B. The Sway of Inhuman Power

We have said above that man is regressing to the *cave dwelling,* etc.—but that he is regressing to it in an estranged, malignant form. The savage in his cave—a natural element which freely offers itself for his use and protection—feels himself no more a stranger, or rather feels himself to be just as much at home as a *fish* in water. But the cellar-dwelling of the poor man is a hostile dwelling, "an alien, restraining power which only gives itself up to him in so far as he gives up to it his blood and sweat"—a dwelling which he cannot look upon as his own home where he might at last exclaim, "Here I am at home," but where instead he finds himself in *someone else's* house, in the house of a *stranger* who daily lies in wait for him and throws him out if he does not pay his rent. Similarly, he is also aware of the contrast in quality between his dwelling and a human dwelling—a residence in that *other* world, the heaven of wealth.

Estrangement is manifested not only in the fact that *my* means of life belong to *someone else,* that *my* desire is the inaccessible possession of *another,* but also in the fact that everything is in itself something *different* from itself—that my activity is *something else* and that, finally (and this applies also to the capitalist), all is under the sway of *inhuman* power. There is a form of inactive, extravagant wealth given over wholly to pleasure, the enjoyer of which on the one hand *behaves* as a mere *ephemeral* individual frantically spending himself to no purpose, knows the slave labor of others (human *sweat and blood*) as the prey of his cupidity, and therefore knows man himself, and hence also his own self, as a sacrificed and empty being. With such wealth the contempt of man makes its appearance, partly as arrogance and as the throwing away of what can give sustenance to a hundred human lives, and partly as the infamous illusion that his own unbridled extravagance and ceaseless, unproductive consumption is the condition of the other's *labor* and therefore of his *subsistence.* He knows the realization of the *essential powers* of man only as the realization of his own excesses, his whims and capricious, bizarre notions. This wealth which, on the other hand, again knows wealth as a mere means, as something that is good for nothing but to be annihilated and which is therefore at once slave and master, at once generous and mean, capricious, presumptuous, conceited, refined, cultured and witty—this wealth has not yet experienced *wealth* as an utterly *alien power* over itself; it sees in it, rather, only its own power, and not wealth but *gratification* [is its] final aim and end.

—Marx, *Economic and Philosophic Manuscripts of 1844,* pp. 125*f.*

C. Communism Equals Humanism

Communism as the *positive* transcendence of *private property,* as *human self-estrangement,* and therefore as the real *appropriation of the human* essence by and for man; communism therefore as the complete return of man to himself as a *social* (i.e., human) being—a return become conscious, and accomplished within the entire wealth of previous development. This communism, as fully developed naturalism, equals humanism, and as fully developed humanism equals naturalism; it is the *genuine* resolution of the conflict between man and nature and between man and man—the true resolution of the strife between existence and essence, between objectification and self-confirmation, between freedom and necessity, between the individual and the species. Communism is the riddle of history solved, and it knows itself to be this solution.

The entire movement of history is, therefore, both its *actual* act of genesis (the birth act of its empirical existence) and also for its thinking consciousness the *comprehended* and *known* process of its *coming-to-be*. That other, still immature communism, meanwhile, seeks an *historical* proof for itself—a proof in the realm of the existent—amongst disconnected historical phenomena opposed to private property, tearing single phases from the historical process and focusing attention on them as proofs of its historical pedigree (a horse ridden hard especially by Cabet, Villegardelle, etc.). By so doing it simply makes clear that by far the greater part of this process contradicts its claims, and that, if it has once been, precisely its being in the *past* refutes its pretension to being *essential.*

That the entire revolutionary movement necessarily finds both its empirical and its theoretical basis in the movement of *private property*—in that of the economy, to be precise—is easy to see.

This *material,* immediately *sensuous* private property is the material sensuous expression of *estranged human* life. Its movement—production and consumption—is the *sensuous* revelation of the movement of all production hitherto—i.e., the realization or the reality of man. Religion, family, state, law, morality, science, art, etc., are only *particular* modes of production, and fall under its general law. The positive transcendence of *private property* as the appropriation of *human* life is, therefore, the positive transcendence of all estrangement—that is to say, the return of man from religion, family, state, etc., to his *human*, i.e., *social* mode of existence. Religious estrangement as such occurs only in the realm of *consciousness*, of man's inner life, but economic estrangement is that of *real life;* its transcendence therefore embraces both aspects. It is evident that the *initial* stage of the movement amongst the various peoples depends on whether the true and for them *authentic* life of the people manifests itself more in consciousness or in the external world—is more ideal or real. Communism begins from the outset (*Owen*) with atheism; but atheism is at first far from being *communism;* indeed, it is still mostly an abstraction.

The philanthropy of atheism is therefore at first only *philosophical*, abstract, philanthropy, and that of communism is at once *real* and directly bent on *action*. . . .

But again when I am active *scientifically*, etc.—when I am engaged in activity which I can seldom perform in direct community with others—then I am *social*, because I am active as a *man*. Not only is the material of my activity given to me as a social product (as is even the language in which the thinker is active); my *own* existence *is* social activity, and therefore that which I make of myself, I make of myself for society and with the consciousness of myself as a social being. . . .

What is to be avoided above all is the re-establishing of "Society" as an abstraction *vis-à-vis* the individual. The individual *is the social being*. . . .

Man, much as he may therefore be a *particular* individual (and it is precisely his particularity which makes him an individual, and a real *individual* social being), is just as much the *totality*—the ideal totality—the subjective existence of thought and experienced society present for itself; just as he exists also in the real world as the awareness and the real enjoyment of social existence, and as a totality of human life-activity.

Thinking and being are thus no doubt *distinct*, but at the same time they are in *unity* with each other. . . .

The transcendence of private property is therefore the complete *emancipation* of all human senses and attributes; but it is this emancipation precisely because these senses and attributes have become, subjectively and objectively, *human*. The eye has become a *human* eye, just as its *object* has become a social, *human* object—an object emanating from man for man. The *senses* have therefore become directly in their practice *theoreticians*. They relate themselves to the *thing* for the sake of the thing, but the thing itself is an *objective human* relation to itself and to man * and vice versa. Need or enjoyment have consequently lost their *egotistical* nature, and nature has lost its mere *utility* by use becoming *human* use.

In the same way, the senses and enjoyments of other men have become my *own* appropriation. Besides these direct organs, therefore, *social* organs develop in the *form* of society; thus, for instance, activity in direct association with others, etc., has become an organ for *expressing* my own *life,* and a mode of appropriating *human* life.

It is obvious that the *human* eye gratifies itself in a way different from the crude, non-human eye; the human *ear* different from the crude ear, etc.

To recapitulate: Man is not lost in his object only when the object becomes for him a *human* object or objective man. This is possible only when the object becomes for him a *social* object, he himself for himself a social being, just as society becomes a being for him in this object.

On the one hand, therefore, it is only when the objective world becomes everywhere for man in society the world of man's essential powers—human reality, and for that reason the reality of his *own* essential powers—that all *objects* become for him the *objectification of himself,* become objects which confirm and realize his individuality, become *his* objects; that is, *man himself* becomes the object. The manner in which they become *his* depends on the *nature of the objects* and on the nature of the *essential power* corresponding *to it;* for it is precisely the *determinateness* of this relationship which shapes the particular, *real* mode of affirmation. To the *eye* an object comes to be other than it is to the *ear,* and the object of the eye is another object than the object of the *ear.* The peculiarity of each essential power is precisely its *peculiar essence,* and therefore also the peculiar mode of its objectification, of its *objectively actual* living *being.* Thus man is affirmed in the objective world not only in the act of thinking, but with *all* his senses.

On the other hand, looking at this in its subjective aspect: Just as music alone awakens in man the sense of music, and just as the most beautiful music has *no* sense for the unmusical ear—is

* In practice I can relate myself to a thing humanly only if the thing relates itself to the human being humanly.

no object for it, because my object can only be the confirmation of one of my essential powers and can therefore only be so for me as my essential power is present for itself as a subjective capacity, because the sense of an object for me goes only so far as *my* senses go (has only sense for a sense corresponding to that object)—for this reason the *senses* of the social man are *other* senses than those of the non-social man. Only through the objectively unfolded richness of man's essential being is the richness of subjective *human* sensibility (a musical ear, an eye for beauty of form—in short, *senses* capable of human gratifications, senses confirming themselves as essential powers of *man*) either cultivated or brought into being. For not only the five senses but also the so-called mental senses—the practical senses (will, love, etc.)—in a word, *human* sense—the humanness of the senses—comes to be by virtue of its object, by virtue of *humanized* nature. The *forming* of the five senses is a labor of the entire history of the world down to the present.

The *sense* caught up in crude practical need has only a *restricted* sense. For the starving man, it is not the human form of food that exists, but only its abstract being as food; it could just as well be there in its crudest form, and it would be impossible to say wherein this feeding-activity differs from that of *animals*. The care-burdened man in need has no sense for the finest play; the dealer in minerals sees only the mercantile value but not the beauty and the unique nature of the mineral; he has no mineralogical sense. Thus, the objectification of the human essence both in its theoretical and practical aspects is required to make man's *sense human*, as well as to create the *human sense* corresponding to the entire wealth of human and natural substance.

Just as resulting from the movement of *private property*, of its wealth as well as its poverty—or of its material and spiritual wealth and poverty—the budding society finds to hand all the material for this *development;* so *established* society produces man in this entire richness of his being—produces the *rich* man *profoundly endowed with all the senses*—as its enduring reality.

It will be seen how subjectivism and objectivism, spiritualism and materialism, activity and suffering, only lose their antithetical character, and thus their existence, as such antitheses in the social condition; it will be seen how the resolution of the *theoretical* antitheses is *only* possible *in a practical* way, by virtue of the practical energy of men. Their resolution is therefore by no means merely a problem of knowledge, but a *real* problem of life, which *philosophy* could not solve precisely because it conceived this problem as *merely* a theoretical one.

—MARX, *Economic and Philosophic Manuscripts of 1844*, pp. 102–9.

D. THE HUMANIST TASK OF THE PROLETARIAT

Proletariat and wealth are opposites; as such they form a single whole. They are both forms of the world of private property. The question is what place each occupies in the antithesis. It is not sufficient to declare them two sides of a single whole.

Private property as private property, as wealth, is compelled to maintain *itself*, and thereby its opposite, the proletariat, in *existence*. That is the *positive* side of the contradiction, self-satisfied private property.

The proletariat, on the other hand, is compelled as proletariat to abolish itself and thereby its opposite, the condition for its existence, what makes it the proletariat, i.e., private property. That is the *negative* side of the contradiction, its restlessness within its very self, dissolved and self-dissolving private property.

The propertied class and the class of the proletariat present the same human self-alienation. But the former class finds in this self-alienation its confirmation and its good, *its own power:* It has in it a *semblance* of human existence. The class of the proletariat feels annihilated in its self-alienation; it sees in it its own powerlessness and the reality of an inhuman existence. In the words of Hegel, the class of the proletariat is in abasement *indignation* at that abasement, an indignation to which it is necessarily driven by the contradiction between its human *nature* and its *condition* of life, which is the outright, decisive, and comprehensive negation of that nature.

Within this antithesis the private owner is therefore the *conservative* side, the proletarian the *destructive* side. From the former arises the action of preserving the antithesis, from the latter, that of annihilating it.

Indeed private property, too, drives itself in its economic movement towards its own dissolution, only, however, through a development which does not depend on it, of which it is unconscious and which takes place against its will, through the very nature of things; only inasmuch as it produces the proletariat *as* proletariat, that misery conscious of its spiritual and physical misery, that dehumanization conscious of its dehumanization and therefore self-abolishing. The proletariat executes the sentence that private property pronounced on itself by begetting the proletariat, just as it carries out the sentence that wage labor pronounced on itself by bringing forth wealth for others and misery for itself. When the proletariat is victorious, it by no means becomes the absolute side of society, for it is victorious only by abolishing itself and its opposite. Then the proletariat disappears as well as the opposite which determines it, private property.

When Socialist writers ascribe this historic role to the proletariat, it is not, as Critical Criticism pretends to think, because they consider the proletarians as *gods*. Rather the contrary. Since the abstraction of all humanity, even of the *semblance* of humanity, is practically complete in the full-grown proletariat; since the conditions of life of the proletariat sum up all the conditions of life of society today in all their human acuity; since man has lost himself in the proletariat, yet at the same time has not only gained theoretical consciousness of that loss, but through urgent, no longer disguisable, absolutely imperative *need*—that practical expression of *necessity*—is driven directly to revolt against that inhumanity; it follows that the proletariat can and must free itself. But it cannot free itself without abolishing the conditions of its own life. It cannot abolish the conditions of its own life without abolishing *all* the inhuman conditions of life of society today which are summed up in its own situation. Not in vain does it go through the stern but steeling school of *labor*. The question is not what this or that proletarian, or even the whole of the proletariat at the moment *considers* as its aim. The question is *what the proletariat is,* and what, consequent on that *being,* it will be compelled to do. Its aim and historical action is irrevocably and obviously demonstrated in its own life situation as well as in the whole organization of bourgeois society today.

—MARX and ENGELS, *The Holy Family* (1844), pp. 51–53.

[6]

ATOMIC INDIVIDUALS AND SOCIETY

The members of civil society are not atoms. The specific property of the atom is that it has no properties and is therefore not connected with beings outside it by any relations determined by its own natural necessity. The atom has no needs, it is self-sufficient; the world outside it is absolute vacuum, i.e., it is contentless, senseless, meaningless, just because the atom has *all* its fullness in itself. The egotistic individual in civil society may in his non-sensuous imagination and lifeless abstraction inflate himself to the size of an atom, i.e., to an unrelated, self-sufficient, wantless, absolutely full, blessed being. Unblessed sensuous reality does not bother about his imagination; each of his senses compels him to believe in the existence of the world and the individuals outside him and even his profane stomach reminds him every day that the world outside him is not empty, but is what really fills. Every activity and property of his being, every one of his vital urges becomes a need, a necessity, which his self-seeking transforms into seeking for other things and human beings outside him. But as the need of one individual has no self-understood sense for the other egotistic individual capable of satisfying that need and therefore no direct connection with its satisfaction, each individual has to create that connection; it thus becomes the intermediary between the need of another and the object of that need. Therefore, it is natural necessity, essential human properties, however alienated they may seem to be, and interest that hold the members of civil society together; civil, not political life is their real tie. It is therefore not the state that holds the atoms of civil society together, but the fact that they are atoms only in imagination, in the heaven of their fancy, but in reality beings tremendously different from atoms, in other words, not divine egoists, but egotistic human beings. Only political superstition today imagines that social life must be held together by the state whereas in reality the state is held together by civil life.

—MARX and ENGELS, *The Holy Family* (1844), pp. 162*f.*

[7]

ON ONE-SIDEDNESS IN PHILOSOPHY, POLITICS, AND POLITICAL ECONOMY

The 18th century, the century of revolution, also revolutionized economics. But just as all the revolutions of this century were one-sided and bogged down in antitheses—just as abstract materialism was set in opposition to abstract spiritualism, the republic to monarchy, the social contract to divine right—likewise the economic revolution did not get beyond antithesis. The premises remained everywhere in force; materialism did not contend with the Christian contempt for and humiliation of Man, and merely posited Nature instead of the Christian God as the Absolute facing Man. In politics no one dreamt of examining the premises of the State as such. It did not occur to economics to question *the validity of private property*. Therefore, the new economics was only half an advance. It was obliged to betray and to disavow its own premises, to have recourse to sophistry and hypocrisy so as to cover up the contradictions in which it became entangled, so as to reach the conclusions to which it was driven not by its premises but by the humane spirit of the century. Thus economics took on a philanthropic character. It withdrew its favor from the producers and bestowed it on the consumers. It affected a solemn abhorrence of the bloody terror of the mercantile system, and proclaimed trade to be a bond of friendship and union among nations as among individuals. All was pure splendor and magnificence—yet the premises reasserted themselves soon enough, and in contrast to this sham philanthropy produced the Malthusian population theory—the crudest, most barbarous theory that ever existed, a system of despair which struck down all those beautiful phrases about love of neighbor and world citizenship. The premises begot and reared the factory system and modern slavery, which yields nothing in inhumanity and cruelty to ancient slavery. Modern economics—the system of free trade based on Adam Smith's *Wealth of Nations*—reveals itself to be that same hypocrisy, inconsistency, and immorality which now confront free humanity in every sphere.

But was Smith's system, then, not an advance? Of course it was, and a necessary advance at that. It was necessary to overthrow the mercantile system with its monopolies and hindrances to trade, so that the true consequences of private property could come to light. It was necessary for all these petty, local, and national considerations to recede into the background, so that the struggle of our time could become a universal human struggle. It was necessary for the theory of private property to leave the purely empirical path of merely objective enquiry and to acquire a more scientific character which would also make it responsible for the consequences, and thus transfer the matter to a universally human sphere. It was necessary to carry the immorality contained in the old economics to its highest pitch, by attempting to deny it and by veiling it in hypocrisy (a necessary result of that attempt). All this lay in the nature of the matter.

We gladly concede that it is only thanks to the establishment and development of free trade that we were placed in a position from which we can go beyond the economics of private property; but we must at the same time have the right to demonstrate the utter theoretical and practical nullity of this free trade.

The nearer to our time the economists whom we have to judge, the more severe must our judgment become. For while Smith and Malthus only had scattered fragments to go by, the modern economists had the whole system complete before them: The consequences had all been drawn; the contradictions came clearly enough to light; yet they did not come to examining the premises —and still undertook the responsibility for the whole system. The nearer the economists come to the present time, the further they depart from honesty. With every advance of time, sophistry necessarily increases, so as to prevent economics from lagging behind the times. This is why *Ricardo,* for instance, is more guilty than *Adam Smith,* and *MacCulloch* and *Mill* more guilty than *Ricardo.*

Modern economics cannot ever judge the mercantile system correctly, since it is itself one-sided and as yet fenced in by that very system's premises. Only that view which rises above the opposition of the two systems, which criticizes the premises common to both and proceeds from a purely human, universal basis, can assign to both their proper position.

—ENGELS, "Outlines of a Critique of Political Economy," in MARX, *Economic and Philosophic Manuscripts of 1844,* pp. 177–79.

[8]

THE SPIRITUAL ELEMENT IN PRODUCTION

[The production costs of a commodity consist, in the last analysis, of] only two sides—the natural objective side, land; and the human, subjective side, labor, which includes capital and besides capital, a third factor which the economist does not think about—I mean the spiritual element of invention, of thought, alongside the physical element of sheer labor. What has the economist to do with the spirit of invention? Have not all inventions come flying to him without any effort on his part? Has *one* of them cost him anything? Why then should he bother about them in the calculation of production costs? Land, capital, and labor are for him the conditions of wealth, and he requires no more. Science is no concern of his. What does it matter to him that he has received its gifts through Berthollet, Davy, Liebig, Watt, Cartwright, etc.—gifts which have benefited him and his production immeasurably? He does not know how to calculate such things; the advances of science go beyond his figures. But in a rational order which has gone beyond the division of interests as it is found with the economist, the spiritual element certainly belongs among the elements of production and will find its place, too, in economics among the costs of production. And here it is certainly gratifying to know that the promotion of science also brings its material reward; to know that a single achievement of science like James Watt's steam engine has brought in more for the world in the first 50 years of its existence than the world has spent on the promotion of science since the beginning of time.

We have, then, two elements of production in operation—nature and man, with man again active physically and spiritually, and can go back to the economist and his production costs.

—Engels, *ibid.*, in Marx, *Economic and Philosophic Manuscripts of 1844*, pp. 187*f*.

[9]

LUDWIG FEUERBACH

A. His Great Achievement

Feuerbach's great achievement is:

(1) The proof that philosophy is nothing else but religion rendered into thoughts and thoughtfully expounded, and that it has therefore likewise to be condemned as another form and manner of existence of the estrangement of the essence of man;

(2) The establishment of *true materialism* and of *real science*,

since Feuerbach also makes the social relationship "of man to man" the basic principle of the theory;

(3) His opposing to the negation of the negation, which claims to be the absolute positive, the self-supporting positive, positively grounded on itself.

Feuerbach explains the Hegelian dialectic (and thereby justifies starting out from the positive, from sense-certainty) as follows:

Hegel sets out from the estrangement of Substance (in Logic, from the Infinite, the abstractly universal)—from the absolute and fixed abstraction; which means, put popularly, that he sets out from religion and theology.

Secondly, he annuls the infinite, and establishes the actual, sensuous, real, finite, particular (philosophy—annulment of religion and theology).

Thirdly, he again annuls the positive and restores the abstraction, the infinite—Restoration of religion and theology.

Feuerbach thus conceives the negation of the negation *only* as a contradiction of philosophy with itself—as the philosophy which affirms theology (the transcendent, etc.) after having denied it, and which it therefore affirms in opposition to itself.

The position or self-affirmation and self-confirmation contained in the negation of the negation is taken to be a position which is not yet sure of itself, which is therefore burdened with its opposite, which is doubtful of itself and therefore in need of proof, and which, therefore, is not a position establishing itself by its existence—not a position that justifies itself; hence it is directly and immediately confronted by the self-grounded position of sense-certainty.

But because Hegel has conceived the negation of the negation from the point of view of the positive relation inherent in it as the true and only positive, and from the point of view of the negative relation inherent in it as the only true act and self-realizing act of all being, he has only found the *abstract, logical, speculative* expression for the movement of history; and this historical process is not yet the *real* history of man—of man as a given subject, but only man's *act of genesis*—the *story* of man's *origin*. We shall explain both the abstract form of this process and the difference between this process as it is in Hegel in contrast to modern criticism, that is, in contrast to the same process in Feuerbach's *Wesen des Christentums* [*Essence of Christianity*], or rather the *critical* form of this in Hegel's still uncritical process.

—MARX, *Economic and Philosophical Manuscripts of 1844*, pp. 45–46.

B. Theses on Feuerbach: The Old and the New Materialism*

I

The chief defect of all hitherto existing materialism—that of Feuerbach included—is that the thing, reality, sensuousness, is conceived only in the form of the *object* or of *contemplation*, but not as *human sensuous activity, practice*, not subjectively. Hence it happened that the *active* side, in contradistinction to materialism, was developed by idealism—but only abstractly, since, of course, idealism does not know real, sensuous activity as such. Feuerbach wants sensuous objects, really differentiated from the thought-objects, but he does not conceive human activity itself as *objective* activity. Hence, in the *Essence of Christianity*, he regards the theoretical attitude as the only genuinely human attitude, while practice is conceived and fixed only in its dirty-judaical form of appearance. Hence he does not grasp the significance of "revolutionary," of "practical-critical," activity.

II

The question whether objective truth can be attributed to human thinking is not a question of theory but a *practical* question. In practice man must prove the truth, that is, the reality and power, the this-sidedness of his thinking. The dispute over the reality or non-reality of thinking which is isolated from practice is a purely *scholastic* question.

III

The materialist doctrine that men are products of circumstances and upbringing, and that, therefore, changed men are products of other circumstances and changed upbringing, forgets that it is men that change circumstances and that the educator

* Engels found these "Theses" in an old notebook of Marx (1845). They were, he says, "hurriedly scribbled down for later elaboration, absolutely not intended for publication, but they are invaluable as the first document in which is deposited the brilliant germ of the new world outlook." (*Ludwig Feuerbach*, Foreword, p. 8).—*Ed.*

himself needs educating. Hence, this doctrine necessarily arrives at dividing society into two parts, of which one is superior to society (in Robert Owen, for example).

The coincidence of the changing of circumstances and of human activity can be conceived and rationally understood only as *revolutionizing practice.*

IV

Feuerbach starts out from the fact of religious self-alienation, the duplication of the world into a religious, imaginary world and a real one. His work consists in the dissolution of the religious world into its secular basis. He overlooks the fact that after this work is completed the chief thing still remains to be done. For the fact that the secular foundation detaches itself from itself and establishes itself in the clouds as an independent realm is really only to be explained by the self-cleavage and self-contradictoriness of this secular basis. The latter must itself, therefore, first be understood in its contradiction, and then revolutionized in practice by the removal of the contradiction. Thus, for instance, once the earthly family is discovered to be the secret of the holy family, the former must then itself be criticized in theory and revolutionized in practice.

V

Feuerbach, not satisfied with *abstract thinking,* appeals to *sensuous contemplation*; but he does not conceive sensuousness as *practical,* human-sensuous activity.

VI

Feuerbach resolves the religious essence into the *human* essence. But the human essence is no abstraction inherent in each single individual. In its reality it is the ensemble of the social relations.

Feuerbach, who does not enter upon a criticism of this real essence, is consequently compelled:

1. To abstract from the historical process and to fix the religious sentiment as something by itself and to presuppose an abstract—*isolated*—human individual.

2. The human essence, therefore, can with him be comprehended only as "genus," as an internal, dumb generality which merely *naturally* unites the many individuals.

VII

Feuerbach, consequently, does not see that the "religious sentiment" is itself a *social product,* and that the abstract individual whom he analyzes belongs in reality to a particular form of society.

VIII

Social life is essentially *practical.* All mysteries which mislead theory to mysticism find their rational solution in human practice and in the comprehension of this practice.

IX

The highest point attained by *contemplative* materialism, that is, materialism which does not understand sensuousness as practical activity, is the contemplation of single individuals in "civil society."

X

The standpoint of the old materialism is "civil" society; the standpoint of the new is *human* society, or socialized humanity.

XI

The philosophers have only *interpreted* the world in various ways; the point, however, is to *change* it.

—MARX, "Theses on Feuerbach" (1845), in ENGELS, *Ludwig Feuerbach,* pp. 82–4.

[10]

THE HEGELIAN METHOD: "THE MYSTERY OF SPECULATIVE CONSTRUCTION"

If from real apples, pears, strawberries, and almonds I form the general idea "Fruit," if I go further and imagine that my abstract idea "Fruit," derived from real fruit, is an entity existing outside me, is indeed the true essence of the pear, the apple, etc.—then, in the language of speculative philosophy I am declaring that "Fruit" is the substance of the pear, the apple, the almond, etc. I am saying, therefore, that to be a pear is not essential to the pear, that to be an apple is not essential to the apple; that what is essential to these things is not their real being, perceptible to the senses, but the essence that I have extracted from them and then foisted on them, the essence of my idea—"Fruit." I therefore declare apples, pears, almonds, etc. to be mere forms of existence, modi, of "Fruit." My finite understanding supported by my senses does, of course, distinguish an apple from a pear and a pear from an almond; but my speculative reason declares these sensuous differences unessential, indifferent. It sees in the apple the same as in the pear, and in the pear the same as in the almond, namely "Fruit." Particular real fruits are no more than semblances whose true essence is "the Substance"—"Fruit."

By this method one attains no particular wealth of definition. The mineralogist whose whole science consisted in the statement that all minerals are really "Mineral" would be a mineralogist only in his imagination. For every mineral the speculative mineralogist says "Mineral" and his science is reduced to repeating that word as many times as there are real minerals.

Having reduced the different real fruits to the one fruit of abstraction—"Fruit"—speculation must, in order to attain some appearance of real content, try somehow to find its way back from "Fruit," from Substance to the different profane real fruits, the pear, the apple, the almond, etc. It is as hard to produce real fruits from the abstract idea "Fruit" as it is easy to produce this abstract idea from real fruits. Indeed it is impossible to arrive at the opposite of an abstraction without relinquishing the abstraction.

The speculative philosopher therefore relinquishes the abstraction "Fruit," but in a speculative, mystical fashion—with the appearance of not relinquishing it. Thus he rises above his abstraction only in appearance. He argues like this:

If apples, pears, almonds, and strawberries are really nothing but "Substance," "Fruit," the question arises: Why does "Fruit" manifest itself to me sometimes as an apple, sometimes as a pear, sometimes as an almond? Why this appearance of diversity which so strikingly contradicts my speculative conception of "Unity"; "Substance"; "Fruit"?

This, answers the speculative philosopher, is because "Fruit" is not dead, undifferentiated, motionless, but living, self-differentiating, moving. The diversity of profane fruits is significant not only to my sensuous understanding, but also to "Fruit" itself and to speculative reasoning. The different profane fruits are different manifestations of the life of the one "Fruit"; they are crystallizations of "Fruit" itself. In the apple "Fruit" gives itself an apple-like existence, in the pear a pear-like existence. We must therefore no longer say as from the standpoint of Substance: a pear is "Fruit," an apple is "Fruit," an almond is "Fruit," but "Fruit" presents itself as a pear, "Fruit" presents itself as an apple, "Fruit" presents itself as an almond; and the differences which distinguish apples, pears, and almonds from one another are the self-differentiations of "Fruit" making the particular fruits subordinate members of the life-process of "Fruit." Thus "Fruit" is no longer a contentless, undifferentiated unity; it is oneness as allness, as "totalness" of fruits, which constitute an "organic ramified series." In every member of that series "Fruit" gives itself a more developed, more explicit existence, until it is finally the "summary" of all fruits and at the same time the living unity which contains all those fruits dissolved in itself just as much as it produces them from within itself, as for instance, all the limbs of the body are constantly dissolved in blood and constantly produced out of the blood.

We see that if the Christian religion knows only one Incarnation of God, speculative philosophy has as many incarnations as there are things, just as it has here in every fruit an incarnation of the "Substance," of the Absolute "Fruit." The main interest for the speculative philosopher is therefore to produce the existence of the real profane fruits and to say in some mysterious way that there are apples, pears, almonds, and raisins. But the apples, pears, almonds, and raisins that we get in the speculative world are nothing but semblances of apples, semblances of pears, semblances of almonds, and semblances of raisins; they are moments in the life of "Fruit," that abstract being of reason, and therefore themselves abstract beings of reason. Hence what you enjoy in speculation is to find all the real fruits there, but as fruits which have a higher mystic significance, which are grown out of the ether of your brain and not out of the material earth, which are incarnations of "Fruit," the Absolute Subject. When you return from the abstraction, the preternatural being of reason, "Fruit," to real natural fruits, you give, contrariwise, the natural fruits a preternatural significance and transform them into so many abstractions. Your main interest is then to point out the unity of "Fruit" in all the manifestations of its life—the apple, the pear, the almond—that is, the mystical interconnection between these fruits, how in each one of them "Fruit" develops by degrees and necessarily progresses, for instance, from its existence as a raisin to its existence as an almond. The value of profane fruits no longer consists in their natural qualities but in their speculative quality which gives each of them a definite place in the life-process of "Absolute Fruit."

The ordinary man does not think he is saying anything extraordinary when he states that there are apples and pears. But if the philosopher expresses those existences in the speculative way he says something extraordinary. He works a wonder by producing the real natural being, the apple, the pear, etc., out of the unreal being of reason "Fruit," i.e., by creating those fruits out of his own abstract reason, which he considers as an Absolute Subject outside himself, represented here as "Fruit." And in every existence which he expresses he accomplishes an act of creation.

It goes without saying that the speculative philosopher accomplishes this constant creation only by representing universally known qualities of the apple, the pear, etc., which exist in reality, as definitions discovered by him; by giving the names of the real things to what abstract reason alone can create, to abstract formulae of reason; finally, by declaring his own activity, by which he passes from the idea of an apple to the idea of a pear, to be the self-activity of the Absolute Subject, "Fruit."

In the speculative way of speaking, this operation is called comprehending the substance as the subject, as an inner process, as an Absolute Person and that comprehension constitutes the essential character of Hegel's method.

—Marx and Engels, *The Holy Family* (1844), pp. 78–82.

[11]

THE YOUNG HEGELIANS

A. Sheep in Wolves' Clothing

Hitherto men have constantly made up for themselves false conceptions about themselves, about what they are and what they ought to be. They have arranged their relationships according to their ideas of God, of normal man, etc. The phantoms of their brains have gained the mastery over them. They, the creators, have bowed down before their creatures. Let us liberate them from the chimeras, the ideas, dogmas, imaginary beings under the yoke of which they are pining away. Let us revolt against the rule of thoughts. Let us teach men, says one [Feuerbach], to exchange these imaginations for thoughts which correspond to the essence of man; says the second [Bruno Bauer], to take up a critical attitude to them; says the third [Max Stirner], to knock them out of their heads; and—existing reality will collapse.

These innocent and childlike fancies are the kernel of the modern Young Hegelian philosophy, which not only is received by the German public with horror and awe, but is announced by our philosophic Heroes with the solemn consciousness of their cataclysmic dangerousness and criminal ruthlessness. The first volume of this present publication has the aim of uncloaking these sheep, who take themselves and are taken for wolves; of showing how their bleating merely imitates in a philosophic form the conceptions of the German middle class; how the boasting of these philosophis commentators only mirrors the wretchedness of the real conditions in Germany. It is its aim to discredit the philosophic struggle with the shadows of reality, which appeals to the dreamy and muddled German nation.

Once upon a time an honest fellow had the idea that men were drowned in water only because they were possessed with the idea of gravity. If they were to knock this idea out of their heads, say by stating it to be a superstition, a religious idea, they would be sublimely proof against any danger from water. His whole life long he fought against the illusion of gravity, of whose harmful results all statistics brought him new and manifold evidence. This honest fellow was the type of the new revolutionary philosophers in Germany.

—MARX and ENGELS, *The German Ideology* (1846), pp. 1*f.*

B. "THE STAUNCHEST CONSERVATIVES"

German criticism has, right up to its latest efforts, never quitted the realm of philosophy. Far from examining its general philosophic premises, the whole body of its inquiries has actually sprung from the soil of a definite philosophical system, that of Hegel. Not only in their answers but in their very questions there was a mystification. This dependence on Hegel is the reason why not one of these modern critics has even attempted a comprehensive criticism of the Hegelian system, however much each professes to have advanced beyond Hegel. Their polemics against Hegel and against one another are confined to this—each extracts one side of the Hegelian system and turns this against the whole system as well as against the sides extracted by the others. To begin with they extracted pure unfalsified Hegelian categories such as "substance" and "self-consciousness," later they desecrated these categories with more secular names such as "species," "the unique," "man," etc.

The entire body of German philosophical criticism from Strauss to Stirner is confined to criticism of religious conceptions. The critics started from real religion and actual theology. What religious consciousness and a religious conception really meant was determined variously as they went along. Their advance consisted in subsuming the allegedly dominant metaphysical, political, juridical, moral, and other conceptions under the class of religious or theological conceptions; and similarly in pronouncing political, juridical, moral consciousness as religious or theological, and the political, juridical, moral man—"man" in the last resort—as religious. The dominance of religion was taken for granted. Gradually every dominant relationship was pronounced a religious relationship and transformed into a cult, a cult of law, cult of the state, etc. On all sides it was only a question of dogmas and belief in dogmas. The world was sanctified to an ever-increasing extent till at last our venerable Saint Max* was able to canonize it *en bloc* and thus dispose of it once for all.

The Old Hegelians had *comprehended* everything as soon as it was reduced to a Hegelian logical category. The Young Hegelians *criticized* everything by attributing to it religious conceptions or by pronouncing it a theological matter. The Young Hegelians are in agreement with the Old Hegelians in their belief in the rule of religion, of concepts, of an abstract general principle in the existing world. Only, the one party attacks this dominion as usurpation, while the other extols it as legitimate.

Since the Young Hegelians consider conceptions, thoughts, ideas, in fact all the products of consciousness, to which they attribute an independent existence, as the real chains of men

* Max Stirner in *The Ego and his Own.—Ed.*

(just as the Old Hegelians declared them the true bonds of human society) it is evident that the Young Hegelians have to fight only against these illusions of the consciousness. Since, according to their fantasy, the relationships of men, all their doings, their chains and their limitations are products of their consciousness, the Young Hegelians logically put to men the moral postulate of exchanging their present consciousness for human, critical or egoistic consciousness, and thus of removing their limitations. This demand to change consciousness amounts to a demand to interpret reality in another way, i.e., to accept it by means of another interpretation.* The Young Hegelian ideologists, in spite of their allegedly "world-shattering" statements, are the staunchest conservatives. The most recent of them have found the correct expression for their activity when they declare they are only fighting against "phrases." They forget, however, that to these phrases they themselves are only opposing other phrases, and that they are in no way combating the real existing world when they are merely combating the phrases of this world. The only results which this philosophic criticism could achieve were a few (and at that thoroughly one-sided) elucidations of Christianity from the point of view of religious history†; all the rest of their assertions are only further embellishments of their claim to have furnished, in these unimportant elucidations, discoveries of universal importance.

It has not occurred to any one of these philosophers to inquire into the connection of German philosophy with German reality, the relation of their criticism to their own material surroundings.

—MARX and ENGELS, *The German Ideology* (1844), pp. 4–6.

* This passage strikingly illustrates the meaning of Marx's famous eleventh thesis on Feuerbach.—*Ed.*

† See Engels, "On the History of Early Christianity," and "Bruno Bauer and Early Christianity," MARX and ENGELS, *On Religion*.—*Ed.*

APPENDIX II

LENIN'S PHILOSOPHICAL NOTEBOOKS

Introduction

LENIN'S *Philosophical Notebooks* comprise a series of quotations, notes, comments, and exclamations jotted down while reading Hegel, Aristotle, Feuerbach, and others, especially during the years 1914–1916.

The studies of these two years represent a third and new stage in the development of Lenin's philosophical thought. His early Marxist studies, in which the philosophical writings of George V. Plekhanov played an important role, enabled him to apply dialectical materialism effectively to complex problems of Russian economic and political development. This is revealed particularly in the work of 1894, *What the "Friends of the People" Are,* three selections from which are contained in the present volume.

The second phase of his philosophical studies began as early as 1899 when he felt the need for a Marxist struggle against the rise and spread of neo-Kantianism. He wrote then, however, that realizing his lack of philosophical education he did not intend to write on such themes until he had done more reading. Interestingly, the secret police noted that on his return from Siberian exile in 1900, Lenin sent his mother books by Spinoza, Helvetius, Kant, Fichte, Schelling, and others. This phase culminated in the years 1907 and 1908 when he devoted himself full-time to the study of Berkeley, Hume, Kant, and their current positivist disciples, in the light of the latest developments in physics. He studied Ernst Mach, Richard Avenarius, Henri Poincaré, Karl Pearson, and other contemporary philosophers in order to combat the growing vogue of "empirio-criticism" among Russian and foreign Marxists. These studies resulted in the publication of *Materialism and Empirio-Criticism* which became, after the Russian Revolution, the most widely read and influential Marxist philosophical work of the 20th century.

His third major philosophical venture, represented in these selections, came during the first years of World War I. In exile in Switzerland, Lenin applied himself to the task of deepening his knowledge of dialectics. With the growth of imperialism and what he regarded as the increasing depth of the contradictions in the capitalist world, expressed by the outbreak of World War among the imperialist powers, Lenin felt that only the most profound knowledge of dialectics could help solve the problems that confronted the working class and socialist movement.

It has generally been assumed that these studies and notes were directed towards a book Lenin was planning to write. That may have been true, but there seems to be no direct evidence of plans for a book, and it is essential to understand that, in any case, Lenin was deeply concerned here with his own philosophical clarification. It is this aspect of these notes that makes them especially interesting. We are seeing a non-professional philosopher, but a professional social revolutionary, studying some of the most technically difficult and theoretically advanced philosophical works of all time. He seeks better to be able to handle complex concepts in the analysis of ever-changing and moving social forces. In these notes we are able to see Lenin's mind at work, trying out every abstract idea he comes across in the effort to test it in the crucible of his own rich experience. His main concern is to reconstruct the Hegelian dialectics on a thoroughly materialist foundation.

The first thing that strikes the reader of the *Notebooks*, or of these excerpts from them, is Lenin's preoccupation with the structure and meaning of a dialectical logic and theory of knowledge. Although *Materialism and Empirio-Criticism* is a fundamental work in the materialist critique of subjective idealism, it nevertheless does not deal with the vast number of dialectical problems that are analyzed in Lenin's *Notebooks*. Lenin's evaluation of Hegel's objective idealism, as in some cases being close to, and at times even transformed into, dialectical materialism by its inner logic, reveals a deep appreciation of the relationship of Marx to Hegel and helps explain why Marx regarded himself as Hegel's pupil. And while Lenin was always the enemy of idealism, he opposed the offhand dismissal of this type of philosophy. As against vulgar materialism, he insisted that philosophical idealism has its sources in the very process of cognition itself. His conclusion was that "intelligent idealism is closer to intelligent materialism than stupid materialism." Thus, these *Philosophical Notebooks* are an indispensable supplement to Lenin's previous philosophical works and observations. Indeed, they constitute a plea for a richer and fuller development of dialectical materialism.

Whether Lenin intended to use these notes as the basis for a work on materialist dialectics or not, we do know that these studies were put to very practical use. In his *War and the Second International,* his *Imperialism,* his polemics on the trade unions, and in almost everything else he wrote after 1914, Lenin employs ideas which are suggested in these notes. Here as elsewhere, Lenin based himself on the unity of theory and practice, which to him was fundamental for the successful pursuit of either. Interestingly enough, Lenin credited Hegel with having brilliant insights into this unity—even though inconsistently. He saw in Hegel some of the guide-lines of Marx's stress on practice as the criterion of truth.

The editors have tried to organize Lenin's notes in such a way as to facilitate the reader's grasp of the main points in the *Notebooks.* This was far from a simple task, as a mere glance at the volume which has now appeared in English for the first time will show. The book contains passages, let us say, from Hegel, and then underscorings, question marks, exclamation points, comments such as NB or *nota bene* (note well), "unclear," "well said," "leaps," "Hegel and historical materialism," "logical categories and human practice." Many of these are interesting from the standpoint of Lenin's reaction to Hegel's texts, but obviously could not be used in this volume. The editors, therefore, had to select those passages which, though abbreviated in many cases, nevertheless could give the reader the quintessence of Lenin's thinking. Then there was the problem of how to present the quotations from Hegel upon which Lenin commented. These were sometimes considerably curtailed by Lenin. The editors felt that in some cases the reader would be helped if Hegel's words were given in fuller form. Sometimes it was the other way around and we quoted less from Hegel than Lenin did. Our one consideration was the maximum possible intelligibility of both Hegel's passages and Lenin's comments.

A word of caution to the reader is necessary. Lenin was the

last person who would expect anyone to take these notes in a dogmatic manner. Consequently, one must avoid isolating this or that note from the elaborate thinking of Lenin as expressed in his published works. We must bear in mind that Lenin wrote down these notes as an immediate reaction to what he was reading. He did not go over them in order to refine his thinking, nor did he revise what he had written. We must look upon them, therefore, as manifestations of a mind hard at work. At the same time, the reader will himself see, on the basis of the preceding sections of this volume, that a first-rate philosophical mind was operating here and that there are highly significant ideas to be derived from a careful study of Lenin's notes.

Texts and translations

All materials from Lenin are taken from *V. I. Lenin: Collected Works,* vol. 38, Foreign Languages Publishing House, 1961, and all page references under Lenin are to that edition.

Lenin used the first German edition of Hegel's *Works,* consisting of 19 volumes, published in Berlin between 1832 and 1887. All excerpts from Hegel, and page references, in this section are from the following English editions:

Science of Logic, trans. by W. H. Johnston and L. G. Struthers, 2 vols., N.Y., Macmillan, 1929. Reprinted with permission of the Macmillan Company.

The Logic of Hegel [the "Encyclopedia Logic"—a later work, published as a part of the *Encyclopedia of the Philosophical Sciences*], trans. by William Wallace, 2nd. ed., Oxford, 1892.

Lectures on the History of Philosophy, trans. by E. S. Haldane, London, Kegan Paul, Trench, Trübner & Co., 1892–96.

A. On Hegel's *Science of Logic*

1.

Hegel, I, 37. "*Consciousness is Spirit as knowing which is concrete and engrossed in externality; but the* schema of movement *of this concrete knowing* (*like the development of all physical and intellectual life*) *depends entirely on the nature of the pure essentialities which make up the content of Logic.*"

Lenin: This is characteristic! Turn it round: Logic and the theory of knowledge must be derived from "the development of all physical and intellectual [natural and spiritual] life." (*88*)

2.

HEGEL, I, 64–66. "... *Method is the consciousness of the form taken by the inner spontaneous movement of the content of Logic.... This is already evident from the fact that the Method is no-ways different from its object and content;—for it is the content in itself,* the Dialectic which it has in itself, *that moves it on....* The necessity of connection *and the* immanent origination *of distinctions must show themselves in the discussion of the subject-matter, for they are part of the self-development of the concept. The one and only thing* for securing scientific *progress*—*is knowledge of the logical precept that Negation is just as much Affirmation as Negation. . . .*"

LENIN: . . . Negation is something definite, has a definite content, the inner contradictions lead to the replacement of the old content by a new, higher one.

In the old logic there is no transition, development (of concept and thought), there is not "an inner necessary connection" of all the parts and "transition" of some parts into others.

And Hegel puts forward two basic requirements:

(1) "The necessity of connection" and

(2) "the immanent emergence of distinctions."

Very important! ! This is what it means in my opinion:

(1) *Necessary* connection, the objective connection of all the aspects, forces, tendencies, etc., of the given sphere of phenomena;

(2) The "immanent *emergence* of distinctions"—the inner objective logic of evolution and of the struggle of the differences, polarity. (*97*)

3.

HEGEL, I, 67. "*Kant freed Dialectic from the semblance of arbitrariness. . . . When Kant's dialectical expositions in the* Antinomies of Pure Reason *are looked at closely it will be seen that they are not indeed deserving of great praise; but the general idea upon which he builds, and which he has vindicated, is the* Objectivity of Appearance *and the* Necessity of Contradiction *which belongs to the very nature of thought-determinations.*"

LENIN: . . . Is not the thought here that appearance also is objective, for it contains *one of the aspects* of the *objective* world? There is a difference between the subjective and the objective, BUT IT, TOO, HAS ITS LIMITS. (*98*)

4.

HEGEL, I, 69. "*It is only through a profounder acquaintance with other sciences that Logic discovers itself to subjective thought as not a mere abstract Universal, but as a Universal which comprises in itself the full wealth of Particulars.*"

LENIN: *cf. Capital.* A beautiful formula: "Not a mere abstract universal. . . ." (all the wealth of the particular and single)! ! *Très bien! (99)*

5.

HEGEL, I, 133 *f* [concerning Kant]. "*We may remark that the meaning of the Thing-in-itself here becomes plain: it is a very simple abstraction. . . . Things are called 'in themselves' in so far as we abstract from all Being-for-other, which means that they are thought of as quite without determination, as Nothings. In this sense it is indeed impossible to know what the Thing-in-itself is. For the question 'what' demands that determinations should be indicated; and since it is postulated that the things of which these are to be predicated must be Things-in-themselves, that is, indeterminate, the question, in sheer thoughtlessness, is so put as to render an answer either impossible or self-contradictory.—The Thing-in-itself is like that Absolute of which we know only that in it all things are one. It is therefore easy to know what is in these Things-in-themselves: as such they are mere abstractions, void of truth and content.*"

LENIN: Thing-in-itself—"a very simple abstraction." The proposition that we do not know what Things-in-themselves are seems sagacious. The Thing-in-itself is an abstraction from all determination (Being-for-other) (from all relation to Other) i.e., a Nothing. Consequently, the Thing-in-itself is "nothing but an abstraction, void of truth and content." This is very profound: the Thing-in-itself and its conversion into a Thing-for-others (*cf.* Engels*). The Thing-in-itself is *altogether* an empty, lifeless abstraction. In life, in movement, each thing and everything *is usually* both "in itself" and "for others" in relation to an Other, being transformed from one state to the other.

Sehr gut! ! If we ask what Things-*in-themselves* are, "the question in sheer thoughtlessness, is so put as to render an answer impossible."

* See above, p. 142.—*Ed.*

Dialectics is the teaching which shows how *Opposites* can be and how they happen to be (how they become) *identical*—under what conditions they are identical, becoming transformed into one another—why the human mind should grasp these opposites not as dead, rigid, but as living, conditional, mobile, becoming transformed into one another. (*108f*)

6.

HEGEL, I, 141, 142. "*Something, posited with its immanent Limit as self-contradiction through which it is driven and forced beyond itself, is the Finite.*" "*Finite things are; . . . but the truth of this being is their end.*"

LENIN: When things are described as finite—that is to admit that their not-Being is their nature ("not-Being constitutes their Being"). "They" (things) "*are,* but the truth of this being is their *end.*"

Shrewd and clever! Hegel analyzes concepts that usually appear to be dead and shows that there *is* movement in them. Finite? That means *moving* to an end! Something?—means *not that* which is Other. Being in general?—means such indeterminateness that Being = not-Being. All-sided, universal flexibility of concepts, a flexibility reaching to the identity of opposites—that is the essence of the matter. This flexibility, applied subjectively = eclecticism and sophistry. Flexibility, applied *objectively,* i.e., reflecting the all-sidedness of the material process and its unity, is dialectics, is the correct reflection of the eternal development of the world. (*110*)

7.

HEGEL, I, 177. "*The ideality of Being-for-Self as totality thus, first, passes into reality, and into the most fixed and abstract of all, into One.*"

LENIN: The thought of the ideal passing into the real is *profound:* very important for history. But also in the personal life of man it is clear that this contains much truth. Against vulgar materialism. *N.B.* The difference of the ideal from the material is also not unconditional, not inordinate.

Obviously, Hegel takes his self-development of concepts, of categories, in connection with the entire history of philosophy. This gives still a *new* aspect to the whole *Logic.* (*114*)

8.

HEGEL, II, 65. "*The determination of Opposition too has been made into a law, the so-called Law of the Excluded Middle.* Something is either A or not-A: there is no third."

LENIN: Hegel quotes this proposition of the excluded middle and "*analyzes*" it. If this implies that "everything is a term of an opposition," that everything has its positive and its negative determination, then it is all right. But if it is understood as it is generally understood, that, of all predicates either a given one or its not-Being, applies, then this is a "triviality"! ! Spirit . . . sweet, not sweet? green, not green? The determination should lead to determinateness, but in this triviality it leads to nothing.

And then Hegel says wittily—it is said that there is no third. *There is* a third in this thesis itself. A itself is the third, for A can be both + A and − A. "The Something thus is itself the third term which was supposed to be excluded." [Hegel, *ibid.*, II, 68.]*

This is shrewd and correct. Every concrete thing, every concrete something, stands in multifarious and often contradictory relations to everything else, ergo it is itself and some other. *(137 f)*

9.

HEGEL, II, 66 *f*. "*But it has been a fundamental prejudice of hitherto existing logic and of ordinary imagination that Contradiction is a determination having less essence and immanence than Identity; but indeed, if there were any question of rank, and the two determinations had to be fixed as separate, Contradiction would have to be taken as the profounder and more fully essential. For as opposed to it Identity is only the determination of the simple immediate, or of dead Being, while Contradiction is the root of all movement and life, and it is only in so far as it contains a Contradiction that anything moves and has impulse and activity.*

"*Ordinarily Contradiction is removed, first of all from things, from the existent and the true in general; and it is asserted* that there is nothing contradictory. *Next it is shifted into subjective reflection, which alone is said to posit it when it relates and compares. But really—it is said—it does not exist even in this*

* All page references in brackets are to the English editions listed in the introduction to this Appendix.—*Ed.*

reflection, for it is impossible to imagine or to think anything contradictory. Indeed, Contradiction, both in actuality and in thinking reflection, is considered an accident, a kind of abnormality or paroxysm of sickness which will soon go away."

[Lenin copied the whole of p. 67 and the first half of 68.]

LENIN: Movement and *"self-movement"* (this *NB!* arbitrary (independent), spontaneous, *internally necessary movement*), "change," "movement and vitality," "the principle of all self-movement" "impulse" to "movement" and to "activity"—the opposite to *"dead Being"*—who would believe that this is the core of "Hegelianism," of abstract and abstruse (ponderous, absurd?) Hegelianism? ? This core had to be discovered, understood, rescued, laid bare, refined, which is precisely what Marx and Engels did.

The idea of universal movement and change (1813 *Logic*) was conjectured before its application to life and society. In regard to society it was proclaimed earlier (1847) than it was demonstrated in application to man (1859). [Lenin is referring to the dates of Hegel's *Science of Logic,* Marx and Engels' *Communist Manifesto,* and Darwin's *Origin of Species.*]

[After copying another page of Hegel, II, 68–9, Lenin adds:]

NB. (1) Ordinary imagination grasps difference and contradiction, but not the transition from the one to the other, *this however is the most important.*

(2) Intelligence and understanding. Intelligence grasps contradiction, *enunciates* it, brings things into relation with one another, allows the "concept to show through the contradiction," but does not *express* the concept of things and their relations.

(3) Thinking reason (understanding) sharpens the blunt difference of variety, the mere manifold of imagination, into *essential* difference, into *opposition.* Only when raised to the peak of contradiction, do the manifold entities become active and lively in relation to one another—they acquire that negativity which is the *inherent pulsation of self-movement and vitality.* *(141–43)*

10.

HEGEL, II, 92–94. *"If it is said of nature that it is the ground of the world, then what is called Nature is, first, identical with the world, and the world is nothing but Nature itself; . . . and if Nature is to be the world, a manifold of determinations is added externally. . . .*

. . . An action may have more Grounds than one; as a concrete, it contains manifold essential determinations, each of which for this reason may be called Ground. . . . For any and every thing one and more good Grounds can be given. . . . What Socrates and Plato called sophistry is just argumentation from Grounds, to which Plato opposed the contemplation of the Idea, that is, the Thing in and for itself or in its Notion. Grounds are taken only of essential *content-determinations, relations, and respects, and of these each thing, as well as its opposite, contains several; and in their form of essentiality one is as valid as another; it does not contain the whole volume of the thing, and therefore is a one-sided Ground, and each of the other particular sides has again its group of Grounds; but not one exhausts the thing itself, which constitutes their connexion and contains them all."*

LENIN: If I am not mistaken there is much mysticism and empty pedantry in these conclusions of Hegel, but the basic idea is one of genius; that of the universal, all-sided, *vital* connections of everything with everything and the reflection of this connection —Hegel materialistically turned upside down—in human concepts, which must likewise be hewn, treated, flexible, mobile, relative, mutually connected, united in opposites, in order to embrace the world. Continuation of the work of Hegel and Marx must consist in the *dialectical* elaboration of the history of human thought, science and technique. . . .

"When all the Conditions of a thing are present, it enters into existence. . . ." [Hegel, II, 105.]

Very good! What has the Absolute Idea and idealism to do with it?

Amusing, this "derivation" of . . . *existence. . . . (146f)*

11.

HEGEL, II, 128, 9, 31. ". . . *Appearance at this point is Essence in its existence; Essence is present therein immediately.*

"Appearance consequently is the unity of Show (semblance) and Existence.

"This unity is the Law of Appearance. Law therefore is the positive element in the mediation of the Apparent."

LENIN: Here in general utter obscurity. But there is a vital thought, evidently: The concept of *Law* is *one* of the stages of the cognition by man of *unity* and *connection*, of the reciprocal dependence and totality of the world process. The "treatment" and "twisting" of words and concepts to which Hegel devotes himself here is a struggle against making the concept of *law* absolute, against simplifying it, against making a fetish of it. *NB* for modern physics! ! !

"This enduring persistence which belongs to Appearance in Law . . . Law is the Reflection of Appearance into identity with itself; . . ." [Hegel, II, 131*f*.]

"This identity, the foundation of Appearance, which constitutes Law, is the peculiar moment of Appearance; . . . Consequently, Law is not beyond Appearance, but is immediately present in it; the realm of Laws is the quiescent counterfeit [reflection] of the existing or appearing world." [II, 133.]

NB: Law is the enduring (the persisting) in appearances.

(Law is the identical in appearances).

NB: Law = the quiescent reflection of appearances. *NB.*

This is a remarkably materialistic and remarkably appropriate (with the word 'quiescent') determination. Law takes the quiescent—and therefore law, every law, is narrow, incomplete, approximate.

"Hence law is essential appearance." [Hegel, II, 132.]

Ergo, *law* and *essence* are concepts of the same kind (of the same order), or rather, of the same degree, expressing the deepening of man's knowledge of phenomena, the world, etc.

The movement of the universe in appearances, in the essentiality of this movement, is law.

NB: (Law is the reflection of the essential in the movement of the universe) (Appearance is *richer* than law). (*150–52*)

12.

HEGEL, II, 140. "*Thus both the Appearing and the Essential World are each the independent whole of Existence. One was to have been only reflected Existence, and the other only immediate Existence; but each continues itself in the other, and consequently in itself is the identity of these two moments.*"

LENIN: The essence here is that both the world of appearances and the world in itself are *moments* [phases] of man's knowledge of nature, stages, *alterations,* or deepenings (of knowledge). The shifting of the world in itself further and further *from* the world of appearances—that is what is so far still not to be seen in Hegel.

NB. Have not Hegel's "moments" of the concept the significance of "moments" of transition?

"Thus Law is Essential Relation." [Hegel, II, 141.]

Law is *relation*. This *NB* for the Machist and other agnostics, and for the Kantians, etc. Relation of *essences* or between essences. *152f*)

13.

HEGEL, II, 157. "*This is apparent in every natural, scientific, and generally intellectual development; and it is essential to understand that the* First, *when as yet Something is internal, or in its concept, is, for this reason, only its immediate and passive existence.*"

LENIN: The beginning of everything can be regarded as inner —passive—and at the same time as outer.

But what is interesting here is not that, but something else: Hegel's *criterion* of dialectics that has accidentally slipped in: "*in all natural, scientific and intellectual development:*" here we have a *grain* of profound truth in the mystical integument of Hegelianism!

Example: The germ of a man, says Hegel, is only internal man, something given up to otherness, the passive. God at first is not yet Spirit. "*Immediately,* therefore, God is *only* Nature." [Hegel, II, 158.]

(This is also characteristic! !)

Feuerbach "links up to this." Down with God, there remains *Nature.* (*154f*)

14.

HEGEL, II, 191–93. "*Thus the Relation of Substantiality passes over into* the *Relation of Causality. . . . Substance attains Actuality only when it has become Cause. . . . Effect contains nothing whatever which cause does not contain. Conversely Cause contains nothing which is not in its Effect. . . . It is the same fact which displays itself first as Cause and then as Effect,—here as peculiar persistence and there as positedness or determination in an Other.*"

LENIN: On the one hand, knowledge of matter must be deepened to knowledge (to the concept) of Substance in order to find the causes of phenomena. On the other hand, the actual cognition of the cause is the deepening of knowledge from the externality of phenomena to the Substance. Two types of examples should explain this: (1) from the history of natural science, and (2) from the history of philosophy. More exactly: It is not "examples" that should be here—comparison is not proof—but the *quintessence* of the history of both the one and the other plus the history of technique.

Cause and effect, ergo, are merely moments of universal reciprocal dependence, of (universal) connection, of the reciprocal concatenation of events, merely links in the chain of the development of matter. *NB:* The all-sidedness and all-embracing character of the interconnection of the world, which is only one-sidedly, fragmentarily and incompletely expressed by causality. (*159*)

15.

HEGEL, II, 196. "*But we may here and now observe that, in so far as the relation of cause and effect is admitted (although in an improper sense), effect cannot be greater than cause, for effect is nothing further than the manifestation of cause. It has become a popular jest in history to allow great effects to spring from small causes, and to quote for first cause of a comprehensive and profound event an anecdote. Such a so-called cause is to be looked upon as nothing more than an occasion or external stimulus; the inner spirit of the event would not have required it. . . . Consequently those arabesques of history, where a huge shape is depicted as growing from a slender stalk, are a sprightly but a most superficial treatment.*"

LENIN: This "inner spirit" is an idealistic, *mystical,* but a very profound indication of the historical causes of events. Hegel subsumes history *completely* under causality and understands causality a thousand times more profoundly and richly than the multitude of "savants" nowadays.

[After quoting a number of passages from Hegel's *Science of Logic,* II, 197–204, on causality, as well as from the *Logic* contained in the *Encyclopedia of the Philosophical Sciences,** Lenin comments:]

Causality, as usually understood by us, is only a small particle of universal interconnection, but (a materialist extension) a

* This work will be cited hereafter as *Enc. Logic.* The English translation, however, as noted in the Introduction to this Appendix, bears the title, *The Logic of Hegel.—Ed.*

particle not of the subjective but of the objectively real interconnection.

"The movement of the relation of causality" = in fact: the movement of matter, the movement of history, grasped, mastered in its inner *connection* up to one or other degree of breadth or depth.

When one reads Hegel on causality, it appears strange at first glance that he dwells so relatively lightly on this theme, beloved of the Kantians. Why? Because, indeed, for him causality is only *one* of the determinations of universal connection, which he had already covered earlier, in his *entire* exposition, much more deeply and all-sidedly; *always* and from the very outset emphasizing this connection, the reciprocal transitions, etc., etc. It would be very instructive to compare the "*birthpangs*" of neo-empiricism ("physical idealism") with the solutions or rather with the dialectical method of Hegel.

It is to be noted also that in the *Encyclopedia* Hegel stresses the inadequacy and emptiness of the *bare* concept of "reciprocal action." (*160–62*)

16.

HEGEL, II, 221. "*And further the Notion must not here be considered as an act of self-conscious understanding, or as subjective understanding: what we have to do with is the Notion in and for itself, which constitutes a STAGE AS WELL OF NATURE AS OF SPIRIT. LIFE, OR ORGANIC NATURE, IS THAT STAGE OF NATURE AT WHICH THE NOTION EMERGES. . . .* [Capitals are Lenin's.]

LENIN: The "eve" of the transformation of objective idealism into materialism.

There follows a very interesting passage (pp. 223–30) *where* Hegel *refutes Kant, precisely epistemologically* (Engels *probably* had this passage in mind when he wrote in *Ludwig Feuerbach* that the *main* point against Kant had already been made by Hegel, in so far as this was possible from an idealistic standpoint)—exposing Kant's duality and inconsistency, his, so to speak, vacillation between empiricism (= materialism) and idealism. Hegel himself arguing *wholly and exclusively* from the standpoint of a *more consistent* idealism.

[After copying the last line of p. 221 and nearly the whole of p. 222 of vol. II of Hegel's *Science of Logic,* with the marginal comments, "Kant belittles the power of reason" and "the more consistent idealist clings to God!" Lenin continues:]

Essentially, Hegel is completely right as opposed to Kant. Thought proceeding from the concrete to the abstract—provided it is *correct* (*NB*) (and Kant, like all philosophers, speaks of correct thought)—does not get away *from* the truth but comes closer to it. The abstraction of *matter,* of a *law* of nature, the abstraction of *value,* etc., in short *all* scientific (correct, serious, not absurd) abstractions reflect nature more deeply, truly, and *completely.* From living perception to abstract thought, *and from this to practice*—such is the dialectical path of the cognition of *truth,* of the cognition of objective reality. Kant disparages knowledge in order to make way for faith; Hegel exalts knowledge, asserting that knowledge is knowledge of God. The materialist exalts the knowledge of matter, of nature, consigning God, and the philosophical rabble that defends God, to the rubbish heap. (*171*)

17.

[Lenin's references below are to Hegel's *Science of Logic,* vol. II: Subjective Logic, The Doctrine of the Notion: Section One: Subjectivity (pp. 233–342) and especially to Chapter II, The Syllogism (pp. 301–442)].

LENIN: These parts of the work should be called a best means for getting a headache! [English in original.]

Kuno Fischer expounds these "abstruse" considerations very poorly, taking up the lighter points . . . but not showing the reader *how* to look for the key to the difficult transitions, nuances, ebbs and flows of Hegel's abstract concepts.

Obviously, here too the chief thing for Hegel is to *trace* the *transitions.* From a certain point of view, under certain conditions, the universal is the individual, the individual is the universal. Not only (1) *connection,* and inseparable connection, of all concepts and judgments, but (2) *transitions* from one into the other, and not only transitions, but also (3) *identity of opposites* —that is the chief thing for Hegel. But this merely "glimmers" through the fog of extremely abstruse exposition. The history of thought from the standpoint of the development and application of the general concepts and categories of the Logic—that's what is needed!

Quoting on p. 306, the "famous" syllogism—"all men are mortal, Gaius is a man, therefore he is mortal"—Hegel shrewdly adds: "Boredom immediately descends when such a syllogism is heard approaching"—this is declared to be due to the "otiose form," and Hegel makes the profound remark: "All things are a *Syllogism,* a universal which is bound together with individuality through particularity; but of course they are not wholes consisting of *three propositions.*" [Hegel, II, 307.]

Very good! The most common logical "figures"—are the most common relations of things, set forth with the pedantic thoroughness of a school textbook, if I may be allowed to say so.

Hegel's analysis of syllogisms (Individual—Particular—Universal: I—P—U) recalls Marx's imitation of Hegel in Chapter I of *Capital.* *(177f)*

18.

HEGEL, II, 309. "*Kant's Antinomies of Reason are just this, that first one determination of a Notion is made the foundation of the Notion, and next, and with equal necessity, the other.*"

LENIN: One would have to return to Hegel for a step-by-step analysis of any current logic and *theory of knowledge* of a Kantian, etc.

Two aphorisms concerning the question of the criticism of modern Kantianism, Machism, etc.:

1. Plekhanov criticizes Kantianism (and agnosticism in general) more from a vulgar-materialistic standpoint than from a dialectical-materialistic standpoint, *in so far as* he merely *rejects* their views from the threshold, but does not *correct* them (as Hegel corrected Kant), deepening, generalizing and extending them, showing the *connection* and *transitions* of each and every concept.

2. Marxists criticized (at the beginning of the 20th century) the Kantians and Humists more in the manner of Feuerbach (and Büchner) than of Hegel.

NB: Concerning the question of the true significance of Hegel's *Logic:* The Formation of (abstract) notions and operations with them *already* includes idea, conviction, *consciousness* of the *law-governed* character of the objective connection of the world. To distinguish causality from this connection is stupid. To deny the objectivity of notions, the objectivity of the universal in the individual and in the particular, is impossible. Consequently, Hegel is much more profound than Kant, and others, in tracing the reflection of the movement of the objective world in the movement of notions. Just as the simple form of value, the individual act of exchange of one given commodity for another, already includes in an undeveloped form *all* the main contradictions of capitalism—so the simplest *generalization,* the first and simplest formation of *notions* (judgments, syllogisms, etc.) already denotes man's ever deeper cognition of the *objective* connection of the world. Here is where one should look for the true meaning, significance and role of Hegel's *Logic.* This *NB.*

Hegel actually *proved* that logical forms and laws are not an empty shell, but the *reflection* of the objective world. More correctly, he did not prove, but *made a brilliant guess.*

Aphorism: It is impossible completely to understand Marx's *Capital,* and especially its first chapter, without having thoroughly studied and understood the *whole* of Hegel's *Logic.* Consequently, half a century later none of the Marxists understood Marx! ! (*178–80*)

19.

HEGEL, Enc. Logic, 322. "*As we first see them* [*the three branches of philosophy; the Logical Idea, Nature, and Mind*] *Nature is the middle term which links the others together. Nature, the totality immediately before us, unfolds itself into the two extremes of the Logical Idea and Mind. But mind is Mind only when it is mediated through nature. . . . It is Mind which cognizes the Logical Idea in Nature and which thus raises Nature to its essence. In the third place again the Logical Idea itself becomes the mean; it is the absolute substance both of mind and of nature, the universal and all-pervading principle.*"

LENIN: Logic is the science of cognition. It is the theory of knowledge. Knowledge is the reflection of nature by man. But this is not a simple, not an immediate, not a complete reflection, but the process of a series of abstractions, the formation and development of concepts, laws, etc., and these concepts, laws, etc. (thought, science = "the logical Idea") *embrace* conditionally, approximately, the universal law-governed character of eternally moving and developing nature.

Here there are *actually,* objectively, *three* members: (1) nature; (2) human cognition = * the human *brain* (as the highest product of this same nature), and (3) the form of reflection of nature in human cognition, and this form consists precisely of concepts,

* Lenin uses the equal mark (=) throughout the notebooks but not always with the same meaning. Sometimes it means literally "is equal to" or "is the same as." Other times it is more of an "*id est*" or "that is to say." Here it obviously cannot be taken in any of these senses, but rather as something like, "based upon," or "dependent on."—*Ed.*

laws, categories, etc. Man cannot comprehend = reflect = mirror nature *as a whole,* in its completeness, its "immediate totality," he can only *eternally* come closer to this, creating abstractions, concepts, laws, a scientific picture of the world, etc., etc. (*182*)

20.

HEGEL, II, 380. "*The End has turned out to be the complementary third term of Mechanism and Chemism; it is their truth. Since it still stands within the sphere of Objectivity or of the immediacy of the total Notion, it is still affected by externality as such; an objective world to which it relates itself still stands opposed to it. From this side mechanical causality (in which generally Chemism must be included), still appears in this End-relation (which is external), but as subordinated to it and as transcended in and for itself. . . . From this results the nature of the subordination of the two previous forms of the objective process: the Other, which in them lies in the infinite progress, is the Notion which at first is posited as external to them, which is End; not only is the Notion their substance, but also externality is the moment which is essential to them and constitutes their determinateness. Thus mechanical or chemical technique spontaneously offers itself to the End-relation by reason of its character of being determined externally; and this relation must now be further considered.*"

LENIN: *Materialist Dialectics:* The laws of the external world, of nature, which are divided into *mechanical* and *chemical* (this is very important) are the bases of man's *purposive* activity.

In his practical activity, man is confronted with the objective world, is dependent on it, and determines his activity by it.

From this aspect, from the aspect of the practical (purposive) activity of man, the mechanical (and chemical) causality of the world (of nature) appears as something *external,* as something secondary, as something hidden.

Two forms of the *objective* process: Nature (mechanical and chemical and the *purposive* activity of man. The mutual relation of these forms. At the beginning, man's ends appear foreign ("other") in relation to nature. Human consciousness, science ("*der Begriff*"), reflects the essence, the substance of nature, but at the same time this consciousness is something external in relation to nature (not immediately, not simply, coinciding with it).

MECHANICAL AND CHEMICAL TECHNIQUE serves

human ends just because its character (essence) consists in its being determined by external conditions (the laws of nature).

In actual fact, men's ends are engendered by the objective world and presuppose it—they find it as something given, present. But it *seems* to man as if his ends are taken from outside the world, and are independent of the world ("freedom"). (*187–89*)

21.

HEGEL, II, 387*f*. "*Further, since the End is finite it has a finite content; accordingly it is not absolute or utterly and in and for itself reasonable. The Means however is the external middle of the syllogism which is the realization of the End; in it therefore reasonableness manifests itself as such—as preserving itself in this external Other and precisely through this externality. In so far the Means is higher than the finite Ends of external usefulness: the plough is more honorable than are immediately those enjoyments which are procured by it, and are Ends. The instrument is preserved, while the immediate enjoyments pass away and are forgotten. IN HIS TOOLS MAN POSSESSES POWER OVER EXTERNAL NATURE, EVEN ALTHOUGH, ACCORDING TO HIS ENDS, HE FREQUENTLY IS SUBJECTED TO IT.*" [Capitals are Lenin's.]

LENIN: The germs of historical materialism in Hegel.

Historical materialism as one of the applications and developments of the ideas of genius—seeds existing in embryo in Hegel.

When Hegel endeavors—sometimes even huffs and puffs—to bring man's purposive activity under the categories of logic, saying that this activity is the "syllogism" (*schluss*), that the subject (man) plays the role of a "member" in the logical "figure" of the "syllogism," and so on—THEN THAT IS NOT MERELY STRETCHING A POINT, A MERE GAME. THIS HAS A VERY PROFOUND, PURELY MATERIALISTIC CONTENT. It has to be inverted: The practical activity of man had to lead his consciousness to the repetition of the various logical figures thousands of millions of times *in order that* these figures *could* obtain the significance of *axioms*. This *nota bene*. (*189f*)

22.

HEGEL, II, 394. "*The movement of the End has now achieved that the moment of externality is posited not only in the Notion, and the Notion is not only Ought and tendency, but, as concrete totality, is identical with immediate Objectivity.*"

LENIN: Remarkable: Hegel comes to the "Idea" as the coincidence of the Notion and the object, as *truth, through* the practical, purposive activity of man. A very close approach to the view that man by his *practice* proves the objective correctness of his ideas, concepts, knowledge, science. (*191*)

23.

HEGEL, II, 395. "*The Idea is the adequate Notion:* objective truth, *or the truth as such.*"

LENIN: In general, the introduction to Section III ("The Idea") of Part II to the *Logic* [Hegel, *Science of Logic,* vol. II, 395–400] and the corresponding sections of the *Encyclopedia Logic* secs. 213–15 [pp. 352–358] ARE PERHAPS THE BEST EXPOSITION OF DIALECTICS. Here too, the coincidence, so to speak, of logic and epistemology is shown in a remarkably brilliant way. (*192*)

24.

HEGEL, II, 399*f* [On "closer determinations of the Idea"]. "*First it is simple truth, the identity of the Notion and Objectivity as a universal. . . . Secondly it is the relation of the Subjectivity, which is for itself, of the simple Notion to the Objectivity which is distinct from it: the former is essentially the impulse to transcend this separation. . . . In this relation the Idea is the process in which it sunders itself into individuality and its inorganic nature, and again brings the latter back under the power of the subject, returning to the first simple universality. The self-identity of the Idea is one with the process; and the thought which frees actuality from the show of purposeless changeability and transfigures it into the Idea must not imagine this truth of actuality as a dead repose or bare picture, spent and without impulse or motion, or as a genius* [*in the Roman sense of an indwelling Spirit*]*, number, or abstract thought. In the Idea the Notion reaches freedom, and because of this the Idea contains even the harshest opposition; its repose consists in the security and certainty with which it eternally creates and eternally overcomes it, coinciding in it with itself.*"

LENIN: The Idea (read: Man's knowledge) is the coincidence (conformity) of notion and objectivity (the "universal"). This—first.

Secondly, the Idea is the *relation* of the *subjectivity* (= man) which is for itself (= independent, as it were) to the objectivity which is *distinct* (from this Idea). . . .

Cognition is the *process* of the submersion (of the mind) in an inorganic nature for the sake of subordinating it to the power of the subject and for the sake of generalization (cognition of the universal in its phenomena). . . .

The coincidence of thought with the object is a *process:* thought (= man) must not imagine truth in the form of dead repose, in the form of a bare picture (image), pale (lifeless), without impulse, without motion, like a *genius,* like a number, like abstract thought.

The idea contains also the strongest contradiction, repose (for man's thought) consists in the firmness and certainty with which he eternally creates this contradiction between thought and object and eternally overcomes it. . . .

NB: Cognition is the eternal, endless approximation of thought to the object. The *reflection* of nature in man's thought must be understood not "lifelessly," not "abstractly," *not devoid of movement, not without contradictions,* but in the eternal *process* of movement, the arising of contradictions and their solution. *(194f)*

25.

HEGEL, Enc. Logic, 352*f*. "*The Idea is the Truth: for Truth is the correspondence of objectivity with the notion:— . . . And yet, again, everything actual, in so far as it is true, is the Idea, and has its truth by and in virtue of the Idea alone. Every individual being is some one aspect of the Idea: for which, therefore, yet other actualities are needed, which in their turn appear to have a self-subsistence of their own. It is only in them altogether and in their relation that the notion is realized. The individual by itself does not correspond to its notion. It is this limitation of its existence which constitutes the finitude and the ruin of the individual.*"

LENIN: Individual Being (an object, a phenomenon, etc.) is (only) one *side* of the idea (of truth). Truth requires still other sides of *reality,* which likewise appear only as independent and individual (existing specially for themselves). *Only in their totality,* and in their relation is *truth* realized.

The *totality of all* sides of the phenomenon, of reality and their (reciprocal) *relations*—that is what truth is composed of. The relations (= transitions = contradictions) of notions = the main content of logic, *by which* these concepts (and their relations, transitions, contradictions) are shown as reflections of the objective world. The dialectics of *things* produces the dialectics of *ideas,* and *not* vice versa.

This aphorism should be expressed more popularly, *without* the word dialectics, approximately as follows: In the alternation, reciprocal dependence of *all* notions, in the *identity of their opposites,* in the *transitions* of one notion into another, in the eternal change, movement of notions, Hegel brilliantly *divined* PRECISELY THIS RELATION OF THINGS, OF NATURE.

Hegel brilliantly *divined* (indeed *divined,* not more) the dialectics of things (phenomena, the world, *nature*) in the dialectics of concepts.

What constitutes dialectics?

Mutual dependence of notions, *all* without exception. Transitions of notions from one into another, all without exception. The relativity of opposition between notions . . . the identity of opposites between notions. *NB:* Every notion occurs in a certain *relation,* in a certain connection with *all* the others. *(195–97)*

26.

HEGEL, Enc. Logic, 358. "*The idea as a process runs through three stages in its development. The first form of the idea is Life. . . . The second form is . . . the idea in the form of Knowledge, which appears under the double aspect of the Theoretical and Practical idea. The process of knowledge eventuates in the restoration of the unity enriched by difference. This gives the third form of the idea, the Absolute Idea. . . .*"

LENIN: The idea is "truth." The idea, i.e., *truth* as a process—for truth is a *process*—passes in its *development* through three stages: (1) life; (2) the process of knowledge, which includes human *practice* and *technique* (see above); (3) the stage of the absolute idea (i.e., of complete truth).

Life gives rise to the brain. Nature is reflected in the human brain. By checking and applying the correctness of these reflections in his practice and technique, man arrives at objective truth.

Truth is a process. From the subjective idea, man advances

towards objective truth *through* "Practice" (and technique). *(201)*

[On Hegel, *Science of Logic,* II, Subjective Logic, Sect. 3, Ch. I. Life (pp. 401*f*) and *Enc. Logic,* sect. 216 (pp. 358*f*).]

The question of *Life* does not belong to "logic as it is commonly imagined." If, however, the subject-matter of logic is *truth,* and "*truth as such essentially is in cognition,*" then cognition has to be dealt with—in connection with cognition it is already necessary to speak of *life.*

The idea of including *life* in logic is comprehensible—and brilliant—from the standpoint of the *process* of the reflection of the objective world in the (at first individual) consciousness of man and of the testing of this consciousness (reflection) through practice—see: "Consequently the original Judgment of Life consists in this, that it separates itself as individual subject from the objective, . . ." [*Science of Logic,* II, 404].

Life = individual subject separates itself from the objective.

Only in their connection are the individual limbs of the body what they are. A hand, separated from the body, is a hand only in name (Aristotle).

"Inorganic nature which is subdued by the living being suffers this because it is *in itself* [*virtually*] the same as life is *for itself* [*actually*]."[*Enc. Logic,* sect. 219, p. 361.]

Invert it = pure materialism. Excellent, profound, correct! ! And also *NB:* shows how *extremely* correct and apt are the terms "*an sich*" and "*für sich*"! ! !

If one considers the relation of subject to object in logic, one must take into account also the general premises of Being of the *concrete* subject (=*life of man*) in the objective surroundings. *(201f)*

27.

HEGEL, Science of Logic, II 426*f* [Speaking of Kant's "thing-in-itself" as an absolute beyond cognition]. ". . . *that empty* Thinghood-in-itself; *the error of taking this relation of the untruth of Cognition as valid has become the universal opinion of modern times.*

"*But Cognition must by its own process resolve its finitude and therefore its contradictions.*"

LENIN: Kant took the finite, transitory, relative, conditional character of human cognition (its categories, causality, etc., etc.)

as *subjectivism*, and not as the dialectics of the idea (= of nature itself), divorcing cognition from the object.

But the *process* of cognition leads it to objective truth. (*207*)

28.

HEGEL, II, 429. "*It is one-sided to imagine analysis in such a manner as though nothing were in the object except what has been put into it; and it is equally one-sided to think that the determinations which result are simply taken out of it. The former idea is of course the thesis of subjective idealism, which in analysis takes the activity of Cognition only as a one-sided positing beyond which the Thing-in-itself remains hidden; the latter idea belongs to so-called realism, which takes the subjective Notion as an empty identity that absorbs the thought-determinations from without. . . . But the two moments cannot be separated; in its abstract form, into which analysis elaborates it, the logical is certainly present only in Cognition; while conversely it is not only something posited but also something which is in itself.*"

LENIN: Hegel against subjective idealism and "realism."

Logical concepts are subjective so long as they remain "abstract," in their abstract form, but at the same time they express also the Things-in-themselves. Nature is *both* concrete *and* abstract, *both* phenomenon *and* essence, *both* moment *and* relation. Human concepts are subjective in their abstractness, separateness, but objective as a whole in the process, in the sum-total, in the tendency, in the source.

Very good in section 225 (*Enc. Logic*) where "*cognition*" ("theoretical") and "will," "practical activity," are depicted as two sides, two methods, two means of abolishing the "one-sidedness" both of subjectivity and of objectivity. (*208*)

29.

HEGEL, II, 460. "*The Idea, in so far as the Notion is now* for itself *the Notion determinate in and for itself, is the Practical Idea, or Action.*"

LENIN: Hegel on practice and the objectivity of cognition.

Theoretical cognition ought to give the object in its necessity, in its all-sided relations, in its contradictory movement, in and for itself. But the human notion "definitively" catches this objective truth of cognition, seizes and masters it, only when the notion becomes "being-for-itself" in the sense of practice. That is, the practice of man and of mankind is the test, the criterion of the objectivity of cognition. Is that Hegel's idea? It is necessary to return to this . . . undoubtedly, in Hegel practice serves as a link in the analysis of the process of cognition, and indeed as the transition to objective ("absolute," according to Hegel) truth. Marx, consequently, clearly sides with Hegel in introducing the criterion of practice into the theory of knowledge: see the Theses on Feuerbach.

[Lenin quotes most of Hegel, II, 460, under the heading "Practice in the theory of knowledge," with the following comments:]

Alias: Man's consciousness not only reflects the objective world, but creates it.

The notion (= man), as subjective, again presupposes an otherness which is in itself (= nature independent of man). This notion (= man) is the *impulse* to realize itself, to give itself objectivity in the objective world through itself, and to realize (fulfill) itself.

In the theoretical idea (in the sphere of theory) the subjective notion (cognition?), as the universal and in and for itself indeterminate, stands opposed to the objective world, from which it obtains determinate content and fulfillment.

In the practical idea (in the sphere of practice) this notion as the actual (acting?) stands opposed to the actual.

The self-certainty which the subject (here suddenly instead of "Notion") has in its being in and for itself, as a determinate subject, is a certainty of its own actuality and of the *non-actuality* of the world.

(i.e., that the world does not satisfy man and man decides to change it by his activity.)

The essence: The "good" is a "demand of external actuality," i.e., by the "good" is understood man's *practice* = the demand (1) also of external actuality (2).

Practice is higher than (*theoretical*) *knowledge,* for it has not only the dignity of universality, but also of immediate actuality. *(212f)*

30.

HEGEL, II, 463. "*. . . Cognition knows itself only as apprehension, as the self-identity of the Notion. . . .*" [Lenin quotes to last line of the paragraph, ending "*. . . Idea of the True.*"]

LENIN: Cognition . . . finds itself faced by that which truly is as actuality present independently of subjective opinions (positing). (This is pure materialism!) Man's will, his practice, itself blocks the attainment of its end . . . in that it separates itself from cognition and does not recognize external actuality for that which truly is (for objective truth). What is necessary is the *union of cognition* and *practice.*

And immediately following this:

"But it makes this transition through itself." (The transition of the idea of truth into the idea of the Good, of theory into practice, and vice versa.) "In the syllogism of action one premise is the immediate relation of the *good end to actuality,* of which it makes itself master, directing it (in the second premise) as external *means* against external actuality." [*Ibid.,* II, 463.]

The "syllogism of action". . . For Hegel *action,* practice, is a *logical "syllogism,"* a figure of logic. And that is true! Not, of course, in the sense that the figure of logic has its other being in the practice of man (= absolute idealism), but vice versa: Man's practice, repeating itself a thousand million times, becomes consolidated in man's consciousness by figures of logic. Precisely (and only) on account of this thousand-million-fold repetition, these figures have the stability of a prejudice, and axiomatic character.

First premise: "The *good end* (subjective end) versus *actuality* ("external actuality").

Second premise: The external *means* (instrument), (objective).

Third premise or conclusion: The coincidence of subjective and objective, the test of subjective ideas, the criterion of objective truth. (*215–17*)

31.

HEGEL, II, 465. "*By the activity of the objective Notion its external actuality is altered, and its determination is accordingly transcended; and by this very process it loses merely apparent reality, external determinability, and nullity, and it is thus* posited *as being in and for itself.*" [Lenin quotes most of the remainder of p. 465 together with the opening sentence of p. 466 (Ch. III, The Absolute Idea).]

"*The Absolute Idea has now turned out to be the identity of the Theoretical and the Practical Idea; each of these by itself is one-sided. . . .*"

LENIN: The activity of man, who has constructed an objective picture of the world for himself, *changes* external actuality, abolishes its determinateness (= alters some sides or other, qualities, of it), and thus removes from it the features of Semblance, externality and nullity, and makes it as being in and for itself (= objectively true).

The result of activity is the test of subjective cognition and the criterion of OBJECTIVITY WHICH TRULY IS.

The unity of the theoretical idea (of knowledge) *and of practice*—this *NB*—and this unity *precisely in the theory of knowledge,* for the resulting sum is the "absolute idea" (and the idea = "the objectively true"). *(218 f)*

32.

HEGEL, II, 473. "*This equally synthetic and analytic moment of the Judgment, by which the original universal determines itself out of itself to be its own Other, may rightly be called the* dialectic *moment.*"

LENIN: One of the definitions of *dialectics.*

[He interprets this passage as containing three elements.]

(1) the determination of the concept out of itself (the thing *itself* must be considered in its relations and in its development);

(2) the contradictory nature of the thing itself (the other of itself), the contradictory forces and tendencies in each phenomenon;

(3) the union of analysis and synthesis.

Such, apparently, are the elements of dialectics.

One could perhaps present these elements in greater detail as follows:

(1) the *objectivity* of consideration (not examples, not divergences, but the Thing-in-itself).

(2) the entire totality of the manifold *relations* of this thing to others.

(3) the *development* of this thing (phenomenon, respectively, its own movement, its own life.)

(4) the internally contradictory *tendencies* (*and* sides) in this thing.

(5) the thing (phenomenon, etc.) as the *sum and unity of opposites.*

(6) the *struggle,* respectively unfolding, of these opposites, contradictory strivings, etc.

(7) the union of analysis and synthesis—the break-down of the

separate parts and the totality, the summation of these parts.

(8) the relations of each thing (phenomenon, etc.) are not only manifold, but general, universal. Each thing (phenomenon, process, etc.) is connected with *every other.*

(9) not only the unity of opposites, but the *transitions* of *every* determination, quality, feature, side, property into *every* other (into its opposite?).

(10) the endless process of the discovery of *new* sides, relations, etc.

(11) the endless process of the deepening of man's knowledge of the thing, of phenomena, processes, etc., from appearance to essence and from less profound to more profound essence.

(12) from co-existence to causality and from one form of connection and reciprocal dependence to another, deeper, more general form.

(13) the repetition at a higher stage of certain features, properties, etc., of the lower and

(14) the apparent return to the old (negation of the negation).

(15) the struggle of content with form and conversely. The throwing off of the form, the transformation of the content.

(16) the transition of quantity into quality and *vice versa* (15 and 16 are *examples* of 9).

In brief, dialectics can be defined as the doctrine of the unity of opposites. This embodies the essence of dialectics, but it requires explanations and development. *(221–23)*

33.

HEGEL, II, 476. "*To hold fast the positive in its negative, and the content of the presupposition in the result, is the most important part of rational cognition. . . .*"

LENIN: Not empty negation, not feeble negation, not *skeptical* negation, [nor] vacillation and doubt are characteristic and essential in dialectics—which undoubtedly contains the element of negation and indeed as its most important element—no, but negation as a moment of development, retaining the positive, i.e., without any vacillations, without any eclecticism. *(226)*

34.

HEGEL, II, 477. "*The first or immediate term is the Notion* in itself, *and therefore is the negative only* in itself; *the dialectic moment with it therefore consists in this, that the* distinction *which it implicitly contains is posited in it. The second term on the other hand is itself the determinate entity, distinction or relation; hence with it the dialectic moment consists in the positing of the* unity *which is contained in it.*"

LENIN: In relation to the simple and original, "first," positive assertions, propositions, etc., the "dialectical moment," i.e., scientific consideration, demands the demonstration of difference, connection, transition. Without that the simple positive assertion is incomplete, lifeless, dead. In relation to the "second," negative proposition, the "dialectical moment" demands the demonstration of "*unity*," i.e., of the connection of negative and positive, the presence of this positive in the negative. From assertion to negation—from negation to "unity" with the asserted—without this dialectics becomes empty negation, a game, or skepsis. (*227*)

35.

HEGEL, II, 477. "*But formal thought makes identity its law, and allows the contradictory content which lies before it to drop into the sphere of sensuous representation, into space and time, where the contradictory terms are held apart in spatial and temporal juxtaposition and thus come before consciousness without being in contact.*"

LENIN: "Come before consciousness without mutual contact" (the object)—that is the essence of anti-dialectics. It is only here that Hegel has, as it were, allowed the ass's ears of idealism to show themselves—by referring time and space (in connection with sensuous representation) to something *lower* compared with *thought*. Incidentally, in a *certain* sense, sensuous representation is, of course, lower. The crux lies in the fact that thought must *apprehend* the whole "representation" in its movement, but *for that* thought must be dialectical. Is sensuous representation *closer* to reality than thought? Both yes and no. Sensuous representation cannot apprehend movement *as a whole*, it cannot, for example, apprehend movement with a speed of 186,000 miles per second, but *thought* does and must apprehend it. Thought, taken from sensuous representation, also reflects reality; time is a form of being of objective reality. Here, in the concept of time (and not in the relation of sensuous representation to thought) is the idealism of Hegel. (*228*)

36.

HEGEL, II, 485. "*For the Idea posits itself as the absolute unity of the pure Notion and its Reality, and thus gathers itself into the immediacy of Being; and in doing so, as totality in this form, it is* Nature."

LENIN: *NB:* In the *Encyclopedia Logic,* addendum to par. 244, the last sentence of the book reads: "We began with Being, abstract Being: where we now are we also have the Idea as Being: but this Idea which has Being is Nature."

This sentence on the last page of the *Logic* [next to last in the English edition] is highly noteworthy. The transition of the logical idea to *nature.* It brings one within a hand's grasp of materialism. Engels was right when he said that Hegel's system was materialism turned upside down.

End of the Logic, Dec. 17, 1914. (*234*)

B. ON HEGEL'S *History of Philosophy*

37.

HEGEL, I, 27. "*As concrete, this [philosophical] activity is a succession of processes in development which must be represented not as a straight line drawn out into vague infinity, but as a circle returning within itself, which, as periphery, has very many circles, and whose whole is a large number of processes in development turning back within themselves.*"

LENIN: A very profound correct comparison! ! Every shade of thought = a circle on the great circle (a spiral) of the development of human thought in general. (*247*)

38.

HEGEL, I, 240 [On the Eleatic School]. "*We here find the beginning of dialectic,* i.e., *simply the pure movement of thought in Notions; likewise we see the opposition of thought to outward appearance or sensuous Being, or of that which is implicit to the being-for-another of this implicitness, and in the objective existence we see the contradiction which it has in itself, or dialectic proper.*"

LENIN: Two characteristics; two typical features.

Here are essentially two determinations (determinations, not definitions) of dialectics:

(a) "the pure movement of thought in Notions";

(b) "in the (very) essence of objects (to elucidate) (to reveal) the contradiction which it (this essence) has in itself *(dialectics proper)*."

In other words, this "fragment" of Hegel's should be reproduced as follows:

Dialectics in general is "the pure movement of thought in Notions" (i.e., putting it without the mysticism of idealism: human concepts are not fixed but are eternally in movement, they pass into one another, they flow into one another, otherwise they do not reflect living life. The analysis of concepts, the study of them, the "art of operating with them" (Engels) always demands study of the *movement* of concepts, of their interconnection, of their mutual transitions).

In particular, dialectics is the study of the opposition of the Thing-in-itself (*Ansich*), of the essence, substratum, substance—from the appearance, from "Being-for-Others." (Here, too, we see a transition, a flow from the one to the other: The essence appears. The appearance is essential.) Human thought goes endlessly deeper from appearance to essence, from essence of the first order, as it were, to essence of the second order, and so on *without end.*

Dialectics in the proper sense is the study of contradiction *in the very essence of objects;* not only are appearances transitory, mobile, fluid, demarcated only by conventional boundaries, but the *essence* of things is so as well. (*252–54*)

39.

HEGEL, I, 264. *"Dialectic is either (a) external dialectic, in which this movement is different from the comprehension of the movement, or (b) not a movement of our intelligence only, but what proceeds from the nature of the thing itself, i.e., from the pure Notion of the content."*

[Lenin quotes most of this para. to middle of p. 265.]

LENIN: Regarding the question of dialectics and its objective significance. . . .

With the "principle of development" in the 20th century (indeed, at the end of the 19th century also) "all are agreed." Yes, but this superficial, not thought out, accidental, philistine "agreement" is an agreement of *such a kind* as stifles and vulgarizes the truth.—If everything develops, then everything passes from one into another, for development as is well known is not a simple, universal and eternal *growth, enlargement* (or simple diminution), etc.—If that is so, then, in the first place, evolution has to be understood *more exactly,* as the arising and passing away of everything, as mutual transitions.—And, in the second place, if *everything* develops, does not that apply also to the most general *concepts* and *categories* of thought? If not, it means that thinking is not connected with being. If it does, it means that there is a dialectics of concepts and a dialectics of cognition which has objective significance. (*255f*)

40.

HEGEL, I, 273 *f* [On Aristotle's critique of Zeno's paradoxes on motion]. "*If we wish to make motion clear to ourselves, we say that the body is in one place and then it goes to another; because it moves, it is no longer in the first, but yet not in the second; were it in either it would be at rest. Where then is it? If we say that it is between both, this is to convey nothing at all, for were it between both, it would be in a place, and this presents the same difficulty. But movement means to be in this place and not to be in it, and thus to be in both alike; this is the continuity of space and time which first makes motion possible.*"

LENIN: *NB* correct!

Movement is the presence of a body in a definite place at a given moment and in another place at another, subsequent moment—such is the objection which Chernov repeats (see his *Philosophical Studies*) in the wake of *all* the "metaphysical" opponents of Hegel.

This objection is *incorrect:* (1) it describes the *result* of motion, but not motion *itself;* (2) it does not show, it does not contain in itself the *possibility* of motion; (3) it depicts motion as a sum, as a concatenation of states of *rest,* that is to say, the (dialectical) contradiction is not removed by it, but only concealed, shifted, screened, covered over.

"What makes the difficulty is always thought alone, since it keeps apart the moments of an object which in their separation are really united." [Hegel, *ibid.*, I, 274.]

We cannot imagine, express, measure, depict movement, without interrupting continuity, without simplifying, coarsening, dismembering, strangling that which is living. The representation of movement by means of thought always makes coarse, kills—

and not only by means of thought, but also by sense-perception, and not only of movement, but *every* concept.

And in that lies the *essence* of dialectics.

And precisely *this essence* is expressed by the formula: The unity, identity of opposites. (*259f*)

41.

HEGEL, I, 292. "*When water in its decomposition reveals hydrogen and oxygen, that means, according to them* [*the natural scientists*], '*these last have not arisen for they were already there as such, as the parts of which the water subsists.' But they can neither demonstrate water in crystal nor oxygen and hydrogen in water, and the same is true of 'latent heat.' As we find in all expression of perception and experience, as soon as men speak, there is a Notion present; it cannot be withheld, for in consciousness there always is a touch of universality and truth.*"

LENIN: Quite right and important—it is precisely this that Engels repeated in more popular form, when he wrote that natural scientists ought to know that the results of natural science are concepts, and that the art of operating with concepts is not inborn, but is the result of 2,000 years of the development of natural science and philosophy.

The concept of transformation is taken narrowly by natural scientists and they lack understanding of dialectics. (*264*)

Hegel's logic cannot be *applied* in its given form, it cannot be *taken* as given. One *must separate out* from it the logical (epistemological) nuances, after purifying them from *Idea-mysticism;* that is still a big job. (*266*)

42.

HEGEL, I, 410 *f*. " . . . *That which is held by me as truth and right is spirit of my spirit. But what spirit derives from itself must come from it as from the spirit which acts in a universal manner, and not from its passions, likings, and arbitrary desires. These, too, certainly come from something inward which is 'implanted in us by nature,' but that which is only in a natural way our own, for it belongs to the particular; high above it is true thought, the Notion, the rational.*"

LENIN: Intelligent idealism is closer to intelligent materialism than stupid materialism. [Lenin then restates this judgment]:

Dialectical idealism instead of intelligent; metaphysical, undeveloped, dead, crude, rigid [materialism] instead of stupid. (*276*)

43.

HEGEL, I, 466. "*That the universal should in Philosophy be given a place of such importance that only the universal can be expressed, and the 'this' which is meant, cannot, indicates a state of consciousness and thought which the philosophic culture of our time has not yet reached. . . . Thought contains only the universal, the 'this' is only in thought; if I say 'this' it is the most universal of all.*"

LENIN: Thereby Hegel hits every materialism *except* dialectical materialism. *NB.*

Hegel seriously "believed," thought, that materialism as a philosophy was impossible, for philosophy is the science of thinking, of the *universal,* but the universal is a thought. Here he repeated the error of the same subjective idealism that he always called "bad" idealism. Objective (and still more, absolute) idealism came *very close* to materialism by a zigzag (and a somersault), even partially *became transformed into it.*

The Cyrenaics held sensations for the truth, "the truth is not *what* is in sensation, the content, but is itself sensation." [Hegel, I, 473.] *NB:* the Cyrenaics and Mach and Co. (Phenomenologists *à la* Mach & Co., *inevitably* become idealists on the question of the *universal,* "law," "necessity," etc.) (*277f*)

44.

LENIN [on Hegel on Plato, *ibid.,* II, 1–117]: The significance of the *universal* is contradictory: It is dead, impure, incomplete, etc., etc., but it alone is a *stage* towards knowledge of the *concrete,* for we can never know the concrete completely. The *infinite* sum of general conceptions, laws, etc., gives the *concrete* in its completeness.

NB: the dialectics of cognition. The movement of cognition *to* the object can always only proceed dialectically: To retreat in order to hit more surely—to fall back the better to leap (to know?). Converging and diverging lines: Circles which touch one another. Nodal point = the practice of mankind and of human history.

These nodal points represent a unity of contradictions, when

Being and not-Being, as vanishing moments, coincide for a moment, in the given moments of the movement (= of technique, of history, etc.)

In analyzing Plato's dialectics, Hegel once again tries to show the difference between subjective, sophistic dialectics and objective dialectics.

Hegel dilates at length on Plato's "Philosophy of Nature," the ultra-nonsensical mysticism of ideas, such as that "triangles form the essence of sensuous things" [Hegel, *ibid.*, p. 86], and such mystic nonsense. That is highly characteristic! The mystic-idealist-spiritualist Hegel (like all official, clerical-idealist philosophy of our day) extols and expatiates on mysticism, idealism in the history of philosophy, while ignoring and slighting materialism. *Cf.* Hegel on Democritus—nil! ! On Plato a huge mass of mystical slush. *(279–82)*

45.

LENIN [On Hegel on Aristotle, II, 117–231]: Incorrect, says Hegel, is the generally held opinion that the philosophy of Aristotle is "*realism,*" "empiricism" in contrast to the *idealism* of Plato (Here again, Hegel clearly squeezes in a great deal *under* idealism.)

In presenting Aristotle's polemic against Plato's doctrine on ideas, Hegel *suppresses* its materialistic features.

Hegel perceives the idealism of Aristotle in his idea of god. (Of course, it is idealism, but more objective and *further removed, more general* than the idealism of Plato, hence in the philosophy of nature more frequently = materialism.)

Aristotle's criticism of Plato's "ideas" is a criticism of *idealism as idealism in general:* For whence concepts, abstractions, are derived, thence come also "law" and "necessity," etc. The idealist Hegel in cowardly fashion fought shy of the undermining of the *foundations* of idealism by Aristotle (in his criticism of Plato's ideas).

When *one* idealist criticizes the foundations of idealism of *another* idealist, *materialism* is always the gainer thereby. *Cf.* Aristotle versus Plato, etc., Hegel versus Kant, etc.

Hegel, the supporter of dialectics, could not understand the *dialectical* transition *from* matter *to* motion, *from* matter *to* consciousness—especially the second. Marx corrected the error (or weakness?) of the mystic.

NB: Not only is the transition from matter to consciousness dialectical, but also that from sensation to thought, etc.

What distinguishes the dialectical transition from the undialectical transition? The leap. The contradiction. The interruption of gradualness. The unity (identity) of Being and not-Being.

"In nature" concepts do not exist "in this freedom" (in the freedom of thought and the fantasy of *man!*). "In nature" they (concepts) have "flesh and blood."—That is excellent! But it is materialism. Human concepts are the *soul* of nature—this is only a mystical way of saying that in human concepts nature is reflected *in a distinctive way* (this *NB:* in a *distinctive* and *dialectical* way!).

PP. 137–53 *solely* on the Metaphysics of Aristotle! Everything essential that he has to say against Plato's idealism is *suppressed!* In particular, there is suppressed the question of existence *outside* man and humanity! = the question of materialism! (*282–85*)

C. A COMMENT ON HEGEL'S *Encyclopedia Logic*

46.

LENIN: The concept (cognition) reveals the essence (the law of causality, identity, difference, etc.) in Being (in immediate phenomena)—such is actually the *general course* of all human cognition (of all science) in general. Such is the course also of natural science and political *economy* (and history). So far, Hegel's dialectic is a generalization of the history of thought. To trace this more concretely and in greater detail in the *history of the separate sciences* seems an extraordinarily rewarding task. In logic, the history of thought *must,* by and large, coincide with the laws of thinking.

It is strikingly evident that Hegel sometimes passes from the abstract to the concrete (Being (abstract)—*Determinate Being* (concrete)—Being-for-itself) and sometimes the other way round (the subjective Notion—the Object—Truth (the Absolute Idea). Is not this the inconsistency of an idealist (what Marx called the mysticism of ideas in Hegel)? Or are there deeper reasons? (*e.g., Being = Nothing*—the idea of Becoming, of development). First of all impressions *flash by,* then *Something* emerges—afterwards the concepts of *quality* (the determination of the thing or the phenomenon) and *quantity* are developed. After that study and reflection direct thought to cognition of identity—of difference—of Ground—of the Essence versus the Phenomenon—of causality, etc. All these moments (steps, stages, processes) of cognition move in the direction from the subject to the object, being tested in practice and arriving through this test at truth (= the Absolute Idea).

If Marx did not leave behind him a "Logic" (with a capital letter), he did leave the *logic* of *Capital,* and this ought to be utilized to the full in this question. In *Capital,* Marx applied to a single science logic, dialectics and the theory of knowledge of materialism (three words are not needed: it is one and the same thing) which has taken everything valuable in Hegel and developed it further.

The history of capitalism and the analysis of the *concept* summing it up.

The beginning—the most simple, ordinary, mass, immediate "Being"; the single commodity ("*Sein*" in political economy); The analysis of it as a social relation. A *double* analysis, deductive and inductive—logical and historical (forms of value).

Testing by facts or by practice respectively, is to be found here in *each* step of the analysis. *(318–20)*

D. On Aristotle's *Metaphysics*

47.

LENIN: A mass of extremely interesting, lively, *naive* (fresh) matter which introduces philosophy and is replaced in the expositions by scholasticism, by the result without movement, etc.

Clericalism killed what was living in Aristotle and perpetuated what was dead.

Highly characteristic and profoundly interesting (in the beginning of the *Metaphysics*) are the polemic with Plato and the "puzzling" questions, delightful for their naiveté, and doubts regarding the nonsense of idealism. And all this along with the most helpless confusion about the *fundamental,* the concept and the particular.

NB: At the beginning of metaphysics the *stubborn* struggle against Heraclitus, against his idea of the identity of Being and not-Being (the Greek philosophers approached close to dialectics but could not cope with it). Highly characteristic in general, throughout the whole book, everywhere, are the living germs of dialectics *and inquiries* about it.

In Aristotle, objective logic is *everywhere confused* with subjective logic and, moreover, in such a way that everywhere objective logic is *visible*. There is no doubt as to the objectivity of cognition. There is a naive faith in the power of reason, in the force, power, objective truth of cognition. And a naive *confusion*, a helplessly pitiful confusion in the *dialectics* of the universal and the particular—of the concept and the sensuously perceptible reality of individual objects, things, phenomena.

Scholasticism and clericalism took what was dead in Aristotle, but not what was *living*, the *inquiries*, the searchings, the labyrinth, in which man lost his way.

Aristotle's logic is an inquiry, a searching, an approach to the logic of Hegel—and it, the logic of Aristotle (who *everywhere*, at every step, raises *precisely* the question *of dialectics*), has been made into a dead scholasticism, by rejecting all the searchings, waverings and modes of framing questions. What the Greeks had was precisely modes of framing quetsions, as it were tentative systems, a naive discordance of views, excellently reflected in Aristotle. *(367–69)*

48.

Lenin [on Bk. M (XIII)]: Aristotle again returns to a criticism of Pythagoras' theory of numbers (and Plato's theory of ideas), independent of sensible things.

Primitive idealism: The universal (concept, idea) is a *particular being*. This appears wild, monstrously (more accurately, childishly) stupid. But is not modern idealism, Kant, Hegel, the idea of God, of the same nature (*absolutely* of the same nature)? Tables, chairs and the *ideas* of table and chair; the world and the idea of the world (God); thing and "noumenon," the unknowable "Thing-in-itself;" the connection of the earth and the sun, nature in general—and law, *logos*, God. The dichotomy of human knowledge and the *possibility* of idealism (= religion) are *given* already *in the first, elementary* abstraction ("house" in general and particular houses).

The approach of the (human) mind to a particular thing, the taking of a copy (= a concept) of it *is not* a simple, immediate act, a dead mirroring, but one which is complex, split into two, zigzag like, which *includes in it* the possibility of the flight of fantasy from life; more than that: The possibility of the *transformation* (moreover, an unnoticeable transformation, of which man is unaware) of the abstract concept, idea, into a *fantasy* (in the final analysis = God). For even in the simplest generalization, in the most elementary general idea ("table" in general), *there is* a certain bit of *fantasy*. (Vice versa, it would be stupid to deny the role of fantasy, even in the strictest science; *cf.* Pisarev on useful dreaming, as an impulse *to* work, and on empty daydreaming.) (*372f*)

49.

ARISTOTLE [*Metaphysics*, Bk. M (XIII), Ch. 2]: "*Again, the solid is a sort of substance; for it already has in a sense completeness. But how can lines be substances? Neither as a form or shape, as the soul perhaps is, nor as matter, like the solid; for we have no experience of anything that can be put together out of lines or planes or points, while if these had been a sort of material substance, we should have observed things which could be put together out of them.*"

LENIN: Naive expression of the "difficulties" of the "philosophy of mathematics" (to use modern language). [But, Aristotle, in Ch. 3] solves these difficulties excellently, distinctly, clearly, *materialistically* (mathematics and other sciences abstract *one* of the aspects of a body, phenomenon, life). But the author does not consistently *maintain* this point of view. (*373*)

SOURCES

Editions Used for Selections

Marx, *Capital,* vol. i, New York, International Publishers (abbreviated as IP hereafter), 1947; vols. ii and iii, Chicago, Kerr, 1906.

Critique of Political Economy. Chicago, Kerr, 1904.

Critique of the Gotha Program. New York, IP, 1938.

Economic and Philosophic Manuscripts of 1844. Moscow, Foreign Languages Publishing House (abbreviated as FLPH hereafter) first impression, *nd.*

Poverty of Philosophy. Moscow, FLPH, *nd.*

Theories of Surplus Value. New York, IP, 1952.

Value, Price and Profit. New York, IP, 1935.

Engels, *Anti-Dühring (Herr Eugen Dühring's Revolution in Science)*. New York, IP, 1939.

Ludwig Feuerbach. New York, IP, 1941.

Dialectics of Nature. New York, IP, 1940.

The Origin of the Family, Private Property, and the State. New York, IP, 1942.

Socialism, Utopian and Scientific. New York, IP, 1935.

The Housing Question. New York, IP, *nd.*

Marx and Engels, *The Communist Manifesto*. New York, IP, 1948.

The Holy Family. Moscow, FLPH, 1956.

The German Ideology. New York, IP, 1942.

The Selected Correspondence, 1846–1895. New York, IP, 1942.

Selected Works. 2 vols., New York, IP, *nd.*

On Religion. Moscow, FLPH, *nd.*

Lenin, *Philosophical Notebooks*. Moscow, FLPH, 1961.

Selected Works. Vols. ix and xi, New York, IP, 1943.

Materialism and Empirio-Criticism. New York, IP, 1927.

The Young Generation. New York, IP, 1940.

BIOGRAPHICAL INDEX

A.

B.

* All book titles in quotation marks are the editors' translations of original titles. All titles in italics are either the original or published English translations.

Aristotelian deductive logic and sought, in his *Novum Organum,* to develop a new inductive logic of discovery.

Barth, Paul (1858–1922) *210.*
German philosopher, psychologist, and sociologist; active opponent of Marxism; author, "Philosophy of History of Hegel and Hegelians up to Marx and Hartman," 1890.

Bauer, Bruno (1809–1882) *226, 236, 279f, 287, 294f, 322, 324.*
One of the leaders of the Young or Left Hegelians; early friend and associate of Marx; a pioneer in modern Biblical criticism.

Bauer, Edgar (1820–1886) *279.*
German publicist, brother of Bruno Bauer; Young Hegelian. Marx's title "The Holy Family" was meant to denote the Bauer brothers and other Hegelians around them.

Bayle, Pierre (1647–1706) *56.*
French philosopher; his *Dictionnaire historique et critique* had a profound influence on philosophers of the French enlightenment.

Bazarov, W. (1874– ?) *64, 66, 68, 84.*
Russian economist and philosopher; author of "Toward a Realistic World-Outlook," 1904.

Beltov, N. (pseudonym for Plekhanov, *see.*)

Bentham, Jeremy (1748–1832) *60.*
English philosopher, jurist, political theorist; founder of Utilitarianism. *Principles of Morals and Legislation,* 1789.

Berkeley, George (1685–1753) *66–75, 77, 148.*
Irish philosopher and clergyman; became a bishop of the Church of England; founder of modern subjective idealism; works include: *Principles of Human Knowledge,* 1710; *Three Dialogues between Hylas and Philonous,* 1713.

Berman, Jakov Alexandrovich (1868– ?) *64, 159.*
Professor of legal and political theory; "The Essence of Pragmatism," 1911.

Bernstein, Eduard (1850–1932) *210.*
German social-democrat; advocate of the revision of the foundations of Marxism; criticized Marxism in *Evolutionary Socialism,* 1898, among other works.

Berthollet, Claude Louis, Count de (1748–1822) *314.*
French physician and chemist; worked with Lavoisier in the reform and unification of chemical terminology.

Blanc, Jean Joseph Louis (1811–1882) *232.*

C.

D.

Diogenes Laertius (2d to 3d century A.D.) *283.*
Unknown author of *Lives and Opinions of Eminent Philosophers,* an important source of our knowledge of the Greek philosophers, especially of Epicurus.

Dodwell, Henry (1641–1711) *58.*
English free-thinking philosopher, author of anonymous pamphlet, *Christianity Not Founded on Argument,* 1742.

Draper, John William (1811–1882) *161.*
American physiologist and chemist; author, *History of the Intellectual Development of Europe,* 1863; *History of the Conflict between Religion and Science,* 1874.

Duhem, Pierre (1861–1916) *82, 160.*
French physicist; emphasized subjective element in physics; author, *Le Théorie physique,* 1906.

Dühring, Eugen Karl (1833–1901) *79f, 108–111, 117f, 126–129, 134f, 137, 156, 231, 260.*
German lawyer, economist, and philosophy teacher (Berlin) of the positivist school; sought to win German socialists to oppose "abuses" of capitalism rather than capitalism itself.

Duns Scotus, John (c.1265–1308) *56.*
Scottish scholastic philosopher and theologian; Franciscan opponent of philosophy of Thomas Aquinas.

Dupuis, Charles François (1742–1809) *59.*
French scholar; wrote "The Origins of All Cults, or Universal Religion," 1795.

E.

Epicurus (342–270 B.C.) *46, 55, 229, 282f.*
Greek philosopher, popularizer of the atomic theory of Democritus; held that the ultimate good is pleasure under the guidance of prudence or wisdom. Only fragments of his many works are extant.

F.

Fechner, Gustav Theodor (1801–1887) *79.*
German physicist and a founder of psycho-physics; wrote on aesthetics and the soul-life of plants.

Feuerbach, Ludwig (1804–1872) *38, 49, 52–54, 56, 65, 79, 84, 158, 162, 164, 226, 228, 231–33, 235f, 243, 243f, 253–56, 278f, 314–18, 322, 325, 340.*
German Hegelian who led the materialist revolt against Hegel;

G.

Goethe, Johann Wolfgang von (1749–1832) *52, 97, 141, 234, 238.*
German poet, novelist, dramatist, and amateur scientist; leading figure of the German Enlightenment.

Grove, Sir William Robert (1811–1896) *166.*
English physicist; contributor to the development of the electric battery.

Grün, Karl (1817–1887) *79.*
German publicist; exponent of "true socialism"; author, "The Social Movement in France and Belgium," 1845.

Guizot, François Pierre Guillaume (1787–1874) *186, 195, 203.*
French historian; Minister of Foreign Affairs and Premier, 1840–1848; author, *General History of Civilization in Modern Europe,* 6 vols., 1829–32.

H.

Haeckel, Ernst Heinrich (1834–1919) *112, 175f.*
German biologist and philosopher; leading exponent of Darwinian evolution; author, *Riddle of the Universe,* 1899.

Hartley, David (1705–1757) *58.*
English physician and speculative psychologist; author, *Observations of Man,* 1749.

Hegel, Georg Wilhelm Friedrich (1770–1831) *18f, 22, 27, 29, 33f, 48–51, 79, 81, 94–101, 103–5, 108–12, 117, 121–27, 130, 132, 137, 142, 149, 158, 172, 176, 183, 186, 192–95, 209f, 213, 215, 236f, 266, 277–82, 287–94, 315, 321–24, 325–62.*
German philosopher, father of modern *objective* idealism; revived dialectics and raised it to a new level; wrote voluminously on philosophy, religion, art, ethics, and logic.

Heine, Heinrich (1797–1856) *124.*
German lyric poet and prose writer, famous for his wit and satire. His *Religion and Philosophy in Germany,* 1834, anticipated features of the Marxist approach to Hegelianism.

Helfond, Osip I. (1868– ?) *64.*
Russian physician and writer; one of the authors of "Contributions to the Philosophy of Marxism," 1906.

Helvetius, Claude Adrien (1715–1771) *56, 59, 325.*
French materialist moral and social philosopher; strongly influenced subsequent advanced thought from the British Utilitarians to Marx; author, *De l'Esprit* (*Essays on the Mind*) 1758; *De l'Homme* (*A Treatise on Man*), 1777.

Expounded nebular theory of the origin of the solar system (1754); his main philosophical works began with the *Critique of Pure Reason,* 1781.

Kingsley, Charles (1819–1875) *224.*
English clergyman and Christian Socialist; best known for his historical novels, *Hypatia* and *Westward Ho.*

Kugelmann, Ludwig (1830–1902) *79.*
Hanover physician; fought in Revolution of 1848; member of First International, in constant correspondence with Marx, 1862–74; *see* MARX, *Letters to Dr. Kugelmann,* New York, 1934.

L.

Lamettrie, Julien Offroy de (1709–1751) *51n, 54.*
French physician and materialist philosopher; author, "Natural History of the Soul," 1745; *Man a Machine,* 1747.

Lange, Frederick Albert (1828–1875) *79.*
German founder of neo-Kantianism; precursor of empirio-criticism and fictionalism; author *History of Materialism,* 1866.

Lamarck, Jean Baptiste de (1744–1829) *52, 168.*
French naturalist, noted for his classification of invertebrates and his theories of biological evolution.

Lankester, Edwin Ray, Sir (1847–1929) *176n.*
British naturalist; professor at University of London, later at Oxford; friend of Marx.

Laplace, Pierre Simon, Marquis de (1749–1827) *33, 62, 165, 242.*
French astronomer and mathematician; author "Mécanique céleste," 1799–1825.

Lavoisier, Antoine Laurent (1743–1799) *86, 167.*
French chemist; a founder of modern experimental chemistry and discoverer of oxygen.

Law, John (1671–1729) *55.*
Scottish financier; became controller general of finances in France, 1720, where his monetary theories and stock manipulations led to ruinous speculation and collapse.

Leibniz, Gottfried Wilhelm (1646–1716) *54–56, 58.*
German philosopher and mathematician; sought to reform science by a universal scientific language and a logical calculus; author, *Monadology,* 1714.

Le Roy, Edouard (1870–1954) *54f.*
A leader of Catholic modernism; philosopher, mathematician; author *Dogme et Critique,* (1907).

Lessing, Gotthold Ephraim (1729–1781) *98.*
German dramatist and critic, called the founder of modern German literature; best known for his play, *Nathan the Wise,* 1799.

Liebig, Justus (1803–1873) *111, 314.*
German chemist; made valuable contributions to agricultural chemistry and led in development of artificial fertilizers.

Linnaeus, Carolus (1707–1778) *24.*
Swedish botanist and naturalist; founder of modern botanical classification.

Locke, John (1632–1714) *31, 54, 56, 58–61, 148, 209.*
English philosopher and political theorist; taught that all ideas have their origin in sense experience; author, *Essay Concerning Human Understanding,* 1690.

Lopatin, Lev Mikhailov (1855–1920) *83.*
Russian idealist philosopher, author, "Positive Tasks of Philosophy," 1886–1889.

Lucretius (Titus Lucretius Carus) (c.96–c.55 B.C.) *46.*
Roman philosophical poet; follower of Democritus and Epicurus; author, *De Rerum Natura. (On the Nature of Things).*

Lunacharsky, Anatol (1875–1933) *64f, 83.*
Russian literary critic, dramatist, philosopher and educator; Soviet Commissar of Education, 1917–29.

Luther, Martin (1483–1546) *215.*
German priest and theology professor at Wittenberg; leader of the Protestant Reformation.

Lyell, Sir Charles (1797–1875) *166.*
British geologist whose theory of uniform and continuous changes in the earth's surface paved the way for Darwinian evolution; author, *Principles of Geology,* 1830–33.

M.

Mably, Gabriel Bonnot, Abbé de (1709–1785) *28.*
French publicist and utopian socialist, brother of Condillac.

McCulloch, John Ramsay (1789–1864) *313.*
Scottish economist and statistician; author, *A Discourse on the Rise, Progress, Peculiar Objects and Importance of Political Economy,* 1825.

Mach, Ernst (1838–1916) *66, 69, 81–84, 148–51, 160, 164, 358.*
Austrian physicist, psychologist and philosopher; leading figure of the new "positivism" known as "Empirio-Criticism;" author,

The Science of Mechanics, 1883; *The Analysis of Sensations,* 1886.

Malebranche, Nicolas (1638–1715) *54, 56, 58.*
French philosopher; tried to overcome Cartesian dualism by maintaining that God is the real ground of all being and knowing; author, *The Search for Truth,* 1674.

Malpighi, Marcello (1628–1694) *154.*
Italian anatomist and physiologist, founder of microscopic anatomy.

Mandeville, Bernard (1670–1733) *60.*
Dutch-English physician and satirical writer on ethics; his work, *The Fable of the Bees; or, Private Vices, Public Benefits,* 1714, was pronounced a "nuisance" by an English jury.

Mantell, Gideon Algernon (1790–1852) *61.*
English geologist and paleontologist; known for his remarkable collection of English fossils.

Mayer, Julius Robert Von (1814–1878) *166.*
German physician and scientist; one of the founders of the theory of mechanical heat and the law of the conservation of energy.

Mehring, Franz (1846–1919) *65, 216.*
German Marxist historian and literary critic; edited many unpublished manuscripts of Marx and Engels, and wrote the biography, *Karl Marx,* 1918.

Mendelssohn, Moses (1729–1786) *98.*
German philosopher; pioneer of the German Enlightenment and of the romantic movement.

Menshikov, Mikhail Osipovich (1859–1918) *151.*
Russian journalist; a former liberal who later defended Tsarism, was frequently called Judas Menshikov by revolutionaries.

Mignet, François Auguste Marie (1796–1884) *195, 203.*
French historian and journalist; friend of Thiers; author, *History of the French Revolution,* 1824.

Mikhailovsky, Nikolai Konstantinovich (1842–1904) *108–110, 172–174, 196n, 199.*
Russian sociologist and publicist, leader of liberal Narodism and opponent of Marxism.

Mill, James (1773–1836) *313.*
English historian, philosopher, and economist; follower of Ricardo; father of John Stuart Mill.

Moleschott, Jakob (1822–1893) *50.*
German materialist, frequently linked with Büchner; main

P.

Pearson, Karl (1857–1936) *82n.*
English statistical biologist; geneticist; writer on philosophy of science; author, *The Grammar of Science,* 1899.

Pellat, J. S. Henri (1850–1909) *88.*
French physicist; writer on atomic theory, electricity, magnetism, thermodynamics.

Petzold, Joseph (1862–1929) *69, 84.*
German philosopher, follower of Avenarius; author, "Introduction to the Philosophy of Pure Experience."

Pisarev, Dmitry Ivanovich (1840–1868) *363.*
Russian literary critic, materialist philosopher and revolutionary democrat.

Plato (428–348 B.C.) *358–61.*
Greek philosopher, founder of the Academy at Athens that flourished for some 700 years; his many Dialogues, including the *Republic,* are available in numerous editions.

Plekhanov, George V. (1856–1918) *66, 68, 85, 117, 130, 145, 325, 340.*
Russian philosopher who turned to Marxism from Populism. His works exerted a strong influence on Lenin and the Russian revolutionary movement; author, "The Development of the Monist View of History," 1895 (Eng. title, *In Defence of Materialism*), published under the pseudonym, N. Beltov and of numerous essays on historical materialism.

Poincaré, Henri (1854–1912) *73, 82f 86f, 159.*
French mathematician and physicist; important figure in European positivism; author, *Science and Hypothesis,* 1902; *Value of Science,* 1905; *Science and Method,* 1909.

Priestley, Joseph (1733–1804) *58.*
English clergyman and scientist; produced experimentally the gas that came to be called oxygen; emigrated to the United States.

Proudhon, Pierre Joseph (1809–1865) *21, 187f, 264f.*
French economist and political theorist; father of French "mutualism" and advocate of "free credit" schemes; author, *System of Economical Contradictions; or, The Philosophy of Poverty,* 1846.

Pythagoras (c.572–497 B.C.) *362.*
Semi-mythical founder of a philosophical-religious school in

T.

V.

ou, Méditation sur les révolutions des empires, 1791, popularized religious skepticism and created much controversy in Europe and America.

Voltaire, François Marie Arouet de (1694–1778) *55, 240.*
Father of the French Enlightenment; attacked all political, religious, and philosophical orthodoxies; best known for his satire on Leibniz's "best of all possible worlds," *Candide,* 1759.

W.

Walpoles, The, *240.*
Robert (1676–1745) British statesman; Horace (1717–1797), Robert's son; essayist, novelist, and chronicler of his times.

Ward, James (1843–1925) *82f.*
English idealist philosopher. Best known for his work, *Naturalism and Agnosticism,* 1899.

Watt, James (1736–1819) *314.*
Scottish inventor whose new type of steam engine was patented in 1769; the *watt* as a unit of electrical power was named for him.

Weitling, Wilhelm (1808–1871) *29.*
German-American Utopian-communist, member League of the Just; published a German language workers' paper in New York, 1850–55.

Wolff, Christian (1679–1754) *104, 168.*
German mathematics professor; popularized conventional philosophy which he treated as based on purely logical-rational laws.

Y.

Yushkevich, P. S. (1873– ?) *72, 85, 90.*
Russian philosopher; author, "Materialism and Critical Realism," 1908.

Z.

Zeno (c.490–c.430 B.C.) *356.*
Called Zeno of Elea to distinguish him from Zeno, the founder of Stoicism; his famous arguments against the possibility of motion sought to prove that the very idea of motion was full of contradictions.